HEALING WORDS

THE COUNSELLOR TRAINING COURSE MANUAL

by Daniel M. Keeran, M.A., M.S.W.

Published by CTI Counsellor Training Institute Ltd.
Vancouver, British Columbia, Canada

Suite 405, 510 West Hastings Street
Vancouver, British Columbia
Canada V6B 1L8

ISBN: 0-9694155-1-6

Contributor of "Theoretical Terms": Bill Halyk, M.Ed.
Layout and Typography: Tehjay B. Fox, Corporate Publishing Group Ltd.
Layout of Appendices: Margaret Lehmann

Canadian Cataloguing in Publication Data

Keeran, Daniel M., 1947-
Healing words: the counsellor training course manual

Rev. ed.
ISBN: 0-9694155-1-6

1. Counselors--Training of. 2. Counseling--Practice.
I. CTI Counsellor Training Institute. II. Title.

BF637.C6K44 1998 158'.3'071 C98-900936-X

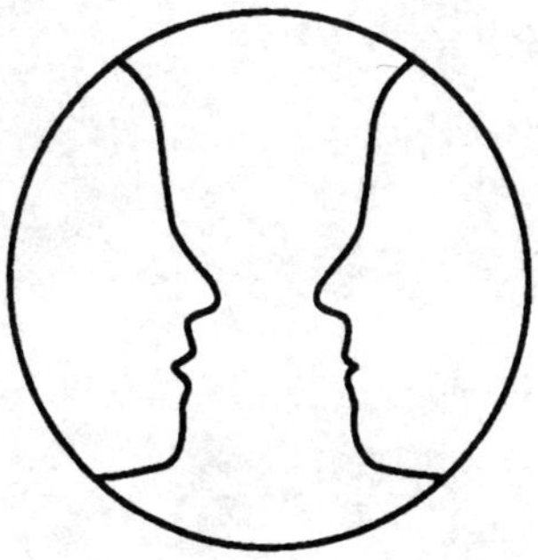

Table of Contents

Chapter Three
Loss and Grief Counselling 181

Chapter Four
Communication and Conflict Resolution Skills 225

Chapter Five
Couple Counselling Strategies 253

Appendices

ACKNOWLEDGEMENTS

Taking the broad view, this manual has been in a process of development for a period of twenty years. The practical concepts, skills, and techniques described here are the contributions of innumerable colleagues and counselling clients, distilled and modified by the author into their present forms. Much gratitude is extended to course participants in the Counsellor Training Institute who have provided opportunities for dialogue and who have been patient during the lengthy preparation of this volume.

Daniel M. Keeran, M.A., M.S.W.

PREFACE

The contents of the Counsellor Training Course Manual are designed to achieve the primary objective of the Counsellor Training Institute which since 1985 has been to make "counselling skills public knowledge for a therapeutic community". Because counsellors themselves benefit personally from their special knowledge of healing, a therapeutic outcome can be predicted for society when counselling processes and skills are made widely available to the public. This book gives away the secrets of the most effective counsellors and therapists.

As a verbatim transcript of the Counsellor Training Course offered on-site in Vancouver, British Columbia, Canada, the format of the Manual is a combination of dialogue between the instructor and course participants, group discussion among participants, and short monologues presented by the instructor. In order to retain a realistic sense of communication and discussion, grammatical errors and the peculiarities of verbal expression have for the most part been left in the text unless clarification seemed necessary.

The purpose of the on-site course, also offered by correspondence for which the Manual serves as the text, is to train counsellors and anyone who wishes to pursue personal growth and recovery. These courses as well as the Manual are available to anyone, in keeping with the philosophy of the Counsellor Training Institute - that everyone who has a sincere desire to help themselves and others, is entitled to acquire the special knowledge and therapeutic skills which are often considered to be the sole property of certain professional groups.

Abundant professional literature is available for heavily theoretical studies in counselling and therapy. As well, bookstores are full of popular literature for understanding various dysfunctions and disorders suffered by individuals, couples, and families. Something more is needed to provide the actual tools and means of healing for the intangible sicknesses of ourselves and our society.

The unique value of this Manual is to give practical instruments which are immediately usable including detailed descriptions and therapeutic wordings of statements, skills, and interventions - healing words - which hopefully will find their way into every public library, physician's office, law office, police station, church and synagogue, school, hospital, business, and into every home "for a therapeutic community".

Chapter One:

Clinical Assessment and Suicide Prevention

Speaker Welcome to the Counsellor Training Course and the Counsellor Training Institute. People enroll in CTI courses for personal as well as professional development, and both are legitimate reasons for attending. Certainly an important point of CTI philosophy is that self-awareness and personal growth and recovery are important for becoming an effective counsellor.

As we begin, I would like to briefly outline the topics we will be covering:

1. Clinical Assessment and Suicide Prevention
2. The Counselling Process and Therapeutic Interventions
3. Loss and Grief Counselling
4. Communication and Conflict Resolution Skills
5. Couple Counselling Strategies

As we proceed through the course you may want to take fairly detailed notes, especially if you intend to take the "Qualifying Examination" which follows courses for the Certificate of Individual Counselling as well as the Counselling Practice Development course. The examination is based largely upon class notes.

Our discussion of Clinical Assessment will be drawn from the Clinical Assessment questionnaire which is the outlined list of questions found in this section of the Counsellor Training Selected Materials. So we will go through the actual questions which are asked in a standard assessment, and we will discuss the reasons for asking each question as well as possible client responses and what these responses may mean.

As we proceed through the assessment, I encourage you to imagine you are being asked these questions as a client. Try to be aware of any discomfort, fear, or anxiety around any questions. This will be important for your ability to empathize with your client's discomfort during assessment.

That was the introduction to the introduction. So I would like to say a few more words before we begin a discussion of the assessment questions. The Clinical Assessment is something that is done in the first meeting with a client. It is a process of information gathering that is important to complete in the first session so that I understand the scope and depth of the client's problem. Otherwise, if I dive into counselling with a client without having done a thorough assessment, I may draw inaccurate conclusions and waste time pursuing issues which are irrelevant or far removed from the client's problems. Having said that, it is also true that assessment is something that is on-going which means that I will continue to gather information about the client's life in the following sessions.

OBJECTIVES

There are three primary reasons or objectives for doing a Clinical Assessment which are listed here. This relates to the first question on the "Qualifying Examination", which is, "What are three objectives for doing a Clinical Assessment?"

CLINICAL ASSESSMENT

1. To understand the story behind the client's presenting problems.
2. To build a therapeutic alliance.
3. To identify goals for counselling.

The first and perhaps primary reason for doing the Clinical Assessment is to gather information from a variety of areas of the client's life which might help me to understand the negative contributing factors to the client's current struggle or difficulty. And so to understand the story behind the client's problems, I am going to ask questions to draw information from the client's recent past as well as his distant past, from his health history, from his family of origin or the family he grew up in, his school history, occupational history, social development, sexual and marital history, and other areas.

It is important that I get as much information as possible near the beginning of the counselling relationship so that I do not draw grossly inaccurate conclusions. For example, if the client is depressed, I may mistakenly conclude from a superficial assessment that he is just upset over losing his job. Whereas, a thorough assessment would reveal that he was abused as a child and also has diabetes which is often a biological cause of depression.

If we discover a possible biological factor related to the client's problems, what would we do then?

Response *Refer the client to a doctor.*

Speaker Yes. Very good. The second reason for doing the assessment is to build what I call a therapeutic alliance. At the same time the counsellor is assessing the client, the client is also assessing the counsellor. And so therapeutic alliance refers to the client's being able to trust and feel safe with the counsellor.

While the counsellor is asking questions, the client is also asking questions often unconsciously. For example:

Is this a safe, private setting?

Is this a counsellor who seems sincere and warm?

Is this counsellor going to be non-judgemental?

Does this counsellor have an accurate understanding of what I'm saying and feeling?

Do I feel understood and supported by him or her?

Does the counsellor appear to know what he or she is doing?

Is this counsellor sensitive to fears and anxieties I may have about being here and about talking about certain things?

If the client has a sense of "yes" about these questions, the therapeutic alliance will begin to develop. Some professionals have said that the therapeutic alliance in the sense of safety and trust, develops within the first three minutes. If safety is not established within the first three minutes, the alliance will take longer to build.

Therapeutic alliance also refers to an underlying phenomenon which often occurs in the counsellor-client relationship. I am speaking of the transference which a client may feel toward the counsellor. Transference occurs when something about the counsellor consciously or unconsciously reminds the client of a significant person in his or her life.

Positive transference occurs when the client sees the counsellor as the caring parent she wishes she had or as the parent with whom the client was overinvolved or double-bonded. Double-bonding may occur when one parent is absent, abusive, or emotionally unavailable, so that the child relies too much on the caring of the available parent.

When positive transference occurs, the client will idealize the counsellor and perhaps view the counsellor as perfect or as being all-knowing and all-caring. In this event the client will often return to the counselling relationship as a child who is looking for the caring parent. And so the therapeutic alliance is based upon this positive transference. A task in the counselling relationship is for the counsellor to provide the nurturing that was missed, or to help the client emotionally let go of the double-bonded parent, and to gradually draw upon the client's own resources for self-nurturing.

Negative transference occurs when the client reacts against the counsellor and perceives him or her as the uncaring or abusive parent from the past. The client may return partly because of a need to change the counsellor into the caring parent and partly because of the client's attraction to what is familiar. This also helps us understand the client's pattern of repeating unhealthy relationships or of undermining healthy relationships by reacting out of negative transference. On the other hand, rather than return to the relationship, what else might happen?

Response *The client might drop out if he sees the counsellor as abusive or uncaring.*

Speaker Yes. And so this means that if the counselling relationship is to continue, the counsellor must work with the negative transference in a way that leads to a therapeutic outcome.

For example, I had a client who reluctantly returned to the second session. About fifteen minutes into the session I realized the client was not able to accept my attempts to reflect her concerns. It was as if no matter what I said, I was not able to be accurate in my understanding of her feelings. I began to feel frustrated because of the sense of struggle and tension that was developing between us. My statement to her was, "As we're talking I'm aware of a sense of tension or struggle between us, and I wonder if you are aware of it." She agreed that she could feel it, so I said,"I wonder if there's some other important person in your life that you have some struggle with." She indicated that this was the problem she had with her supervisor at work. After discussing this briefly, I said, "Who is the first person in your life that you experienced a similar kind of struggle with?" She said, "That would be my father. He has always been critical of everything I do and he still is. We fight to this day."

So by this example, negative transference was approached by first acknowledging and identifying the client's feelings toward the counsellor; second, by identifying another struggle in the client's adult life; third, by identifying the first struggle in the client's life. In this way the client is no longer stuck in the negative transference with me and is able to gain insight into the pattern of struggle and its origin.

The third objective of the assessment is to identify goals for counselling. Goals are identified near the end of the assessment, and these goals must be identified primarily by the client. Counselling must be goal-directed and client-centered.

Counselling must be goal-directed in order for progress to be evaluated by both the client and counsellor as the counselling process continues. Without goals which are regularly refocused perhaps in every session for a while, the counselling process may be unproductive, and the dependent client may be easily exploited.

Counselling must be client-centered which means in part that goals must be identified by the client to support the client's ability to direct his own process of healing, to support the client's responsibility for his own progress and in a larger sense his own life, and to empower the client. What do you imagine might happen if the counsellor imposes his or her own goals or agenda on the client?

Response *She may feel her needs are not being met and decide not to return.*

Speaker Yes, exactly. If the counsellor disregards the client's agenda and directs the client to pursue some issue which the client perceives as irrelevant, the client may not return. On the other hand, a very passive dependent client may accept whatever the counsellor says, and in this case the counsellor would be feeding into or supporting an unhealthy pattern.

It is alright for the counsellor to suggest some possible goal areas but only after the client has identified his own goals, and even then the counsellor would phrase his suggested goals in a tentative way that could be easily rejected.

CRISIS INTERVENTION

When the client arrives or in the first phone contact, the client is informed that the first session will be for assessment or for gathering information about his life experience. The exception to this is when the client is in crisis. How do I know if the client is possibly in crisis?

Response *The client seems upset or crying.*

Speaker That's right. The client appears to be preoccupied with painful feelings, crying, very silent, fidgeting, and so on. If this is happening, what do we do with the assessment?

Response *Nothing. You don't do it.*

Speaker That's right. If the client is in crisis, I will set the assessment aside and attend to the painful emotions. In crisis intervention, the process is to first, support the painful emotions, then when these have subsided, take time to sort out what has happened, the causes or variety of issues or experiences which may have occurred, then finally to look at choices and directions in order to instill some hope. Some brief assessment is done to gather information related to the crisis, but the in-depth assessment would be delayed until the next session.

PRESENTING PROBLEMS

If the client is not in crisis, I will say, "What have you been feeling lately or what problems bring you to counselling today?" This is usually how I will begin the first session, by asking for the presenting problems with this wording of the question.

I begin with presenting problems because this allows the client to vent his feelings and address his needs. At the same time I am able to demonstrate my ability to be supportive and understanding as well as other counsellor qualities which are important for the building of safety and trust in the therapeutic alliance. I will stay with the client's presenting problems long enough for him to feel a sense of support.

As he talks about his problems, I am making a mental list. For example, he may say, "I just don't feel myself, and I don't seem to have any motivation to do anything. And I just don't seem to have any direction in my life. And I've been crying sometimes." As he speaks, I will use reflective statements and validations, and I will invite him to say more.

Then I will begin to structure the assessment process with the following statements:

"Rather than counselling, I would like to use the first session to ask you a series of questions about your life experience so that I can get a broad understanding of problems you are having. Is that OK?"

In order for the client to accept the process of assessment in the first session, he must be properly prepared. Otherwise, the client who expects counselling and gets assessment without being prepared, may be disappointed and not want to return for another session. This preparation of the client is accomplished with the use of structure and permission.

The client is then informed about note-taking, brief responses, and confidentiality, and the following statements are used:

"I would like you to give just brief responses."

This helps to complete the assessment within the first session.

"I would like to take short notes as we're talking."

This tends to decrease the distraction of note-taking, while on the other not informing the client will increase the client's distraction and will undermine his safety.

"Everything will remain completely confidential."

This provides a boundary around the counsellor-client relationship which contributes to the client's feeling of safety.

"Is that OK?"

Asking for the client's permission, again supports the client's safety and power to choose which is a basic objective of the counselling process. Obtaining the client's verbal permission for note-taking and assessment can be done in the initial phone contact or following a discussion of presenting problems during the first session or following a discussion of the history of present illness.

With this permission from the client, I will begin taking notes and recording the information on the blank form entitled "Clinical Assessment" found in the Counsellor Training Selected Materials. This form has the same outline as the questionnaire and has blank space between headings where relevant information can be recorded.

The information will be recorded in the client's own words as much as possible, beginning with the presenting problems which will be taken down in point form. For example:

1. "I don't feel myself."

2. "I don't seem to have any motivation."

3. "I don't have any direction in my life."

4. "I've been crying sometimes."

These will be recorded as separate problems because they may in fact have different origins or beginnings.

HISTORY OF PRESENT ILLNESS

This section is a history of the presenting problems, taking each problem separately. The questions in the order of asking are as follows:

"How long have you experienced this?"

This question should be asked for each problem presented because the time frame may be different for each. The client may have had crying spells for a few months, yet he may have been lacking direction and motivation all his life.

"What happened at the time you began feeling this way?"

This question is asked in order to discover a precipitating event or factor, something that may have triggered or caused the problem. Examples of precipitating events would be a car accident, illness, marital separation, death of a loved one, job loss, or others.

"Since you have been feeling this way, do you feel worse or better now?"

This is an attempt to determine fluctuations in the severity of the problem. The person who has been severely depressed may be at greater risk for suicide when he is beginning to feel better because he has more energy than before to carry out a suicide plan. This may determine whether the client has been in crisis as well as changes in circumstances or mood.

"When was the last time you felt something similar to what you are feeling now?"

This question helps to reveal previous episodes of the problem and whether or not the problem is recent or is characterized by a repetitive cycle going back to an earlier point in life. Repeated episodes going back many years may indicate what?

Response *That the person's problems are deeply entrenched and may require a long period of counselling.*

Speaker Yes. And so I will ask, "When was the last time you felt this way?" "When did you feel this way before that?" And so on, until I have discovered the earliest episode the client can recall, perhaps going back to early childhood for example, or adolescence, or some other period.

"What happened at the time you decided to come for counselling?"

Here I am trying to determine factors which may have precipitated or motivated the client to seek help. For example, a marital conflict and threat from the spouse that she would leave if he did not get help. Or it may have been pressure from parents in the case of an adolescent client. Another example is the client who attempted suicide and realized that his situation is desperate, motivating him to seek help.

The motivation of the client falls into two categories: 1) the client who is in counselling for himself and 2) the client who is in counselling to please someone else or from outside pressure.

In the second case, the therapeutic alliance will be based upon the counsellor's ability to support and validate the client's resistance to being in counselling, perhaps beginning by asking the client to talk about his feelings about not wanting to be in counselling. Then say, "It makes sense you wouldn't want to be here and that you would feel annoyed, and I think you have every right to feel as you do." In other words, the client's feelings of annoyance or of pressure can be treated as his presenting problem.

IDENTIFYING INFORMATION

After the History of Present Illness, I will go to the questions for Identifying Information. To introduce this section, I will say, "Now I'd like to ask a few questions about your current circumstances if that's OK." As we proceed through this section and throughout the assessment, we are looking for two broad categories of types of life experiences. These include significant conflicts and significant losses, and we are looking for indications that these may be unresolved and still affecting the client's life. I will present the questions in this section and discuss each one. The first question in this section is:

"What is your age?"

The client's age may relate to certain issues common to this period in human development. For example, the adolescent client is struggling with forming a unique identity, emotional separation and conflict with parents, and forming relationships with the opposite sex perhaps. The client in his twenties and thirties may be dealing with issues of marriage or mate selection, career development, independent living. The client in his forties and fifties may be looking at whether life goals are being achieved, loss of youth, planning for retirement. The client in his sixties and seventies and upward is facing issues of retirement, loss of spouse, abandonment, and preparation for death. Notice that various types of losses accompany each stage of development.

"What is your marital status?"

The client may be separated or divorced or single. What type of experience is separation or divorce?

Response *It would be a loss.*

Speaker Yes. Being single may also be a loss if being married is a desired expectation which remains unfulfilled. And being married may be a loss if the client is not fulfilled in the relationship. At this point I would like to point out that as I am going through the assessment and certain losses are being identified, I am also wondering what painful feelings the client might be experiencing with the loss. There is the possibility that the client is experiencing any or all of at least seven primary painful feelings. We will refer to these at times during the course, and I will list them here as: fear, anger, guilt, sadness, emptiness, low-self-worth, and despair. The nonsense word "FAGSELD" is a way to remember these feeling words.

The next item in this section refers to sex, race, and ethnic identity. It will not be necessary to ask a question regarding sex. However, it will be important to keep in mind issues which are gender related. For example, women face issues of discrimination in employment, sexual harassment, fear of assault, childbirth, premenstrual syndrome (PMS), hysterectomy, mastectomy, and being homebound. Men face issues of loss of children in custody decisions, vasectomy, impotence, and unemployment.

In terms of race and ethnic identity, I may ask about the country of origin or cultural background by saying, "Where were you born?" or "What is your cultural background?" This may be relevant for a number of reasons. Certain cultures have experiences or practices which relate to the individual client. For example, many Native Indians in North America have experienced the loss of their traditional language, culture, and way of life because of the residential school experience. Removal of children from their families and subsequent physical, sexual, and emotional abuse resulted in the breakdown of the native family and culture. For example, children were beaten to make them stop speaking their native language. This kind of abuse together with sexual abuse and the loss of nurturing parents, resulted in alcoholism and the perpetuation of abuse in the native communities when the children grew to adulthood.

East Indians who emigrate to North America experience the loss of their cultural milieu, and the adolescent children are often caught between the Eastern values of parents and the Western values of peers. This leaves them often feeling torn and alienated, not fitting into either culture. Despair, depression, and suicide may be the outcomes.

East Indian, Chinese, and other Oriental cultures may have the expectation that young single adult children should remain in the family home even after marriage. To live as a single adult in the community is considered shameful, and so this would not be considered a sign of dependent behaviour as it would in white culture.

"What are your children's names and ages?"

This is an attempt to find out if the client has children whose ages may imply particular parental obligations. Young children may require more time and attention than older children, and adolescent children are presenting the challenge of emotional and social separation from parents. Also I may discover that the children are not with the client, which may imply a loss issue.

"What is your employment? How long have you been employed (or unemployed)?"

The client's type of employment may contribute stress, and unemployment may be a significant loss experience.

"Do you live alone or with someone?"

If the client is living alone, this may indicate the lack of a support system. A depressed client or a client who is facing difficult issues in counselling may be going home to stare at four walls which may place the client at increased risk for attempting suicide.

With the information I have gathered so far, I can determine whether or not the client fits the profile of a high suicide risk group which would be the male who is over 50 years old, unemployed, separated or divorced, and living alone. This profile together with presenting problems related to depression, implies the need to carefully assess and prevent suicide which we will cover later in the assessment.

What is another high suicide risk group?

Response *Teenagers... and men who are HIV positive.*

Speaker Right. Teenagers who may be experiencing a difficult adjustment with issues of identity, low self-worth, hopelessness, and loss of parental caring. And people who are terminally ill possibly with the prospect of a long period of suffering.

"Do you have any religious affiliation?"

Religious or spiritual orientation suggests three possible implications. First, active involvement with a religious group may be an important part of the client's support system. Second, religious or spiritual orientation provides a sense of identity and an existential framework, meaning that it answers question about the meaning of life such as "Who am I? Why am I here? Where am I going?"

Third, involvement with a very rigid religious group, may mean that the client will not be supported in his counselling with someone who is not a member of that religious group because of suspicion that the non-religious counsellor will undermine the values and beliefs of the group and of the client. Their suspicion is well founded because they may have heard stories of so-called professional counsellors who have recommended divorce, infidelity, leaving the religious group, and so on. Similarly, cultural and ethnic communities may also discourage the client from taking problems outside the family or cultural group.

The next brief category is Mode of Admission. This refers to how the client came to the counselling service. I want to determine whether the client came by word of mouth from another client. This may mean my counselling practice is providing a valued service. Referral from a physician implies the need to perhaps obtain a medical report or to contact the physician for relevant information, with the clients signed release of information.

Question *Can you explain what to do when you sense someone is suicidal?*

Speaker To cover that we have to get into assessing his mental status. Basically you need to ask him very directly if he's having any suicidal ideas. We'll discuss that more as we get into that part of the assessment.

PAST HISTORY

Okay, lets move into the past history of this client. You will notice I'm beginning this category with another kind of introductory statement, which is something like: "I would like to ask a series of questions to get a broader understanding of your situation. Would that be okay?" And again, I'm getting his permission, and then I go into the following questions. Most of these questions have to do with past history which relates to the client's past contact with helping and counselling professionals.

SURGERIES

The first question is: "Have you had any surgeries at any time in your life? And how old were you? Were there any complications?" Because depending on the type of surgery, it might constitute a conflict and loss experience.

So, for example, a person says he has had a back condition or back surgery, or brain surgery, heart surgery, a hysterectomy, or a mastectomy. That might have very significant implications because of the painful feelings that come up around that experience.

So as I'm moving through the assessment, and a person identifies something like a previous surgery, I'm asking myself things like: what painful feelings might this person still be experiencing bits of, around that kind of surgery? If the surgery happened early on in her life, it might have had a more far-reaching impact or a different kind of impact than surgery which occurred in adult life.

For example, imagine a person who said he had surgery to have a testicle lowered or to have an eye condition corrected. What you do imagine that person might feel having those conditions, maybe from birth?

Response *He might feel disabled, abnormal, not as effective as others.*

Speaker Yes, all right.

Response *Also, as we found with our own youngsters, abandonment. They didn't understand being left in the hospital....*

Speaker All right, a long period of being in the hospital as a child away from the family is an early separation experience. And, depending on the type of condition that brought on the surgery, a person might have been left feeling low self-worth, especially if it was a congenital condition. He may think there is something wrong with his genes that he could pass on to his own children.

HEALTH PROBLEMS

I will be asking: "Do you have any health problems at all?" And I will give examples like diabetes, or epilepsy, M.S. or any kind of ongoing health problem or struggle which would constitute a kind of a loss-experience, an ongoing loss of physical ability.

Also, as I said earlier we need to be aware that certain types of health conditions contribute biologically to depression. For example, diabetes brings about changes in body chemistry that can contribute to a kind of biological depression. Epilepsy and M.S. may also affect mood, anxiety, and personality.

PREVIOUS COUNSELLING

"Have you had any previous counselling at any time in your life?". I'm interested in any experience a person may have had seeing a guidance counsellor, a school counsellor, a minister, a clergyman, or a psychologist or psychiatrist or other professional counsellor. I'm interested in the chronology or the time frame for that.

If a person was seeing a counsellor as a child that might be an indication that there was a problem very early on that really is a background to what they struggle with right now.

For example, a person might have seen a school counsellor because their marks were low in school. Their marks might have been low because they were pre-occupied or depressed about some family problem. So it might indicate that the family of origin was dysfunctional, in some way that related to the problem.

And then if I sense or hear the client telling me about seeing counsellors at different times since then, I might begin to see an outline of their involvement with different types of helpers or counsellors. That's going to have implications for that client's ability to benefit from counselling and for how significantly I can expect to help that person.

A client who has been involved a long time in counselling over many years and has seen many counsellors might have the system down so pat that his defenses are well established. His resistance for making change could be enormous.

There are two extreme types of clients that might not benefit as much as they could. One is the client who has had extensive involvement in counselling before coming to see me, seeing a number of counsellors over a number of years perhaps going all the way back to childhood; the other is the client who has never seen a counsellor before — this is their first involvement.

Both of those types of clients might not be able to benefit as much as the client who has had some experience — who has been on the road of personal growth and recovery for a shorter amount of time. That person might be more highly motivated and have more realistic expectations.

What often happens with a new client? Does any body have any ideas? What would you imagine would be the case with the new client?

Response *Fear to disclose things.*

Speaker Okay. He might be afraid to talk about certain problems.

Response *A lack of trust.*

Speaker Yes, lack of trust.

Response *Lots of testing.*

Speaker Testing kinds of things. What are you thinking about there?

Response *I'd want to see if this counsellor could really do what I want. I'd run little tests.*

Speaker Okay, so that person might have expectations that aren't realistic about what counselling is going to do for them, or what counselling is about. Often times a new client has the idea or notion that the counsellor is going to fix them and they're going to be a passive participant in the process.

They may think counselling is like going to see a witch doctor who will prescribe a certain magical or miraculous cure. The counsellor is going to do some magical thing, or say some magical words and it's going to make it all better and they can go away after one session and go on their merry way.

Response *So they haven't come to the stage where they've accepted responsibility for it. They would rather pass on their problem for the counsellor to take care of.*

Response *Would you, as a counsellor, disclose in the beginning how much time and work it might take?*

Speaker It would be very important to talk with that client about what to expect in counselling. You might say things like: "It sounds like it has taken some time for these problems to develop, so it's going to take time for things to change" or, "There aren't any quick fixes to your problems — its going to take work. There are no miracle cures in the growth process or the counselling process." Make sure they have a very clear notion of that so that they don't go away feeling disillusioned about counselling.

New clients will often come one time, and if those unrealistic expectations are not addressed carefully, won't come back. They will have expected if they came once or twice, then they should have gotten all better. And that's simply not the case.

Response *I think that also a new client might be testing to see how safe it is for them to disclose what they think is their miserable self. That could be the underlying thing, that they feel they're so bad that people can't tolerate them. You have to get at problems that go back to childhood. And so he will test the water to see how far he can go and how safe it is.*

Speaker Exactly, yes. And you were saying earlier the new client is experiences counselling as an unknown so he does a certain amount of testing to see what this is like and what this counselling process is about.

Response *It would seem to me to that in the beginning a lot of disempowering things are said, like the person is down on themselves and feels beyond help. A lot of negatively charged words are spoken. I think a counsellor has to be very aware of what is a disempowering statement.*

Speaker Yes, and part of the ongoing assessment is to pick up on a client's language and patterns of beliefs about himself and others, negative self-talk, devaluation of others, and things like that.

DIVERSION ABOUT SEEING A CHILD IN COUNSELLING

Response *I'm thinking of a person who saw me last week because his mother sent him to see me. And I don't think he really wants to be there. The mother is expecting him to get fixed by coming to see me. I don't see his marriage as a happy one either.*

Speaker Well, often times it's very important to meet with the family and other people related to the client to make sure everyone is clear in their expectations of what counselling is going to achieve.

Response *She wants him to get better. He just lost his dad. He's difficult to handle in school.*

Response *Is that process focused on what he wants? Is that something where you take the parents aside, rather than work with them together? When I was young I went to a counsellor and I found it was quite intimidating to have my mother sitting beside me.*

Speaker Working with children requires some different considerations. After we've seen the family together, we will need permission from parents to see the child individually if this is going to be helpful and to get parent's permission to allow the child confidentiality in order to establish trust. Later the child will be encouraged to share the counselling issues with parents perhaps in a family session. Maybe we could speak about that more later.

Response *But isn't it easy to tell if a client has seen counsellors regularly? And maybe they've had really good counsellors too, but have to work through a lot of bad experiences. It's not that they don't want the help, but they have a lot of working through to do.*

Speaker Yes, but I'm getting the sense that when I'm hearing they've seen a variety of people who are well trained professionals over the years, that I might not be able to help them much. I guess what I'm thinking is that my ability is probably not going to be significantly superior to any of those other counsellors. And so it helps me keep my expectations at a realistic level. I'm going to do what I can to help that client, but I'm not going to expect more than what's realistic.

Response *Would it be a good idea to ask a question like: "You have seen many professionals before — what do you think I can do that they haven't been able to do?"*

Speaker Right. Or, "What's been missing from the counselling you've had?"

Response *You do this so that the client can actually experience some results and some success.*

Speaker Yes, I think it's very important to outline their expectations.

PREGNANCY HISTORY

Speaker All right, let's go down to the next category, which is miscarriages, abortions, or post-partum depression. What type of life experiences are these?

Response *Losses. Grief.*

Speaker That's right. Oftentimes those aren't acknowledged as significant and yet they are for many people. And post-partum depression might accompany the birth of a child whether it be the first child or the second child. It's a hormonal change that takes place at childbirth. It might trigger a biological depression, but oftentimes it works in combination with other factors. For many women this may last for a few hours to a few days or a week. For some women, a post-partum depression may complicate an existing depression or begin a period of chronic depression lasting many years. Many of the female clients I see who have post-partum depression have also experienced being the oldest responsible child of the family of origin. In other words, they missed out having their own childhood, and now they are having a child, or having their second or third child, so that the prospect of their ever having the sort of carefree life that a child deserves is lost and gone. And often-times I see the additional factor of the unsupportive spouse — the person is having another child and the husband is not there to provide support. Or if he is in the picture, he's simply not emotionally available. She may have chosen this partner unconsciously because of her familiarity with not getting the support she needs or with the role of the responsible person in the family of origin. Those can be some contributing factors to post-partum depression, which can last for years and can become a chronic depression triggered off by a birth.

The next questions is: "When did you begin menstruating?" This is important because the late onset of menses can be related to stress and conflict in the family of origin. By late onset we are talking about what might be considered late for the women of that family — but I'm thinking about 18 or 19 would certainly be considered late. Another condition that can cause an absence of menses is anorexia. One of my clients enrolled her teenage children in ballet, and one daughter has not been menstruating at all. She had one period at the start, but has not had a period since then. She is very thin, doesn't eat properly. My concern is that she is anorexic. In this situation referral to a physician and psychiatrist would be important for the child's progress since anorexia is a potentially fatal condition.

Then I will ask, "Do you have any venereal diseases?" This may indicate either the instability of the client's relationships, or the instability of her sexual partner's relationships. If it is the latter, this may say something about the client's attraction to abusive or unhealthy partners. Are there any questions about past history?

Response *Are we looking at past history roughly as cause and effect?*

Speaker In this particular category, we're just looking at their past contacts medically, psychiatrically, surgically. And yes, whether the cause is being in surgery, or a health problem, we are wondering about the effect in terms of how it relates to their current problem situation.

Response *So we're looking for trauma?*

Speaker That's right. We're looking for possible factors from their medical and counselling history — painful feelings from past losses and previous attempts to get help which are related to their current problem situation.

FAMILY HISTORY

The next category is "Family History and Relationships", and this is often considered to be the core of the assessment. Oftentimes the issue the client struggles with in a current life situation had its beginnings in the family of origin.

I'm going to start this category by saying, "Now I'd like to ask you some questions about the family you grew up in." This invites them to speak clearly about the family they grew up in. I don't want to get responses about their current situation, such as their own nuclear family.

As we move through family history and relationships, I'm looking for experiences of closeness and distance in relationships and, in particular, parental relationships. I'm also looking for conflicts and losses, and extremes in the family origin. I'm looking at whether there was any extreme conflict or the lack or avoidance of conflict, for example. That would be significant. And I want to know if there was distance in the parental relationship.

Response *Is the question establishing which family that we are dealing with? For instance, I grew up with a few families. Would you use the family that you spent the most time with and the one that is the most influential? How do we look at that?*

Speaker That's an excellent question, which comes up when you're working with a client who maybe was put into a foster home at an early age and proceeding from there had multiple foster home experiences, and things like that. What I would want to do with that client is to get an outline by asking, "How old were you when you left the family that you were born into, and then how long were you in the family that you stayed with after that? How old were you when you left that family?" I try to get a chronological outline.

Response *Accuracy is sometimes a difficult thing. It's not really so important as the things that do come up as you are listening.*

Speaker It's more important to observe and listen for emotions that come up for the client than to get accurate information about dates and years in certain homes. Sometimes I'll get a sense about a feeling of confusion that the client experiences when they try to recover the facts and information. But do you want to say more about that?

Response *No, that pretty much gives me the idea.*

Speaker So basically I'm looking for a rough outline of the different family experiences when the client was growing up. Then I have the client describe their relationships with who they perceive as the people they were closest to, or the most intimate relationships that were the longest in duration. Maybe they spent time in one family experience and were abused, and I would want to know about that.

With this first question, the idea of extremes comes up: "How many brothers or sisters do you have? I'd think it was significant if a person indicated that they were an only child, either that extreme or if there were of a large number of siblings. Does anybody have any ideas about what an only child might experience?

Response *Being spoiled; loneliness; sheltered; around adults a lot.*

Speaker So that may affect their social development.

Response *Introspection.*

Speaker More introspective maybe. Perhaps keeping issues to themselves. Oftentimes the only child is sad and lonely because of the lack of siblings. It may also have an influence on social skill development that comes from being able to interact with other siblings. Now that may not be the case with the only child. So it's very important to acknowledge who the expert on that person's life is as you're doing assessment. Who would that be?

Response *The client.*

Speaker The client is always the expert on what they've experienced. So it's one thing for us to have a hypothetical or theoretical understanding of what may have been the experience or for us to have that in mind. Ultimately we need to be getting that information and record that information from the client themselves and go with that. The person that was in a large family might feel something similar to the person who is an only child. What might that be?

Response *Same thing — there are too many other people.*

Speaker So lost in the shuffle, maybe lonely.

Response *Or an economic impact — there wasn't enough money to go around.*

Speaker Likely related to that as well. Not getting parental attention. It's hard for parents to give attention to everybody in a large family — I'm talking of a family of ten, twelve or more people — perhaps eight could be considered a large family.

Response *I have an older sister I looked at as a mother figure rather than my mother. My issues were more around her than they were around my mother.*

Speaker So you saw an older sister as more of a mother. There still may be implications about feelings of mother not being there for you. This is true for other issues we're going to explore.

The next question is, "Which one are you in the line of birth?" We're looking at the person who is the first born, the middle child, and the last born, and the significance of those positions. The second born or the second to last born might be significant as well. What often times is the experience of the oldest child?

Response *To lead; responsibility.*

Speaker Yes, to be the responsible child or the assistant parent. Often the oldest child misses out on childhood because of being responsible for looking after the other children. We find that this child often turns out to be the giver, the doer, the provider, the person in charge, the controller, the fixer in subsequent relationships. It's a role that is often perpetuated throughout a lifetime and becomes part of the life pattern. And it may also be part of the background for depression because that's what happens to a people when they don't take care of themselves, when instead they're into a pattern of looking after other people in their lives. They become depressed.

What might be the experience of the person who is born last in the family?

Response *Everybody takes care of him. He is self-focused and may not be sensitive to other people's hurts and problems or needs. He may be given a lot of freedom because parents have invested more energy and anxiety in raising the older ones. He may get the hand-me-downs — the seconds. He may get less pictures taken of him. He inherits.*

Speaker Right, he inherits things from the other members of the family that are passed down. The last child might have been unplanned. And the same could be true of the first child. The first child may be the reason for parents getting married — may have been the cause of feelings of pressure. The last child might come along as a mistake or an unplanned pregnancy. So either of those two people, and for that reason, might feel what?

Response *Unwanted, unloved.*

Response *They also get away with a lot — the last kids.*

Speaker So feeling unloved and unwanted might take a toll on their self-esteem. Getting away with a lot of things, as you just mentioned, might also take a toll on their self-esteem. They might feel that nobody really cares because they're allowed to do whatever they want.

Response *On the other hand if there was a previous death of a sibling or parents' feeling guilty because of an unplanned pregnancy, parents may over-protect, restrict or control the child. And if the child is adopted, the adoptive parents may be permissive out of fear that the child will feel rejected if disciplined.*

Speaker Excellent comment. Very insightful. And in those situations the child is missing the caring that he or she needs. What may be the experience of the middle child?

Response *He just gets overlooked. All the emphasis is on the other two children.*

Speaker Right, absolutely. So the oldest gets special attention as the one and only until the second child is born, and even then may continue to receive special attention as the favourite, or the example for other siblings, or the responsible child, the caregiver. Also, the last born gets a kind of special attention as the last baby who often gets protected as we discussed. Those two people have special positions. The middle person often doesn't have a special role or position and doesn't get any special kind of attention.

The same would be true of the second born or the second to last born. The second to last born had a special role before the last one was born and then lost that. So the second born and last born may be resented by the first born and second to last born respectively because attention was taken away.

The oldest child may feel resentment in losing a special position when the second child is born, and this might be part of some sibling rivalry. The relationship between the first and second, and the second to last with the last, may have much in common, both being characterized by conflict and resentment from those who lost attention by the birth of the next born.

Response *It gets so complicated because it also depends on the gender. So, regardless of the position in the family, I think that's a factor.*

Speaker Yes, exactly — whether you're an oldest female, or a oldest male could mean different expectations and a special role as the first female or first male.

Response *There are ethnic groups too. Certain ethnic backgrounds would rather have boys than girls.*

Speaker That's right. There's more value attached to the birth and death of the first male child in some cultures — such as eastern cultures — than the birth and death of the first female child.

The next question I ask is, "How many years separate you from the other siblings nearest you." Again we are looking at the extremes, but mostly the extreme of distance in years between siblings on either side.

For example, I had a client whose older sibling was eight years older and his next younger sibling was eight years younger. So he grew up as if he was an only child. If there is an age difference of four or more years, then it is almost as if a separate family is formed. So this has implications for closeness and distance in the family of origin. And if there was distance in the family of origin, that might have implications for distance in other significant relationships in that person's life and the ability to be intimate.

The next question is: What are your siblings work and marital situations?" What are we looking for there?

Response *Jealousy.*

Speaker Okay, maybe jealousy or sibling rivalry. There may be a history of that. What else?

Response *Maybe low self-worth, for example your brother is a doctor and you are a garbage collector?*

Speaker What if we find that siblings are having trouble in their work life and in their nuclear families or their social life? For example, there's a history of separation or divorce, or unemployment, or both. It might indicate a pattern that implies something about parental relationships as it impacted not only on the client, but on siblings as well. And if the client is different from the siblings and has problems functioning socially and occupationally, this may impact greatly on feelings of low self-worth or inadequacy too. He may feel very different — that he is somehow the black sheep of the family.

The next question:

"Who were you closest to when growing up?" This is simply a general question to get at whether the person was close to anyone in the family. If he indicates that he wasn't close to anybody, then that may be very significant and be part of the background for current difficulty achieving or maintaining intimacy in relationships.

The next question is: "Are your parents still living and if not, what was your age at their death?"

I might also want to ask this additional question:

"Are you your parents' natural child?" We need to understand whether the person was adopted or not, early on. Adoption is what kind of a life experience?

Response *Loss*

Speaker Loss, yes. Being adopted may influence the child's pattern of rejecting or being rejected in relationships. And if the parents are not still living, their deaths would also constitute a loss. We're asking what was the client's age at their parents' deaths. The earlier the deaths, especially if they occurred in childhood during particular developmental years, the greater will be the possible impact on the development of maladaptive behaviours or dysfunctional life patterns or ways of coping and relating that don't work well. The death of a parent that happened more recently in adult years would normally have less impact.

In fact, I've found in my work that schizophrenic clients have often lost a parent around the age of eight. The death or the abandonment of a parent, especially father, around that age of development can be critical.

Response *Are there any reasons?*

Speaker Well, I think when a child experiences a traumatic separation or loss at that age, his way of coping might tend to be one of withdrawal into one's self or withdrawal into a fantasy life.

Response *What would cause it at that age or around that age? What would be the reason for that age specifically?*

Speaker I think that a young child's way of coping with stress is to make use of fantasy in play activity.

Response *So there's more pressure suddenly placed on the child.*

Speaker Yes, and this is because the bonding with father for example is very important at this stage of development. So when a parent dies its a very difficult, painful experience. The bond or need to bond is disrupted, and a child's way of coping might be very dysfunctional.

I'm not sure about all of the reasons for why a person might become schizophrenic from that. There is probably more than one factor, but I think it is interesting that a number of my clients have had a loss of a parent, especially father, around that age. I don't understand what it's all about. Of course as we'll discuss in a short while, there's also thought to be a genetic link with some types of schizophrenia.

The next question in assessment is: "Describe your father's personality and your relationship to him when you were growing up. Were you close? Not so close? Distant? Affectionate?" The parental relationships are what I consider to be the core of the discussion of family history relationships.

Parental relationships are most significant because of their impact on the development of personality and coping abilities. It's in the closeness and caring with parents that a client derives feelings of self-worth or what may be termed ego strength that comes from his experience and knowledge of being loved and accepted unconditionally.

The person who did not have a close, caring, nurturing relationship with parents is apt to have a low sense of ego strength which may well affect his ability to deal with current stresses in adult life.

There are actually two separate questions contained in one. The first is an attempt to get the client's perception of father's personality. "What was he like when you were growing up?" The second is an exploration of the client's relationship with father in terms of closeness or distance, and affection as well. The essential content of this question is, "How would you describe the kind of relationship you had with father when you were growing up?"

The extremes in the client's response are going to be significant to me. If a person says, "Oh he was just a perfect father," or "a perfect mother," or, "My father was a monster," those extreme perceptions are going to be significant.

Often in dysfunctional or alcoholic families, the client will idealize one parent and devalue the other. The alcoholic parent often is devalued and the enabling parent is often idealized and seen as wonderful, strong, virtuous, or good.

There is often a black and white perception of the parents. If a client gives me a very brief response and says, "Well, we were close," then that's going to be significant as well. I'm going to say things like, "Tell me a little bit about some of the kinds of things that happened when you were growing up with Dad that have left you thinking that you were close to him." Often I find that the client has difficulty recalling any experiences of closeness, which means that he is protecting Father by saying they were close. He is protecting Father or protecting himself from feelings of resentment and hurt. So I might be picking up on what I call a protection racket going on. We can call it denial — some form of defense which protects the client from feelings that he has towards the parent.

Often I see clients who are caught in a conflict with a parent, who they will describe as bad in so many words. I may need to address the "stuckness" which the client has in conflict with that parent and help him to let go of the conflict. This is because it is quite possible that unresolved conflict with the parent is being brought over into current relationships. This client is caught in the anger toward an uncaring or abusive parent. It's causing a distortion of the client's perception of current relationships, authority figures such as employers, or partners in relationships.

The other type of client, or maybe the same client, is protecting the enabling parent or protecting both parents by giving reasons or rationalizing why he should not feel angry toward the parent. I might want to work with that client to let go of the protection so that he can access his resentments.

By protecting the parents he may also be affecting current relationships. The unaddressed, or unspoken hostilities may be tunnelling from the parental relationship and surfacing in a current relationship. If the person did not deal with the anger felt toward a parent, he may be transferring it to a current relationships and dumping it on someone in adult life. He may need to be helped to experience and direct the anger toward parents so he can let go of it and see the connection between the parental relationship and the current relationship.

Response *It's not always a dumping thing is it? Sometimes if you have a relationship with your father and there's no communication and you feel it's unresolved, you try to resolve it by treating it in your partner. An example is an adult child of an alcoholic marrying an alcoholic and trying to fix what he wish he could have fixed in father. He might keep choosing alcoholic partners in an effort to change them.*

Speaker Yes, there can be a compulsion to repeat the conflict until it can get resolved. That's a good observation, but what often happens is the person ends up simply repeating it and not being able to resolve it. The resolution would be to change the alcoholic so that she can get the caring she missed from alcoholic father. This would be a way of changing father which she felt powerless to do as a child, and yet the resolution is illusive.

Response *Because they're using the same techniques.*

Speaker They're using the same approaches, using anger and control. The only person who can change the alcoholic is the alcoholic himself. Even if the alcoholic changes, the client may become bored or frightened by the prospect of intimacy which is unfamiliar and so the relationship may end thereby repeating the loss of caring. Are there any questions or comments about the parental relationships?

Response *Do men deal with men — like father issues, and women with mother issues. Is that common?*

Speaker I don't find that there is necessarily a correlation there. What happens often is that the parental relationship that is most unresolved in terms of loss of caring, whether it's with mother or with father, is the one that gets perpetuated or repeated.

Response *So it doesn't matter what sex?*

Speaker It doesn't matter what sex. A male client might have an unresolved conflict with his father and pick or be attracted to a woman who has qualities similar to father.

Response *That's kind of the same thing as when we have a physical attachment to someone — maybe they have a nose or ears that's like their father's — or something like that. Some attraction, some emotional charge.*

Speaker That's right. It triggers the attraction. I find generally that it's something about the personality type more than the physical appearance that will attract the client.

It's going to be significant when the client describes parental relationships in which there was some kind of distance that had been due to open conflict, criticism, lack of approval, lack of affection, lack of being present. The parent could be a workaholic or addicted, or physically absent. Or it could be that the parent was very passive and simply didn't interact and talk much with the client — or never talked, or talked rarely if ever, on any level of depth to the client about needs, feelings, or personal concerns — emotionally unavailable. Maybe the parent was overly humorous, jovial, light or superficial. All those kinds of things would indicate distancing.

Then we can speak of the parent who is physically or sexually abusive, as well as verbally abusive or critical of the child. These characteristics constitute the loss of parental caring and closeness.

Now the next question is, "What was your family like, that is, economically, socially, and culturally?". With this question we are exploring where the client fit in his community, or how his family related to others around him in his community. This is particularly important with people who come from families that are culturally different, or ethnically different, or economically different from the norm. The child from a different culture may feel distant from parents as he assimilates, or he may feel distant from peers. Differences in economic status may also result in distance from peers. For example, a client whose parents were doctors and who lived in an expensive house felt ashamed to bring friends home, and so he was a loner among peers.

An addiction in the family might have affected the financial resources of the family so that a person growing up in that situation didn't enjoy what his peers enjoyed, as far as entertainment or any other recreational activities. This may result in an obsession with pursuing material success in adult life.

The next question is, "What was your role in the family when you were growing up. Think of a word." And with this I'll give the client a list of words for them to choose from. "Were you a peacemaker, a black sheep, a victim, a responsible child, the invisible one, the worker, or some other word that might describe the kind of role you had when you were growing up?"

Response *You give him or her the word?*

Speaker I'll give them the list of words and I'll say, "I wonder if one of these words might fit the kind of role you had in your family — or if there's another word you can think of that will fit the role you had." Or I might say "roles", since there may have been more than one role that the person had when they were growing up.

The importance of this question is that it tells us about the life patterns that the person may have developed from the family of origin. For example, the victim role may be one that the client still perpetuates in relationships. Or it could be the responsible child role, the assistant parent role, the worker role, or the invisible person role. That role might repeat itself or show up in group situations, such as the workplace, the nuclear family (the family of one's marriage), at school, or groups like this one involving you as participants in this course.

The role may change from the family of origin to the school setting for example. In the family of origin, the client may have been an invisible child or an outsider, and in the classroom the role may be that of a responsible child who looks to the teacher for the caring and approval that is missed at home.

The person who has a conflictual life pattern in adulthood, may have been a rebel in the family of origin. I had the experience of a course participant being the rebel, the barracuda, wanting to sabotage the experience of the group. She sometimes threw verbal darts at me as the leader. And in one situation in which that happened this person then shared something of her own family experience in which she was extremely physically and emotionally abused. Her life was actually threatened by a step-parent who she says tried to bury her alive.

So there's a story behind all behaviour, and when we're doing an assessment we're trying to understand that story. The role of the client in the family may be seen as a significant part of the beginning of the story about why a client relates to others in a particular way.

Response *Doesn't the therapist's explanations of certain behaviour vary depending on the theoretical frame that the counsellor is operating from?*

Speaker It certainly might. That's why I think it's very important for counsellors in training and counsellors in practise to have a broad exposure to a variety of models and approaches and not be so narrowly focused. For example, a counsellor who thinks of a strictly behavioural approach might be more symptom oriented and be more focused on just changing current behaviour, and not really be interested in the story which goes back farther than the last few weeks or months in that person's life — or at most recent years. A counsellor using a psycho-dynamic approach would be more concerned maybe with the early life experience and less focused on actual behaviour change. Although I think that's included with psycho-dynamic approaches.

A person with a cognitive approach might be very focused on understanding the person's thought patterns: self-defeating thoughts, self-blame, self-limiting thoughts, erroneous beliefs, and so on. That counsellor might tend not to be as focused on supporting and validating painful feelings related to unresolved grief and loss, for example, that might still be affecting the client.

A little later on we'll see how the different models can be brought into an integrated process in order to meet the needs of the client.

Response *Couldn't the client think they're, say, the peacemaker, but they really aren't? That's just how they've been thinking.*

Speaker Yes, it might be kind of a misperception or an unbalanced perception of themselves. They might see another role as they're talking that they haven't identified, and which might be a more dysfunctional kind of role or a more prominent role. We need to be able say things to generate the client's insight.

Response *How would you do that, or is that too far down the road?*

Speaker That's something we'll do later when we look at the counselling process and therapeutic interventions. The next question is: "Describe your parents' marriage. Were they affectionate? How did they deal with conflict?" Here we are looking also for the extremes in terms especially of how they dealt with conflict. Were the parents highly conflictual, chronically conflictual, frighteningly conflictual, or did they avoid conflict altogether? Were they both very passive and silent when it came to conflict? With either extreme we can expect it to have an extreme impact on the client. So as a rule of thumb, extreme experiences in the family of origin result in extreme behaviours in the client. For example, a person who grew up in a highly conflictual or violent home — what impact might that have on the person?

Response *If he grew up in a violent home? He would see that as a way of getting things done — that would be normal.*

Speaker And he would follow that example or model himself after it and be violent sometimes?

Response *Would he also be self-abusive? Is that the same thing?*

Speaker He may perpetuate self-abuse in various ways, especially if he was a victim of that violence. What's another possible outcome?

Response *He rejects that as a model and goes the other way.*

Speaker Exactly. He reacts with the opposite extreme of avoiding conflict at all costs — keeping the anger in, suppressing his own anger, deciding anger is no good because it's so destructive from what he has seen. He might develop a very passive style with the occasional explosive outburst — that's another possibility. If he tries to stop expressing his issues and his anger for a long period of time, there can be a sudden explosive outburst. And then that will just demonstrate to him how bad anger is and he may stuff it again for a period of time until it builds up to another explosive encounter. There may be extremes in his ways of dealing with conflict.

Response *Anger by itself isn't really the destructive thing but how it is expressed.*

Speaker It's the way that the person copes with it or deals with it or expresses it.

Response *The opposite is also true when the person tries to model avoiding conflict by avoiding conflict in himself as well.*

Speaker That's right, exactly.

Response *There will be emotional outbursts. This has been my observation. The emotion is so strong it seems like it needs to get out and they're trying to model this calm non-conflicting parent but it's very difficult to hold all that in. So it will be okay at times, but there will be times of explosions.*

Speaker That's right. The client may adopt the style of the parent he feels sad for, or the parent he sees as the victim, or the parent he sympathizes with. A child may adopt the style of the aggressive controlling parent who is trying to change an alcoholic partner whom the child also resents. Or the child may adopt the style of the passive parent whom the child perceives as a victim of an aggressive dominating parent. In the latter case the adult child may be generally passive with the occasional aggressive outburst.

If both parents are generally passive and avoiding conflict, the child may model this behaviour and be frightened by an aggressive partner. When parents do not demonstrate skills for coping with conflict, it is no surprise that the adult child lacks the skills to cope.

So clients are usually either overly or generally passive, or generally or overly aggressive and destructive and don't seem to have the assertive option in their repertoire. One of the things we want to help clients with is acquiring communication skills so that they can express themselves in a way they can feel good about, and that works better than what they've been using.

Now if a client also never saw his parents being affectionate with each other, then it might make sense that he's having difficulty achieving intimacy in giving and receiving affection in his own relationships. On the other hand, if he didn't receive affection or see affection given in the parent's marriage it might be something that he craves so much he becomes smothering or overwhelming with people in relationships and so pushes them away.

It could have a distancing effect because he seems to want or need too much, so that he repeats the loss of caring.

Response *Where does the distancing come in?*

Speaker In either case there are these extremes perhaps in different individuals but resulting from the same type of parental relationships, first, keeping others at a distance by withdrawing from affection and second, distancing by smothering others with affection.

Speaker And so that has implications for what we're going to help the client gain insight into — those distancing kind of patterns that may perpetuate from the family of origin.

Then the next question is, "Did any one in the family or extended family ever become hospitalized for emotional reasons or commit suicide. Is there any mental retardation in the family?" So there are two things that are important about this question — maybe three. Does anybody have any ideas of what might be the significance of this question?

Response *If it has happened to someone else in the family then it could be genetic or a pattern.*

Speaker Right, there might be a genetic link or factor contributing to the clients problem that is evidenced by a relative or family member being hospitalized, for example. Hospitalization, suicide, or mental retardation also constitute significant losses with associated painful feelings which the client may experience. There are four types of disorders that are thought to have a genetic as well as environmental factors oftentimes. I'll just list and define them very briefly.

One is schizophrenia, which is a psychotic disorder in which the person often has paranoid ideas that he is the centre of a conspiracy, maybe a world wide conspiracy. He also may have auditory and visual hallucinations, and believe he can see things other people don't see and believe they can hear voices. That is actually his experience. The schizophrenic hears voices not inside his head but as if they are outside his head. In a typical psychotic episode, the subject may hallucinate that he is being spoken of in the third person by two other voices, who may be commenting negatively about his behaviour.

A visual hallucination is actually seeing something. It's not just imagining seeing a face in the wood grain of a door or something like that — it's actually being able to see something that isn't there. So that's schizophrenia. The disorder may begin at any age but instances of genetic disorder may begin in late adolescence or early adulthood and continue in a chronic course.

The other kind of schizophrenia is often characterized by a single acute episode that's temporary and goes away. The person may never have another recurring experience.

The second disorder is manic depressive illness, in which a person experiences periods of extreme elation. During that time he exercises very poor judgement — spending his money, having sex with various people, quitting his job, partying, things like that, maybe getting a divorce during that period. If he was on medication he might stop taking it, because in a manic phase he feels so high that he thinks he doesn't need to take it. The medication required is Lithium which must be regularly monitored by a psychiatrist.

And then he experiences extreme suicidal lows or depressions. If relatives did have manic depressive illness, in most cases they would have been hospitalized, and so you would know whether anyone in the family had the illness by asking these questions.

It's also important to ask about suicide. If someone committed suicide in the family, or among relatives, that might set a precedent. It might also be an indicator of some type of disorder that might be genetic — like borderline personality or manic depressive illness or schizophrenia. Those types of disorders occasionally result in a suicide.

The third disorder is the borderline personality which is thought to be genetic in some cases. It's characterized by extreme feelings of emptiness and abandonment, lack of identity, and extreme shifts in mood — intense mood swings, intense angry outbursts for example. Also, suicidal gestures or attempts would not be uncommon in a borderline person, especially when they're feeling abandoned in the breakup of a relationship.

The anti-social personality disorder is the fourth type and is thought to be genetic in a number of cases. It is characterized by violating the rights of others. This person might have difficulty with impulse control, might gamble his money away, might have multiple sexual partners, engage in conning or lying behaviour, unlawful behaviour, assaulting behaviour, maybe doesn't accept responsibility for his children and things like that.

We go more into the details in the advanced counselling course. These disorders are thought to have a genetic link because when a person placed in a nurturing adopted home environment immediately after birth, it has been found in significant numbers of cases that the person develops the same disorder that the natural parents were known to have.

One of the early indicators of a possible genetic factor for anti-social personality is hyperactivity in childhood and treatment with medication, i.e. Ritalin. If the child has attention deficit disorder, hyperactive disorder, that's often a pre-disposing factor or pre-curser of anti-social personality disorder that develops in adulthood. If a child's behaviour can be managed without Ritalin, then he does not have Hyperactive Disorder.

In addition, if we see indications of anti-social behaviour in parents and grandparents, a history of arrests and incarceration, this may contribute to a picture of possible genetic factors. Certainly an important environmental cause of anti-social personality is absence of parental discipline. And so in the disorders I'mdescribing, we need to consider both environmental as well as genetic factors — nature as well as nurture.

Response *Sometimes hyperactivity is thought of as caused by poor nutrition and lots of sugar.*

Speaker Well, it's more than that when there's an actual attention deficit. There's more involved than just poor nutrition or sugar problems.

Response *How much do diet, drugs, and alcohol use affect genetic changes?*

Speaker This is getting into an area where there's ongoing research and no firm conclusions right now, so it's a bit controversial about how much genetic material is affected by eating behaviours and things like that. Certainly we know that certain drug use might cause changes in genes or birth defects. That's still a very controversial area.

And concerning mental retardation, if a person has family members who are mentally retarded, it might affect his own self worth or he may think there is something wrong with his genes. This might indicate that we need to send our client for neurological, psychological, or genetic testing, or testing to determine a learning disability or something like that. There could be something related to the client's problems that might be of a genetic or biological nature, and it will be important to identify this if possible.

"How do the family members relate to each other?" is simply a general question to try to assess the nature of relationships in the family and to allow the client to elaborate or give a general impression of the family.

The next question is: "How were feelings of anger, sadness, fear and guilt expressed?" This question helps us to understand whether or not feelings were expressed in healthy kinds of ways, in destructive ways, in passive ways, and whether or not there was permission to express feelings.

For example, if a client cried as a child was he allowed to cry? Was there permission to cry? Was he always sent to his room? Did he feel understood when he was crying? Was he told to be quiet and shut up?

If a parent was a rage-aholic, the client may model that behaviour or react against it and become passive. If mother used tears to manipulate or cried often, a client may model that behaviour or react against it and become heavily defended against her own outward expression of painful feelings. Remember that extreme behaviours of parents often result in extreme behaviours in the adult child who either models the behaviour of the parent or reacts against extreme parental behaviour or both.

Have the client describe the who, how, why of the discipline experience. In other words, "Who disciplined you? How were you disciplined and why were you disciplined?" This tells us which parent was more involved. Maybe they were both involved. Maybe only one was involved. We learn about parental caring from this because it requires caring in order for a parent to discipline, in a healthy, effective kind of way. It takes time and patience to do this properly. "How were you disciplined?" For this I might ask for an example of a time when the person was disciplined. Maybe he thought he was disciplined severely. Here we might learn about whether the discipline was abusive or not. Were physical things used? And look for the why of the discipline — did it fit the severity of the child's behaviour or not?

For example I had a client who was lectured for hours and hours by her father for a small offence, and there has continued to be a significant unresolved conflict. She never felt accepted, loved or cared for by him.

So we are looking for extremes in discipline. On the one hand, abusive or rigid discipline and discipline without affection or reassurance of love. Over-restriction and over-protection may give the child the message that the world is a scary place, people can not be trusted, and the child is not capable of taking care of himself. On the other hand permissiveness or extreme lack of discipline may have been the case. All of these approaches constitute a loss of parental caring.

The next question is: "What personality features do you have that your parents also have?" This might indicate which parent your client felt closest to and adopted personality features from. It may also be the key to who the client felt most distant from. There are times when I hear a client saying that he was like the parent who was most abusive, or most distant, or who was gone from the family altogether. For example, the client says he is most like his father who "wasn't around."

Sometimes people adopt personality features, or think of themselves as having personality features of a parent because they are wanting to be connected or close to that parent.

What other questions or comments do you have at this point?

Response *Do people sometimes take on characteristics of loved ones who die?*

Speaker So you're suggesting a client might adopt certain personality features as a way to hang on to a parent or to keep him alive. I had a client whose father died when he was eight. The client was a schizoid type of fellow. He didn't have a full schizophrenic disorder, he wasn't psychotic but he did have some paranoid delusions. His father had left the family when the client was eight and then died in a motorcycle accident that same year. Father had been a railway man and an alcoholic. My client also had a motorcycle and when he rode up for treatment, he was dressed in railroad clothes and had a railroad cap on. He also had a drinking problem. So it seemed very striking to me that there were those kinds of similarities with his father. So this illustrates your point that a person might take on traits of a loved one who has died.

The next question is: "Who was there for you when you were hurt as a child?" This explores the caring and nurturing that was in the family. The client might say there was no one. That would be a sign of the loss of parental caring.

The next question is: "What message about your worth and the worth of others was communicated by your parents?" Here we're interested in both verbal and non-verbal messages communicated by the parents. The client may say for example, "Well my father was never around, so...." or, "My mother was always warning me about boys. That they're only after one thing," or, "My father was always drunk, so I guess he cared more about drinking," or "I could never do anything right."

The next question is: "How old were you when you left home and why did you leave?" What is the significance of this question?

Response *How you felt at home and how dependent you were.*

Speaker Yes. We might find from this that the client left home because of conflict and family dysfunction, or he stayed home to a late age because of being over-protected or manipulated to stay home. The parent may say or communicate in so many words that if the child leaves, then the parent will die, or become depressed or will lose her health. The parent is too dependent and will "guilt trip" the child. Or the parent may overprotect the child by giving him the message that he is not able to look after himself out there in that cruel world, that the world is a frightening place to be.

If there was abuse in the family of origin we might not be surprised to find that the child left home during early adolescence or earlier to get away from alcoholism or the emotional or physical abuse that was taking place. We might get the reasons why he left at the age he left. The anti-social personality who experiences conflict with authority figures may have left home as a teenager after a physical fight with father for example.

For a person from an Eastern culture, there would be a different significance if he left home at a later age. Because as I was saying earlier, if he is of Chinese or East Indian heritage or culture, it would be considered shameful shame to live as a single person in the community. People stay at home until they're married. Then they might continue to live in the parents' home or with the parents in an extended family arrangement.

Response *I guess older clients could be in the same situation if they came through the depression when people did stay together longer because there were no jobs and there were no places to live, no money.*

Speaker Yes. Nowadays for a person from Western culture it would more likely be an indication of dependency.

Near the end of exploring family history, we will ask the following question:

"If you had miraculous power to change your family and childhood experience in any three ways what would you choose?"

This is one of my favourite questions because it really focuses on what we might term the core issues that the client struggles with, and that often form the background for his current struggles and problems.

Some typical answers here are things like, "Well, I wish my family had been closer. I wish we had communicated better." Or, "I wish my father hadn't been an alcoholic. I wish my parents didn't drink or wish my parents hadn't fought so much. I wish there hadn't been so much conflict." Or, "I wish we had more money." Often times this is related to the conflict between parents who fought over the lack of money.

And so almost always we'll hear a client mention things that have to do with the loss of caring and closeness in the family of origin. When they say, "I wish we communicated better," or, "I wish my parents hadn't fought so much," that's an issue of closeness in the family.

There also may be issues of loss that the client mentions, such as, "I wish my parents hadn't divorced or my father hadn't died," or, "I wish my mother hadn't died", or things like that.

Sometimes a client will say, "I can't think of anything I would change about my family." My response to this is, "What might you change even in some minor way." This makes it easier for the client to identify something. Another common client response is to say, "I wouldn't change anything because I am who I am today because of what happened." My response to this is, "So I'm hearing that you've been able to make these difficulties work for you. What are some examples?" This rephrasing supports the client's way of adapting and still identifies some core issues. Another approach is to ask the client to describe the ideal family and then to talk about how his family was different.

Otherwise, the next question will help the client to connect his family experience with what's happening now. This is a little bit of what you're going to be doing in the counselling process — helping the client gain insight into his life patterns and the connection between past and present experiences.

This question is: "If your family experience had been different in the ways you mentioned, I wonder if you can imagine how your life might be different today." A response for example may be, "If we communicated better and been closer when I was growing up I think it would be a lot easier for me to approach people and to form relationships and to be closer, not be so frightened or shy." So the client is establishing a link between how the family experience has affected his current functioning and implies an area he may need to work on in counselling.

A common question I hear is, "What do you do when your client begins to express some emotions in responding to a question during assessment?" Do you have any ideas about that?

Response *You'd want them to let the emotions be expressed, and create a safe space for that to happen.*

Speaker Yes. It's important for a while to attend to any feelings that come up but not to stay too long with them, unless of course the client is overwhelmed or in crisis. It is important to acknowledge the pain the client has. Initially I would say, "Just let yourself feel that right now." And then I would say something like, "This sounds like something that maybe would be important to explore in your counselling." In other words, validate the importance of the area being touched on and underscore that as something the client might want to come back to. You don't want to take time during assessment to focus on any particular area, but you do want to acknowledge painful feelings.

Another thing that happens in the assessment that drags it out is when a client gives lengthy responses and becomes over-talkative. You need to be able to say things that can move the assessment along, such as making a reflection of what the client is talking about and then introducing the very next question.

So for example I'll interrupt the client by saying something like, "Let me see if I understand what you're saying so far." And then I'll say, "So it sounds like what you're talking about is that you weren't very close to your father, he was very critical, he didn't give you the approval or the understanding that you needed and that's been a kind of ongoing issue for you even now. Is that what you're saying?"

So the client will then acknowledge that this is an accurate reflection, and then I will introduce the next question by saying for example, "The next question I'd like to ask you is what was your mother's personality like?" It's important to be able to lead right into the next question, to be assertive and caring with the over-talking client. Otherwise you might not be able to finish the assessment.

Response *You need to establish some order or some containment.*

Speaker Correct. We have to keep the client moving within the structure of the assessment because the main objective is to gather information, not to do counselling. It's a little like running along side a moving train to jump on. By this I mean you have to start talking as the client is talking in order to break into the flow of words, and you need to do it with the kind of intervention I described. Are there any questions about family history before we move on?

Response *When you're doing family history and you come up against an absolute brick wall, too much anger or emotion or anything, would you go to personal history and then back to family history? Or would you keep working at the family history?*

Speaker I am careful to acknowledge that discomfort or pain and if there are tears I say, "Just take some time to feel that." When painful feelings are triggered it's important to acknowledge, validate, and allow some silent space for the client. This maintains the client's safety and trust, whereas if I were to ignore the painful feelings, how might it affect the therapeutic alliance?

Response *Safety might be lost.*

Speaker Exactly. Then I might say, "So there's some hurt around this, and maybe it will be important to explore this further in your counselling." It is very important to acknowledge the value of the issue and to structure it by referring it to the counselling process which will begin in the second session. It might be tempting to take too much time with the issue and to lapse into counselling. If the client appears to be in crisis, we will of course set the assessment aside and do crisis intervention. But otherwise it's important to move along with the assessment, yet to provide enough support for the client when painful feelings are engaged. I might then say, "Do you feel OK about continuing?"

If the client refuses to answer a question, I say, "Maybe it is difficult for you to respond to that right now and that's okay, that's understandable. Maybe that's an area we could come back to at another time." What might I do next?

Response *Give him the option of continuing.*

Speaker I might, and then go right down to the next question. Or I might say, "I wonder if you could just say a little bit about this for now." In other words, present it to him in a way that is less threatening by encouraging him to say just a little bit. What I find happens with people who are very frightened or resistant about pursuing an area of their life experience, if you just invite them to say a little bit, they will usually say all they need to say or all you need to know for now. But it helps them feel safer because it lets them know that you are not expecting them to say everything or a whole lot about it.

PERSONAL HISTORY

The next area is personal history. With this I'm saying, "Now I'd like to ask you some questions about your life mostly apart from your family. Is that okay?"

BIRTH AND DEVELOPMENTAL HISTORY

The first category is birth and developmental history, and the first question here is, "Do you know if your mother had any problems with your birth?" I'm looking for not only what happened but also the parental message that might have gone along with what happened.

There are two things that I'm really interested in here. The first is whether the client has any information about complications or problems such as the umbilical being wrapped around the neck, or experiencing oxygen deficiency, or something that may indicate a need for neurological testing.

The second area is what was said about the birth that could relate to the client's self concept, or messages or beliefs about the self that may have originated very early on.

For example, a client might say to me, "Yes, my mother told me that I took a lot of trouble to deliver and I've been trouble ever since." Something like that — a very negative sort of message.

"Were you a planned pregnancy?" As we said earlier the unplanned child often feels unwanted and has low self esteem.

"Did your parents ever tell you what kind of baby you were? Easy or difficult?" Again there's a parental message that's involved, and often I see a client having an adult personality that corresponds directly to how they were described as a baby. So the easy baby is often the passive, laid back client. The difficult baby or crying baby is often an aggressive adult, outspoken and conflictual. Now whether that's due to genetics or environment or parental message, is up for debate.

Question *And what about the opposite, the person who has been told he was an easy baby but became demanding later on?*

Speaker Yes, that's possible too. I'm simply suggesting that often there is a correlation, and sometimes there isn't. The next question is: "Did you have any experience of bed wetting after early childhood?" What are the implications of this question?

Response *Nervousness or anxiety may have caused it.*

Speaker Okay, what else?

Response *Conflict in the family — a dysfunctional family.*

Speaker All right, it might have been something like that, related to stress. Recent research indicates the possibility of physical or biological factors. Perhaps more importantly, we're interested in how the client felt about themselves around the bed wetting and what was the parental response or way of coping with the bed wetting. Did the client get rejection messages? Did he feel shame or low self worth? Were the parents nurturing and understanding about it, or not? And when we say after early childhood, we're talking about bed wetting that goes on into the pre-teen years and maybe in the teenage years, or maybe even later than that.

The next question:

"Did you learn to walk by age one or talk by age two?" Those are the normal developmental milestones for walking and talking. So if a person has slower development in those areas, it might be an indicator of some type of learning disability, or neurological problem for which they might be referred for testing or examination. Early development may set up high expectations for the child which he must meet or face disapproval from parents whose caring is conditional.

The next question:

"Any long high fevers or convulsions as a child?" Convulsions are usually related to oxygen deficiency and brain damage. This might imply a need to refer them for neurological testing to determine any possible biological factor contributing to the presenting problems.

Response *So if someone says that he had convulsions, how do you determine whether you need to refer him or not?*

Speaker Well if he had convulsions I would refer him just to rule out the possibility of any organic or biological factor. I would continue to work with him but I would set him up to get some type of examination so that I could add that to my understanding of what the client is going through.

SCHOOL AND INTELLECTUAL HISTORY

The next area is school and intellectual development. "What was the first day of school like?" Why is that a significant question?

Response *Because when school begins they're being cut off from the family, in a sense.*

Speaker That's the first separation experience from the family of origin often times, and possibly frightening for a child.

Response *These days we ask, "What was the first day of day care like?" Often kids are separated from their families before they go to school.*

Speaker That's right, it's very different nowadays with pre-school, day care and things like that. I think in some ways it's not as traumatic although it probably is in some situations. As these adult children begin counselling they can tell us how day care has affected their lives.

The next question:

"How many moves and school changes occurred during school years?" Certainly this is a type of loss experience. Why is this important?

Response *Stability in the family.*

Speaker Okay, it might indicate something about the instability of the family. What else? What are the effects of multiple moves?

Response *Being afraid to get to know people.*

Speaker Right. So it might get in the way of social development and forming close personal attachments to others. The client may have thought, "What's the point in getting close if I'm going to be uprooted again?"

And it might be part of a larger picture of problems with intimacy in adult relationships. If a person has a combination of some of these factors we've talked about so far, say he had multiple moves and wasn't close to the parents, then we're seeing two very important factors contributing to his difficulty of maintaining closeness in current relationships.

Next ask, "Describe your relationship with peers in school." And we may hear him say that he was the outsider with peers. He really wasn't connected or he felt victimized in school. Then that might be also part of that larger pattern of difficulty in being close in current adult relationships.

The next question:

"Describe your relationships with teachers." Here we are looking for the extremes of the overly conforming child who was the teachers pet and the conflictual person who's in trouble with the teachers and authorities in school. What personality in the family of origin is very conforming and dutiful in classrooms?

Response *The responsible child.*

Speaker We might see that pattern being perpetuated in the occupational history when we ask, "How do you get along with bosses?" The responsible child perpetuates that role. He's staying a long time perhaps in jobs and reporting that he always gets along very well with bosses — he doesn't rock the boat.

Response *There would be exceptions though.*

Speaker Oh yes.

Response *There may be different reasons why a person would stay with a job.*

Speaker Say more about that.

Response *Well, people who stay in a job because opportunities are limited or who stay in jobs that they dislike, but just because it's an easy job.*

Response *By contrast, I talked to a friend of mine who felt fear over establishing a pattern that was predictable or steady, and wanted to avoid this responsibility. "Thank you, no I just want to go at my own pace." So would change jobs.*

Speaker So whether a person stays with a job or changes frequently, there's a story behind that behaviour. Sometimes people do flip in ways and in their patterns. They move from one extreme to another. They go from being an overly responsible person to being the party animal — the wreckless carefree extreme. Often times I see the person who has been the responsible child and in order to make progress in recovery, needs to let herself have a childhood and be irresponsible before she can really let go of the loss of her childhood during the growing up years. So for that person we might get her involved in contact sorts of play. Volleyball is something that is traditionally done with clients who have been overly rigid or controlled or overly responsible. This gives them a chance to play and have fun and loosen up, to laugh and jump, to bump into other people, and to be a child. Volleyball provides an opportunity for the child in the client to come out and play.

Question *Is that mid-life crisis? I mean in men or women — men in particular get to a certain age and have been working at a job for a while and they become childlike. They go out and buy sports cars, they dress in flashy clothes.*

Speaker Yes they might make a major shift there in their mid-life.

SOCIAL DEVELOPMENT

The next area is social development. Here we are going to see these life patterns being extended. We're going to see more evidence of patterns of distancing and things like that.

The first question here is: "Did you have a group of friends during the first six grades?" That would be normal development or expected development to have a group of friends during ages 7 to 11. But if a person reports he didn't have that, we might see that as part of his current difficulty that he didn't experience adequate social skill development which comes from interacting with the group during those years as a child.

A person who has had multiple moves during school years also may have difficulty forming a group of friends. It takes a while to be in a place in order to have a group.

The next question is: "Did you have one or two very close friends as a teenager?" That would be expected development for teenagers, not to have a group, but rather to have one or two very close friends. If a person said that he didn't experience that, that would be a significant factor.

If we saw combinations of these things around difficulty being able to form close relationships in these various categories, the contributing factors would begin to mount. So we can then see a broad picture, or story, behind our client's current difficulties.

The next question is: "Did you tend to be a follower or leader with friends?" The follower tends to be an internalizing individual, tends to not be the outspoken decision maker, tends to be more passive, tends to allow others to decide. So the follower may be dependent, and because of internalizing feelings, he may tend to be depressed and withdrawn under stress.

Question *What do you do when a person is confused about that? I know if I was to answer that, I couldn't be too sure because there were times when I was a follower probably because I didn't want the responsibility of making decisions for other people. But I also adopted the role of the leader sometimes because no one else would. There could be a lot of confusion there.*

Speaker So a person might give you one of three responses: "I was generally a follower" or, "I was generally a leader" or, "I was both depending on the situation". If he reports both, I'm seeing it more as a balanced picture than the person who is generally the follower, or generally the leader.

The leader may be too controlling or aggressive. That means there might be a pattern of demanding, telling people what to do too much, making too many decisions for others, doing too much, giving too much, taking care of others too much. The responsible child or the assistant parent in the family of origin might be a leader or a follower. In extreme cases both the follower or leader may not get his needs met because of a tendency to focus on others, either to please others or to look after others or both.

Sometimes a client might respond that he was neither a follower nor a leader. How is this possible?

Response *Maybe he was a loner.*

Speaker Exactly, and this may be the case with the victim or outsider in the family of origin or among peers, or if there were many moves, for example.

The next question is: "How old were you when you first dated?" Again we are interested in extremes. An early age might indicate a lack of parental guidance.

Speaker This is not necessarily implying first sexual contact. So essentially what we're wanting to know is, is there contact with the opposite sex at that level of social development. Was it too early or was it too late?

Question *How do you judge what's too early and what's too late?*

Speaker That's changed over the years depending on our social expectations or social practices, but a person who starts dating regularly at age 12 or 13 can be considered early. The odd date or the first time date might normally happen that early.

My little girl had her first time experience going out with a friend from school when she was 11 to a family square dance. We tagged along and sat at the other side of the school auditorium, and she hasn't done anything like that since and probably won't for a few more years. Age 14 would be a usual early age to begin dating perhaps on an occasional basis..

Response *I guess that depends on if you're hurt too. If you start a relationship and experience a loss, that might stop you from doing dating.*

Speaker Yes, that's right. It can get scary. And then we are also looking for the person who starts dating at a much later age. Maybe he's 19, 20, 21 or even older by the time a he has a first date, which might indicate some kind of block or fear of the opposite sex. The young man that grew up with a dominating mother and didn't have any sisters might find females to be threatening, too frightening. The male or female client who started late may have been overprotected by parents or given the message that something bad will happen, such as pregnancy, for example.

Question *About dating, what would be the implications of starting really young?*

Speaker If a person was into regular dating patterns at an early age it might be a way of looking for caring that is missed in the parental relationship or a way of escape from an abusive or conflictual family. This might lead to sexual involvement because the need for caring is often sexualized. If a child is sexually abused in the family of origin, early involvement may proceed from her belief that she is good for only one thing and therefore a way to define self-worth.

Having said all of this, it is important not to draw conclusions from early dating or late dating but to see if it fits a larger picture or pattern of what may have been happening in the family of origin.

Another point here is that sexuality is not just sexual intercourse but interaction with the opposite sex, so we're talking about this happening too early in puberty so that the child is not able to have fun with peers of the same sex for a long enough period of time.

So the child moves along prematurely into opposite sex relationships. It may be important for adult development for the child to remain in sexual innocence for a longer period of time. Regular dating might also involve other sexual experiences that would take away from that person's need to be sort of ignorant and innocent rather than doing adult things too soon. It can take away from her childhood.

Question *Is our current notion of childhood different from what it was say 100 or 150 years ago? Let's say a family then was on a farm and the kids needed to be put to work to help on the farm, whereas now they don't have, other than going to school, that same kind of responsibility. During the industrial revolution they were even put to work in the mines. Has that concept of childhood changed?*

Speaker It seems it has. Years ago children were expected to work and take on adult responsibilities at a very early age.

Response *I find it's the same nowadays, only it's coming from a different source. You go out into the world and you have to grow up quick because there are so many signals. You just look at television and the expectations of what kids should look like. You look at the commercials and see how kids should dress. I mean there are always these sexual innuendos built into the clothing that they're wearing. And these kids are about eight or nine years old.*

Speaker That's right, and they are already being seduced, facing responsibilities, becoming pregnant for example, before having the training and emotional readiness.

The next question is: "Do you have friends or acquaintances now?" We are interested in what the client's social network is like now and whether this is part of a pattern of not being able to form social relationships. Does this person have a support system?

Next question:

"Is this a satisfactory network of friends?" The person who is the expert on the adequacy of the social network, of course, is the client. If the person has one or few friends and says that's satisfactory, then who are we to say that it isn't?

The next question is: "How do you describe the type of people you associate with?" Are these people part of the problem? Are they drug friends or booze buddies? Are they long distance friends? Are these friends people with problems who the client looks after or counsels? So this question may tell us something more about the kind of role the client takes on in relationships.

I had a client who said she had a lot of friends. I asked, "How often do you see them or associate with them?" She said not very often because they live in all the other major cities in Canada. That told me that she really has no one here. Her network is really scattered. If a person has friends who are associated with his current problems, then it might mean that if he is to recover from his problem, he may have to lose those friends.

Response *That would be quite an issue if someone had an alcoholic problem. That would make it a double issue. Someone would have to go through letting go of the booze plus changing or losing the circle of friends.*

Speaker So it's a double loss. He has to replace his addiction and replace his social network. What would you do first?

Response *Take care of the network I suppose.*

Ross drinks with his brother ... his best friend.

Speaker Or both at the same time.

Response *When they change their addiction, often times there's a friend they used to hang out with, and might be uncomfortable hanging out with any more.*

Speaker They don't have that thing in common.

Response *He can find out who his true friends are.*

OCCUPATIONAL HISTORY

Speaker The next category is occupational history. The first question is: "How old were you when you first went to work?" Again, we're looking here at perhaps a loss of childhood through work at an early age. Again, we look at extremes — the early age and the late age.

The early age implies a loss of childhood. I'm not talking about babysitting but work that the family depends upon. For example, one of my clients was abandoned by his father when he was eleven and had to go to work to help support the family out on the prairies. He appeared for counselling with his wife who complained that he was non-communicative, and this seemed to fit with a pattern of looking after others and not addressing his own needs from an early age.

And then the client who went to work at a late age maybe was kept at home or protected, and remained dependent in that way. He may have been given a "the world's a scary place" message or not encouraged to step out, perhaps meeting some emotional need of the parent.

The next question is: "What kinds of jobs have you had, and how many?" Here we're looking for stability in the work place and on the level of occupational experiences. Have they been short-term jobs with periods of unemployment? This may be part of a pattern of dependency or difficulty accepting adult responsibility. The other extreme of remaining a long time on the job without a promotion may also be part of a pattern of dependency.

The next question is: "Why have you left jobs?" Has the person been fired? Maybe that's part of the picture of conflict with authorities. Had they become bored?

The next question:

"Describe your relationship with bosses." We're looking for whether the person has been overly conforming or overly conflictual. The responsible child may stay a long time on the job, stay late to work, and respond to this question with, "I always get along very well with bosses." This type of person makes a good employee but may not be getting her own needs met, may be self-sacrificing. The conflictual client may respond with, "I don't like people telling me what to do or looking over my shoulder." To be a good employee, it's important to accept your boss telling you what to do, and so this may be part of a larger problem of the way he relates to authorities going back to the parental relationship in the family of origin.

The next question:

"And are you realizing your potential? Do you feel fulfilled?" A negative response might be an indicator for low self worth, and may be a contributing factor in burnout or depression. Has a person been many years in a job he dosen't like or a number of jobs that he dosen't like? Does he seem to be unable to find his niche? Is it because he doesn't know what his own needs are? Or if he does, what's getting in the way of fulfilling his needs? Does it have to do with negative beliefs about self and self worth? Often that is the case.

Of course we can also say it's because of the person's own stage of personal development that he hasn't found the jobs fulfilling. The young adult for example is still searching and experimenting. Are there any questions or comments up to this point?

Question *How can the assessment be done in an hour or an hour and a quarter?*

Speaker It takes a lot longer to discuss the rationale as we're doing than it does to do the assessment with a client.

Response *I've worked with this type of format and asked similar questions in a smaller degree and even at that I find that it's time consuming. It's a combination of building rapport and developing trust and safety, and finding the hidden issues of why the person is there. Then of course after all of that, getting to the solution.*

Response *This takes practice doing assessments and becoming familiar with the process of gathering information.*

Speaker A lot of practice and really getting the assessment down in your head so you don't have to take a lot of notes. Note-taking is the most time consuming.

Response *But you'd have to take some kind of notes on some areas so you know to come back to them. If you only see the client for an hour you'd have to get something down.*

Speaker That's definitely the case if you're seeing multiple clients, such as when I'm seeing six clients a day, three in the morning and three in the afternoon.

Response *You might confuse your stories.*

Response *It is time consuming but it does seem to be necessary.*

Speaker Absolutely, some form of note-taking is necessary at least after the client has left.

Question *Couldn't you just take down a few notes? Like if a person says that they've had no real problems with alcohol or drugs, couldn't you just skip that whole section?*

Speaker Yes you can. You can abbreviate and skip some areas maybe that have already been answered by your client because sometimes your client will respond to a few other questions in response to one. You can skip over a section, or a question or two here or there if it has been answered previously.

Also, if you have the assessment outline in memory, then you can simply sit down after a session and write down the significant information on the assessment form and under the appropriate headings.

Speaker So let's see if we can move down through the rest of our assessment, briefly, and then I'll have a demonstration in the last part of today.

HOBBIES AND SIDE INTERESTS

We're now asking about hobbies and side interests. The question is: "What are some of your side interests and activities." Often times clients are having problems because they have all their eggs in one basket. If something happens to that basket, they lose all their eggs. The person who has diverse interests is probably going to be able to cope better with things like losses.

We're also going to be asking, "Has there been any change in the level of your interest lately?" With this we're looking for depression because with depression there's a loss of interest in usual pleasurable activities.

SEXUAL AND MARITAL HISTORY

We move on to sexual and marital history. The question I ask is, "Describe your personality during the early teen years." Sometimes people are stuck at that stage of their development as it relates to their social and sexual feelings — a person who was very shy around the opposite sex may still be shy as an adult.

One of my male clients about age 32 said he felt afraid of girls from age 15 or 16 and attributes this to the lack of a close relationship with father, not being told about sexuality by his parents, and not having sisters. He had one older brother, and said his brother had a similar problem until he moved from the parental home. My client was still living at home at this late age and seemed very frightened of moving out. There appeared to be overprotection and overinvolvement by the mother, double bonding with one parent which often occurs when the relationship with the other parent is distant.

The next question:

"What were your feelings about menstruation and wet dreams?" Here, we're going for some of the experience or emotions that may have occurred during puberty, around those events. What would you imagine are the feelings or emotions that come up for some people around, say, their first menstruation. What's it like at the beginning?

Response *I imagine that it's scary.*

Speaker What's that fear about?

Response *Am I going to stop bleeding?*

Speaker Okay, yes, the fear that she might bleed to death, that she might die, especially for the girl who is not prepared, who wasn't informed. That might indicate that she wasn't close to her mother or a female parent figure. In some families, looking at the other end of the scale, often times it's an occasion for celebration, a special event. The family goes out to eat or something special happens.

With a boy having wet dreams, the trauma might not be as significant.

Response *You still celebrate... go out to eat? (laugh)*

Speaker What are the feelings that a boy may have with his first wet dream experience?

Response *I know if you're a strong Christian, that could be bad or dirty.*

Speaker Yes. Absolutely. There could be shame associated with it. The person might feel there's something wrong with him.

Response *Embarrassment?*

Speaker Yes. Feeling guilty.

Response *The thought that there could be something wrong.*

Speaker There could be something wrong with your genitals or sexual organ... something's broken... or, "I'm becoming a sex deviant. I'm having these sexual dreams. What's happening to my mind?" So, if you have older brothers or a father who you can talk to, it becomes easier.

The next question is: "What was your first date like?" Was it scary? Was the client nervous? It would make sense for a person who had a conflictual opposite sex parent, or an unaccepting, critical opposite sex parent, or a distant non-communicative parent, that it might be scary to date. If you were a boy and didn't have any sisters, the unknown might be scary. You might have all these ideas about how different girls are but not really know how they're different.

Response *How about expectations, like getting excited and it being nothing special at all?*

Speaker Yes, there may be a lot of unknowns.

Response *The emphasis our society places now on sex and sexuality as being the be-all and end-all in advertising and films and so on would come into play.*

Response *In music — teenagers' music — there's a lot of that too.*

Speaker You mean the fear of not performing, fulfilling expectations for sex in the dating relationship? Alright. So we're looking for the level of discomfort. We want to know if it was a positive or a negative experience.

The next question is: "How old were you with your first sexual experience?"

Response *Do you leave that up to the client as far as what sexual experiences are?*

Speaker Yes, I do initially. I want to see what he comes up with as his first sexual experience and how old he was exactly. He might report a childhood sexual exploration or experimentation from preschool days, for example. He might come up with a sexual abuse experience, being sexually abused by somebody, or his first sexual intercourse.

I'm interested in what is presented in response to this and if she doesn't refer to sexual abuse or sexual intercourse, I'll ask specifically about those two things by saying, "Were you ever sexually abused? Touched in a way you didn't like sexually?" and, "When was your first sexual intercourse experience? How old were you and what was it like?"

I had a client recently whom I asked whether or not she had ever been sexually abused. She thought she had been but she never told anybody about it before. She didn't come back for the next session. She phoned and cancelled, but I did have a chance to talk to her, and she said that she realized when she told me she was sexually abused that that's what she had to deal with but she felt more comfortable talking about it with a female counsellor. I supported her in that by saying: "That's certainly understandable. I encourage you to pursue that with a female counsellor."

It was very important, I think, that I ask that question because often times when people go for counselling, they're not asked certain questions because the counsellor may feel too uncomfortable. The other approach which makes sense and which some counsellors use is that if the counsellor asks too directly about sexual abuse before the client feels safe to disclose it, the client may feel too frightened or ashamed to return. Asking, "What was your first sexual experience?" gives the client an opportunity to disclose sexual abuse without feeling controlled. Otherwise, maybe she will disclose it later when she feels safe enough.

Response *Are you saying be more direct then?*

Speaker Be more direct taking into account that you may be opening a painful issue prematurely. Now, with the first sexual intercourse, I want to know what it was like. Was it okay? Was it unpleasant? Was it a case of date rape or something like that? Because often the first sexual experience or of sexual intercourse might actually colour all subsequent sexual encounters — if it was a very painful experience, physically and emotionally.

I may ask about vaginismus which is a contraction of vaginal muscles preventing intercourse. The fear of incest or of sexual abuse or intercourse may be in the background. For example, a client whose father attempted intercourse with her as a child following mother's death, was married as an adult but did not have intercourse with her husband for eight years due to vaginismus.

The next question is: "How many sexual partners have you had over time?" I'm simply going for the level of sexual stability. I'm interested in the history of sexual relationships which may indicate multiple partners, periods of promiscuity, monogamy, or no sexual involvement. In the extreme cases of promiscuity on the one hand or no sexual involvement on the other, problems with intimacy may be indicated.

The next question is: "What is your sexual preference or orientation?" Is the client homosexual, bisexual, or heterosexual? Now, there are some varying schools of thought around this question.

One of them is that sexual preference is genetic, another is that it is simply a matter of choice unrelated to previous life experience, and the third school of thought is that it is related to early life experience. That is, that there has been a block in relating to the opposite sex on a sexual level. This is why he or she chooses a same sex preference.

There also may be a contributing factor of sexual abuse earlier in life during developmental years.

Response *So, you're not saying that they are gay just because they had such a bad time with whoever they were with of the opposite sex, that they then choose a partner of the same sex?*

Speaker Well, for example, you have a person who grows up in a family where her father died when she was four. Within the next few years she was molested by her uncle and, subsequent to father's death, her mother became emotionally unavailable and unaccepting of her. So, she had abuse experience by a male and abandonment by a male (the death of her father), and subsequent to that had a distant relationship with the mother. Since then in her adult life, she has sought the caring of same sex individuals.

It makes sense that she would be having a lesbian preference in light of that story. It makes sense that she would be blocked in her ability to trust or to be intimate with men, and it makes sense that she would seek the caring that she was missing in her relationship with mother.

Often times there are dual factors: when the same-sex parent is emotionally unavailable and the opposite sex parent is often either over-involved, smothering, sexually abusive, or highly violent, or rejecting. Contributing factors to same sex preference are, for gay males: same sex childhood exploration, distant or absent father, sexual seduction by an adult male, a smothering or controlling mother, a sexually abusive mother, or a castrating mother who put men down by saying for example that men are only interested in "one thing", i.e. sex.

For lesbian preference — traumatic sexual abuse by a male, same sex childhood exploration, physically or emotionally abusive father, emotionally unavailable or rejecting mother. In male or female gay preference, once pleasure is derived from same sex activity or same sex fantasies, changing to heterosexual preference may not be wanted or thought possible by the homosexual person.

Another client's father was alcoholic, violent, abusive toward mother and always put mother down. Mother was always passive and emotionally unavailable to this client. I don't know that the client was sexually abused but it made sense that she would go in the direction away from opposite sex relationships toward seeking the caring that she needs from mother by forming same sex relationships.

I've seen this repeatedly. But it is a controversial area so I do present varying schools of thought on that.

Response *I would think also that in your first example of the woman's relationship with both the two men and her mother, that she might seek to drop out of any relationship with anybody because she could feel abandoned with her mother just as she felt abandoned with her father.*

Speaker So what may occur then is that the person has repeated attempts to get the caring from same-sex partners. And because of familiarity with loss of caring, the client is attracted to partners who are needy and have difficulty maintaining relationships so that the loss of caring is repeated again and again. The male homosexual may have up to 500 sexual partners in a lifetime. For Lesbians the number of sexual partners is much fewer.

Response *You don't ask how often the client masturbates.*

Speaker No. That's a question that often goes into a clinical assessment. I don't put it here because sometimes I feel that it's too intrusive. You have to decide when its appropriate to ask questions about things like frequency of masturbation. Another question that's not here is. "Do you have vaginal or urinary tract infections — kidney infections?"

Often times yeast infections in women accompanies stress. The female client becomes quite susceptible to yeast infections because of chronic stress, and frequency of masturbation might also be related to anxiety disorders and lack of an available sexual partner. So, it can be worthwhile asking that.

Some people might also have feelings of low self-worth around their masturbation behaviours, and it might be getting in the way of their relationships. For example, a person may prefer an auto-sexual activity to heterosexual or marital-sexual activities. I think that it is important to ask those questions in these situations.

Response *There are religious views.*

Speaker There are religious views opposing masturbation. Yes. And then there are religious views encouraging masturbation.

Response *The comment I was going to make here is about dealing with gay relationships. I don't think of them as a dysfunctional arrangement because I haven't formed any conclusion on this. For instance, I have a friend, a very well-balanced individual, and she's made her preferences for women known and she's also very accommodating with men. She's a very friendly and warm person. If that wasn't an issue or a dysfunctional situation it would be something I would have a tendency to leave behind unless it came up somewhere else.*

Speaker That's right. Absolutely. That's a very important point that we don't address the sexual preference as a problem or an issue unless the client identifies it as a problem area she wants to work on.

When a client indicates a same-sex preference, however, I can't help but think about what the psychological origins might be. And often times I do see patterns common to a number of clients. But it is very controversial.

Response *How could we rule out the genetic or some sort of pre-disposition superimposed on the family of origin? Because even if a person from the beginning is gay, and he doesn't have a traumatic childhood, he's still going to be gay, and it won't be caused by the trauma?*

Speaker Genetic factors would be involved in such a tiny fraction of homosexuals that the incidents would be insignificant. And in cases where it might be a factor related to the presence of opposite sex physical or biological characteristics, the individual is sterile or perhaps mentally retarded. Another contributing factor that is often pointed out is early childhood sexual experience with the same sex which sets up pleasure related sexual fantasies involving the same sex.

As with many behavioural life patterns, the early development is not by choice but a matter of the child's adapting in order to survive. However, the continuation of a pattern in adult life is a matter of choice, and patterns can be changed by choice. If we argue that homosexual behaviour is not a choice but somehow genetic, then what do we do with heterosexual behaviour and other sexual behaviours and preferences?

No, there is always a story behind the behaviour that allows it to make sense. Sexual preference does not just fall out of the sky. If you have a male client who had early sexual experiences with the same sex, and you have a father who was distant and unavailable and a mother who was smothering and over-involved, then it might make sense that he would perpetuate a same sex preference without necessarily being consciously aware of how he developed that preference.

Many clients would not be interested in identifying homosexuality as a problem because they associate pleasure with same sex experiences. Why change something that you find pleasurable? They don't identify it as a problem, even though it can contribute on another level to social instability.

Just a rule of thumb about sexual questions. Don't ask questions that you are uncomfortable asking. It will show through and your client will feel unsafe with you. And what I would recommend when you go through sexual questions is to ask them matter-of-factly without any emotional reaction on your part. In general, use the questions in the assessment. Ask them matter-of-factly without any non-verbal or verbal reaction on your part. Show caring and support and empathy, but don't show any sort of negative reaction.

Response *Don't show judgement.*

Speaker Yes, no verbal or non-verbal judgement on your part. I had somebody in training ask, "When was your first sexual experience of sexual intercourse?" And the client said, "Oh, I didn't have sex until I was married," and the counsellor did something non-verbal to indicate shock and surprise. And the client wasn't aware of feeling anything about that just then but she thought about that through the week and when she came back she said that she couldn't be with that counsellor again because of that reaction.

She couldn't feel safe with that person. She, herself didn't feel good about not having had sex before she was married. She felt like she was too much of a goody-two-shoes and she saw that as part of her problem, so she didn't want anybody to see her the way that she saw herself. She felt ashamed for being a virgin before she was married, which may also say something about our social expectations today.

The next question is: "Describe your partner's personality in your current relationship." Here we're trying to identify the current relationship, because in the next question, "Describe previous meaningful relationships, personalities, and why they ended", we're going to see if there's a pattern between what's happening now and what was happening in the previous meaningful relationships. We're looking for patterns of distancing, of repetitions of experiencing unmet needs.

For example, if the person was in an alcoholic family — an alcoholic, maybe violent father — the first person she attaches to is perhaps alcoholic and violent. But then she decides she's not going to subject herself to that again and so she finds someone who's passive and quiet and gentle — very laid back. But that doesn't last because passive people may not communicate. So she's gone from one extreme to the other and in both cases what is she left with?

Response *Something that doesn't make for a very satisfying relationship — doesn't meet her needs.*

Speaker That's right — an unsatisfying relationship that doesn't meet her needs. Exactly. That's what happened in the family of origin, and this is being repeated in current relationships, loss of caring.

"Describe the family including how you and your partner and the children relate as a family and as individuals." I want to explore just a little bit what the nuclear family is like. Are people close? Who is closer than others within the family? Does the client have a sense of enjoying being with one child more than another? Is a parent deriving support from a child that should be coming from the spouse?

Are there conflicts with some family members more than with others? This is especially important in the blended family situation where you have children from other previous families or marriages being brought into the same family. Most often there is unresolved grief over the loss of the parent that is missing and a rejection of the parent who is taking the missing parent's place.

There is often conflict in blended families between the step-children and step-parents because of unresolved grief. And there might be abuse or sexual abuse issues between step-children and step-parents. In single parent families, maybe the mother is directing anger toward a child who resembles or reminds her of the ex-husband.

ALCOHOL AND DRUG HISTORY

Now we come to alcohol and drug abuse history.

The first question is: "What about your use of alcohol and drugs? How much and how often?" I want to know about quantity of alcohol consumption to determine the degree of dependency. So I may ask,"Do you use liquor or beer, wine and how much? How often?"

Next I want to ask, "Why do you use it?" To relax? To wind down after a hard day? If a client says, "I just feel like I want it or I need it after work," he's perhaps indicating a craving or desire to have a drink which leads to finishing, for example, the whole bottle of wine, or everything in the house. Knowing when the client drinks, helps us to identify the "Critical Time Zone," when craving occurs.

He may also say, "I drink to loosen up in certain situations just so I can talk more easily". What he's telling us is that he's using booze as a way to cope. He hasn't found another way that works better, a healthier way maybe.

The next question is: "How long have you used it? And what changes have occurred?" I had a client who started doing some drugs when he was a teenager because of his parents' marital problems. He started out with one type of drug then moved to another type of drug, then to booze, and so on. So there was a progression or a continuation moving from one type, such as marijuana, LSD, or booze, to another.

To determine how much of a problem the drinking has become, I may ask, "Have other people complained about your use of drugs or alcohol?" Because if anybody has been giving him feedback or complaining, that probably indicates that it is a problem. "Has your use of this gotten in the way of work or family or social relationship responsibilities?" This last question might be inviting a denial.

He may not be willing to say it's affected him in this way at work or family or social outings, but the first question will give you an idea if other people are saying it's getting in the way of his everyday activities and level of performance. Has his boss commented on it? Or a colleague? Or a friend? A family member?

If use has been a problem, if I'm hearing this problem through the assessment of my client I may encourage him to stop for thirty days before I continue counselling.

When alcohol or other drug abuse is assessed, it should be addressed as the primary issue. All other issues will have to come after the abuse issue.

Response *If you should identify this as a problem and he comes back how do you know if he has actually stopped?*

Speaker Most likely when it's identified as a problem I'll be working with the family. I'll have a family interview early on so that the others members can aid in the identification. The treatment for this often involves a family intervention approach and is an advanced topic.

Briefly, it works like this: I'll have a family meeting and identify the issue as something the client may need to work on, and I'll elicit how the drinking affects them as family members and then give the client feedback on it. I may meet with the family without the client and prepare them to meet with the client so that the feedback can be given without dumping but in a caring way. And then I'll outline a treatment approach or a treatment plan with the entire family involved in it.

If the client thinks that he can control his drinking, I'll make that Step One, which means restricting the time, place, amount, and people he drinks with. I might allow two glasses of wine per weekend or per Friday night or Saturday night with a meal at home or at a restaurant with the family. That covers time, place, amount, and people.

I'll then say, "What if you can't control the drinking, what will happen then?" If the client is able to control the drinking, fine. If not, then we'll go to Step Two. The steps increase in confrontation or consequence. Step Two is to stop drinking altogether.

Response *In the initial Step One do you set the parameters or do you invite the client to set the parameters? What if he says, "Well, I'll have a six-pack every weekend"?*

Speaker I'll have the family set the parameters.

Response *It'll vary then from family to family as to what is acceptable.*

Speaker That's right, and it might have to be renegotiated after time. It might be that the amount is too much, and has to be reduced.

Response *I guess a co-dependent type of family would just allow the client to drink as much as he wants.*

Speaker That's right. So I'd be meeting with them again to see how things had been going — to see what their report is. And they'll be letting me know or I'll be picking up on whether they'd been letting him get away with violating the limits.

Response *They might say, "But he only had an extra drink."*

Speaker Yes, that's right. "It was only an extra drink." So I'll be picking up on whether they're enabling his use in some way and I'll point that out to them. And then I'll recommend total abstinence if control doesn't work. So I'll say to the family, "If abstinence doesn't work, what will happen then?" Step Three then is to recommend residential treatment so that the substance is unavailable and so that he can begin to identify underlying issues.

Then I'll say, "So suppose he refuses to go for residential treatment or relapses following treatment?" I'll talk about restricting the client's involvement with the family. It might mean separation from the family or exclusion to a varying extent from the family. The client might not be permitted to drive the kids or the grandkids anywhere any more, or be left alone with him.

Response *Will they accept that when you put that down? Something like, "You can't drive the kids any more?"*

Speaker Well, I'm going to have them state the restrictions, but I'll outline at the beginning what they are like. I'll say, "If you're not able to control your drinking, then there will be various degrees of consequence going all the way up to separation from the family, does that seem reasonable?" It's important to get the client's validation of the plan.

Response *So this is very much structured around trust, and the client's willingness to cooperate?*

Speaker Yes, his willingness is motivated by seeing what the effects of his drinking have been for the family and what the effects will be for him if he continues. His being able to see what's out ahead of him in terms of increasing confrontation and consequences, is designed to motivate him while preserving his dignity and power of choice.

Response *Once he is in the treatment centre it will be harder for him to forget the limits when there's someone waiting on the other side who's down the road in recovery saying this is what it looks like over here, it's much easier now. Go for it.*

Speaker Exactly. But the enabling family is a problem as was pointed out. They're going to be giving double messages; they're going to be saying, "Well, his drinking really upsets us", but the other message is, "He seems to need something to relax" or "it was only one more drink" or things like that. So we need to point out the fact that they're giving double messages.

We can help them sort out double messages by saying, "What effect does that have on the person who is having the problem? How is it helping? Or how is it undermining?"

LEGAL DIFFICULTIES

The first question is: "Have you had any past arrests, warrants, charges or suits against you? Do you have any outstanding debts?" The anti-social personality has a history of past arrests, particularly for assault or theft or some unlawful activity. This might help us decide whether we want to work with the client or not.

If the person has a history of assaulting behaviour or if he is into conning and lying then they may be going to do that in the counselling relationship. Personally, I am not going to work with a person with those behaviours.

Response *What do you do if you're a counsellor who is hired for mental health services by the government and you don't really have a choice?*

Speaker It depends on your setting. You'll have team meetings in many settings and you can say that, "I've got this client that I really don't think that I want to work with because I don't have the necessary skills. Is there someone here who might want to take on this person?"

Response *Do you have the right to refuse clients?*

Speaker Not always. In government settings the counselling service is provided without a fee. If you're the only show in town and you're refusing to work with certain clients, the funding source is going to look at that and maybe not renew your contract or whatever arrangement you have.

But if it's a case of assaultive behaviour, that person might best be treated in a forensic type of setting where there are legal boundaries on his behaviour and consequences that he is aware of, if he gets out of hand.

A female counsellor may especially not want to work with a client who has a history of assault. Also, a history of not meeting financial obligations may indicate that the client will have difficulty paying your fee.

DEMONSTRATION OF AN ASSESSMENT SESSION

Speaker What I'd like to do now is demonstrate the brief assessment, and we have someone in the group who has volunteered to be my client. So I'll ask that person to come forward now.

(The client is a male, and he is sitting across from me at a slight angle so that he can look past me without turning his head. We are both seated facing the group.)

Speaker Okay so the way I'd like to start this afternoon is just by asking you to talk about any sort of issues or concerns or problems you've experienced lately, minor or major.

Client *Career changes.*

Speaker Uh-huh.

Client *Going out on a limb...risking.*

Speaker Okay. So say a little bit more about that.

Client *I'm not too sure if I'm ever going in the right direction.*

Speaker Uh-Huh. How long have you had that sense of uncertainty?

Client *Since I quite my last job.*

Speaker And how long ago was that?

Client *A month.*

Speaker Uh-huh. Alright. What were you doing then?

Client *I was working in a wholesale business. For about thirteen years.*

Speaker Okay. And so what are some of the feelings that go with that uncertainty? It sounds scary.

Client *Its scary that I don't really have any professional experiences except working within that field. Doing something new sounds scary.*

Speaker Uh-huh. Okay. So has it been about a month since you left that kind of work?

Client *Yeah...control is gone now.*

Speaker Alright. I wonder if you experienced that kind of uncertainty at any other time in your life.

Client *Not that comes to mind.*

Speaker Okay. So what I'd like to do this afternoon is ask you a series of questions about your life experience to sort of give me a broader picture of what makes you tick, where you're from and what you're about. Will that be okay?

Client *Sure.*

Speaker Alright. How old are you?

Client *Thirty-two.*

Speaker Okay. And you're alone or with someone?

Client *I have a partner.*

Speaker Okay. How long has that been happening?

Client *Almost two years in December.*

Speaker Alright. And any children?

Client *No.*

Speaker Alright. What about a religious affiliation... any religious connections or spiritual...

Client *No, not really...spiritual, yeah.*

Speaker Okay. Do you belong to some group of some kind?

Client *No. Pretty loose right now. Nothing conclusive yet.*

Speaker Alright. How would you describe your spiritual identity, just briefly.

Client *Well, something that really encompasses my beliefs probably the best would be — I don't know if you're familiar with Aikido — some of the Eastern philosophies. Eastern ways of looking at things.*

Speaker Uh-huh. Okay. Alright. So it's sort of an Eastern perspective on life and things.

Client *Yin and yang.*

Speaker Balance... alright. So maybe right now in your life you don't feel a good enough balance. Would you say that's accurate?

Client *I'd say that's accurate.*

Speaker Okay. I'd like to ask you a few questions about your health and past surgeries and things like that, if that would be alright.

Client *That would be alright.*

Speaker Have you had any past surgeries in your life?

Client *No*

Speaker Have you had any health problems that you're aware of?

Client *No.*

Speaker Okay. And have you been to see a counsellor any other time in your life?

Client *No this is my first time.*

Speaker Okay. And now I'd like to ask you a series of questions about the family you grew up in if that's alright?

Client *Okay.*

Speaker How many brothers and sisters do you have?

Client *I have one brother and one sister. Younger sister, younger brother. I'm the oldest.*

Speaker Okay. And how many years separate you from the next.

Client *Two years between us all.*

Speaker Alright. And are you your parents' natural child?

Client *Yes.*

Speaker And are they still living?

Client *Yes they are.*

Speaker Alright. Have your parents always been together?

Client *No they were separated and divorced when I was four years old.*

Speaker Okay. And so did you stay with one parent during your growing up years, were you back and forth, or how did that go?

Client *For the first couple of years I was living, no, not even the first couple of years...probably the first year, I stayed with my dad and next year I stayed with my mother, and then after that we went into foster homes.*

Speaker Okay. So at what age did you go into a foster homes?

Client *Just after four.*

Speaker Uh-huh.

Client *So, actually they were separated before I was four.*

Speaker You sort of went back and forth for a short period of time and then went into a foster home.

Client *Uh-huh...a short period of time.*

Speaker Were you in the same foster home or did you go to different homes when you were growing up?

Client *Different homes. Probably about the longest I stayed in one place was two years and the others were just temporary places.*

Speaker Alright. Until what, age 17/18?

Client *Uh....10.*

Speaker Age 10? And then what happened?

Client *Boy...memories here! Ummm...*

Speaker What are your memories?

Client *Actually I lived with my mother for a year between 10 and 11.*

Speaker Uh-huh. Okay. And then....?

Client *Then I went into a group home.*

Speaker Okay. And give me an outline of where you went from age 11 until age 18.

Client *Okay. I lived in the group home till I was age 15. And the service that I belonged to at the time saw fit to let me loose when I was 15. And so I lived on my own for about a month and got married.*

Speaker Alright. And so then how long were you married?

Client *Two years maybe.*

Speaker Okay. Until you were about 17 or 18?

Client *That's right.*

Speaker Okay. And do you still maintain some contact with your parents?

Client *Yes as a matter of fact, I keep in touch with my father. He's a big supporter of me in the direction I'm taking right now, and occasionally I phone my mom. But I was much closer to her before. This is a new thing with my dad.*

Speaker Okay. So this happened relatively recently and up to recently you've been closer to Mom?

Client *Yes, spiritually for sure. Dad was kind of stodgy about that kind of stuff.*

Speaker Okay. Do you still maintain your contact with Mom?

Client *Uh-huh.*

Speaker Alright. Okay. What's it like talking about this so far today?

Client *Weird. This is uncomfortable actually.*

Speaker A little scary?!

Client *Yeah.*

Speaker Alright. Well that makes sense. It sounds like you've been through a lot of changes during your growing up years.

Client *Oh yeah! Still. Big changes in one year.*

Speaker Uh-huh. What's striking to me is that you're able to stay in one place for thirteen years. In one sort of job. Is that what you're saying?

Client *Yeah. I hadn't figured that out yet.*

Speaker Okay. How would you identify the kind of role that you had during the years when you were growing up? Would you say you were a victim, invisible or responsible. What kind of words come to mind when you try to put your finger on that?

Client *Close to responsible for awhile. Because I was the example of being the oldest kid. And I would say that I acted responsibly. And I felt the responsibility.*

Speaker Alright. Okay. And what was your relationship with your younger brother and sister during those growing up years? Did you get separated? Were you staying together?

Client *Separated.*

Speaker Okay.

Client *So my brother and sister are actually closer to each other than to me.*

Speaker Okay. What I'd like to ask you now is, if you had miraculous power to change your life experience growing up in any three ways, what do you think you might want to change in some small way or some large way about that experience. If you had the power to make it a perfect childhood.

Client *Well its just that I'm pretty happy with how it turned out. I don't look back on it and want anything changed because then I'd be different.*

Speaker Uh-huh. Okay. So you feel you benefitted in certain ways. In what ways do you feel you haven't benefitted as much as you wish you could have or might have?

Client *Stability.*

Speaker Uh-huh.

Client *I practised for thirteen years though.*

Speaker Yes, you were quite stable on that level in work.

Client *In some sense. I stayed with the job. But then there are all the things that come along with it. When people work thirteen years, they usually put away a little money, or they have some sort of career or some idea of what they want to do. I don't think I got that down pat.*

Speaker Uh-huh.

Client *I put in the time.*

Speaker Alright. If your family had stayed together and your siblings and your parents were able to have a close relationship, and that had been your experience, I wonder if you can imagine how your life might be different in any sort of way today.

Client *I don't know...a little more stable.*

Speaker Uh-huh.

Client *Now that I'm actually thinking of it, there are a couple of times where the feeling of abandonment is quite strong. I would have lived with my father when I was fifteen and that didn't work out. He didn't show up. So for a long time I held on to that. I'll do things my own way. So if that didn't happen, that issue wouldn't be there.*

Speaker So experience around abandonment, difficulties with that, struggling with that. The whole idea of stability.

Client *Uh-huh*

Speaker Okay. Now I'd like to ask you a few other questions about your life, mostly apart from your family, if that would be okay? The first one is, do you know if your mother had any problems with your birth?

Client *Absolutely! She had pneumonia and I think I had pneumonia too... I was purple anyway. And I was caesarian.*

Speaker You were caesarean?

Client *Yeah. So were the rest of the kids. Back in those days I think it was easier for the doctors to do a caesarean.*

Speaker Okay. And any experience of convulsions as a child that you know about?

Client *No*

Speaker Okay. And what about your first day of going to school. Do you recall what that was like?

Client *Yeah. I do actually. I enjoyed it. I enjoyed getting out of the house.*

Speaker Uh-huh. How many moves did you have during school years growing up?

Client *Quite a bit. I probably averaged two years, if that, maybe only a year and a half between moves. I went to quite a few schools.*

Speaker So it sounds like there were quite a few shifts and changes over those years.

Client *Uh-huh*

Speaker What was your relationship like with teachers in school?

Client *Some good, some pretty bad. I didn't really like the authoritarian type of teacher, but the teachers that would kind of come down and relate to you on a different level, I can relate to them.*

Speaker Alright. And how did you get along with peers in school?

Client *I had the groups I hung around with. People who wore the tank tops in school when you weren't supposed to wear tank tops.*

Speaker So a little bit of a rebel identity. Okay. Did you achieve as well as you think you could have in school?

Client *No*

Speaker And how far along did you get in school years? Were you able to finish grade twelve?

Client *No. I got as far as grade seven. Then I went to vocational school and wrote my grade nine there so I could get into high school.*

Speaker Okay. Did you have a group of friends between ages seven and eleven?

Client *I had a few friends.*

Speaker And what about as a teenager? One or two?

Client *I didn't hang around in groups so much but, one or two, yes.*

Speaker Were you a follower or leader with friends?

Client *A little bit of both.*

Speaker A bit of both. Alright. How old would you say you were when you first dated ?

Client *Ten.*

Speaker About ten. Okay. Do you have friends and acquaintances now?

Client *Yes.*

Speaker And would you say that that's a satisfactory network?

Client *Oh, absolutely.*

Speaker Good friends. Good. Now, how old were you when you first went to work?

Client *Fifteen.*

Speaker And what was that kind of work that you did then?

Client *It was in a factory making heels — plastic heels.*

Speaker So between then and your job that you had for the thirteen years was there another period of time that you worked a single job, or did you move around?

Client *I moved around a lot. Probably the longest that I ever kept a job before that was one year — maybe two, but that would be stretching it. That was in construction and that's sort of all over the place.*

Speaker Tell me about this job that you had for thirteen years. It's striking that you stayed with it for that long.

Client *Well, it's interesting because when I first came to Vancouver I went to the Manpower office and told them that I was interested in taking a job that required some training, because I had just finished getting out of construction and that really wasn't doing anything for me. The manager of the business actually knocked at my door three times. He had gotten the information from the receptionist at the* *unemployment office that this guy's really gung-ho, keen to learn and stuff like that. He knocked on my door and asked me to work, caught me on the third try and I guess I felt some loyalty.*

I guess that was his intention too and worked there for... it was about eleven years and then I went to the competitor's and worked there for the following years. It was something I was good at. I got to work with people — it was a social environment. And that was about it. I wasn't spiritually satisfied, but it kept the bank happy.

Speaker So then you decided to leave that job. What happened around leaving?

Client *Why did I leave?*

Speaker Yes.

Client *I wasn't... like I said, I wasn't spiritually satisfied. So I thought I'd try it somewhere else.*

Speaker Okay. How would you say you have gotten along with bosses?

Client *Good. I remember one boss... not so well, but generally it's been good.*

Speaker In terms of your relationships with various partners, people you've been close to: you've been involved with this person for a couple of years. How would you describe this person's personality and the kind of relationship that you have.

Client *Strong. Very strong personality. Self-determined. Motivated. Independent.*

Speaker I wonder if there have been other previous meaningful relationships that you can speak about?

Client *One previous to this one.*

Speaker And what happened in that one, in terms of what that person was like and why it ended?

Client *Practically the opposite type of character.*

Speaker And so that's the reason it ended?

Client *I think so. We were too much alike in some areas, and there was no one there to tell you that what you were doing wasn't right.*

Speaker Any meaningful relationships before that?

Client *Yes.*

Speaker And how long did it last?

Client *Two years.*

Speaker And why did it end?

Client *Really, that's a good question. We were not very settled. I didn't have any idea of what I wanted.*

Speaker How's your mood these days? Where would you rate it yourself — zero being life's not worth living and ten being life is great.

Client *Oh, life is great.*

Speaker So, you're a ten.

Client *Yes.*

Speaker Having reviewed much of your history and your background I wonder if you have some understanding of the story behind this uncertainty that you're experiencing right now. Do you see it as being only related to this immediate time or do you see it as being related to anything else that's happened to you in your life?

Client *Actually, I think a little bit of both because after jumping around so much the instability is there. Also, after thirteen years in a secure situation I wasn't willing to give that up so easily, but I'd already had the experience of jumping around a bit.*

Speaker So because you had the experience of having instability you welcomed this period of stability, and now there's this period of instability. Maybe it's scarier than it would have been otherwise?

Client *It's taken more than a month.*

Speaker Well, that makes sense to me that you'd have that level of fear and anxiety after what you've been through in terms of the instability and then the long stability in your life. You didn't have the opportunity to be in one place with a family or other stability growing up until those last thirteen years that you've described.

Speaker So if you were to continue your counselling I wonder what your goals might be and what you'd want to achieve if you were to take it further?

Client *There's a lot of baggage and stuff that has to be cleared up, and there's some addictive behaviour that's been carrying on that I'd like to look at.*

Speaker Can you be a little bit more specific?

Client *Drug addictions. Alcoholism in the family. I don't have alcoholism but I've had some contact with drugs and addictive behaviour.*

Speaker When you say baggage what are you referring to there?

Client *Things that either I'm not comfortable with or things that I feel are burdens — that feel heavy.*

Speaker What would you say is the major thing — the biggest piece of excess you'd like to let go of, to work through to let you get on with things.

Client *I don't think I have an answer for that. There's a few things I haven't looked at.*

Speaker That's a big area that might contain a lot of things you want to explore.

Client *Yes. I don't think it's just one thing, one or two things.*

Speaker So there is the addiction issue and then the baggage around it.

Client *Family.*

Speaker Family experiences. That sort of instability that you've mentioned.

Client *I've just recently worked things out between me and my father. We hadn't really had that much contact over the years and he is an inaccessible person, but I phoned him up one day and had a fantastic talk with him and I guess in response to that he's supported me through this course. So that's sort of balanced things out.*

Speaker So what I'm hearing here is that maybe one issue is the loss of the closeness that you experience with father over the years. Maybe the family too — other members of the family?

Client *That's possible.*

Speaker Well, those sound like very important goals and issues to explore and I encourage you to do that in your own personal journey of growth. What's this been like talking today?

Client *My heart's going.*

Speaker It's going pretty fast?

Client *Pretty fast. My palms are sweaty.*

Speaker Well, it certainly takes courage to do what you're doing, to volunteer and to share yourself on this level with a group of strangers; people you don't even know. So you're to be commended for that.

Client *Maybe it's easier because of that.*

Speaker What I would say also in closing a counselling session is, "I wonder if you'd like to meet again and take those goals, those very important areas that you identified, just a little bit further?" Then we'd sort out a time to do that if you wanted to and that would be our closing. So maybe we'll stop at this point. Is that okay with you?

Client *Absolutely. (Volunteer client takes a seat in the group.)*

Speaker At this point perhaps we could have some discussion about how you saw me working with the client and some of your observations of what the assessment process is like.

Response *You make it look so easy. It must help to have done a lot of assessments so you don't have to take notes or refer to your questions.*

Speaker Yes. However, until you have done many assessments, it will be important for you to take notes and refer directly to the questions on the questionnaire. What else?

Response *You used a lot of reflective statements and a lot of validation. You sort of let him know what you heard him saying.*

Response *I liked it when you checked out with him what it was like to answer the questions up to that point. That added to the safety.*

Speaker Yes.

Response *I thought it was effective to see how you handled his response to the question about what he would like to change about the family of origin. He presented a defense and you worked around it.*

Speaker Yes, I reflected and validated his defense by saying he had benefitted from events related to the family, then I asked in what ways he hadn't benefitted in ways he wished he could have.

To the Reader: Notice the significant factors revealed by the client in this assessment.

1. The presenting problems are: "career changes" and feeling "scared",and he says,"not too sure I'm ever going in the right direction," and "control is gone."

2. He reported initially not having experienced that kind of uncertainty any time previously, but at the end of the assessment, he was able to relate this feeling to the instability he experienced when growing up.

3. He's drawn to an Eastern philosophy that provides a concept of "balance."

4. He is the oldest of three siblings.

5. Parents were separated when he was four, and he experienced numerous placements in foster and group homes until his short marriage at about age 16.

6. The client is not close to parents or to siblings.

7. He relates to the role of "responsible one."

8. He states that working for thirteen years in one job was a way of "practicing" stability.

9. He felt abandoned by father.

10. There were multiple moves and school changes.

11. He related to rebels in school and did not finish.

12. He dated at age 10.

13. He went to work at an adult job at age 15.

14. Sexual partners have been either parental or childlike.

15. He mentioned his addiction history which I had not asked directly about.

16. Not feeling "spiritually satisfied" in his work.

Summary: The client's struggle with instability is especially an issue now since the loss of his lengthy employment of thirteen years against the background of family breakdown and living in numerous homes as a child. He worked and married early which adds to the picture of loss of childhood. He appears to be looking for the parental caring he has missed indicated by early marriage, and his last employer who demonstrated "loyalty" may have been a parental figure. Stability and parental caring appear to be the elusive goals in his life. Therefore, he is not certain of "ever going in the right direction."

FUNCTIONAL INQUIRY

Speaker Today we will complete our discussion of clinical assessment beginning with the Functional Inquiry. One of the things I need to check out with the client is whether or not he has had a recent physical examination, and so I will ask him if he has had one within the last six months, or possibly a year. If he hasn't, I ask him to have one, and I'll get a report from the doctor. In order to get the report have your client sign the "Release of Medical Information" form provided in the "Counsellor Training Selected Materials."

Question *I often find myself in the situation where social workers are referring people to me for a variety of reasons who may not even want to be there in the first place. They're there because the social worker has some leverage to get them there, so would it be appropriate to ask for a physical examination under those circumstances?*

Speaker You can ask; it doesn't mean that he will go. And it's not necessary to make it a condition, but you're really hindered if you don't get a physical report on your client. The simple reason is that often times a person's problems are related to physical problems, and if you don't know about possible physical factors, you can waste a lot of time. You might find out that he has a thyroid condition or some other physical problem that's impacting on his personal issues.

Response *It might come up as a barrier to the client and something that he'll turn around and complain to his social worker about. This guy's talking about a physical examination, forget it.*

Are these going to be young people that you're dealing with?

Response *Mostly, although it's going to be a combination of young people and families.*

Speaker Well, you can use your own judgement. You'll have to try to determine as well as you can whether the client seems to be in good health or not. But you can't always be sure unless he gets a physical and even then you can't be completely sure. This is just a safety factor in assessment.

GENERAL INQUIRY

Speaker Now let's look at allergies, medications, appetite, sleep, weight, and energy questions. Allergies are often exacerbated by stress or produce stress themselves. About medication — ask what medications the client uses, why, and for how long? The person might let you know about prescribed medications that he is taking.

For example, some common medications that have been used in the recent past are valium and other forms of tranquilizers or anti-depressants. If the person tells you that he is taking those kinds of medications for specific reasons related to the way he is feeling then that's going to be important for your assessment. It means that the doctor has picked up on his mood and has prescribed medication. It also might indicate over-medication or the possibility of addiction; sleeping medication, for example is often abused. If this is part of the problem he may need to stop using some medications in order to create some hope. I will also ask about over-the-counter medications which are commonly taken for headaches, coughing, allergies, and other symptoms and which are abused by clients with addiction problems.

Appetite and Weight. What might be the significance of a person losing ten pounds in two or three weeks or a month?

Response *She could be bulimic or have some other eating disorder.*

Speaker It could be an eating disorder. What else?

Response *Depression.*

Speaker Depression, yes. Significant weight loss or weight gain might indicate depression. Some people overeat when they're depressed, others lose their appetite and stop eating or eat much less than usual.

Dieting and vomiting. What kinds of disorders might be associated with dieting or vomiting?

Response *Bulimia.*

Speaker Okay. And what else?

Response *Anorexia.*

Speaker Anorexia, right. The bulimic will binge eat and vomits; the anorexic diets. Anorexics feel fat or think they're fat even though they appear emaciated. That distorted body image is the key to diagnosing whether a person has anorexia or not. If a person is more than fifteen percent under the low range of her normal body weight, that's another indication of anorexia. If that's the case she needs a referral to a physician immediately because anorexia can result in irreversible damage to vital organs and death if it continues. We are looking at a life threatening disorder, and the client may need to be hospitalized.

Bulimia can also be a very serious, life-threatening condition. In severe cases there's the danger that frequent repeated vomiting could result in hemorrhaging of the stomach lining, which can cause death.

Sleep. Does the client have any problems getting enough sleep? Sleep loss is often an indicator of depression. I am talking about insomnia, waking up in the middle of the night or early in the morning and not being able to get back to sleep. By "early morning" I mean maybe two,three, or four o'clock in the morning.

The fundamental question here is, "Do you feel rested in the morning?" Some people sleep five hours a night, but they still feel rested in the morning. So they don't have a sleeping problem. Keep in mind also that poeple who over-sleep may be depressed as well.

Energy. The question I will ask is, "What has your energy level been like?" Low energy is another indicator of depression. I'm looking for an accumulation of these indicators: loss of weight or appetite, sleeping problems and low energy level. These physical symptoms will tell me if the person is perhaps depressed.

SYSTEMS INQUIRY

Speaker Under "Systems Inquiry" I am going to simply ask the following questions very briefly. "Have you ever injured your head or neck?" Injury to the head or neck might bring about personality changes — angry outbursts or depression, things like that. And if he has had that kind of injury we need to see if there's been an EEG (electro-encephalogram) or some other type of neurological testing done, and if not we need to send him to have that done to find out whether or not there has been an injury that's affecting his behaviour and the way he is feeling.

The next question is, "Any problems breathing?" A person with anxiety or panic disorder might have episodes of problems with breathing. "Any heart or chest pain?" might go with panic disorder as well.

"Any problems with bowels?" Stress, anxiety can cause problems with bowel movements such as constipation or diarrhea. Gastroenteritis is often stress-related.

"Any problems urinating?". Frequent urination may be related to diabetes. "Any weakness or stiffness in joints?" may be related to arthritis. "Any headaches or dizziness?" may be related to a brain tumor. Certainly all these symptoms are possibly related to stress or anxiety.

It's known that prolonged stress brings about changes in the central nervous system, which affects the physical health of the person, lowering his immune defenses. The result could be ulcers or tumours, or any of the other signs and symptoms that we've just looked at. Certainly these conditions also in turn contribute to stress.

If the client responds positively to any of these questions, I will need to send him for a physical. If he has had a recent physical, I will send him for another one to rule out the possibility of a physical cause for these physical signs and symptoms.

Personality. "How would you describe your personality?" With that I get an idea of the person's own self-image or self-concept. I might help him out by saying, "Are you a follower or a leader? Shy or outgoing? How else might you describe yourself?" This is a question that people don't often respond to. They're not often asked this so you have to give them a little time to think.

MENTAL STATUS

Speaker The last part of the assessment is Mental Status. Assessing "General Behaviour and Appearance" doesn't involve asking the client any questions. It simply has to do with my observations of the client's behaviour, mannerisms, eye contact, whether fixed or avoidant, for example, and so on.

I may notice seductive behaviour or manner of dress and whether or not the person appears unkempt or extremely neat.

Question *When you are assessing seductive appearance, do you say it's "seductive" behaviour or do you just write down what you observe?*

Speaker That's a good question. Write down what the behaviour is. For instance, I might note that the blouse is unbuttoned or the female client is sitting with legs apart, tight pants, for example. Describe what you see rather than placing a name or judgement on it. Also, if a person came in with cowboy hat and cowboy boots and a shark's tooth around his neck, I'd make a note of that. That would be a unique dress that might be significant — it might correlate with the personality type.

For example, some antisocial personalities are street people, and they often times have a form of dress that corresponds to being a street person. Having tattoos on the arms might be an example.

What might unkempt appearance indicate? For example, the client's hair appears unwashed, in tangles, shirt tail hanging out.

Response *Maybe low self-worth or depression.*

Speaker Yes. Or Psychosis. What if the person appears extremely neat, every hair in place?

Response *Perfectionistic. Obsessive-Compulsive.*

Speaker Quite possible. What might fixed eye contact signify?

Response *Maybe the client is hostile or aggressive.*

Speaker Yes. And what if the client avoids eye contact?

Response *Maybe he's afraid or passive. Low self-worth.*

Speaker Yes. The person who dresses below his stated age. Let's say a person in his 50's appearing with a mickey mouse shirt, may also have dependent behaviour.

Speaker Listen for anything unusual about the person's speech. For example, I had a client who spoke of past experiences in the future tense. She said things like, "When I shall be lying in my hospital room, the attendant shall be coming into the room etc." I thought that was unusual. It turned out that this woman was a schizophrenic in remission.

Schizophrenics perhaps have the most striking kinds of unusual speech content, "word salad" which is a combination of words that have no association with each other, and non-sensible rhyming. For example a client said, "I went to the mall, walked down the hall, climbed the wall," things like that. I was visiting in a psychiatric setting, and there was a man who was sweeping the floor saying, "I don't care if I die-dee-die-dee-die".

Anything unusual about talk should be noted with a written sample. Also, note the tendency to over-talk, under-talk, talk fast, talk slow, talk in tangents, talk with excessive detail, and talk circumstantially without answering the question.

MOOD: SUICIDAL AND HOMICIDAL ASSESSMENT

To assess mood, you're going to be asking the client to rate his mood on a scale from zero to ten saying, "Where would you rate yourself on a scale from 0 to 10, zero meaning life is not worth living and ten meaning that life is great and you're feeling optimistic and hopeful about the future? Where would you put yourself right now on that kind of scale?" If a person has given you signs of depression in presenting problems or in the functional inquiry, it's very important to have him rate himself on the mood scale.

If a person gives you anything less than a five, consider him depressed. It's then very important to ask him the following series of questions to assess suicidal ideas and intent.

The first question I'll ask is, "Have you had any suicidal ideas?" If the person says "Yes", then I'll ask him the next question, which is very important. "I wonder if you have thought about how you might commit suicide."

That's a question that goes for the intent or the plan. If a person indicates he has a plan, that means the risk is increased, and so then we need to ask the next crucial question which is: "Do you feel safe with yourself?" And if a person indicates he doesn't know, which is very common, I'll take that as a 'no' answer. "I don't know" means, "No, I'm not safe with myself."

Now if the person is living alone, then it's especially important to go to the next step which is to recommend that he goes to the hospital emergency room, so he can get some temporary relief from the depressed mood.

If a person is living with others, such as family, he may have a support system he can spend time with through the night. You can try to involve the friends or family and make them aware of the client's suicidal ideas and plans. However, my approach is to have the person hospitalized even if he has a support system. I still wouldn't want to take the chance that he might follow through with any plans.

To get a client to the emergency room, I would make a summary reflective statement. "So what I'm hearing, Bob, is that you're thinking about suicide, you've thought about how to do it, and you're also telling me that you might kill yourself. You're feeling really down and you're in a lot of pain and anguish right now. I think it's important that you get some immediate help, so I'm recommending that you go to an emergency room at a nearby hospital so that perhaps they can give you some medication or something to help you feel better during this tough time you're going through. I can either go with you to the emergency, or maybe a friend or a member of the family could go with you. Who would you prefer?"

The crucial question is whether the client is willing to go or not, because if he is not willing, I have to take the next step. I make sure somebody is watching him, maybe a colleague or a secretary, and then I'll go to another room and phone either a crisis unit or the police. My practice is to usually phone the police.

Question *Do you have any problem with the police? They'll come and do that?*

Speaker There's no problem as long as I explain each question that I asked my client and give the client's verbatim response. So for example, recently I had to phone the police, and I said, "I'm a therapist in the community and I have a client who is very suicidal right now. I was talking to him on the phone just a few moments ago and I asked him if he's having suicidal ideas and he said that he was. I asked him if he had a plan in mind and he said that he did. He said he thought of driving his truck over a cliff, and he has his truck with him now. And I asked him if he was safe with himself and he cried for a while and said at first said he didn't know, and then said no, he wasn't. And I asked if he would go to the emergency room on his own, with his friend with him, and he said he would not go. And so I'm phoning you now to see if you're able to go out and escort him to the emergency room."

When I made the request in that manner, the police were very cooperative. If I was to just phone the police and say I have this client who's suicidal, will you go out and help him, take him to the hospital, they may not be very cooperative. They need the facts, because they're bound by certain policies and legislation that are designed to protect the individual from the invasion of privacy.

Often times this situation happens over the phone, because when I have a client who has been very depressed, I'm going to get a suicide contract with them. I'll say, "I'd like for us to have an agreement that if you ever feel so down that you feel like committing suicide, that you'll phone and talk to me personally before you carry out any ideas or plans to harm yourself or kill yourself. Can you agree to that?" If a person says that he is committed to talk rather than act on his suicidal ideas, maybe he is saying he does feel safe enough with himself.

I'll still make the suicide contract even if he has no attempt or plan, but he just has suicidal ideas.

Question *It's verbal, not written?*

Speaker The suicide contract or agreement itself is verbal.

Response *Where I work we have a written one. It's also used for insurance purposes.*

Speaker That's right. It's good to have it in writing to cover yourself legally. Even if you make the agreement verbally it's important that in your client's file you write down exactly what you did, including the questions you asked in assessing suicide, the responses, and the verbal suicide contract. Date it and sign it.

Now I also explain along with that verbal contract that it's not good enough just to leave a message on my answering machine, and if I can't be reached the agreement is that you won't follow through on any ideas of committing suicide until you talk to me personally. Alternatives in the agreement are that he will go to hospital or phone a Distress Line.

If I couldn't get that agreement from a client — and it has never happened that I couldn't — I wouldn't be able to work with that client. I would have to refer him to another service. Any questions about suicide?

Question *Do you tell them that if they don't agree to it that they will be referred to someone else?*

Speaker No.

Question *So who do you refer him to? You've got somebody who is ready to jump off the bridge but he won't agree to the contract.*

Speaker Well, actually if he said that he is going to jump and won't go to hospital, I'll involve the police for intervention.

If he just has suicidal ideas and is not willing to make the contract, I would see him as a highly manipulative client. I wouldn't be able to work with that person anyway. I'd recommend he approach his family doctor for a referral to a psychiatrist.

Question *Do you ever get a client just using suicide as an excuse to call you about any other area that he has difficulty with?*

Speaker If he makes a statement that he is going to commit suicide or feels suicidal, I'll take it at face value.

Question *How do you know what his final intention will be?*

Speaker Even if it's a manipulative way of getting attention, I will still see him as feeling desperate and treat it as a serious intention.

Speaker Before involving family it is very critical to assess how much support is there. If we see that the family is not caring and not being very supportive then we'll have to make appropriate arrangements.

Response *It's not always easy for the family. A friend of mine was very depressed once, and talked a lot about suicide. Her family was very supportive, and loving, and understanding, and she got through her depression. Three years later she became depressed, and her family was worried that this was happening all over again. They talked to her and she said, "Oh no, everything is fine" and a few days later she took her own life. Was there some element missing, some reason they weren't enough of a support system for her?*

Speaker Well, sometimes the Cry Wolf syndrome sets in. If a person expresses suicidal ideas too many times it doesn't really get her the help that she needs. People don't give weight to her statements any more.

I think every individual situation is different, and I wouldn't know what happened in that situation unless I talked to those people. But in some situations of chronic suicidal ideas and periods, relatives and friends simply give up. They don't know what to do anymore. And then the person may feel totally abandonned and commit suicide.

Borderline Personality Disorder might be something that you're describing. With this disorder, suicidal attempts or gestures might be frequent, sometimes as an attempt to get reassurance of caring, but it's hard for this type of person to take in the caring even if it is sincerely expressed.

You may sometimes have a client who was suicidally depressed the last time you saw her, and then the next time you see her she's saying that everything's fine and she doesn't think she needs to come back. This is the kind of situation you described in your comment. The woman said, "Everything is fine."

When there's that dramatic shift in the way that person is feeling, you need to be very concerned about the possibility that she has resolved to kill herself, just as the family was in relation to the depressed woman.

In that situation I would say to the client, "It's very striking that last time we met you were thinking of suicide and today you're saying that everything's great, life's wonderful, and you don't think you need to come back any more because your problems are solved. I'm wondering what happened between last time we met and today. Could you just tell me what happened when you left my office last time? What happened that evening? What happened the next morning? What happened that day or that evening? The next morning, that day and evening?"

Have her give you a blow by blow description of what happened, because unless you do that, the client is not going to be able or willing to fill in the gaps. In this way, the client may then report having made the decision to kill herself, or when she can't fill in the gaps, that's going to increase your suspicion.

I might say, "Sometimes when people report feeling so much better after being suicidal, it's because they've decided to kill themselves." And then I'll watch the client's non-verbal reaction. Any eye shifts or tears or voice changes should be immediately attended in an attempt to draw out the feelings.

Of course, if a client is giving a false reporting of feeling better, maybe it's because he wants you to elicit the suicidal feelings. Otherwise, he wouldn't bother to contact you.

If a client is really intent on killing himself, you may not be able to prevent it. You can only do your best, and do all you can. Sometimes every appropriate measure still isn't enough to prevent the suicide.

The opposite of the person who internalizes and has a very low, possibly suicidal mood is the person who externalizes intense anger and hostility. That might be the case with a client who has a history of assault.

The most extreme form of that behaviour is the homicidal person. So we need to assess on the same basis. You can say, "Have you had any homicidal ideas or ideas of doing harm to others? Have you thought about how you might do it?"

Question *Are you using the mood scale with this as well?*

Speaker We use a scale related to anger to find out whether or not to ask further questions. "So you're telling me that you're feeling quite angry lately. On a scale of zero to ten — zero being that you're just a little bit annoyed and ten being that you want to kill someone — where would you put yourself?" If he puts himself at a five or greater I'd ask him, "I wonder if you've had any thoughts of wanting to kill that person? Have you thought about how you might do it? Can you commit yourself to talking rather than acting on those ideas? Is that person safe with you?"

Question *So you're saying if it's over five that's when we start to think of homicidal tendencies?*

Speaker Yes.

Question *So, it's the opposite?*

Speaker It depends on how you want to design the scale. I've just designed the assault scale opposite to the depression scale. But it doesn't matter as long as you communicate your design clearly.

If a person can't make a commitment to talk rather than act on those feelings then I'm under legal obligation to warn the victim. This is a very important legal point. There was a test case recently in the United States, and the same situation may occur in Canada leaving you open to a law suit, in which the counsellor failed to warn the victim. He had a lawsuit filed against him, and he was found guilty of aiding and abetting the crime that was committed.

The situation was that the client's girlfriend had left him for another man. The client told the counsellor that he intended to kill the girlfriend, and the counsellor then failed to warn her.

So in the cases of suicidal or homicidal feelings and intent, we need to document our questions, the client's responses, and the fact that we informed the potential victim in the case of homicidal threat. We also need to question clients for about four sessions after the last report of their having no suicidal or homicidal feelings regardless of intent. We need to document that we questioned the client, then date and sign each entry.

Question *Would you talk to the victim yourself or would you get the police involved?*

Speaker I would talk to the victim myself. For example, a man was in treatment on Vancouver Island, and he threatened to kill his wife who was my client. The professionals involved with the husband informed the referral source who contacted me and asked that I warn my client which I did that same day. How you warn the potential victim is not as important as the fact that you warn her immediately and document that you made contact or reported to the police. I would also likely refer the client to a physician who would refer to a psychiatrist.

Are there any questions about assessing and reporting suicidal and homicidal ideas?

Question *I'd like to back up just a bit to where you stated that, in a situation where you had a resistant, suicidal client, you would contact the police. Would you tell that client that you had done that?*

Speaker That's a judgement call. My general practice is not to tell the client, as long as I think there's a chance that he might bolt from my office or run from wherever he is calling me.

Question *Once he is hand-cuffed then we don't have him as a client any more, do we?*

Speaker Well, actually I have had to do this, and what I've found is that the client does return to me. Any ideas why?

Response *Because you knew what they were going to do — you understood them.*

Speaker That's right. He saw it as a caring thing and it contributed to his feeling of safety with me. It increased his confidence in me as a professional working with him.

Response *After he had gone through that immediate crisis he would be no longer immediately thinking about killing himself.*

That's right. It's sometimes important to allow clients to go through the whole process of hospitalization so that they can experience what happens when they are suicidal or uncooperative.

Response *We had a teenage girl who was living with us as a foster child. She took some pills and we didn't know how many but I really didn't think that she intended to kill herself. I took her to the hospital and on the way I said, "You don't really want to die do you?" And she said, "No." She went through it all: swallowing the charcoal, the vomiting, the whole nine yards. After that she became closer to me.*

Speaker Okay. This is one of the most important areas for us to be very clear about in working with our clients. The assessment of suicidal and homicidal intent are matters of life and death.

COGNITION

Speaker Let's move on to "Cognition". The term cognition refers to the thinking processes. The first point, orientation, is really designed to assess psychotic disorder.

Orientation has to do with a person's time and place sense. The psychotic person is out of touch with reality and doesn't know who you are and won't remember your name, or the date, or where he is.

So we ask him, "What's my name? What's today's date? And where are you?" I may not ask this if there is no doubt that the person is not psychotic.

Delusions and misinterpretations. The question here is: "Do you believe that strangers are out to get you?" This is to assess paranoid ideas. Another question is: "Do you think people are always talking about you negatively or talking about you behind your back?" Also,"If you walk into a room full of people who are laughing do you think that they're laughing at you?" Again, paranoid ideas.

Hallucinations-auditory and visual. This is designed to assess psychosis which essentially involves auditory and visual hallucinations. The questions here are: "Do you hear voices other people don't hear? Do you see things that other people don't see?"

The voices people hear are experienced as coming from outside their head and may involve two or more voices speaking in a derrogatory way about the client in the third person. Visual hallucinations involve actual visions, not simply seeing a face in the clouds.

Question *Will people honestly answer that if they do?*

Speaker Yes, they'll usually be very straightforward about that.

Compulsive phenomena. The question is:"Are you a perfectionist?" Only if he answers 'yes' to that will I ask the following questions: "Do you have set routines which is upsetting to you if they are interrupted? Do you check and recheck the stove, locks, lights?" And this is multiple or frequent rechecking. The obsessive-compulsive person checks and rechecks frequently, and often she is referred to as a "checker".

Another question is: "Do you have unwanted thoughts repeating in your mind? Thoughts that you wish you did not have going around and around and around that you just can't seem to get rid of?"

For example, a client found that whenever he dug in the garden, he was obsessed with the thought that he was digging into his daughter's face. And he was so obsessed with the safety of his daughter that he would follow her to school every day, making sure that she didn't notice that he was following her. And this is a girl who's not in kindergarten, but ten or twelve years old — able to walk by herself. But he just couldn't seem to get rid of these thoughts.

General information. I'm going to say, "Now I want to ask you some questions to see how well you've been remembering and concentrating lately." The depressed person often has difficulty with memory and concentration. We may need to say, "It's not an intelligence test."

I'll say, "Who is the Prime Minister of Canada?", "Who is the Premier?", "Name three capital cities in Europe," and, "Name five large cities in Canada." (For U.S. clients make these questions fit the context.) Now if the person is a recent immigrant he wouldn't be expected to know these things. An American just moved to Canada wouldn't know the difference between the Prime Minister and the Premier, so you have to make allowances.

Question *Is there any problem with multiple personalities here, where one personality might know all this stuff but another one wouldn't?*

Speaker Alright. That's an interesting disorder, and we deal with it more in the advanced counselling skills course. The person who is severely abused as a child — sexually, physically and emotionally abused — that person might develop a multiple personality disorder. We might see shifts in the person's personality during the assessment. It could become apparent that there is another and different personality talking, and because it is being recognized more frequently than in the past, it is one we need to be aware of.

Maybe some of you are familiar with the Trudy Chase story. There's been a movie made of her recently and she's been on some talk shows. It's an interesting example of a multiple personality disorder. Because of severe childhood abuse, the child Trudy became virtually non-existent and was replaced by a host of other personalities who existed primarily to defend Trudy against the strong pain of her abuse. Each personality is distinct, some know more about Trudy's life than the others know, and the personalities may or may not know about the other personalities.

Intelligence is the next topic, and it is your own subjective assessment of the client's general level of intelligence. There are no questions to ask here. You simply assess whether the person has below average, average, or above average intelligence, and you make a note of that. The person with below average intelligence may not be able to benefit from insight or know how to approach problems analytically. So it may mean that you'll have to confine your work to a behavioral approach — just helping them change their problem symptoms and behaviours.

Memory. "How's your memory been lately?" The depressed client has difficulty with memory, such as telephone numbers.

You might say, "How well have you been able to concentrate lately, for example reading or watching TV programs?" You can also use what's known as the Babcock Sentence as a test of concentration.

Introduce the sentence by saying, "Now I want to give you a sentence and see if you can repeat it back to me. I'll repeat this sentence up to three times" Then you say:

"The one thing a nation needs in order to be rich and great is a large, secure supply of wood."

Have the person repeat it. If he has trouble, say it again and ask him to repeat it. We give the client three opportunities. This sentence is designed in such a way that it requires a pretty high level of concentration in order to be able to remember and repeat it. Even a person who is not depressed has to concentrate pretty well in order to remember and repeat this.

Speaker Proverb interpretation is designed to assess concrete versus abstract thinking abilities. And so we give the person a proverb to see how he interprets it.

"People who live in glass houses shouldn't throw stones." The concrete thinker says, "If they do they'll break their windows." The abstract thinker says, "If you criticize others they might criticize you."

Question *Is that a function of culture as well? Or would that be cross-cultural?*

Speaker The ability to think abstractly is cross-cultural, but the proverb itself might be culturally limited. The person from an Eastern culture might not be able to respond to that proverb, for instance. We need to be flexible and certainly consider culture in doing the assessment.

Question *What value does assessing concrete versus abstract thinking have?*

Speaker If a person tends to think more concretely it implies that our counselling approach will be less insight oriented and more behaviorally oriented. Counselling will have less to do with the cognitive and psychodynamic approaches and more to do with behaviour modification approaches.

This question is one of the ways you can check your assessment of the client's intelligence. Some people appear to be below average intelligence, but in reality that appearance is only a defence.

Response *In other words it can be difficult to determine general intelligence.*

Speaker Yes. For instance, you might have assessed a client as having low intelligence, but if she can interpret the proverb abstractly then we can pretty well conclude that she only appears to have low intelligence. It is perhaps an old pattern of behaviour that is there for a reason — maybe a way of internalizing negative messages or low parental expectations of the client as a child, for example.

Response *It's also a way of not taking responsibility.*

Speaker That's right. It may be a defence against taking responsibility which might be very frightening for the client.

Response *Alcohol and drug addicts do that a lot.*

Speaker Yes. It might also be related to low self-worth. He been told that he is stupid and dumb, and then he acts as though he has low intelligence. If this person is able to understand the story behind his problems, and point out links between past and present and those kinds of things, then we can see that he has the ability to think abstractly and that the appearance of low intelligence is only appearance.

The person who is very dependent might also come across as having low intelligence. In other words he might leave blanks in his sentences as if he doesn't know the word to put in it, and he will wait for you to supply the word. That's very dependent thinking; he is appearing to be helpless, maybe as a way of getting parenting that he missed.

The last question is simply asking the client, "Have you been able to make day-to-day decisions?" A person who is depressed can have difficulty with deciding what to do on a daily basis.

CLIENT'S ETIOLOGIC FORMULATION

Next we look at the client's etiologic formulation. The word etiology means a knowledge of the origins, sources, causes or beginnings. It is the client's knowledge or understanding of the causes, sources, origins or beginnings of the problems that the client began talking about. This is how we can assess how much insight or self-awareness the client might already have about his situation.

So I will put it to him in this way: "Having reviewed much of your background today, I'm wondering if you might have just a little bit of insight or some understanding of the story behind the problems you began talking about today." Or, "Having reviewed much of your background I wonder if you have just a little bit of a handle on, or some insight into the story behind the problems that you began talking about today. And about how you came to have the problems you spoke of."

If the client is able to bring together a story encompassing a long period of time integrating past and present experiences, then that would say to me that he may have a higher level of insight or awareness than if he were to just relate the problem to a recent event. Of course, that is assuming I am seeing other significant contributing factors in the background.

Question *If your client did just focus on a recent event, how would you respond?*

Speaker I would say something like, "You know, as you've been talking today I've been seeing a theme or a pattern in your life relating the past to the present, and I wonder if you see that. I won't tell him what it is; I will allude to a theme or a pattern. In doing that I am starting to generate insight that may not have been there previously.

CLOSURE: CLIENT'S GOALS

"If you were to continue your counselling what would you want to achieve and what would be your goals?" So this is where I identify the client's goals, and this is where the client begins to take the lead.

The following are some common goals: "I'd like to improve my communication." "I'd like to feel better about myself." "I'd like to be happy."

Sometimes people state their goals in a very general way, and that is okay to start with, "I'd like to be able to deal with my anger better." "I'd like to be able to feel comfortable around people in social situations." When a client gives me some goals, I will repeat them and maybe develop a numbered list, by saying,"So I'm hearing three goals, first you would like to deal with your anger better, second you would like to be more comfortable in social situations, and third you would like to feel better about yourself and work on your feeling of self-worth."

If he only gives me one goal, then I will say, "I wonder what would be another goal", unless it is very clear that he is here for one very specific reason — maybe it's to deal with the death of a loved one that happened recently, for example. In that case I will not pursue any other goals. I will just reiterate that as being his primary goal.

Now if it became clear to me during the assessment that there were some other unresolved losses or issues, I might suggest the possibility that he look at something that he did not mention as a goal. That might be a loss, or a conflict, or some other life experience, maybe being sexually or physically abused. I will suggest it as something he might want to look at, and I will see if he can acknowledge that as an important goal.

For example, I would say, "When you were talking earlier you mentioned your mother's death and there were some feelings that seemed to come up, so I'm wondering if that's an area you might want to explore a little bit at some point."

Response *What if he says, no, I don't want to go over that?*

Speaker Then I would not impose it. I might see it as directly related to his stated goal, in which case I am confident that it will come up during the counselling process.

Once I have reviewed the goals I'm going to say, "Which of these goals is most important to you?" I prioritize the goals because I want to be sure to address what the client feels is the most important goal so that he will have a sense that his needs are being met, and his reasons for seeking help are being addressed.

CLIENT'S EVALUATION OF THE SESSION

Then I am going to say, "What's this been like today talking about your life and problem areas?" The person will validate the session or he may say it has been difficult.

He might say, "I'm not used to talking to people about my problems." He might validate it in a back door type of way by saying, "I don't like to talk about my problems, but I know I need to." Or he might say, "It's really good to be able to talk about these things because I haven't talked about some things for a long time."

INVITATION TO RETURN

If the client is able to validate the first session, it is much more likely he will come back for the second session.

After he has responded I will say something like, "I wonder if you might like to meet again and take your goals a little bit further. Especially that most important goal of wanting to feel good about yourself, of working on your self-worth. Is that something you want to do?"

I put that to the client as a choice. Give him the opportunity to say, "Yes I think I would," or, "Well, no I don't think I want to right at this time — maybe at some other point".

It's important to reinforce the client's power of choice. Let him take responsibility. Very dependent clients in particular will be submissive to any suggestion on my part such as stating I think he should come back and see me. I do not want to feed into that kind of behaviour.

If a client is experiencing significant difficulty in his life, and he expresses uncertainty about returning to counselling, I will say, "I would encourage you to seek help from someone and to continue your counselling, whether it is with me or with someone else you can trust. If you want to continue with me I would certainly be available to you, but if not I would encourage you to see someone who can give you the help you need. What do you think you will do?"

When a client expresses the desire to meet again, I will close by saying, "Is this a good time for you next week?" If my time options are limited, I will suggest times for the next session and allow the client to choose. It is important identify at least a tentative time, and then put a period at the end of the session by saying, "Maybe we can stop now, and I will see you next week."

ASSIGNMENT: PRACTICE SESSION

The assignment is to practice conducting the assessment with a volunteer client who may be a friend, a training participant, or a family member. The objectives of the assignment are: 1) To experience what it is like to ask the assessment questions, 2) To experience the pacing or time required to complete the assessment, 3) To experience what it is like to have to take notes while establishing rapport or therapeutic alliance.

Use the following guidelines:

1. Prepare your client by saying, "Rather than counselling, I would like to use this time today to ask questions about your life experience, and I would like you to give me short answers, is that OK?" And "Is it OK if I take notes?"

2. Use your watch to measure the time you take in each category and to pace yourself. You would not do this in an actual assessment, but our training objective is to pace the session. Try to finish in one hour. Remember that assessment is only a brief sketch of the client's life.

3. Remember that with the talkative client you will need to interrupt with, "I would like to see if I understand what you are saying." Then make a reflection, get confirmation of accuracy, then introduce the next question.

4. Do not belabor or extend discussion of the client's responses to certain questions. If you do, the assessment will become a counselling session, and you will not finish soon enough.

5. Do not react in any judgemental way either verbally or non-verbally to what the client discloses. Do not infuse humour or any emotion which the client does not initiate. Your role is to mirror or follow the emotion of the client, not to lead.

6. If you do not finish the assessment in the first hour, wherever you are in assessment with ten minutes remaining, move down to a review of the client's goals and bring closure. It is important to review goals even if you are not finished with the assessment because this will tend to instill hope and help the client to look forward to the next session.

7. To elicit Presenting Problems with the volunteer client, you could suggest that he might think of some minor problem, or let him know that everyone has problems of one sort or another. And say, "Just take your time to think about it."

8. Remember that the client does not have to respond to questions that he chooses not to answer. However, it is important that you ask the question anyway.

9. If any strong emotions arise around certain questions, take time to acknowledge and validate the pain, then refer it to the counselling process. For example, "There's some hurt there, some pain around your relationship with father. Maybe it will be important to explore that further in your counselling." And ask permission to continue with the assessment, "Is it OK to continue? It's important to take time for feelings when they come up."

10. Avoid opening the session with, "How are you today?" The client is likely to say, "Fine," and this is untrue or the client would not be in counselling. It is setting up a denial defense.

11. Avoid closing the session with thanking the client. For example, "Thanks for coming." "Thanks for sharing that." "I'm glad you shared that today." This puts the client in the position of sharing for your benefit rather than for his own benefit.

12. Avoid attempting to support the client with your own self-disclosure of problems. This takes time away from the client, leaves the client with possibly comparing his experience with yours, opens the door for other personal questions, takes away from the transference relationship, leaves the client with having to protect you if you appear fragile to the client. In summary, counsellor disclosures may erode the client's safety.

13. In the case of an assessment which is to be submitted as a written assignment for this course, assure your client that his name and information which might identify him will be inked over so that confidentiality will be maintained. The volunteer client has a right to see the information you have recorded and must give permission for your supervisor to review it for training purposes.

COUNSELLOR'S SELF-ASSESSMENT

After completing the assessment, record your answers to the following questions:

a. What was it like doing the assessment with this client?

b. What questions did you find difficult or uncomfortable to ask?

c. What was it like taking notes while trying to make eye contact?

d. How far did you get in completing the assessment?

e. What was it like to open the session?

f. What was it like to close the session?

g. If you had it to do again, what would you have avoided or done differently?

h. What was it like to stay with the assessment rather than to do counselling?

i. What special challenges did this client present? For example, overtalking, expressing emotions, etc.

j. Were you able to see life patterns and contributing factors emerging from the information your client disclosed? Explain.

COMPLETION: When you have finished the assessment of your volunteer client as well as the above questions for the "Counsellor's Self-Assessment," submit the written copy to your supervisor.

Chapter Two:

The Counselling Process and Therapeutic Interventions

Speaker This module of the course describes the counselling process and therapeutic interventions. I will be discussing qualities of the counsellor, cycles in counselling, working through the pain, understanding life patterns, and changing life patterns. As we review cycles in counselling and parts of the counselling process, I will suggest specific therapeutic interventions and the actual wording of statements to use in counselling.

Genuineness, empathy, and warmth are regarded as the core counsellor qualities, and I will define those just very briefly.

GENUINENESS

By genuineness I am referring to sincerity, and this is something that is conveyed by means of eye contact and facial expression. I am communicating non-verbally that what my client has to say is of the greatest importance and I am truly interested in it. So I speak of genuineness as opposed to being mechanical; a counsellor who uses stock phrases or who uses too much or misplaced humour and does not take the client seriously enough is not going to be able to come across with genuineness and sincerity.

Response *Being real.*

Speaker Yes. Being real; genuine. Which carries along with it the importance of being one's self instead of putting on some kind of role. In other words the way you are as a counsellor in terms of your overall style and the way you come across needs to be the way you are in any relationship or situation. It is not a role, or a hat that you put on and take off. What might indicate a lack of sincerity?

Response *When the counsellor looks away, being easily distracted, looking at his watch, yawning.*

Speaker Yes, showing by these behaviours that he really is not interested in the client's issues. The professional literature indicates that the most common reasons for client's dropping out of therapy is when there is unresolved anger toward the counsellor and when the counsellor is perceived as insincere indicated for example by clicking his pen or looking at his watch. The first reason may be related to the second reason.

Question *Is this sincerity and genuineness a cultural thing? Or is it cross-cultural? Because I've heard that in North America there seems to be an emphasis on sincerity in relationships. If someone's not sincere in a relationship people don't like it as much, whereas in Europe there's more give-and-take and they take on roles more easily.*

Speaker Yes. There might be different signals of sincerity. For example, in some cultures the emphasis on eye contact wouldn't be as great as in the Western culture. In native culture, or black culture, and some other cultures there's a noticeable lack of eye contact or different eye contact as compared to Western cultures. For example, in some non-white cultures, the person might look at you when talking and look away when listening which you might interpret as not listening if you are not aware of the custom.

Response *Eye contact can be different for men and women — women tend not to look men in the eyes.*

Speaker That's right, yes. Especially in some Eastern cultures which are patriarchal.

SEATING ARRANGEMENT

Another point to make here is regarding seating arrangement and body language in counselling. In addition to frequent eye contact, sitting with your legs uncrossed and with your arms uncrossed resting on the arms of the chair, may communicate a relaxed openness to the client. Also, in terms of the angle of the chairs, about a 100 degree angle or a little more than a 90 degree angle tends to maximize the comfort of the client because this allows him to look past the counsellor without turning his head away. Whereas if chairs are directly facing each other, this may set up a sense of confrontation. The distance of the chairs should be no more than three feet and not closer than two feet. This range communicates support, whereas if the chairs are too close, I may communicate intrusiveness or if the chairs are too far apart, I may communicate a lack of support for the client. Non-verbal rapport is important to the counselling relationship.

EMPATHY

The next quality is empathy. I am speaking specifically of accurate empathy, the ability to be connected to the feelings, to the emotions of the client. So if the client is feeling sad, the counsellor needs to have a sense of that sadness and be able to mirror it in voice tone and facial expression.

For example, I had a client whose little boy was killed by a city utility truck, and as she talked about the incident she was feeling sad and I felt very sad as well. Now I think it was easy for me to connect because I have a little boy, and at the time he was six or so, about the age her little boy was. I found that I was able to feel very sad. In fact it was all I could do to keep from breaking down and crying.

A rule of thumb with your empathy is not to allow your own feelings of sadness to overshadow the expression of your client's sadness. So if I were to break down and cry and my client is just feeling sad, but not crying, then that might have a particular effect on my client. Can you imagine what that might be?

Response *She'd feel like she had to cry.*

Response *She becomes a care-giver.*

Speaker So the roles get reversed. She could become the care-giver. The focus would be taken away from the client. Also, I might be seen as fragile and as someone who needed to be protected from the client's pain. So the client might tend to hold back her own painful experiences for fear that I might break down and cry. I might appear to be overly sensitive and fragile.

Empathy is conveyed in non-verbal ways such as tearing or a frown if the client's feeling is sadness. Keep in mind that empathy must also be genuinely felt and genuinely mirrored. Any insincerity from the counsellor will erode the client's feeling of safety.

Essentially I will be mirroring the emotional content or the emotions of my client whether the feeling is anger, sadness, fear, or some other feeling. Some counsellors have said that empathy is the most therapeutic counsellor quality because it lends support to the client's pain.

Empathy may also be conveyed verbally in the voice tone. And so I will speak with empathic reflections. This is a statement that reflects back what the client has been saying, accompanied by a feeling word. An empathic reflective statement would be "So you're feeling sad because your good friend just moved away, is that what you're feeling?"

Question *When you as the counsellor show tears what does the client perceive? Is the client going to think you don't really understand or is he going to become defensive?*

Speaker If your tears are an accurate reflection of the client's feeling, and if your expression of feeling is a little bit less than the client's expression of feeling, your empathy is likely to be accepted as support. However, something else that may happen is that the client's own engagement of emotion is scary for him so that he withdraws. This is an issue of the client's not feeling safe with himself or perhaps with you, which I will speak about in a few minutes.

WARMTH

The next quality is warmth, and here I am talking about non-possessive warmth, as opposed to cool detachment. Warmth is caring that is conveyed in a soft and gentle voice tone and facial expression.

Warmth may be conveyed in a non-verbal way and a non-possessive way. Now what would possessive warmth be? Does anybody have any ideas?

Response *Smothering.*

Speaker Too touchy-feely. Smothering in that way. In a physical way, giving too much physical caring. Sometimes a counsellor will like to give out hugs or want to hug a client more for the counsellor's own needs than for the client. And so that can become possessive.

Response *A female counsellor was mentioning that she would touch and sometimes have it misread. It wasn't a prolonged contact, just a touch. So the client was interpreting any physical contact as something possessive.*

Speaker This could easily occur. I want to talk about touching a little more when we get down to boundaries — touching is a boundary issue.

Question *So you're talking about warmth here in a verbal sense?*

Speaker That's right. Verbal warmth can be experienced as possessive if it is excessive in terms of the warm voice tone or in terms of verbal content if it is overstated. This may be perceived as lacking sincerity or as superficial and shallow, or if it is perceived as sincere it is experienced as being too mothering and protective or condescending, treating the client too much as a child.

We can understand warmth by its opposite quality which is to be cold. In this case the voice tone is emotionally flat, detached and mechanical, and verbal content may tend to understate the client's plight. It is a style which communicates aloofness, distance, and unconcern.

UNCONDITIONAL POSITIVE REGARD

Another important attribute is unconditional positive regard. Some people believe that this is the most curative or therapeutic thing that a counsellor can provide. This implies a particular mental attitude: that the client's problems and feelings are of the greatest importance, this session is the most important session for the client, and the client himself is as valuable as the most highly respected person on earth even if he does not believe that he is.

I am regarding the client's behaviour, no matter how self-destructive or even destructive of others it may be, as having a story behind it that allows it to make sense, that makes it understandable even though the client is responsible for choosing it.

The belief is that a person will make choices that are best for himself if he is aware of all the possible choices. If I have the ability to convey unconditional positive regard it will be possible for me to sincerely validate my client, to bring all my best ability and expertise to the session, to listen and focus on the client, and to accept the client's pace and process of recovery.

Response *That would be like having Charles Manson, the mass-murderer as a client. Yes, he killed a lot of people, however, he may have the possibility or the potential for change.*

Speaker Yes.

Response *And he can overcome that. So he's there and my task is to help him to be the best person that he can be from what appears to be the most disturbed person.*

Speaker Exactly.

Question *Does that go along with separating the person from the problem?*

Speaker Absolutely. You see the person as having intrinsic value apart from his behaviour, and you see his behaviour as having an understandable story behind it. And that will allow us to be able to remain in a helping position with our client.

There might be some types of people, such as Charles Manson, that we would not be able to maintain an unconditional positive regard for. What are some other types of clients that you might have trouble with?

Response *Sexual offenders.*

Speaker Serial killers. Rapists.

Response *Child abusers.*

Speaker Child abusers. Okay. Molesters. That type of behaviour.

Question *Could that perhaps be why they are some of the hardest to cure or change?*

Speaker Yes. It's hard to find people who are able to work with those types of individuals.

Response *I think that's why the problem keeps going. It's difficult, I think, for someone to get out there and work in those circumstances and still separate themselves to such an extent that they don't become part of it, or that they become a part of the solution rather than part of the problem.*

Speaker Alright, yes. And its difficult to keep from reacting judgementally and lose your effectiveness in that way. So what should we do if we can not maintain unconditional positive regard for a client?

Response *Have him seek someone else, perhaps. Say, "I'm not sure I'll be able to help you as much as you may need."*

Speaker That's right. Make a referral and own it as your problem.

Response *Yes. Rather than blaming the client.*

Speaker When you say to the client "I don't feel that I have the skills that you need to get the help that you need" you show you are accepting responsibility for your limitations, rather than blaming the client.

NON-JUDGEMENTAL

Along with that goes the ability to be non-judgemental. I need to be able to regard the client's behaviour in terms of behaviours which work well and which do not work well for the client relative to his functioning, rather than in moral terms. So we need to be aware of the range of judgemental terms to be left out of the counselling relationship and left out of our counselling vocabulary.

Rather than say to a client, "Do you think that's wise or do you think that's right?" I'm going to say, "Does that work well for you?"

Response *So it's non-judgemental on a certain level, but I see it being judgemental on another level. We're saying this behaviour is effective and this behaviour is not effective to meet the client's needs.*

Speaker The question is what works well and what doesn't work well, rather than what behaviour is right or what behaviour is wrong. Terms like inconsiderate, or imprudent, or unwise, irresponsible, right or wrong, good or bad, are judgemental terms.

Response *And I think having unconditional positive regard and being non-judgemental are inseparable. I think those two really work together.*

Speaker Unconditional positive regard goes beyond being non-judgemental and most certainly includes being non-judgemental. The client usually brings too much self-judgement with him, so he does not need ours added to his. To take it further, judgementalism from the counsellor is likely to do with his counter-transference which will be discussed later in the course.

Response *Unconditional positive regard I see as having to extend from myself — the way I regard myself. I can't have that for another person if I don't — If I'm not able to see myself in that light.*

Response *Actually, you have it for the client to the degree you have it for yourself — that same degree for someone else. So I think it's a matter of degrees... possibly to realize how silly it would be and I'm at 60 or 70 percent of my ability to be non-judgemental and that's the way it is — and putting aside that and still being as totally open as possible. I mean there's no 100%.*

Response *But is there a point where you choose not to be judgemental. I might feel judgemental but a client doesn't have to know that. I can choose not to be express it — I can filter that out.*

Response *The choice of leaving your stuff behind and going there without your stuff so it doesn't get in the way of your work with the client.*

Speaker The client is already self-blaming enough — already bringing enough self-judgement and guilt with him, so he doesn't need your judgement of him. The dependent client may allow you to judge him and he will return to the session. In any case, judgement tends to erode safety.

Response *I sort of see the counsellor as a defence lawyer who is appointed by the court to defend and support the client. You can't make any judgements and you give unconditional support. It's as if the client tends to be his own prosecutor and presents the negative self-talk, for example.*

Question *Isn't unconditional positive regard judgement? Like okay, I judge everybody as good.*

Speaker Well, it has to do with a fundamental view of humanity that everyone is sincere and well intentioned and that people have problem behaviours for understandable reasons. In other words, a client may not have been responsible for beginning his unhealthy patterns, they were adopted as a means of surviving painful life experiences. However, although the person was not responsible for starting the patterns and although they seemed to work well during childhood for example, the client is responsible for perpetuating those patterns in adult life, and they do not work well now or he would not be in counselling. Maybe there was an abusive background or there was unhealthy parental modelling, there was a tragic loss of a loved one, for example, and these experiences resulted in some adaptive behaviour which does not work well in adult life and relationships.

Response *You stated that you have to know the client's story, that there's always some sort of logic for the behaviour.*

Speaker Exactly, there's always a story there that allows it to make sense and that allows us to remain non-judgemental of the client and to maintain positive regard.

I recently heard a counsellor tell a client during the first session, "What are you complaining about? What are you complaining about now?" Well that's a very judgemental way to approach a client, to assign to her problems the word "complain" or "complaining".

Response *That's a negative judgement there.*

Response *It's a parental means of dealing with the client.*

Speaker Some counsellors might justify that by saying they are trying to elicit a transference reaction. In my view what they are doing is abusing the client to encourage the expression of feelings the client has been unable to deal with. But the end does not justify the means. It does not justify a non-professional approach — a destructive, abusive approach which could harm the client. If I cannot predict a therapeutic outcome of my statement, I am not engaging in professional counselling.

MAINTAINING BOUNDARIES

This is a very important area for discussion because maintaining boundaries is essential for creating a safe enough atmosphere for the client. There is a boundary around the counselling relationship as well as boundaries between the counsellor and client that are important for safety. What kind of boundary surrounding counsellor and client is important for maintaining safety and trust?

Response *Confidentiality.*

Speaker Yes, confidentiality. That's right. So that is a primary boundary around the counsellor and the client. The client needs to be assured that whatever he discloses will remain confidential, that nothing will be revealed without his signed written permission. Exceptions to this include any behaviour which is a life-threatening danger to himself or others, or information related to the physical or sexual abuse of a child.

Another related issue arises when the client who is being seen within the context of a service agency attempts to split off the counsellor from the other professional staff by saying, "I'm going to tell you something and I don't want you to tell any of the other counsellors." The boundary of confidentiality in this case surrounds the service agency rather than just the individual counsellor-client relationship. This is because the counsellor needs to be able to confer with the other professional staff regarding the progress of his client.

Now we need to look at the boundaries that need to be there between the counsellor and the client. So I will list these and discuss each one.

1. Never say "I care for you" or "I care about you", or "I love you" to a client.

2. As a rule, do not touch a client.

3. Do not accept gifts from a client.

4. Do not disclose information about your personal life.

5. Do not express thanks to a client for disclosing or working in the session.

6. Do not engage in extended phone calls unless the client is suicidal and phoning to keep the suicide contract.

7. Do not engage in a social, sexual, or business relationship with a client.

8. Do not express anger to a client.

9. Do not reveal your personal spiritual views.

10. Do not extend a counselling session beyond the agreed time.

11. Do not accept substitutions for the fee for service.

Beginning with the first boundary issue, no direct verbal statements of affection such as "I care for you or about you" or "I love you" or statements which could be taken as sexual messages, should be given. Why is that important?

Response *Because you don't want any emotions that can just add to the problems.*

Response *It opens up a relationship — it sure changes the level of relationship from a professional one to a personal one.*

Response *You could get into trouble sexually.*

Speaker Yes, it could be taken as a sexual message. Also, it could be taken as offering false hope for your client. The client may take it as meaning that you are going to be there for her indefinitely. That is simply not possible. If you present a message that raises false hope, and then for some reason you terminate the relationship, a particularly sensitive client may become suicidal.

Response *But it seems to me that the whole process of counselling is saying to the person "I care about you" but it's not verbalized.*

Speaker That's exactly right. You are being caring but you are not verbally saying "I care".

Response *So you never say "I care".*

Speaker That's right.

Response *Do you say "I care about what happens to you?"*

Speaker You don't need to say that. You're demonstrating it by being there for him. You don't want to create any false hope for your client that you will always be able to be there for him. Let your caring be communicated by your counsellor qualities of genuineness, empathy, warmth, and unconditional positive regard.

Response *Quite often the client might fall in love with you. This kind of statement,* "I care about you," could really fuel that kind of emotion, which is not what you want.

Speaker The client may already have that tendency because of her vulnerability, her neediness. Because of a loss of parental caring and closeness, she may have a pattern of sexualizing the need for caring. So for you to say something like that — especially if you're the opposite sex to the client — but also with homosexual clients, might lead to that kind of sexual or romantic attraction to you associated with the need for caring. That is what is meant by erotic transference.

Question *How would you answer someone if they asked you "Do you care about me? How do I know if you care about me?" How are you going to answer that?*

Speaker You could say "I'm here". However, what I might prefer to say is "So what I'm hearing is that you have your doubts. Maybe you are wanting some assurance. And I wonder if that's a new experience for you that people who you've wanted to care for you, or expected or hoped would care for you, that somehow they haven't." So I put it back on the client to explore her own experience with the loss of caring.

If we verbalize our caring for the client in a direct way, the resulting erotic transference could be so powerful that the client is no longer able to progress. Her motive for coming to sessions is to pursue the counsellor romantically.

In addition, if the counsellor ends this relationship without adequately working through the transference, the result could be a suicide attempt by this client who now feels abandonned.

Another boundary issue is not to touch a client, as a rule of thumb, for the same reasons. The very vulnerable, needy client who missed parental caring and closeness might sexualize that, and you are just going to feed into an erotic transference.

Now sometimes a same sex touch on the client's arm when the client is crying, or on the shoulder, might be alright. But if a client has been sexually or physically abused, even that might create anxiety for a client and cause her to feel unsafe. So as a rule of thumb, I would say abstain from touching. It is a safe policy. You can convey your caring through your counsellor qualities.

Question *Wouldn't touching as well have a calming effect? If you have a client who's going through an extremely emotional or painful thing and they're crying or sobbing, you could put your hand on them and touch them. Isn't that okay because it has a calming effect?*

Speaker It might actually have the effect of interrupting her engagement of the pain.

Response *There are some times when that will induce the emotions to fully come out, to fully clear. You want the emotion to come up and be released. I think it takes a great deal of discernment though — whether that is appropriate.*

Speaker And maybe you can check it out with your client. After a client has cried, for instance, you have provided that kind of comfort, you could say "Was it okay for me just to put my hand on your shoulder. What was that like for me to do that? Is that okay for you? Does it feel supportive or not?" However, if you touch first and check it out later, the damage may already have been done, and safety is lost.

Have a frank discussion about it. But I would say that because the outcome is unpredictable, no physical contact is the rule of thumb unless all of your other verbal interventions and your counsellor qualities make such contact completely safe, and depending upon what the assessment and history of your client might indicate.

We hear about so-called professionals who play with fire on this issue, and the complaints from clients are to be found in the newspapers, in court reports, and in membership files kept by professional associations.

Another boundary issue is not to accept gifts from a client but rather encourage him to put it into words. Some types of clients, especially the borderline personality which is discussed in a later course, may want to give you gifts and money for you and your family. This may be a way of attempting to manipulate her way into your life. I might also add here to avoid having your family pictures in your office. This may trigger feelings of jealousy, abandonment, and the need to cling to you and your family.

Question *How do you turn down a gift?*

Speaker You can use it as an opportunity to validate the client's intentions and to define the boundary. You might say, "It was very thoughtful of you to choose this gift. Maybe this is a time when I can let you know about a boundary that exists between us as counsellor and client, which is that it is not possible for me to accept gifts. What's it like hearing me say that?" After reviewing the feelings around this boundary, I will say, "What is the message you are giving me by wanting to give this gift?"

One of the fundamental things I am wanting my clients to do is to put their feelings into spoken word, to give verbal expressions to their emotions and their needs. This could be used as an opportunity to use the gift-giving in a therapeutic way. Sometimes I will accept the gift the first time, then explain the boundary.

You can also define the boundary when a client is either requesting a hug, or when he is asking you personal information about your life.

As a general rule, do not self disclose to a client. If your client asks you personal information, use that as an opportunity to define the boundary and ask him what it is like hearing you describe that boundary. He might report feeling frustrated that there is a kind of a barrier there that he can not break through or get past.

And so I tend to want to use that therapeutically, first by validating and reflecting the client's feelings and views, then by linking the client's feelings to an earlier experience. I might say, "It makes sense that you'd feel that frustration because in a social relationship you would perhaps have mutual sharing of personal experiences. In our counselling relationship I'm not able to answer personal questions because of professional boundaries. I wonder if there's somebody else who was important in your life whom you couldn't get close to or who was distant from you or who wouldn't share personal experiences." The client will probably identify a parent whom he was not close to.

So the key here in exploring the client's transference reaction is to first fully support and validate the client's current feeling of rejection or frustration with the boundary, then reach for a link to the past. If you do not first support the client's current frustration with you, any attempt to link with the past will likely meet with strong resistance.

Now there are settings and situations in which self disclosure is a very important part of the therapy. I am thinking about alcohol and drug counselling by recovering addicts.

Speaker Essentially I am talking about peer counselling rather than therapeutic or clinical counselling. Self-disclosure by the counselling addict, of his own personal recovery process, is often effective in helping another addict to embark or proceed with the recovery process.

Response *That's basically my situation. What works in the treatment centre for me mostly is when I'm disclosing about myself— it allows the clients to feel comfortable that somebody else has gone through it. They do feel alone until someone tells them they aren't, and I'm an authority figure because I'm a counsellor there. However, I understand that when I disclose my experiences, I'm really doing peer counselling which erodes the client's time in the session and which leads to the client's making comparisons.*

I'm also starting to cut back on accepting gifts . I say "Okay, listen, I can't accept this gift and I don't want to hurt your feelings, but maybe you can tell me someone else in your life who's done the same thing."

Speaker Or ask her to put the gift into words, because you want to know what the client is saying when she gives a gift. What do you think she is saying to you?

Response *That I appreciate you — appreciate what you're doing.*

Response *Where I work, a lot of clients do give gifts to counsellors because they go through a process in five weeks that to them is miraculous. But I'm starting to say no to that and I can see the reasons why now.*

Speaker When a person expresses appreciation or thanks to you it's important to say, "You're most welcome." I would not say "I am glad I can help you" because it sounds as though I am saying, "What you've done has benefitted me — what you have done has been for my benefit instead of for your own benefit."

For the same reason I won't say to a client "Thank you very much for sharing what you shared" or for coming to this session" or things like that because this also conveys the message that the client has done the work for my benefit.

Question *So how do you respond?*

Speaker "You're most welcome."

Question *What's the difference?*

Speaker Well, if you are saying "thank you" you are implying that what the client shared benefitted you and that he came to counselling for your benefit. "So thank you very much for coming to me." When I say "you're welcome" it is acknowledging that what I've given to you, you are welcome to have.

Response *It's like if I give you a gift, you'll say thank you but I won't say thank you back, I'll say you're welcome.*

Response *Yes I understand that. Well let's say if someone gives me some information, I'd thank her. I'd say "Thanks for giving me that information." Is that wrong?*

Speaker It's not a question of right or wrong but a question of the predictable effect on the client.

Response *That's not information for your benefit, but for the client's benefit.*

Speaker What are you thanking her for?

Response *For being honest, open and letting me know.*

Question *But who benefits from her being open and honest? You don't. So why are you saying thank you?*

Response *I'm thanking her for giving me the information.*

Response *But she's there for her. She's not there for you.*

Speaker Exactly. She's there for her. And you're there for her. She's not there for you. It's a ritual way of speaking at the end of a social visit to say, "Thanks for coming." We just have to be very aware that counselling is not a social visit, not for mutual benefit, but for the therapeutic benefit of the client. So our language needs to change to be consistent with that objective. Many clients are people pleasers, seeking approval. If you express thanks to them, they will want to give you disclosures in order to get your approval, and so this will feed into an unhealthy pattern which may characterize their ways of relating to people generally, that is, wanting to meet what they perceive to be other people's needs more than their own.

Question *You were saying that if somebody asks you something about your own personal life, to try to turn it around back to him?*

Speaker Use it as an opportunity to define the boundary and say "So you want to know where I went on holidays and what I did and where I went, and if we had a social relationship, I would be able to tell you about that. Because we have a counselling relationship, I'm not able to talk about my personal life."

Question *Just to tell them about a vacation?*

Speaker That's right. If you start disclosing your personal life on one point, it may be more difficult to establish the boundary later, and the negative transference will be stronger than if you were clear at the beginning.

Question *Doesn't the client sometimes feel they've shared so much that they'd like a little sharing in return?*

Speaker Yes, and I wonder if you're aware right now of feeling a little annoyed or frustrated with this boundary.

Response *Yes. A little.*

Speaker It's not unusual for people in the class to react emotionally or to have a negative transference when we discuss these boundary issues.

Just to add another reason for not self-disclosing to clients, I have had a number of clients who last saw a psychiatrist, psychologist, or other professional counsellor, and the client is saying, "I saw this counsellor and he ended up telling me all about his problems, so I never went back." So there was a role reversal, and the client was put in the position of helping the counsellor. Who's paying who for what?

Even in the case of sexual abuse counselling or addiction counselling, if I begin to disclose that I was abused or addicted, what will I be asked to disclose next? Where will it end? And if I disclose that I am not in recovery from such experiences, what happens to my credibility? It is better for the client if I simply define the boundary from the start.

The client has a need because of her own situation to get some other kind of caring from you, to have some other kind of involvement.

The borderline personality in particular has very obscure boundaries. That is part of the problem in that disorder. And it is important for that client, any client really, to feel safe. He needs to know that this time is his time only, and you are not going to let him give up his time because of his own neediness or perhaps as a defense against focusing on his own difficult issues.

If the borderline wants to be a member of your family, one of the ways she may do that is by giving gifts and by phoning you at inconvenient hours or other times outside the session.

So there is another boundary issue. Do not allow the client to phone you except for suicidal feelings, and when she phones and wants to talk say "I think that's a very important thing you're talking about, and maybe it's going to be important for you to discuss that in our next session. Rather than talk further now, I would recommend that we continue in our next session." Then in the next session I might re-state the boundary issue and explore the client's feelings about it. Another approach that helps to limit phone counselling is to say, "Maybe what we could do is agree on a fee for phone counsellng, does that make sense?"

Question *So you limit your contact with the client to the agreed upon time and place.*

Speaker Yes. Do not see a client socially. Do not do business with a client. In small communities it might be difficult. For example, counsellors in small native communities often find difficulty in maintaining a professional role because they are related to many of the people.

Response *You go to the store and there is the client, shopping.*

Speaker Right. In small communities there needs to be a recognition of the unique role of the counsellor and the unique boundary surrounding his role or function. This can be done through community education about the role of the counsellor. Another option is for a counsellor to provide services in another community or reserve.

Question *If someone saw you in the supermarket in a city like Vancouver, what would you say?*

Speaker I'd keep it light and superficial. If I met a client I wouldn't ask, "How are you today?" Because you might get a long explanation.

Question *What would you say?*

Speaker I would say "Hello. Here we are, shopping again." I would make small talk. I would make a statement rather than a question.

Another thing that I need to mention here is when you start a counselling session never say "How are you today?" That's a ritual question, and what's the ritual response?

Response *I'm fine. How are you?*

Speaker Right. So you're setting up a denial defense right at the start.

Response *Do you know how many people ask that question?*

Speaker I'm sure many do.

Response *They'll ask it in the doctor's office:"How are you today?" If I was fine I wouldn't be here.*

Speaker So we start by saying "Tell me what's been happening" rather than "How are you today?"

So, back to the boundary regarding no social, sexual or business relationships. If these relationships existed prior to being approached by a client, this person is to be referred to another counsellor, and if these kinds of relationships develop during the counselling relationship, safety for the client will be lost, and a referral must be made. Otherwise to see a friend or relative or someone you've done business with, introduces hidden agendas or the need for the client to protect himself or to protect you and your special relationship. This means the client will not feel safe to be himself and perhaps to share difficult issues.

The next boundary issue on our list is to avoid expressing anger toward a client. The counsellor's anger may be experienced by clients as being very powerful. The counsellor's anger would be a counter-transference reaction to the client's behaviour, and the client's negative transference triggered by this may be insurmountable.

Do not disclose your personal political, religious, or spiritual views. Clients are vulnerable and want to please you as was stated earlier, and so they are easy to convert to your religion. To do so would be considered abuse of the client, exploiting her vulnerability. If the client knows your particular spiritual or religious views before seeing you because perhaps your counselling service includes a reference to your views, e.g. "Christian Counselling Services", then there is no boundary violation. But if you disclose these views only after the therapeutic alliance is established, then this is abuse.

Do not extend the length of the session beyond the established time. This is something the saviour or the counsellor who fears rejection by a needy client, might do. The client who wants more time in the session and keeps introducing material, may feel unsafe if the counsellor allows her to continue or may perceive the counsellor as lacking confidence. We need to think of ways to end the session in the face of the client's pressure. The simplest approach is to make a summary reflection of what the client has talked about in the session by saying,

"So today you've been talking about....." and "What's it been like doing this today?"

These statements lead the client into closure. To structure the closure a little more, I might say,

"We will need to close the session in about five or ten minutes, and so maybe we could just summarize the work you've been doing today."

The most difficult situation is when the client waits until the last ten minutes to engage painful emotions. When this happens I might say,

"You're feeling the pain now, and that's important. I encourage you to let yourself feel that especially when we meet again. Right now we're going to end the session in a few minutes. I wonder what it's like to end the session just when you're feeling this. It's not easy to feel the pain and then to have to end the session."

In other words, I am supporting and validating the client's pain, and then I am taking the client into a cognitive level of thinking about it rather than feeling. I am also helping the client to process the experience of ending the session soon after engaging painful feelings. This makes it OK for the client. Notice that I'm moving the client from the emotional level to the cognitive level as much as possible before closure. We may need to do some educational work with a client so that she accepts the fact that a counselling session may sometimes end with her feeling worse than when she came in. Checking out support systems and encouraging the client to share her feelings with someone between sessions or to do some journalling, may also be helpful.

Another point to make here is that the length of time within which a client can benefit most is 50 to 60 minutes. Beyond this time, the session becomes counter-productive or too draining, or too much for the client to integrate. Sometimes counsellors think a client needs more time to get down to business. However, the opposite is true. The more time we give that type of client to address important issues, the more time he will take before he addresses those issues. If we stay with the limited time, the client is likely to get the message that if he wants to benefit from the session, he had better get to the point.

The last boundary I will discuss is that there should be no substitute for the fee for service. Sometimes the less professional counsellor will allow a client to do office work or house work. In this case the client may want to protect herself in order to preserve this privilege. If the office work or house work is unsatisfactory, this issue may remain hidden by the counsellor or the anxiety about performance may not be identified. The threat to the client's feeling safe in counselling is increased. It is much easier to simply allow the client to meet every two weeks or to reduce or eliminate the fee.

There may be some other boundary issues but these are the ones that frequently arise.

SELF-AWARENESS

Self awareness is the next topic and has to do with being aware of our own core issues, our own painful life experiences, our own conflicts and losses. And we need to have embarked on the path of our own recovery, our own journey of personal growth. We need to be far enough down that road to be able to help somebody who is behind on the road. We need to be farther along than our client.

Response *Sometimes clients report having read certain self-help books as evidence of having begun their own process of healing.*

Speaker Self-help books tend to focus on the individual only. People who have used self-help materials might think of themselves as ahead. They might think that they're down the road. You may have clients who are very aware of the issues on an intellectual level through their own research.

But clients who have done their own work often times have only done it only on an inner level. They haven't done the work of sharing that with anyone.

Healing takes place when an individual takes the risk to open himself to share the pain with another, and then receives validation. It's difficult for a person to come up with a validation for himself. Validation and support, at least initially, seem to have to come from outside.

Response *That's the way we all start out in the world. Our parents validate us.*

Speaker That's right. And then our ego strengthens as we mature and grow, and we can begin to validate ourselves. But it's difficult if a person hasn't had the parenting that he needed, to give himself that validation without first getting it from outside.

Question *Are you saying we should all go for counselling before we become counsellors?*

Speaker I really believe in that. I believe that everyone, no matter how recovered you think you are, can benefit from counselling.

If the counsellor has not grieved his own losses, he may not appreciate the importance and benefit to the client of grieving his losses. If the counsellor is very cognitive and intellectual, he may not be able to help the client engage in the process of integrating painful feelings from past experiences. If the counsellor has his own blind spots or defenses, he may not recognize them in the client. If the client is overly passive for example, he may not be able to help the client change his own dysfunctional passivity, because the counsellor is in fact modeling passivity.

Speaker I think the point to be made is that ultimately there's no division between the client and the counsellor. Every counsellor is a client, and that's the point that we need to make here about the need to be aware of our own issues.

One of the primary reasons for doing our own work is so that our client doesn't trigger off too much of our own stuff, which could leave us being pre-occupied with those issues and ineffective or unable to focus on the client.

COUNTER-TRANSFERENCE

On the other hand, if we react to our client in some way, our own counter-transference might be triggered, and we might become bored or resentful, or annoyed, or frustrated with our client. It's important to engage in self-exploration and ask yourself, "What type of client really turns me off?" And we might answer, "Well, it's this person who talks unceasingly. I can't get a word in edgewise." And when you answer that question, you'll be working on your own counter-transference, or perhaps your own frustration with your lack of skills which is projected onto the client.

Question *But isn't there value in reacting sometimes? For instance, if a client is constantly evasive, you might become really firm in stopping that pattern.*

Speaker If you're doing it as a conscious deliberate choice, that's not a reaction. Counter-transference is when we react impulsively to a client. Keep in mind, as we discussed clinical assessment, we said counter-transference is when something about the client reminds the counsellor of someone in his own past.

Whenever we have expectations of our client, to respond or progress in a certain way, then this is our counter-transference. It is important that we approach the client without having expectations for him. It is when the client does not do what we want or expect, that we then feel frustrated, bored or whatever, and then we can no longer focus on the client's struggle and remain non-judgemental. It is then that the client is experienced as not meeting the counsellor's needs perhaps to be effective, to be adequate, competent, approved, cared for, and validated. When the counsellor expects the client to do anything or become something, the client is placed in the position of being present for the counsellor rather than for himself. And this brings us to the saviour counsellor who needs to be needed or to be liked.

Now it may also be the case that the client's behaviour leads to a reaction in the counsellor which affects many others in the same way. If the counsellor's reaction is not exaggerated but seems in fact to be reality-based and fits the situation or behaviour of the client, then the counsellor can use that emotional response in himself as a way of assessing and identifying the dysfunctional behaviour or pattern of the client. If the client's behaviour turns me off and distances me, I am going to wonder if my reaction is my counter-transference or if my reaction is a clue to the client's dysfunctional way of relating to others generally. To distinguish these, I can ask myself whether or not my reaction is something about which others have given me feedback, or I can ask the client what happens when he demonstrates similar behaviour with others and what feedback he has received. Keep in mind also that in a given situation, the counsellor's counter-transference may be triggered by the client's dysfunctional pattern or transference and vice-versa.

SAVIOUR SYNDROME

Speaker One of the main things that comes up in the area of self awareness is the saviour syndrome. We need to focus on this because people are often attracted to the counselling profession out of a need to take on a saviour role.

Many people who are attracted to counselling as a profession want to use clients to work on their own problems. That's a reality. There are also counsellors who are the oldest, responsible child in the family of origin or who have had a role in the family of origin that corresponds with the counselling role. People from dysfunctional families who were peacemakers, assistant parents, caregivers, or fixers might end up being attracted to counselling as a profession.

The saviour is characterized by wanting to fix the client prematurely. She allows the client to extend the session beyond the agreed time. She allows the client to phone and engages in phone counselling rather than limiting the client's work to the session. Facing the counsellor and working within the hourly session may be difficult for the client. She tries to make it easy for the client and feeds into the client's neediness.

She wants to take the difficulty or the struggle away when in fact what's going to help the client is to be in the position of doing what's most difficult, facing the pain, taking the difficult scary risks. The saviour is going to want to rescue the client from all of that and in effect to support the client's defenses which serve to protect the client and preserve the dysfunction.

Response *So if the counsellor's motivation is to get the client to face all that, then they're not a saviour type?*

Speaker That's right. The saviour is the person who gives answers, who tells the client what to do instead of having the client explore his own options. The counsellor who fills in the blanks for the client. When a very dependent client gives a partial sentence and waits for the counsellor to complete it, the saviour counsellor will complete it.

But what the counsellor needs to do is hang back and maybe say "You know, I notice that now and then as you're talking, you'll stop in the middle of a sentence and look at me. I wonder what that's about?"

The saviour wouldn't work in that way. The saviour counsellor would go on completing sentences and filling in blanks for the dependent client, perhaps because the saviour is afraid of being rejected if he doesn't do what the client expects or wants.

The saviour counsellor will pass the tissue too soon to the client. Why is that a saviour behaviour?

Response *Because it keeps the client from feeling the feelings.*

Speaker All right, it saves him from the pain. As soon as the person blows his nose and wipes his tears, he's wiping away the pain as well. The crying stops, the pain stops. So it's important to let the nose run a little while. Let the tears flow. Let the client feel uncomfortable with that, but not too uncomfortable. When it gets to the point of being messy, the client begins to feel unsafe. Then hand him the tissue. But we need to practice hanging back.

Response *I have difficulty with that. My own thinking was when they start to cry, by my giving them the tissue or putting it near them, I'm saying "Here's a tissue, go ahead and cry." And you're saying they may not get that message?*

Speaker Yes. What I'll do is put the tissue box just out of his reach so that he has to exercise some effort to get it. I'm very concerned that as soon as he wipes his tears, then the crying will stop. I've seen this happen many times. Instead I'll lend comfort and consolation by saying "It's okay to cry. Just let yourself feel that right now. Just stay with that feeling."

Question *So you verbalize it?*

Speaker I'll verbalize the permission in a consoling way.

Response *The point I have a hard time with is the period of silence. I know that I have to allow some silence and I do that. How do you do it? How do you know? Is there a sign there that says this is enough silence? Do you count seconds or minutes or anything like that?*

Speaker It's definitely a judgement call. But during that silence it's important to help the person to engage the pain. So if I see a non-verbal indication of it, like tearing, I'll say "Just let yourself feel that right now." In fact, I might say "Just take some time in silence, and let yourself feel that."

Question *So you do speak?*

Speaker I do speak but I may instruct the client not to speak. "Take some silence without using any words. Just let yourself feel that right now." That kind of intervention doesn't require a verbal response. In fact it's just the opposite. It requires the client to stay with what he's feeling. Then the next step is to encourage. Say "That's it, just let yourself feel that." And when the crying seems to diminish, I'll say "Now just begin to put those feelings into words. What are the tears about?" That's the next step. This is a question on the qualifying examination — what do you do as soon as you see a sign of painful feelings surfacing, or tearing, crying? What's the first thing you do with that? And the second and third thing? What are the steps? What are the interventions, in their proper order?

Question *What are the steps again?*

Speaker First, "Just let yourself feel that."

Then second, use silence. Wait for the crying to diminish. Third, say "What are the tears about? Put that into words now. Are they sad tears, angry tears, what kind of tears?"

Fourth, when the client identifies the kind of tears, say "Is it OK to feel that?" In any case, the counsellor will say, "You have every right to feel that," or some wording of validation.

Finally, the counsellor will extend the invitation to talk, "Say more about that feeling."

Remember, the saviour is going to say "What are the tears about?" as soon as the tears start. And what level does that take the client to?

Response *Cognitive.*

Speaker Cognitive level, exactly. It takes him right out of his feelings. And so the order and wording of the interventions or statements to the client, are very important.

The saviour will spend too much time in problem solving and cognitive and behavioural work. He'll skip over facing the painful feelings. For many clients the tough work is facing the pain.

The saviour will also attempt to give his own insights to the client rather than elicit insight or generate insight from within the client. So the saviour will make interpretations, such as "You know it seems that what you're feeling has to do with all that unresolved anger toward your mother," instead of saying things like "So you had a strong reaction in this situation. What's the story behind that?"

For example, I had a client who was talking about performance anxiety. He said he was being observed by a supervisor and he just froze up. He couldn't speak, and I said "What was it about that situation that triggered such anxiety that you were immobilized?" He responded that he saw the supervisor as being cold, mechanical, critical and distant. So I said to him "What other important person in your life would you describe as having been cold, mechanical, critical or distant?"

In this example I used his words in describing the current situation that triggered his exaggerated response. I asked him about what other important person in his life had similar characteristics. And it didn't take him long to come up with his alcoholic father whom he saw as being very successful, and who had high expectations of him and was very cold and critical. Father gave him no approval and no caring, only criticism.

And so there's the root of his performance anxiety. He'd been struggling with that for years. He couldn't hold a job or relate to authority figures. It was a very debilitating reaction. The point I'm making with this example is that this kind of intervention allowed the client to come up with his own insight and make his own connection. We need to learn how to help the client generate his own insight instead of making the connections for him.

The saviour counsellor may save the client from pain, from insight, and from choices. Instead of allowing the client to develop his own strategy or action plan, the saviour will tell the client what to do. It works well for the counsellor to suggest choices only after the client has had an opportunity to create his own. And then, in order to support the client's power and self-reliance, the counsellor needs to say, "Among these choices, which seems most workable to you?"

The saviour counsellor is parallel to the overprotective parent who deprives the client or the child from facing the difficulty, the struggle, and from making his own choices and mistakes, which is a process whereby the client or the child is able to learn and grow.

CYCLES IN COUNSELLING

Speaker As we begin talking about cycles in counselling, you may remember that when we discussed crisis intervention, we identified the three parts of the client as being the feeling-emotional part, the thinking-understanding or cognitive part, and the behaviour-action part of the individual, the doing part. These correspond to three questions which summarize the entire counselling process. Nearly everything you say as a therapeutic intervention relates to these three questions, and they are:

1. "What happened?"

2. "What are you feeling?"

3. "What are you doing?"

In a counselling process, we might work with those different parts of the client and introduce these three questions at different times, in a cyclical manner.

The first question, "What happened?", can refer to every experience in the client's life from conception to the present moment. In fact, the entire assessment is about "what happened".

The second question, "What are you feeling?", is to do with the painful emotions associated with what happened. In other words, you are saying, "What are you feeling as you talk about what happened?"

The third question, "What are you doing?", is a way of exploring the defenses and thought and behaviour patterns which come from the painful feelings. In other words, the counsellor is saying, "What have you done with the pain?"

This exploration may go further with, "Has what you've done worked well for you?" and "What could you do that might work better?"

When a client works on painful feelings for a while, he has a tendency to want to withdraw from that work because it's difficult and painful, perhaps frightening. That might be a time to take the client to a cognitive level because he may feel safer to work intellectually and explore insights and patterns of behaviour rather than to engage pain. But that can also be scary at times. The client may see connections and get a sense of how pervasive the problem is.

He might say, "I thought it had only to do with this current situation and now I'm becoming aware that it really goes all the way back to my childhood."

So we need to process that with the client when we take him into a deeper level of awareness of himself. Maybe the client will be able to do that kind of work after he has done some intense, emotional work. And then he might be ready to take the risk to change old patterns that he has gained insight into. So then the counsellor can take him to the behavioural level. Maybe he can be given assignments or look at choices and be invited to take risks.

PARADOXICAL INTENTION

Speaker When the client is very stuck in old patterns, the counsellor may attempt an approach which involves prescribing a symptom, or assigning a behaviour that the client wants to get rid of, telling him to do what he is still doing, in a way that motivates him to change.

For example, if I say to a client, "Maybe you're not ready to change yet and that would be understandable, because you've been having those patterns of old behaviour for many years — they're part of your life — and, from what you've been through, it's understandable that you'd struggle with that. Maybe you need to work more for a while, maybe just talking about it or looking at the painful feelings around it before you attempt to do anything differently, or make any changes."

I'm prescribing in a sincere, supporting, validating way that he stay "stuck" for a while in the old patterns. Now after he has heard that enough, what might he be feeling about that?

Response *Anxious to move on, to do the opposite?*

Speaker It starts motivating him and he begins taking the risk to do something different. When you prescribe a symptom, when you use paradoxical intention, which is the other term for it, it's important that you are sincere, that you mean what you're saying. And you can be sincere because in fact old patterns are difficult to change. It takes time, and often there is a need to validate and engage old pain a little bit more or a lot more in order to integrate and move beyond it.

MODELS OF COUNSELLING AND PSYCHOTHERAPY

Speaker Let's have a look at some other models or approaches in counselling which focus on parts of the counselling process. Some therapies which focus largely on working through painful feelings include Psychodrama and Gestalt. A technique suggested by J.L. Moreno and Fritz Perls is one in which the client may be assisted to talk to a significant other by directing statements or "unfinished business" as if the person were sitting in an empty chair. In this way the client may access and verbalize emotions and say things which were internalized or misdirected in unhealthy ways.

Pounding pillows or punching-bags to purge or release the pain or rage may be used. Physical methods such as punching or pounding may be used to help the more passive client to access anger and rage which have been internalized and protected against. Moreno brought forward the concept of catharsis, from a Greek word meaning "to purge or cleanse", and suggested that emotional healing is facilitated by re-enacting painful life experiences so that the pain can be released.

Primal Scream Therapy advocates focus exclusively on emotional release as the cure and speak of the "pool of pain" which may proceed from as early as pre-natal experiences. From this concept, some practitioners have focused on the pain of conception and birth and speak of "rebirthing" as a necessary step in healing. Some proponents of Therapeutic Massage also suggest that release of emotional pain is the core to healing and can be facilitated by touching or moving joints and muscles of the body where emotional pain has been stored causing physical tension, stress, and physical illness. A major hazard of this approach is that physical touch may trigger erotic transference in some clients.

Response *It's got to be frustrating, I think, from a client point of view, to hear that all you do is just scream for a while.*

Speaker Yes. And, if you haven't gotten better, often you're told the problem is that you haven't screamed enough. You've got to scream some more, a little harder.

We need to bring in a combination of therapies that impact on all three parts of the individual and the counselling process.

Someone may add the spiritual aspect as a fourth part. But spirituality is actually on a cognitive level because it has to do with values and beliefs or ideas, the thinking part. It has implications for feelings and behaviour, but it's fundamentally cognitive.

Some therapies that focus on the client's ways of thinking and understanding are: Cognitive Therapy, Rational Motive Therapy, and Positive Thinking. These are similar therapies which explore thinking patterns such as self-defeating and self-limiting thoughts, false perceptions and beliefs about oneself and others, critical self-talk, emotional triggers for new behaviour patterns, and affirmations. A best-selling book called Your Erroneous Zones by Wayne Dyer, describes a form of cognitive therapy known as Rational-Emotive Therapy. Aaron T. Beck, a major contributor to Cognitive Therapy, wrote Cognitive Therapy of Depression in which he states that working to correct distorted thoughts and beliefs is most effective in treating depression.

Much Psychoanalysis and Psychodynamic Therapy are done on a cognitive level. Concepts which involve understanding transferences in relationships, including phenomena in the counselling relationship, and gaining insight into patterns of thought and behaviour which come from early life experience, for example stemming from the family of origin, all have to do with cognitive processes.

Transactional Analysis is a cognitive approach, concerned with helping the client gain an understanding of parts of the self including the adult, child and parent ego states, which have been shaped and influenced by the family of origin. We will examine these ego states more closely at a later point in the course. TA is actually in many ways a popularized version of Psychodynamic Theory, and is designed to help clients gain insight into long-standing dysfunctional patterns, so that the client can change these patterns as a conscious choice rather than continuing to be swept along by the unconscious compulsion to repeat unhealthy ways of relating.

Hypnotherapy also belongs in the category of cognitive therapy because it utilizes memories, mental images, and the ability to concentrate, which are cognitive functions. The ability to imagine and to fantasize are cognitive abilities.

Response *I have a question about affirmations. I read a book recently by Robert Fritz, and his idea was that affirmations are wrong or negative because they encourage people to affirm something that is not really true in the here and now. You're supposed to say "I am now happy and healthy" or whatever, and he argues "Well, you're lying to yourself."*

Speaker That's right. If the counsellor is a hard core cognitive therapist, therapy is often times bolstering defenses, using denial defenses. In fact the emphasis of Neuro Linguistic Programming, which is a marketing term for a set of cognitive techniques, is to strengthen denial defenses and to disconnect emotions. The idea is, "Deny your pain. Tuck it away. Suppress it. Put it behind you. Imagine the painful event never happened."

N.L.P.

Response *Sooner or later, it's got to erupt.*

Speaker Old unresolved pain which has been defended is likely going to be triggered off by a current situation, or the stress will continue to be internalized and appear as physical illness. Dysfunction in reltionships is likely to continue.

Response *Well, I think the point here is to identify the problem. And I think it really needs to be a conscious effort to understand, "Okay, yeah, this is the problem" and admitting it. Feeling the problem — actually being with the problem — and then moving on, so that you don't get stuck there and just create more problems.*

Speaker Okay. Letting go of the pattern as a way of letting go of the loss. Suppose the person hasn't taken the step of working through the pain yet and then you try to impose the cognitive belief that everything is now okay. It's probably not going to work too well. It's like the person raised in the chicken coop being told "Well, you just have to believe that you are as important and worthwhile as anyone else. The counsellor needs to say,"Yes. Yes. Yes. Yes. Yes. Yes," to the pain... for a long enough period of time and then say, "...and so now what will you do?". The cognitive therapist, doesn't say "yes" long enough to the pain. As long as the pain is defended against, then a part of the client is split off or denied. This means that the pain will not be recognized when it is triggered by a current situation, so that the client will then continue to repeat the old pattern. Engaging the pain is necessary to gain insight into patterns proceeding from it. But more than that, engaging the pain allows the client to be in charge of the pain rather than the pain being in charge of the client.

Rather than reacting out of the pain impulsively, the client will be able to respond to situations as a conscious deliberate choice. Secondly, engaging the pain is directly related to self-worth, because when the pain is engaged it can then be supported and validated. When the client is able to bring the pain forward and engage it, he is saying, "My pain is OK. This pain fits what I've been through. I'm entitled to it. I'm OK." When the client or therapist minimizes, splits off, or defends against the childhood pain for example, then this is equivalent to saying to the wounded inner child, "Shut up. Go away. Go to your room." He is treating himself as he was treated by the uncaring parent, for example. On the other hand, acknowledging the pain validates the child because it says, "You have every right to feel that." Cognitive therapy is important as part of the overall process and after the client has already done the work of validating the wounded self. If cognitive approaches come prematurely, they will further defend and distance the client from himself and from others.

If I distance myself from my pain, I distance myself from myself. If I distance myself from myself, you can not get to know me. By the same means that I distance myself from my pain, I also distance myself from others.

The process of integration involves engaging the pain so that it can be supported and validated. This process results in self-acceptance, the strength to cope more effectively with current difficult struggles, and the ability and desire to bring my whole self and my whole potential to the challenges life has to offer. As well, self-acceptance enables me to support and accept others, which leads to satisfying, intimate, balanced relationships.

Perhaps there needs to be a distinction made between release of pain and integration of pain. Release of pain implies a need to express, verbalize, and externalize pain which has been held in, resulting in stress, tension, anxiety, depression, and illness for the client. Integration of pain implies a need to accept, acknowledge, support, and validate the pain that can not be completely released. This may be old pain that is triggered by current situations which resemble the past experience. Integration means to recognize, support, and validate the old pain when it is triggered by a current situation. Paradoxically when the client is able to do this, he is better able to let go of the pain which now has less power. One of the primary goals of counselling therefore is to help the client nurture and support himself, including the wounded inner child.

There are counsellors who simply focus on behaviour change, on symptom change, which certainly is an important part of the process. But if that's all we do, we might see a substitution of one symptom for another because the underlying problem might be low self-worth which for example may be the pain that comes from the family of origin, and hasn't been dealt with. So it will still give rise to more self-defeating behaviours.

For instance, the person who is stuck in his grief may feel guilt, and he may not believe that he deserves close relationships, so he will continue to behaviourally sabotage his relationships by being overly passive or overly aggressive, overly conflictual, overweight, not using proper hygiene, addictive, or whatever it is that is a distancing behaviour.

We can focus on and change the behaviour, but if we haven't dealt with the underlying problem, we haven't really provided service — an adequate service — to our client. Having said that, behaviour change is an essential part of the process because if we facilitate extensive catharsis, engaging the pain, and the person gains elaborate insight, but still doesn't change the dysfunctional behaviour, then how has he benefitted?

Behavioural approaches may involve the use of assignments, assertiveness training, communication skills training, journalling, the use of rewards and consequences, the self-monitoring and recording of problem behaviour or of attempts to adopt new behaviour. Anytime you ask the client to do anything, you are strictly speaking using a behavioural approach.

We need to bring to bear intervention techniques on all three parts of the process: emotional, cognitive, and behavioural. I think we have a professional responsibility to learn about all kinds of models and skills and approaches and techniques that are available so that we can use what's going to work for our client, whatever our client needs. So we are talking about an integrated holistic approach, which may also require biological, medical, or physical approaches, such as physical examination and medication. This may require interfacing with or referring to a physician or related practitioner. The holistic model may include addressing spiritual issues related to the presenting problems, which require a referral to the client's clergyman for spiritual counselling.

Response *So I hear you saying, "Well if this doesn't work, try something else." It's a mixed bag.*

Speaker Yes, that's right, proceeding from a planned but flexible treatment strategy. Where you are with the client, in the process of therapy, determines the approach. The client may have already done a fair amount of work related to painful feelings, and she is now ready to focus on behaviour change. Or the client may have engaged in insight, cognitive, or solution-focused therapy and still needs to work through some painful feelings. The counselling process has been compared to an onion or a spiral staircase, always ascending in a circular manner, or peeling deeper to the core.

SPIRITUAL/MYSTICAL EXPERIENCE

Question *You said that spirituality would fit into the cognitive part of life. What about mystical experiences that a person has? How does that fit in? It seems to me that it tends to transcend an intellectual cognitive understanding, and it has to be expressed in a metaphorical way in order for it to be communicated to people.*

Speaker Alright. Mystical experience has to do with mental images and belief — whether you believe that you've had a mystical experience or not.

Response *Whether you believe that it's mystical?*

Speaker The belief about the experience is still very much on a cognitive level. The experience itself consists of mental images or hallucinations. It is a projection, sometimes symbolic or metaphorical representation of a belief or thought or emotion or memory. So, if you believe that something mystical happened, then you are talking about a belief regarding making some kind of spiritual connection with some intangible personal or animal or plant element or force in nature or in the universe, and the belief that something happened of a spiritual nature or a mystical nature might be accompanied by emotion, which in effect is a projection of the self onto the object of "mystical" connection. Hallucinations, by definition, belong to the realm of cognitive experience and may be similar to what occurs in a hypnotic trance or a psychedelic LSD trip.

ENGAGING PAIN AT THE TIME OF CLOSURE

Response *With regard to talking about the counselling session and when you're at the end of it, sometimes you've touched some old pain, and you're finished the interview but they're not finished yet.*

Speaker So, you're saying "What do you do when a person saves her painful feelings or experiences her painful feelings near the end of the interview, and it's time to stop?

Speaker That's an excellent question; one that I addressed earlier and worth discussing further. I think it's very important to do a number of specific things. It's important to acknowledge what the client has been doing and acknowledge its importance. Encourage him to stay with that from the time he leaves the office and maybe to share it with someone he feels safe with, and then continue to do that kind of work in the next session. Another option is to explore at some point what the client normally does with painful feelings, and then prescribe that he do what he normally does if it works well enough. It is also important early on in the counselling relationship to discuss with the client the fact that sometimes he may leave a session feeling worse than when he came in and that this is to be expected if the client is talking about things that are difficult or things that have been buried for a long time.

Using a warm supportive voice tone, I might say to a person who is crying or upset and feeling a lot of painful feelings near the end,

"There's a lot of pain and hurt about what happened. What you're doing right now is very important, allowing yourself to feel that pain. It's not easy. It takes courage, and I encourage you to continue to explore these feelings next time we meet. We're going to have to close our session in a few minutes now."

In fact, I would probably want to give the client some indication that the end of the session is coming five or ten minutes before the end. You can't always do that or you won't always do that. So it's important to acknowledge or validate that what he is doing is important, and then I would be inclined to want to bring him from the emotional level to a cognitive level just before we end, by saying "What's it like having to end our session when you're feeling this pain?"

So with this statement, I am bringing the client up to a cognitive level, to think about the session and to evaluate it and to distance from the painful emotions. Notice that I have done this after supporting and validating the client's pain.

Response *What if it isn't okay for him to end the session then?*

Speaker Then I'm going to give him an opportunity to say what it's like to end, and then validate what he says. Sometimes he will say, "Well I'd really like to stay longer," or "I'd like to stay for another half hour".

And I'll say, "So maybe it's a little frustrating knowing that we're going to have to end just when you're facing something that's important."

This shifts the client's focus to another feeling related to the process rather than the loss he was grieving up to now. Then to provide some structure, I may say, "What I'd like to do is talk about what to do with the feelings that have been coming up just now. Is that OK? Maybe one choice could be to try doing some journalling and write about the feelings you are left with today. Something else you could do might be to share these feelings with someone you trust."

A support group might already be in place as part of the treatment plan, and the client could be encouraged to share feelings with the group.

Response *That's cognitive.*

Speaker That's cognitive — addressing the process, acknowledging and reviewing what he's feeling including possibly the frustration about having to end, and saying, "What's it been like talking about these things and letting yourself feel these things?" I'm going to say that to lead more into closure by distancing from the engagement of pain associated with issues presented near closure.

I'm also going to provide a summary of what the client has been talking about throughout the session — not just the last few moments, and this distances the client from the most recent pain.

I'll say, "So today we've been talking about the relationship with your father and how that's very similar to your relationship with your husband, and you've been talking about feeling rejected and not cared for by both your father and your husband, and how that's left you feeling very angry and abandoned, and sad. You've allowed yourself to feel some of those painful feelings and to grieve the loss of the caring that you wish you'd had from your father. What's it been like doing this today?"

So I'll provide a summary, ask her what it's been like, and she'll respond to that and then I'll say, "I wonder if you'd like to take this a little bit further in another session?" This is the invitation to return.

Usually I'll put it that way, "take it a little bit further" because it helps the client continue to feel safe to know that the process will be moving slowly through painful experiences.

THE ONE-HOUR SESSION

Response *You're still limited by time, aren't you? Because they want to do a lot but suddenly their hour's up. Do you always stick to the prescribed time?*

Speaker Yes I do. Some counsellors will extend it another 15 or 30 minutes or even another hour. And that's really feeding into the client's dependent behaviour. Also, it reinforces the idea that he doesn't have to do the work that he needs to do early on in the session. He just starts beating around the bush and using all sorts of defenses for the first hour, because you're going to give him another half hour. Once you set that precedent, he's going to expect it again and again. It's important to hold to the boundary of the limited time.

If the client works hard all the way through 90 minutes, it's likely to be too overwhelming.

If the client learns he can push or extend the limits of the session, he will perhaps lose his sense of safety and confidence in the counsellor who is then perceived as passive and easy to manipulate or needing the client's approval and so gives in to the client. This client may lack the self-control he needs, and when he perceives the counsellor's lack of self-control, the client decides not to return.

Keep in mind the saviour will tend to want to do too much for the client. Substantial growth takes time in smaller pieces for the process of integration. Even what we regard as small steps may be big steps for a client. And moving too fast or doing too much in one session may not get integrated and simply serves as a defense. But do check it out with the client; say, "What's this been like? Are your needs being met so far?"

Response *How is it arrived at? Is it because an hour is a time that everybody's comfortable with? I mean, there isn't any sort of clinical evidence that an hour is the right length of time, is there?*

Speaker Well, I guess experience has taught us that the client benefits most within one hour and after that the ability to benefit begins to diminish. I mean, to extend it beyond an hour, we're allowing more time for defenses to be used. A person who knows they only have 35 or 45 minutes will be so much more motivated to get down to work.

Response *Do you ever cut sessions short, if it seems that all the work has been done?*

Speaker Yes. If it feels like the person has done a lot of work in, say, 30 minutes, and it feels as though we're coming full circle and then going into a completely different area that will require another sort of time frame then I might end it at 45 minutes with the client's agreement.

That might be especially true later on in the counselling relationship when you have sensed that the client has made progress. She doesn't always seem to need as much time.

GESTALT AWARENESS CYCLE

Let's continue on with our discussion about the counselling process and the cycles involved. One of the most important cycles in counselling is the Gestalt Awareness Cycle, which has to do with the client's work with painful feelings.

GESTALT AWARENESS CYCLE

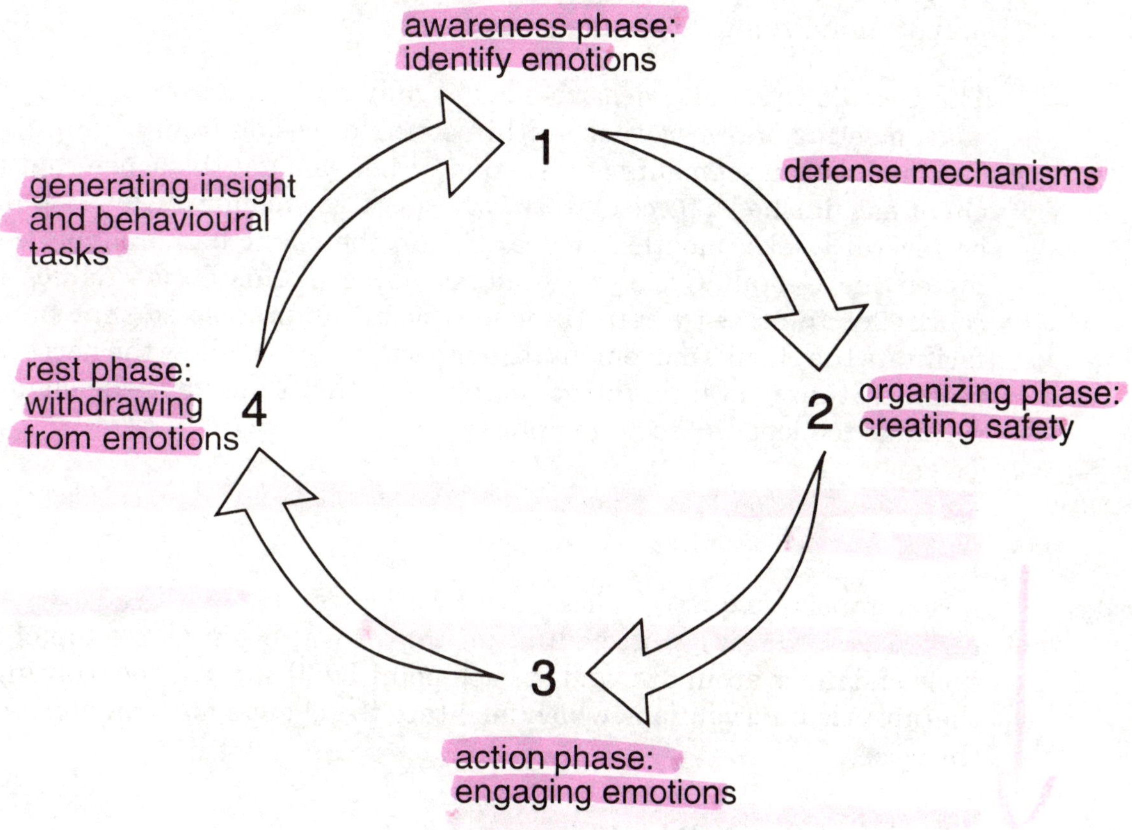

This cycle refers to the process whereby the individual recognizes his needs, organizes himself to meet his needs, takes action or meets his needs, then withdraws or rests from the action.

For example, I start becoming aware of feeling hungry, I look for food and cook it, I eat it, then I take a nap. This cycle can be applied to an entire life experience: I start life by becoming aware of my life goals, this overlaps with preparing and organizing myself to meet the goals by going to school and training myself, then I fulfill my career and my potential, then I retire and rest.

Applied to the entire counselling process, the Gestalt Cycle describes: 1. the early stages of assessment and building a therapeutic alliance; 2. identifying core issues, working through painful painful feelings, gaining insight; 3. taking risks to change; and 4. consolidation of gains and preparation leading to closure.

The Gestalt Cycle also describes what may happen across several sessions meeting once per week, within a single session from beginning to end, and within segments of a session. When you get the sense that the client has finished a piece of work, whether it is one minute, one session, or several weeks, months, or years, then the client has probably completed the Gestalt Cycle. An understanding of this cycle enables the counsellor to assess where the client is in his process so that he can facilitate the client's movement through the cycle and allow the necessary rest or withdrawal from the action phase rather than force the client to continue too long in the action phase.

Response *This is really helpful to know about. How does the counsellor move the client through the cycle?*

Speaker A very important question. To answer your question, I would like to apply the cycle to working with painful feelings. I will begin at the top of the cycle and move around it, and at each point I will suggest the wording of therapeutic interventions which facilitate the client's movement around the cycle.

IDENTIFYING PAINFUL EMOTIONS

Speaker To help the client become aware of painful feelings as he is talking about what happened, I will say:

"What are you feeling right now as you're talking?" Then I provide a feeling list of words.

"Is it fear, anger, guilt, sadness, emptiness, low self-worth, despair, or some other feeling?"

Give him a list and allow him to choose from it. What I'm doing is helping him to become aware on a cognitive level, an understanding level, what he is feeling in the moment. I am aware that he is engaging some feeling, to some degree, so I am having him identify that.

This is very important when working with a client who's new to counselling or new to your counselling relationship, because he may not be aware of his feelings. He may be disconnected from emotions or he may have used so many defenses so effectively, such as intellectualizing, that he is completely out of touch with feelings and has no words for painful feelings or emotions. So I educate the client initially by using the feeling list. It's going to be very important for you to be able to remember this feeling list of seven primary painful feelings, so that you can you this intervention. Something you might try is the non-sense word FAGSELD. Each letter of this non-sense word is the first letter of each of the feeling words.

After the client becomes familiar with the list, I may simply say, "What feeling is coming up inside you right now as you're talking?" and the client will respond with a feeling word.

Take a closer look at the wording of this question. Notice I'm saying "what" rather than "how". Suppose I were to say, "How are you feeling?" What is the client often likely to say in response?

Response *"Oh, I'm fine" or "I'm OK with that."*

Speaker Exactly right. So instead, when I word the intervention as, "What are you feeling?" the client is placed in a position to identify an emotion. Notice the further wording in the above statement: "...is coming up inside you..."

This helps the client to focus on emotion sensations in the body. Another body-oriented intervention to help the client become aware of emotions is to say, "Where do you feel that emotion in your body? In your head, your chest, your stomach, your neck, your back? Where would you say?"

Finally, notice the last words from the previous statement: "...right now as you're talking." These words help the client focus sharply on the present moment in time connected to what happened or the event being described. In this way the past is brought into the present and connected with the painful feelings associated with it. That which is split off and defended against is in a process of being integrated so that the client can engage in a process of being fully self-accepting.

Now, as a person becomes aware of his feelings, defense mechanisms are going to be coming up to stop him from engaging those feelings. This also is a normal part of the self-awareness cycle. After we have outlined some basic interventions to move a client through the cycle, we will discuss some primary defenses and suggest the wording of statements to help the client integrate and move beyond his defenses.

ORGANIZING PHASE: BUILDING SAFETY

The next step in the the cycle is the organizing phase. During this phase, the client is assessing whether he feels safe enough to engage or openly feel the emotions which have been identified.

He's assessing whether or not he feels safe enough with himself, safe enough with the setting, and safe enough with the counsellor. If a client feels safe enough, he can heal himself.

A person with very painful life experiences might feel very unsafe with himself and have a fear of losing control or going crazy if he allows himself to engage the pain. Also, if the setting has too many distractions, such as noises coming in from outside the room, a phone ringing, or people knocking on the door, the person may not feel safe. Privacy is important to safety, as is decor, which should be non-distracting, simple furnishings in basic colours.

Of course, safety with the counsellor is essential.

As I said earlier, the client assesses how safe he feels with the counsellor in the first few minutes. This depends upon the counsellor's ability to project confidence in his own skill and expertise, his warmth, empathy, genuineness, and unconditional positive regard for the client. Safety with the counsellor is perhaps most important, because if the client has confidence in the counsellor and feels safe with her, then he is likely going to feel safe enough with himself to face very difficult, painful issues. The client is thinking, "If I start exploring some new or frightening areas, I know this counsellor will stay with me and support me through it."

The defenses and the client's resistance are about not feeling safe enough, and so the defenses are designed to protect the client from the pain which is too frightening to engage.

We can recognize the client's lack of safety by his verbal report and by the observation of his behaviour. For example, he may appear quiet or respond with few words. He may present superficial issues. He may say, "I don't want to talk about it," referring to a difficult issue.

The fear attached to the lack of safety, holds the key to building safety. The wording of interventions for working through this fear might be:

"Maybe it's a little scary to talk about this, and that's understandable. It's not easy."

"I wonder if you feel safe enough to talk about the things you need to talk about today."

"What gets in the way of feeling safe enough today?"

"I wouldn't want you to talk about anything if you don't feel safe enough."

"Talk about what's getting in the way of talking about it."

"Instead of talking about what's difficult, maybe you could say a little about what gets in the way. It sounds a little scary."

The primary step is to identify the fear or reflect the feeling of "scary". Another component is to validate this fear by saying "it's not easy". Another approach is to invite the client to say "a little" because this feels safer than saying a lot. Still another approach is to invite the client to talk about "what gets in the way of" talking about what's difficult. The idea is to support and validate the fear, and when this has been done effectively, the next step is to say, "What's it like talking about this so far?" This elicits from the client a validation of the process. Once the client can validate that it's OK to talk about the fear, then I will move the client beyond it by saying, "I wonder what feeling is under the fear? Maybe a little anger or sadness or guilt or some other feeling." Notice the non-confrontational choice of words like "I wonder" and "maybe".

A soon as the client is able to identify a feeling other than fear, he has become safe enough. The key to working through the lack of safety is to put the fear into words.

If the client feels unsafe due to the counsellor or the setting, these reasons also must be validated and supported. If the client directs a criticism to the counsellor, it is important that the counsellor not react but rather support and validate the feedback. Lack of safety for these reasons is often, not always, a transference issue which must be worked through in a therapeutic way in order for safety to be restored. In the case of unsafety coming from transference, the client is in actuality bringing forward a past experience of unsafety with a significant other, which will appear as an exaggerrated feeling of distrust or lack of safety with the counsellor. A series of interventions may follow in this way:

"What is it about me that leaves you feeling unsafe?"

The client responds with something about your appearance, your demeanor, or something you said or did. The counsellor then may say,

"You have every right to feel that. Say more."

The idea here is to fully support and validate the client's transference reaction rather than react against the client out of counter-transference. When the client feels supported, the counsellor may say,

"What other important person in your life left you feeling unsafe or did or said something similar to what you saw in me?"

This takes the client to a link with unresolved core issues related to earlier life experiences. If the client goes to the core issues, he is now feeling safe and has actually achieved something therapeutic by simply verbalizing the lack of safety to the counsellor. This is precisely what the client has needed to say to the significant other, and he has just done so by addressing the issue to the significant other appearing in the counsellor, as it were.

ACTION PHASE: ENGAGING THE PAIN

If the client feels safe enough, he'll then be able to move to the third part of the cycle which is to engage the painful feelings, to be with and express the pain, to cry, to verbalize his anger or what have you, to grieve significant losses. This is where the intense work takes place — being with the pain. This is an essential goal for any client, and the intensity of that pain is going to be very individual depending upon the client's issues.

Speaker The pain is what the client has been defending against, and the defense mechanisms are what get in the way of her relationships and the ability to get on with her life. The pain gives rise to defenses, thoughts, and behaviours which also constitute unhealthy or maladaptive ways of relating to self and others. Therefore, the essential task of the client is to face the original pain in order to adopt healthier ways of coping. The very process of facing that pain is the first healthy step because in facing the pain, the client is giving up dysfunctional defenses. The counsellor can facilitate this process by wording a variety of interventions. When the client has identified a feeling or when there has been some non-verbal signal of pain such as tears, mouth quivering, pausing in a sentence, shifting in the chair, head or eye movements, changes in voice volume, the counsellor can say:

"Just take some time right now and let yourself feel that."

"Take a moment of silence and just feel that now."

"That's it, just let yourself feel that. Give yourself this time."

"Just let it come. That's it."

"Let it out a little more. Stay with it. That's important."

"It takes courage to face that pain."

If the pain seems to be engaged at a low level, the counsellor may say:

"Just feel whatever feeling is there even if it's a little bit."

feeling not cognitive

Notice that these interventions do not require a verbal response from the client but simply support and validate the client to feel the pain. It's what every child needs to hear when he's skinned a knee or falls down and gets hurt.

The counsellor is modelling the nurturing parent so that the client can internalize the nurturing parent within himself and eventually nurture himself.

WITHDRAWAL PHASE

Once a person has engaged her pain, then she will move into the fourth phase, which is withdrawal from that work or to rest from it because it can be very draining.

The client will withdraw or rest because engaging the pain has been frightening or because she has done significant work or feels finished with it, as if the burden has been lifted. She is ready to disengage from that kind of activity and begin the cycle again.

The withdrawal phase can be used therapeutically because while the client may not want to engage painful feelings again just yet, she is now able to move into cognitive and behavioural parts of the counselling process. We can help her gain insight into old patterns of behaviour, into the kinds of defenses she uses, what she has done in the past and is still doing to protect herself against pain, how she copes with fear, anger, guilt, sadness, emptiness, low self-worth, and despair.

UNDERSTANDING PATTERNS

We can help her gain a greater awareness of and insight into patterns of thought and behaviour which have not worked well. These may include patterns of self-criticism, patterns of protecting or rescuing or dumping, patterns of sabotaging relationships, patterns of being overly passive or overly aggressive, patterns of choosing unhealthy partners, reacting out of earlier pain rather than responding as a choice in situations, patterns of doing to himself and to others that which has been done to him, patterns of giving too much or taking too much in relationships and the list goes on.

Interventions for exploring patterns may include saying:

"So what I'm hearing is that you reacted strongly in a way that didn't fit what happened. Is that what you're saying? What's the story behind that strong reaction? Where is it coming from?"

"What was it about that person or situation that pushed your buttons?"

"If you were to review your life from early days to the present time, what other important person in your life did or said something similar?" or

"That sounds familiar, like someone or something you've talked about before." or

"I wonder if this is the first time you felt that?" or

"How long in your life have you struggled with this problem?"

Other statements for exploring patterns might be:

"What do you do when you feel that kind of feeling? Do you keep it in, or dump it on someone? What happens? Where does the feeling go?"

"I wonder if you can imagine what your life might be like today if that hadn't happened?"

CHANGING PATTERNS

Apart from insight into patterns, the withdrawal phase may be used to focus on behaviour change or changing the old dysfunctional patterns. We may challenge the person to take some risks, to do something different, to look at choices. If the behaviour change is too big a step or too frightening, the counsellor may suggest smaller steps or may explore and support the fear or may use the fear as a therapeutic trigger or signal to move forward and take a risk.

The key intervention series for changing patterns is:

"What are you doing?"

"Does that work well for you?"

"What could you do that might work better?"

The following dialogue between counsellor and client, talking about difficulty expressing anger to a partner, serves to illustrate how the process can work:

Client: "My husband just doesn't listen when I talk to him."

Counsellor: "What emotion comes up inside right now as you talk about that? Frustration, anger, sadness, what feeling?"

Client: "Frustration."

Counsellor: "I wonder if you've been able to tell him that you feel frustrated."

Client: "No."

Counsellor: "What gets in the way of letting him know?"

Client: "I'm afraid of what he might say, he might criticize me, or I'm afraid he might leave."

Counsellor: "So what I'm hearing is that when you feel angry or frustrated, you have a pattern of feeling afraid and keeping the anger inside because of what you think he might say or do. Is that accurate?"

Client: "Yes, that's right."

Counsellor: "What happens when you keep the anger inside? Do you feel better or worse? Is your relationship better or worse for not letting him know?"

Client: "I feel worse, and our relationship doesn't get any better."

Counsellor:"So the fear could be your key or signal to becoming more assertive. When you feel the fear you can withdraw as you have in the past, or you can use the fear as your signal to take a risk to move forward and let him know about the frustration. Which will you do?"

In this illustration there is an exploration of emotional reactions as the client is talking. Fear appears to be blocking the healthy expression of frustration toward the husband. The counsellor uses "reframing" by making the fear a positive feature or "signal" to the client to "risk" new behaviour. There is also an assessment of the negative effects of withholding the anger, so that the client is motivated to take the risk. An additional feature of this approach may be to suggest that the client acknowledge, validate, and support herself when she feels fear, then to move forward and be assertive. The idea is to "feel the fear and do it anyway," which by the way is the title of a book in stores now.

Depending upon other background factors, the client may need to come to terms with childhood fears of confronting parents and early abandonment and rejection issues which are brought into this relationship from the family of origin. In addition, the client may need to see assertiveness modelled by the counsellor and may need to practice assertiveness to develop a sense of mastery before actually expressing angry feelings to her husband.

Another effective example of a cognitive-behavioural approach is the use of mental imagery or visualization in which the client is guided through a past experience of a time when she engaged in the old pattern. She is asked whether she feels strong or weak when she withdraws. Then she is told to imagine that someone comes into the mental picture who is confident, bold, and assertive and who speaks to the husband by saying, "I feel annoyed when you don't look at me when I'm speaking to you, because then I don't know whether or not I'm being heard." The counsellor then asks the client, "What's it like seeing this person speaking to your husband this way?" The client will report feeling good and wishing she could speak the same way. Then the counsellor invites the client to imagine she is speaking the same way, with confidence and boldness. This approach may be used before enacting or role playing the event using an empty chair or using the counsellor to take on the part of the husband so that the client can practice the new skills.

The idea is to visualize using the skill before enacting the skill.

If the client's fear is still too great, the client may withdraw from the skill, indicating a need to move the client into parts of the counselling process which help the client to face painful emotions arising from the abusive parental relationship and to gain insight into behaviour and thought patterns arising from the family of origin. The counselling process is often one of moving the client from present to past to present to past, from emotions to insight to risking new behaviour, then back to emotions, and so on in a process of integrating the parts of the self, exploring the childhood pain, the child within and integrating this child with the protecting, reassuring, confident adult self which is underdeveloped.

The client is carrying around the internalized parent, and this is where the negative, devaluing self-talk arises, from the critical verbal and non-verbal messages which were taken into the self by the client. Hanging on to the negative self-talk is directly related to low self-worth and is a way of hanging on to the uncaring parent.

The guided imagery or visualization technique could take the client back to a childhood experience in which the parent was uncaring or abusive. The client imagines an adult who enters the scene to speak for, protect, and reassure the child. The counsellor models or provides the lines for the adult. When the client reports feeling good about the support of the adult, the counsellor suggests the client can try doing this for herself. In fact, the assertive, nurturing adult is simply an undeveloped part of the client which is blocked by the frightened child part. Paradoxically the adult self is strengthened when the client supports and asserts for the frightened child self rather than to abandon the child self in repetition of the original childhood experience. Does that make sense?

Response *That sounds very effective. It makes a lot of sense. And I've never heard that process described in such clear, simple terms. I was just wondering, when do you give your clients homework?*

Speaker Homework is a way of strengthening the adult self and supporting the hurt child. You can give him homework during the withdrawal/rest phase or even during the period of emotional engagement, for example, to suggest journalling the issues and feelings that are coming up. And give him opportunities to try on new behaviours both in the session and in his social situation outside the actual counselling session. Be alert to recognize changes however subtle or minor which the client is demonstrating in the session itself so that this can be brought to the client's attention and given acknowledgement and validation.

It's important to be able to determine where your client is in the cycle so that you can let him have the necessary distance at its end, rather than continuing to push.

The need to withdraw may occur when the focus has been on emotions, or insight, or behaviour change. The client may indicate the need to withdraw from emotions by being analytical and intellectual in a session. He may indicate a need to withdraw from insight by missing a session, complaining that nothing is changing, or by wanting to do something rather than just talk. He may indicate a need to withdraw from behaviour change by reporting anxiety about an assignment or by not completing a task.

In any case, the counsellor can utilize the client's need to withdraw from one part of the counselling process by moving him into another part. And this can be done as the client's conscious choice which is elicited by the counsellor first summarizing the content, then saying, "So we can either focus on exploring feelings that you carry around, or we can explore and understand old life patterns which have not worked well, or we can look at what you can do to make things work better. And we can either focus on what's happening now in your life or we can look at how the past is still affecting you life now, or both." The approach of outlining choices for the counselling session works well for the experienced, motivated client who knows how to move himself through the process and who simply needs the counsellor's cooperation.

Keep in mind that the client may go around the cycle within a few minutes, during the session, or maybe over the course of two or three sessions. He may spend one session on intense emotional work and another on more intellectual, analytical, cognitive work, and then another session on reporting and reviewing behaviour change, risks taken, and assignments or homework completed.

Also, the cycle may be run over the course of the entire counselling relationship. There may come a point in the relationship when he feels that he has done a lot of work and now he is ready to rest or to withdraw. He has had enough counselling for a while.

And he may say it just that way, "I think I've had enough counselling for a while. I'd like to take some time off." What he's telling you is that he has come around to this withdrawal phase. The chances are that he will reach another point when he's ready to do some more intense work, especially if he has significant core issues to work through. He is not likely going to do it all in one counselling relationship. It's going to take time, maybe years and perhaps seeing different counsellors.

RATIONALE FOR THE COUNSELLING PROCESS

Let's return to the basic premise of the counselling process, the description of the kind of work that we're doing with the client. Everything that we're doing with our clients is based on this truth which is:

Everyone has a tendency to repeat or perpetuate aspects of significant unresolved conflicts and losses.

This is simply a description of the human condition. You can't avoid loss. You can't avoid conflict. These are parts of our human experience. It's also true that because we've experienced these kinds of painful events in our lives, we will have a tendency to perpetuate or repeat aspects of those most painful conflicts and losses if they remain unresolved. It's the pain that makes these events "significant"; the more painful the event the more significant it is. Because of the pain, we have a need to protect ourselves from feeling the pain because no one likes pain. The "aspects" that we have a tendency to repeat or perpetuate are the defenses, the means of protecting ourselves from the pain. Those defenses or those means of protection become the unhealthy ways of relating, to distance ourselves from ourselves and from others, which results in more pain.

Resolution occurs in a process of three parts:

1) To identify, engage, support and validate the painful feelings associated with original painful life experiences,

2) To gain insight into the defenses, the unhealthy patterns of thoughts, beliefs, and behaviours, ways of relating to self and others, which proceed from the pain, and

3) To take risks to adopt new attitudes and ways of coping and relating.

The pain leads to maladaptive thought and behaviour patterns which result in more pain. Yet the pain we know is preferable to the pain we bury and hide from our consciousness. Cognitive and behaviour therapies focus on the thought and behaviour patterns which arise from the earlier pain, and the premise in those therapies is that getting better means changing the secondary thoughts and behaviours rather than going back to the primary pain.

I recently heard an expert on addictions say that he believed people are addicted because they refuse to be with their pain. Addiction is only one kind of defense among the many forms of defense against pain.

Response *When you say unhealthy, do you mean self-destructive?*

Speaker By unhealthy I mean behaviours and attitudes that don't work well, that get in the way of what the person needs, which can include intimacy, being able to work with other people, being able to resolve conflict with a positive, productive outcome when that is possible, and being able to grieve and get on with one's life.

The third part of the process is to risk a new adult attitude in ways of relating rather than perpetuate the childhood patterns. This is where behaviour change takes place.

So, these three points correspond with the three parts of the individual and the three parts of the counselling process that we've been talking about so far: the feelings, the thoughts, and the actions.

All change is frightening because it involves risk-taking, doing something new and unfamiliar to the client. Although a way to facilitate behaviour change is to draw upon similar experience or strength from the client's past and bring it forward with a cognitive-behaviour technique known as "anchoring". In this technique the client is taken through three steps: 1) the client recalls a time when he was bold, for example, 2) then the counsellor suggests that he feel the sensation of boldness, 3) then the client is directed to use a word or or to touch a designated part of his body as a way to bring the feeling of boldness to a present situation.

Nonetheless, the behaviour which arises from this may be frightening to enact and so the element of risk is still involved although perhaps somewhat reduced because of the now conscious realization of the ability to perform the behaviour.

Response *What would be the antithesis of fear?*

Speaker Antithesis of fear? I'm not sure. That's a good question. Maybe confidence, mastery, empowerment.

Response *What I've found is that fear stays lodged if I just sit there and do nothing. But if I do something, no matter what it is, as long as I am taking action, I realize how illusionary and how false the fear is.*

Speaker So when the client succeeds in taking a risk, he discovers that his fear was exaggerrated. You will have some clients who are very resistant to dealing with their painful feelings. It's very important, I think, to have an understanding that the resistance and blocking are related to fear which is there for a valid reason and needs to to be explored and validated. The resistance served to help the client survive in the first place and can be framed as a strength even now.

Sometimes, we can begin to help that person access his painful feelings if we can minimize them by saying "I wonder what you might be feeling just a little bit of, right now?" It's easier and safer for that person to admit to a little bit of that feeling than a lot of the feeling. A lot of feeling is frightening, but a little of the feeling is safer and manageable from the client's perspective.

Response *Sometimes I have clients who can not communicate their feelings. They don't have the words. They're not even in touch with them a lot of times because they've buried them for so long. I'm just wondering if there's some way of helping them open up.*

Speaker If they don't have words for their feelings, that implies the need for education. And that's what you're doing when you say, "What are you feeling right now?" and then give them the feeling list. That's an educational intervention.

Response *So that's okay to do that?*

Speaker Oh yes. Because they don't have the words. They don't have them in their vocabulary.

Response *Is it possible to go through the whole counselling process without expressing painful feelings?*

Speaker If there are painful life experiences in the background, a whole process means moving through that level which gave rise to the problem behaviour.

Response *Couldn't somebody understand that they have pain but not feel safe in that setting, and still have insights?*

Speaker If a person is not willing to engage his pain, he may gain some or even considerable insight and still remain depressed for example. Or maybe he has great insight but has taken no action to face what most difficult or frightening for the inner child, and so the inner child continues to dominate the client's behaviour because the assertive adult self is undeveloped. If he remains distant from a significant part of himself, the emotional part, what is he saying about it?

Response *That he doesn't like it.*

Speaker That he doesn't want to support this wounded child inside. What else is he saying?

Response *That it's too scary to feel.*

Speaker He is saying it's too scary which is the inner child dominating. If the client is to develop a self-nurturing adult self, he must go into the fear with the child. So the child self is saying that it's not okay to engage or openly disclose the pain. Engaging and disclosing the pain holds the key to closeness in adult relationships, because emotion is an essential part of what makes us human, and the acceptance of this part of us is tied to self-acceptance and acceptance of others. Painful emotion is part of what we are.

It's worth repeating. When we allow ourselves to express our pain, that leads to acceptance and validation of that pain and of our whole human selves. It's essential in allowing us to experience intimacy.

Speaker There's no such thing as intimacy without the sharing of painful feelings or emotions. So, if I'm using whatever mechanisms I use to disconnect myself from those feelings, to that extent I'm not going to be able to be intimate.

Response *Could it be intimacy with yourself as well as intimacy with other people?*

Speaker Excellent point. It could be self-intimacy or being open with self as well as being open with others, which is the meaning of intimacy. In order to share myself with others, I must first be open to, get to know, and share myself with me.

Response *When one person faces all the pain and suffering alone, they become, in essence, a different person, a different human being. Who are they then? How far back do we have to go before we're in touch with who we are?*

Speaker I think it's a life long process of integrating ourselves, rather than splitting off the painful parts of our life experience.

In the counselling process, what we're trying to do with the client is to integrate his experiences, help him explore his pain and ways of surviving so that he can validate himself and accept himself fully.

He then becomes more fully present and capable of more intimacy and of achieving life's goals and challenges. He no longer has to use up so much energy containing, denying, and splitting off a part of himself. He can now, by being fully accepting, move forward in life by bringing himself fully into the present and thereby utilize more of his potential, including the strengths acquired from surviving the past difficulties.

Response *So then I would arrive at a place of greater "wholeness".*

Speaker Yes. Wholeness has to do with integrating insight, emotions, and conscious choices. The counselling process therefore is a process of integrating parts of the self: the range of emotions past and present as well as awareness of choices past and present.

We've talked a lot about integrating emotions, and people are also less than whole because of rigid choices and perceiving that things can only be done one way. The choice is either black or white. It can't be a third way or a fourth way or a fifth way. They don't have an expanded notion of choices. So another thing we're trying to do with the client is to expand his choices and to increase his awareness of what he has done in the past. His old way of choosing has been limiting and inhibiting, although understandable as a way of surviving. Our approach will be to validate the old choices, to look at what has worked, and to integrate those behaviours in ways that will continue to work well and on a conscious level, as well as to explore new choices.

REFLECTIVE LISTENING SKILLS

Another way to educate the client who is unaware of emotions is to use what Carl Rogers has termed the "reflective statement" which I am wanting to underline as one of the core counselling skills.

This means to simply take what the client has said and reflect it back to him including a feeling word, because often times when the client is recalling a painful event he may not use feeling words, as we were discussing earlier. He doesn't have these words in his vocabulary, and if we offer the words we can help him begin to identify painful feelings. The reflective statement is also the key skill for conveying an understanding of the client's problems. Rather than saying "I understand", which must be avoided and which is a clear mark of the amateur counsellor, the counsellor will use a reflective statement which demonstrates what he understands.

Reflection of what the client is saying helps him to feel understood and therefore also supported and validated. In addition, being able to hear what he has just said, helps the client to clarify his problems for himself. Reflection is a way of utilizing the clients own strength to heal himself. The counsellor in this capacity is simply acting as an alter-ego, another "client self" helping the client to hear himself.

An example might be a female client who says she had a fight with her husband because he wasn't doing his share of the household responsibilities, which they agreed would be his. I might make this kind of statement:

"So maybe you feel annoyed with him because he didn't follow through with the tasks that you have agreed on, and that's made more work for you. Is that what you feel?"

A reflective statement is a statement, not a question. Usually I start a reflective statement with "So maybe you feel..." and then a feeling word.

Often times if a person has blocked the feeling or hasn't identified it, I'll reach for a little bit of the feeling. I'll say, "So maybe you feel a little...." Minimizing a feeling in this way usually results in the client maximizing it by responding, "I feel more than a little annoyed. I'm furious!"

When a client owns or identifies a feeling from our reflection, I will focus on it by saying, "Say more about feeling furious" or "Go on".

We need to have a broad vocabulary of feeling words so that we can make accurate reflective statements. With the first part of the reflection we supply a feeling word, and then we reflect the meaning. If we have an understanding of what a client has said, we need to reflect both the feeling and the meaning. A reflection may be overstated to help the client feel more supported. An understatement of the client's point leaves him feeling unsupported. However, be careful that your overstatement does not become an interpretation which contributes too much to the client's process and begins to sound like putting words into the client's mouth.

Then we can check out whether our reflection is accurate or not by saying something like, "Is that what you're feeling?" or "Do I understand you?" or "Is that what you're saying?" If the client continues to correct our reflections, then the key is to repeat the client's exact words while sincerely attempting to mirror the client's tone so that he feels joined and supported.

People who use the Rogerian model strictly might argue that that's all one needs to do in a counselling session. And, in fact, I think you can carry on a counselling session just by using reflective statements and invitations to say more.

The client will then respond to your reflection by elaborating more, by correcting your reflection, saying "No, that's not quite what I said." Whatever her response is, you can respond by saying "Can you say a little more about that?" After she has elaborated, make another reflection and so on. We can pretty well carry on an entire session with just reflections and invitations to say more. So if you are ever at a loss about knowing what to say to your client, remember these two simple interventions.

LEADING OR FOLLOWING

Another benefit of reflective statements is that they tend to allow the client to lead the session, because a reflection follows the client's feeling and thought. On the other hand, a questioning approach, especially close-ended questions which lead to a one-word response, tend to direct, lead, and control the session, because this type of questioning presents the counsellor's agenda. Examples of close-ended questions are one's which begin with “who”, “when”, “do” or “did”, “where”, “are”, “can”. Examples of opened-ended questions begin with “what” and “how”. These questions allow the client to elaborate, to speak at length, and to lead the session. If the counsellor leads the session, the client will feel unsupported and will not be able to develop a sense of his own power, responsibility, and self-reliance.

Keep in mind that one of the fundamental goals in counselling is to help the client put her life experiences and feelings into spoken words, to get it from the inside to the outside of herself. Some of you reported that when you did the assessment, that’s exactly how you benefitted, just by having that full hour to talk about nothing but your own life experiences.

Once we’ve reflected the client’s feelings, we need to draw them out. We’re doing that by using the feeling list and by inviting the client to say more about the identified feeling; “Say more about the sadness” or “Say more about the anger.” That’s what I mean by drawing it out, focusing on the feeling, having the client talk about the feeling. “What’s that feeling about? What’s the sadness about?” The process of integration refers also to exploring, acknowledging, and validating each separate and distinct feeling which may be present in the client.

Be aware of helping the client feel safe in counselling. We discussed that already in terms of counsellor qualities, but we can reinforce safety especially when exploring a new difficult area with a client by saying things like “What’s it like talking about this so far?” If a client is very resistant, not willing to talk, what he’s telling usually is that he doesn’t feel safe enough to talk about whatever he needs to talk about.

And so I’ll say to him, “I wonder if you feel safe enough here to talk about the things that you need to talk about?”

Response *I’ve also experienced people who’ve said they didn’t think of anything worth talking about. They didn’t think anybody else wanted to listen because they’ve had a history of nobody listening.*

Speaker You can make a reflection of that. You could say “So maybe you’re saying that what you have to say is not worth talking about, or you think other people don’t care about what you have to say?” Is that what you mean?

Response *Yes. That’s what they have said. It’s the feeling that they don’t have anything worthwhile saying.*

Speaker I’d want to hear more about that. I’d say “Say more about that. Where is that coming from? What’s that about?"

or "What important person in your life gave you a similar message?" or "Who else in your life said you don't have anything worth saying?"

Response *So I reflect that back to them and keep the process going. "Talk more about that."*

FACING THE DIFFICULTY

Response *If you have some difficulties and you have someone who, say, is aware of counselling tools and they just don't want to let go, can you try a different angle, like talk about something on the surface that's not really connected and loosen them up with something safer?*

Speaker Yes. You might engage her in lighter conversation, something that's easier to talk about, something safer. That might be feeding into the defense, though.

Response *Wouldn't that be helping them de-focus?*

Speaker That's right. It's saving him from the difficulty. And maybe that would work so that the client feels safe talking about something that is easier than something that is difficult. If the client is especially defended and persists, I might be wanting to say, "Maybe you're feeling a little uncomfortable about talking about this right now? Is that accurate? You're getting a little afraid or uncomfortable about discussing this now?"

See if she acknowledges that and if so, I would say, "Say a little about what's scary about this. What the discomfort is about?" The key to helping a person feel safe is to have a talk about the fear and the un-safety.

And I might make a validating statement such as, "It makes a lot of sense that you would feel a little afraid of talking about this. You've been through a tough time and so that's normal and understandable. Say a little about the fear, the scary feeling." If she can begin to talk about that scary feeling or that fear, then I would support that, reflect that.

Then I could say, "I wonder what you might be feeling beside the fear. Would it be sadness or anger or..." As soon I've got her past the fear to identify another feeling, she has gone past the safety issue. She is now feeling safe again. Working through the fear is the key to feeling safe.

Response *So you don't want too many options. You don't want to provide them ways out.*

Speaker That's right. I don't want to allow her an escape from facing what's most difficult but I don't want to put him in a position of facing too much too soon. So, if I get a sense he's too frightened, I'll slow him down but still invite him to keep going in a forward movement, toward the pain. The client needs to hear, "Whatever is most difficult to talk about is the key to your progress."

DEFENSE MECHANISMS

This leads to a discussion of defense mechanisms and helping the client to get past fear and resistance to facing difficult feelings and life experiences. The counsellor is wanting to see the client's defenses and allow them to appear in the counselling relationship. The defenses are tied directly to those means which the client has developed to survive, to protect himself, and which are therefore the keys to understanding dysfunctional patterns which constitute the current presenting problems and struggles.

The defenses must be identified and validated as methods which perhaps worked well in childhood and which may work well even now in some situations. So the objective is to identify ways that the defenses can be integrated as strengths which work well sometimes and don't work so well other times. This insight allows the client to utilize the defenses more effectively as conscious choices rather than unconscious compulsions or habits. The format for our discussion will be to define the defense and then give an example of how to work with it.

DENIAL

The first and most common defense is denial. A classic example of this is a 38 year old female client I had whose father had died when she was age ten. I was using the empty chair method, having her put some things into words toward father, who she imagined was in the chair. The first thing she said to him was, "I'm glad you're still alive." The denial was striking. I said to her, "So for you, your father is still alive and that's neither right nor wrong. Maybe you're in a stage of denial about his death, and that's okay. Maybe it's just helpful to know where you are in your grief." Essentially I labelled the denial, called it what it was, and supported her use of the defense, rather than to confront the defense by saying for example, "Your father died 28 years ago."

The next time I saw that woman she was openly grieving her father's death. She was no longer in denial because in order for her to accept my support, she had to accept the fact that she was in denial. So it's very important for me to say it's "neither right nor wrong", and that "it's okay for you to be in denial," but for her to accept the "okay-ness" of it, she also had to accept the reality of the denial.

When she accepted the support for her denial, in that moment she actually moved past it. When I presented that to her in that way and supported her denial, she became quiet - the wheels were turning. There was no attempt to resist.

So the approach with denial and generally with resistance is to label, support, and validate the resistance. Supporting and validating, allow the client to own, accept, and admit the defense which has been labelled. Simply to label the defense without giving validation, will likely result in increased resistance.

RATIONALIZATION

Rationalization is a defense in which the client presents a reason for not feeling the painful emotions. The implied meaning usually not explicitly stated is, "The reason I shouldn't feel so bad is that...." Some clients will say things like, "Other people have had it worse than I have." This is the client's attempt to minimize his pain by comparing himself to others and focusing on others.

The counsellor can approach that simply by bringing the focus back to the client by saying, "Just talk about yourself."

People often rationalize the behaviour of their parents. Where there is an abusive parent or a dysfunctional family situation, a client might say, "Dad couldn't have helped abusing me because he was abused himself and had a very tough childhood." Giving Dad a reason, giving Dad an excuse for what he did, that's rationalizing. In other words, the client is saying, "The reason I can't feel sad or angry is that Dad had a hard time." Again the focus is on the difficulty Dad had.

Response *It's almost permission.*

Speaker Yes, excusing him or justifying Dad. This is in effect what the enabler does: protects, justifies, excuses the behaviour of the abuser rather than making him responsible. I would say, "It sounds like you might be protecting him a little bit, and I wonder what you might feel toward him if you didn't protect him."

I am phrasing the intervention in terms of the hypothetical. I'm not saying, "What do you feel?" but "What might you feel". Yet in response, the client will say what he does feel. Notice also that I refer to protecting Dad "a little bit". This makes it easier and safer for the client to own.

So the client may identify resentment, or anger, or sadness or something. And then I'll say, "Say more about that resentment". I'll keep the client focused closely upon the painful feeling he has just identified. Because what I want to help him do is to own his anger, and feel it instead of protecting it.

The client who protects the abusive parent, may have a generally passive personality, or he may dump the anger he feels toward Dad, onto other people who resemble Dad in some way but on whom he feels safe to dump the anger, a spouse for example. Identifying the original anger and properly directing it toward Dad, can help the client separate and distinguish this anger rather than add it as an exaggerrated transference reaction to the anger which fits a current situation. Another scenario is that the client may not only be protecting Dad, he may also protect other people from his feelings, so it's going to be very therapeutic for him to own his anger toward the most significant person who has mistreated him. This form of protection which is generalized to others, may come from a fear of being hurt which comes from Father's physical or verbal abuse of the client as a child. If the client can move past his fear of Father, he may be able to stand up for himself, not just in relation to Dad or in relation to parents, but in other situations as well. It's very important for this reason to engage the original emotion of anger toward Dad for example.

Now when the client owns his anger or resentment, what other feeling might he move into?

Response *Guilt.*

Speaker Alright, yes. He may feel very guilty especially if he has seen that parent as a pathetic victim, who was abused and now the client is beginning to direct what feels like more abuse toward the parent. The passive individual believes this anger is destructive. So he feels very guilty.

The classic case is the alcoholic family in which the non-drinking enabling mother was responsible for perpetuating the alcoholic behaviour of the father. Often in this kind of family, a child is chosen by the enabling mother to be her support, her parent. This parental child feels very protective of the enabling mother and perceives her as strong and virtuous for putting up with father for all those years.

INDIVIDUATION FROM PARENTS

So what we need to do is help that person own her anger and resentment toward mother for enabling the alcoholic father. When that person begins to own her resentment, she then feels very guilty because she has previously viewed mother as a pathetic victim of alcoholic father.

Now she's angry at Mom too. It feels as though she's heaping more abuse on this pathetic, but "virtuous" woman. Often after the client expresses anger, she begins to tear. So then we can say, "What are the tears about? Are those sad tears or angry tears?" And the client will say "sad tears".

Then, and this is very important, we need to say, "Who is that sadness for? Is it more for yourself, or more for Mom?" And the client is going to say she feels sad for Mom. So that sadness is not for herself but for Mom, even though the previous anger was for herself toward Mom. So the client flips back to the protection mode.

To help this person continue grieving the loss of parental caring which was lost when Mom enabled father, we need to say ,"Which is easier to feel? Sad for yourself or sad for Mom?" She will say,"Sad for Mom."

So then we'll say, "Talk about the sadness that you feel for yourself. What's that about? What did you miss out on because Mom allowed your father to drink and abuse you and the family? Where did that leave you?" Bring the focus back to what the client lost instead of what Mom lost. The protecting client or the person who rationalizes in that way, finds it much easier to grieve for other people than for herself. Our task is to help the client grieve for herself. Sometimes we can use the client's pattern of grieving for others more than for herself by saying, "If you saw a little girl being abused and the one person who could protect her stood by, what would you feel?" When the client accesses anger on behalf of another child, we can say, "That little girl is you." Or "Who do you wish had protected you from the abuse?" This places the client in the position of identifying the enabling mother as a responsible adult, and allows the client to access feelings of anger. Are there any questions about that?

Another approach focuses on the process of integrating the client's love for the parent with the feelings of anger. The protecting client may tend to use guilt to split off the feelings of anger. The client believes that love and anger can not co-exist, and that they are mutually exclusive. Therefore, the client who feels sad for a parent and who wants to rationalize or justify the parent's neglect or abuse, feels guilty when anger is accessed. The process of integration might occur in this way:

Counsellor: "Who do you wish could have protected you from father's abuse?"

Client: "My mother I guess."

Counsellor: "So maybe sometimes you feel a little disappointed or annoyed at Mom for not protecting you. Is that accurate?"

Client: "Yes." (Client begins to cry.)

Counsellor: "Just feel that now." (Silence.) "What are the tears about? Are they sad tears, angry tears, or both?"

Client: "Sad."

Counsellor: "Is the sadness for yourself or for Mom."

Client: "For Mom."

Counsellor: "Say more about that."

Client: "Mom had such a hard life. She was never able to do what she wanted. She was always held back, because my dad was so dominating."

Counsellor: "So what I'm hearing is that you feel annoyed at Mom for not protecting you, and at the same time you love your mom and care about her because you saw her being oppressed by your father. Is that what you're saying?"

Client: "Yes."

Counsellor: "So I wonder if it's possible to love someone and feel annoyed at the same time?"

Client: "Yes. I guess so."

Counsellor: "Say more about the anger or feeling annoyed at Mom. What's that about?"

The objective here is to help the client integrate the feeling of anger with the feeling of love. Notice also that the protection of Mom is reframed as caring or love for Mom.

As soon as the client identifies feeling disappointed and annoyed at Mom, she begins to cry. This is sadness for Mom rather than for herself because the client can not integrate anger and love, so the client flips back to protection of Mom and feeling for her. Then the counsellor reframes the sadness for Mom as caring for her and introduces the integrating intervention which is, "I wonder if it's possible to feel angry and feel love at the same time for the same person." If the client can acknowledge this possibility, integration has occurred, and the counsellor can then focus more on the client's feeling of anger about the caring she missed from Mother.

It's a very important process, because the client not only needs to grieve the loss of caring of the abusive father but also the loss of caring of the mother who did not protect the child.

Question *Is that one of the bigger or major issues current in our society? The relationship between the client who is an adult child and his parents?*

Speaker Yes, and facing the issues in this relationship is at the very core of the deeper process of recovery for each of us. The two types of relationships that create unhealthy ways of relating and dysfunction for adult children of alcoholic or dysfunctional families are: 1) protecting the parent, for example the enabling, passive, or victim parent, and 2) being stuck in a struggle with the rejecting, abusive, or alcoholic parent.

Just to summarize the process in each case, the protecting client needs to move into anger and sadness for herself and to grieve the loss of parental caring. The struggling client needs to express the anger, then move into sadness in order to grieve and let go of the loss of parental caring. And finally seek to understand the story behind the parent's behaviour. The protecting client empathizes prematurely with the parent, and this empathy become a block to expressing anger and sadness for self. The struggling client must move from anger to sadness for himself, and then empathize with the parent which is most difficult.

Some clients are stuck in the struggle with a conflictual parent or an alcoholic parent. We need to help that person move from her anger into her sadness. It's a lot easier for that person to feel angry than to feel sad, but we need to move her to sadness so she can let go of the struggle. The anger and the struggle are about fighting to get the caring, the understanding, the approval, and the support that the client has always wanted, needed, and deserved. In this case, anger hangs on, and sadness lets go. The anger is a defense against facing the sadness and emptiness underneath.

But the client is afraid. If she lets go of the struggle what is she left with?

Response *Nothing. No parents.*

Speaker No parents. So the client will have nothing left because the only kind of relationship she has is based on the struggle. If she gives up the conflict or the struggle, she is left with emptiness and nothingness. The struggle was an attempt to get caring, and it has resulted in the client continuing to look too much outside herself for the parental caring she has missed. This has resulted in being dependent in a passive way or in a struggling aggressive way. Grieving and letting go of the need for parental caring, allows the client to mature emotionally and to become self-reliant, to give herself the caring she has missed rather than looking too much to others.

Question *In a case like that, what do you say to a client who goes through their own sadness and finds their relationship with their parent is really gone? It must be very painful for someone to go and see their parents then. They would like to see the relationship established perhaps on a more loving level, but it's not possible for the parents.*

Speaker We need to help him say, "Goodbye Mom" or "Goodbye Dad" and "Hello friend." Or maybe the parent is not even the kind of person that the client would choose as a friend. Maybe the parent is abusive. So it might be "Goodbye Dad" and "Hello occasional acquaintance." In some cases, it's just goodbye. There's nothing really left and nothing salvageable simply because the parent who was very abusive is very closed, and has been closed for many, many years. And there's no possibility or likelihood that the parent is ever going to become open, because after all, the parent is stuck in his own wounded child and is not in a process of recovery.

That's a reality in some situations. We have to help that client grieve the loss of that relationship, and not only the loss of the parent-child role, but the relationship as a whole in some cases.

When a client can face the parent with the painful feelings, rather than protect the parent, the client is moving out of the child state and into the adult state. The child within is frightened of facing the parents with unresolved issues. The child runs away. The adult goes to the parent and shares, but doesn't dump on the parent. The child either runs away and hides, or fights and dumps. The adult self does neither, and the client will need to grieve the childhood loss of caring fully enough so that he can come from his adult self.

Question *Would you usually use the empty chair method?*

Speaker If the parents aren't available, maybe because they've died or they live at a great distance so there's no possibility of seeing them for a very long time, the client can still work on that issue by using various psychodramatic or gestalt methods such as the empty chair. And then the client can incorporate that adult behaviour into other relationships.

If the client hasn't grown up in relation to parents, hasn't worked that through, then he probably hasn't grown up in relation to other adults. He is childlike, particularly to authority figures perhaps, or to people who are perceived to be parent-like figures. Even if parents are unavailable, the client cannot avoid meeting his parents as they appear in others.

Imagine the client who is protecting one parent and stuck in anger with the other, then grieves the loss of parental caring with each. Now he is left with emptiness and aloneness, abandonment. This is precisely the pain that the client has been working so hard to defend against, defenses which simultaneously consist of and result in the perpetuation of childlike dependency and loss of effective, meaningful, intimate adult relationships.

The task now is to help the client reconstruct his life perhaps initially by finding a supportive network, a family to replace the family of origin. The counsellor is a parent figure but may not be enough support for the client. Then the client needs to leave home as it were and become independent and self-reliant. This has been a lengthy discussion but important for understanding the deeper core processes in counselling to do with the client's individuation from parents.

INTELLECTUALIZATION

Let's go over some of these other defenses now.

Intellectualizing is when a person talks about a painful life experience in a news reporting style, without any emotion. The client often does this because he is not connected to his feelings, so we say things like, "What are you feeling right now?" Then giving him the feeling list helps him choose a feeling word and move past intellectualizing.

Or I might say, "That might leave a person feeling a little..." and then a feeling word, for example sad, scared, annoyed, and so on. Notice the reference to "a person". This wording allows the client to identify the feeling as his own because it is less confrontational than saying, "So you might feel..." Also notice the wording "a little" which allows the client to safely own a feeling.

Another approach is to listen and observe the client's subtle non-verbal cues or signals. For example, an intellectualizing client related the death of her child and briefly paused when referring to the "power truck" that killed the child. I noted this reference and in another session said, "There was a power truck." At this point, she began to grieve openly.

This is making use of what can be termed "key words". These are the client's words spoken immediately adjacent to the engagement of painful feelings and which the counsellor later repeats in order to elicit the same pain.

PROJECTION

Projection is when the client assigns his own feeling to the counsellor or to someone else. For example, I had a client who was constantly angry and he came to a session and started out by staring at me intently and saying, "You're angry aren't you, I know you're angry about something." And I said, "No, I'm not aware of feeling any anger. I wonder if you're aware of feeling a little angry right now?" It's important to invite the client to identify his own feeling rather than focusing on the counsellor.

Question *What about the use of someone saying "Well, you know when you do this then you feel..." instead of saying "I"?*

Speaker Okay, that's another common defense. It's easier for me to say that "people out there" feel this than "I" feel it. If I have to own it as my feeling, it's a little scarier. It's a little riskier.

So we need to ask the client to change 'you' to 'I' and repeat what he said. I may say, "Say that again and change you to I."

INTROJECTION

Introjection is when a person swallows whole anything you say to him — any interpretation. That's why it's important not to make interpretations, especially to very dependent clients. If I ever make an interpretation, it will be very tentative by saying, "I wonder if maybe there's a possibility that there might be a link between your experience growing up and what's happening now?" Notice the tentative expressions "I wonder" and "if" and "maybe" and "possibility" and "might". Even with these expressions which make it clear your statement is not carved in stone, the dependent client will introject to avoid taking responsibility for his own insight and his own conclusions. With this defense people simply agree with whatever you suggest.

Another approach is to point out that you've noticed a pattern of the client agreeing with anything you say and then exploring what that's about. Introjection is characteristic of the need for approval and the need to please the counsellor by making him competent and right. The co-dependent saviour counsellor engages in too much interpretation because of his own need to fix, to be right, for approval. The most effective approach is to say, "What's it about?" and "What's the feeling?" allowing the client to come up with his own responses from scratch rather than using reflections which may suggest too much to the client and which he then introjects by saying, "That's right...yes..."

Question *So you end up telling them how they feel.*

Speaker That's right. Yes. And you can observe this when you make a reflective statement and you get a sense that it's not possible for you to make an inaccurate reflection to this client. All your reflections are 100%. And you get a sense that you're actually leading this client; he's not leading you any more. In that case he is probably engaging in introjecting.

Question *So they tear then because you've told them that they're sad in a reflective statement.*

Speaker That's right, in extreme cases. So it's important to get the response generated or initiated by the client.

RETROJECTION

Retrojection is when a client says that he feels something toward or about himself that he actually feels toward you. This commonly occurs in relation to anger. For example, I had a client who was right on time for an appointment but I was late from an appointment with a previous client. When she came in she said, "I did it again, I screwed up again. I came at the wrong time." And I said, "Well, it seems to me you came right on time and I was late with the last person I was seeing. You have every right to feel annoyed, and I wonder who you might feel a little annoyed with if you weren't feeling annoyed with yourself. Who would that be?"

Response *It's you.*

Speaker So that's the way I work with that retrojection. She was able to admit that she felt a little irritation toward me.

As soon as she owned the feeling of irritation, I immediately said, "Is it OK to feel irritated with me?" She responded, "I guess so," and I said, "I think you have every right to feel irritated and to say so, and I apologize for being late." It's very important to reach for a validation of anger in this situation because the client has a strong pattern of fear of asserting her anger. She has just stated her anger toward me, a significant parental figure, and this risk is an important therapeutic step which needs to be validated. The validation is the key to integrating the feeling. The retrojection defense is often a fear of speaking up, arising from the parental relationship in the family of origin, and so the anger is turned inward toward self and contributes to negative self-talk and depression.

The client may be modelling a parental figure who also used retrojection, or the client may be protecting against the fear of retaliation from an emotionally punitive parent.

OVER-TALKING

Over-talking is a very common defense. A person will talk, talk, talk, because she doesn't want me to reach for any feelings. The client uses that verbal wall, a way of controlling, as a defense. One approach is to interrupt the client and say, "I'd like to stop what's happening right now and just take a look at what has been happening between you and I. It seems that so far today, you've been saying some important things and you've had a lot to say about those things. What I've noticed is it's been difficult for me to intervene in any way, or to make any statements to you to help you explore the things you've been talking about. And I wonder what that's about." So we'll have some discussion about the process. Another approach is to say, "I wonder what would happen if you were to slow down." A client once responded very clearly, "Dan, I'm afraid if I did slow down I might feel things I don't want to feel."

In this case I reflected by saying, "So maybe that's scary to think about feeling those things," and then continued to explore the client's fear and safety issues.

Still another approach is to say, "I wonder if you use words to take away the feelings." The client may become silent or smile as if to say, "Yes, that's right." Then I will say, "What's the feeling coming up?" In other words, identify, describe, or label the defense, then reach for the feeling. This approach in general, is what the counsellor can do with most defenses.

I may also explore the pattern more broadly by saying, "I wonder what happens when you do this with other people. What feedback or reaction do you get?" Keep in mind that the defense, whatever form it takes, is a key to understanding the client's dysfunctional and distancing patterns of behaviour outside the counselling relationship.

Question *So they're filling up as much space as they can in an hour.*

Speaker That's right.

CHANGING TOPICS

Response *Also, by changing the topic they always have something to talk about so neither of you has a chance to deal with anything in depth. They can just stay on the surface.*

Speaker That's right. The client can be in control of what's talked about as well as the depth of the discussion. But sometimes, when the client changes topics I'll say, "A moment ago you were talking about the death of your brother and now you're talking about your plans to go to school next year. What's the connection between those two?" Sometimes I'll take that approach. Sometimes there is a connection that I've completely missed. In this case for example maybe the client is talking about getting on with her life after the death, or the topic shift may be a defense against the pain she feels when talking about his death.

Another approach I'll take is to say, "I wonder which of those topics is easier for you to talk about?" And he may say, "I guess my plans to go to school." I'll say, "So say more about your brother."

RED HERRINGS

Red herrings are superficial issues. A client for example was talking about grocery shopping, seeing the dentist and so on. By pursuing those issues, you can sometimes get to a client's core issue. Every once in a while she'd sigh as she said, "Oh I've got to go to the dentist, I've got to take the kids skating". And it was as if these were really important heavy issues.

But I cued in to the sigh and I said, "It sounds as if life is really a burden to you. You've got a lot of things on the go — little things, tasks and chores to do. And I wonder how long you've felt life is a burden?"

And she said, "All of my life".

I then said, "Say more about what happened when life first began to be a burden. How old were you?"

So even though her first issues sounded like red herrings, the sigh was a window into a core issue from the family of origin. She was then able to talk about how she was the oldest responsible child singled out to do adult work in the tobacco fields from eight years of age in while her younger brothers and sisters were allowed to play and have social lives with peers. And that's been her life pattern. Her mother died when she was 16 years old which left her with more responsibility. She's never moved out of that role so that now in the nuclear family she continues to lead a martyr's life. She found a husband who is no support, and she is distant from the children and complains about looking after them.

Another approach to red herrings is to first validate the red herring issues by saying, "So you've been talking about... and that may be important for you to talk about," and then say, "If you were to review your life from early days to present, what would be most difficult for you to talk about today?" That cuts right through the red herring defense, because the client is directed to the painful experience. He might say, "I don't want to talk about it," and I'll say, "The thing you find most difficult to talk about, or least want to talk about is the very thing that you most need to talk about in order to get on with your therapy. So I wonder if you can say just a little bit about it."

Response *You keep working at them.*

Speaker I find that works very well. I stress the importance of facing the difficulty in relation to progress, and then invite the client to say a little bit.

VAGUENESS

Vagueness is the defense of talking in vague generalities about the situation — the discussion almost sounds philosophical. The key here is to say, "What's an example of something that happened?"

The client does not want to give an example because then he would have to connect to the pain associated with that example, or that experience. It's a lot easier or feels safer and less painful to be vague and general.

Response *What if a client just says, "I don't know."*

Speaker Not knowing is a denial defense. The client does know. I repeat my question or state my question in a different way. If I were to be more confrontational, I might even say, "That's not really an answer. What I'm asking you is...," and then repeat it. So I identify that as a non-answer.

Another approach which is non-confrontational and which usually works better, is to say, "Just take some time and think about it. There's no hurry." This supports the resistance and allows the client to let go of the struggle.

Response *Sometimes when I respond I say, "Just guess, what do you think?" It's amazing what comes up.*

SOMATIC COMPLAINTS

Speaker Alright, yes. Next, somatic complaints refers to physical complaints — headaches and so on. "Soma" is a word referring to the body. For example I had a client who talked about a headache and bowel pains she'd had for the last three days and which occurred periodically. I asked her to have it checked out by a doctor, which she did, and the report came back negative. The doctor said there was nothing wrong with her physically. It was stress-related he thought.

I said to her, "So the doctor's report is that there's nothing wrong physically. Sometimes painful emotions take on the form of physical pain — physical manifestations. What might those painful feelings be about? Maybe fear, anger, guilt, sadness, some other feeling?"

This appeals to the client's sense of the hypothetical. "Sometimes... what might..." It's similar to your intervention of, "If you were to guess, what might be a possibility?" Notice also that the intervention is tied to the doctor's report. It's very important that any physical complaints be checked out by a doctor. Then that report becomes the basis for the intervention with somatic complaints. Incidentally, some recent research indicates that internalized painful emotion or stress leads to physical illness and even cancer. The personlity type for cancer is the passive behaviour which keeps one's own pain inside, suffering in silence, attending to others more than to self.

EYES CLOSING

Speaker Eyes closing. When a person closes her eyes, often times it's when you're exploring something that is painful, and she wants to withdraw from that. It's a key to her unhealthy pattern because she is internalizing. And what you're seeing with that behaviour is how the client becomes depressed. The client withdraws, closes her eyes, internalizes, and starts brewing up a depression.

Sometimes closing the eyes is intended to increase concentration or to contact emotions or memories, so we're sometimes a little unsure when first working with a client whether it's one or the other, but we'll be able to see over time in our relationship, which it is. I'll allow the client to close her eyes for a while if it's an internalizing, withdrawing behaviour. Then I'll say, "Now I'd like you to open your eyes and put that feeling into words. What is it you are feeling when you close your eyes?" It's a simple direction. One of the chief objectives of counselling is to put feelings into words, to bring feelings from the inside to the outside as a way of taking care of them for oneself.

PHILOSOPHIZING

Speaker Sometimes the client will philosophize by referring to grand themes which seem very distant from himself such as love, peace, social injustice as examples. A client of mine once began a discourse on the corruption of Western Civilization. Then he spoke of the corruption of the world. I listened for a while, reflected what he was saying, then said, "So I wonder if you were to review your life from early days, what important person in your life was someone you saw or experienced as being corrupt." He identified his father and began talking about his childhood relationship and his experience of feeling rejected by his father. This client also then proceeded to connect experiences of conflictual relationships with supervisors and other authority figures.

At one point this client was delusional and perceived himself as an alien from another planet which illustrates how far from the pain a person will distance himself. When delusional thoughts emerge, suicide may also be contemplated. This client attempted suicide following a rejection by a lover, which also followed a divorce from his wife.

RELIGIOSITY

Speaker This defense is characterized by using religious or spiritual beliefs to avoid pain. For example, a client may say, "I won't decide. I'll just pray about it." Making a decision is too difficult, too frightening, too risky. So rather than take action, the client waits, and waits, and waits. Spirituality is important for a sense of purpose and direction in life, and when it is used as a defense, the client is unable to move forward. This is the pattern of the dependent personality. An intervention for this may be to make a reflection which presents the implications, for example, "So there's nothing you can do but wait for a long time." The client may respond by limiting the time frame. Or I may say, "So you are wanting someone else (God) to decide for you, and I wonder if this is part of an old pattern." And ,"What does that leave you feeling about yourself?"

Another example of religiosity is the belief presented to me recently when a client said, "I can't be angry with my father who sexually abused me because I believe I chose to be born into that family." I replied,"So maybe you were born into that family to express the anger."

Sometimes it helps to know something about the client's religion in order to understand how he is using religion as a defense, how he is distorting his belief, and how to respond with a statement that will therapeutically challenge the client.

CORE COUNSELLING SKILLS

Speaker Now I want to discuss some core skills and interventions that I want you to use in your practice sessions. Refer back to our previous discussion for a review of reflective listening, identifying feelings, and engaging feelings which are essential to facilitate the counselling process.

VALIDATING INTERVENTIONS

An example of a validating intervention would be, "Is it okay to feel that?" In other words my first approach to validation is to elicit it from the client himself, or herself. "Is it okay to feel that sadness?" "Is it okay to feel that anger?" If he says no, I'll say, "What gets in the way of your feeling okay with that? What's that about, not feeling okay?" And he will talk about it.

And then I will make a validation even when he doesn't validate himself. I'll say, "It seems to me you have every right to feel that". There's a validation statement. "What you're feeling, or what you did makes sense. It fits with what you've been through. It seems to me you are entitled to that." You might also say, "It takes courage to take that step, to feel that, to face that pain".

"It's okay to cry, just let it out." There's a validation combined with engaging a feeling. "Just let it out" is engaging. "It's okay to feel, to cry" —is a validation. Validation is the key to integration and self-acceptance.

INSIGHT INTERVENTIONS

"What is it about that situation that pushed your buttons? And what other person or situation in your life had similar characteristics?" The phrase "pushed your buttons" implies the exaggerated response or reaction, or the hypersensitive reaction. Or I might say to a person, "As you're talking, it's striking to me that this isn't the first time this has happened to you. You're telling me that in this situation, you are a helpless victim. That's not the first time you were a helpless victim. Can you think of another time when you were a helpless victim?"

In other words I'll suggest there was another time that the client was a helpless victim but I won't tell him when it was. I will suggest it especially if the client previously mentioned, on assessment for example, a similar experience in early childhood. And then I'll leave it up to the client to make the link with another experience as a way of gaining insight into patterns.

Question *When you're giving suggestions like "Can you tell me another time in your life that you were a victim?", does it matter whether it's actually accurate that they were a victim or is it just their perception that matters?*

Speaker The client's perception is what's most important to work with. It's easier to work with examples. But I had a client who was talking about feeling controlled, that she had no power in her life, that things just kept happening to her since she'd been assaulted about three years ago. She was afraid to go places. She turned down going to a concert because she was afraid the person who assaulted her might be there, even though the chances were almost nil. And she talked about being afraid that the person who assaulted her was coming around her home, had been tinkering with her car, leaving the gas cap off or leaving the oil cap off and the door open, and so on. She was getting quite paranoid.

She came across generally as a helpless victim. As we talked about that, having done the assessment, I was aware of other situations in her life when she had been a helpless victim. I said, "You know, it seems to me this isn't the first time you've felt like a helpless victim." Another way I might put it to a client is, "Is this the first time you have felt like a victim of other people, that you were treated unfairly?"

She thought of another situation and talked about that for a while, to do with an ex-husband. Then I said, "Can you identify another situation? And another?" And she accumulated six or eight different situations.

There was a series of experiences in her adult life, and she was able to identify other experiences going back even to childhood, from the time her mother kept two younger siblings and gave her up to be taken care of by her grandparents. So she felt like her mother's victim. It's been a life pattern.

CHANGE INTERVENTIONS

One of my favourites is the paradoxical intention, saying "It's understandable that you wouldn't be ready to change yet," when a person is very stuck. We've already looked at that. But essentially when we're looking at change, we're helping a person look at choices. And then we're going to help her take the risk to implement a choice or combination of choices.

Part of that movement toward change might take on this kind of picture. You'll be saying to a person, "Is what you did in that situation working well for you?"

So I might say to a person for example, "What did you feel in that situation when your husband put you down?" She responds, and we'll sort it out, maybe by using a feeling list. She says, "I felt resentment". I respond, "What did you do with that resentment? Where did the resentment go?" She says, "I guess I kept it inside". So I say, "I wonder if that's a pattern of how you cope with your feelings of anger and resentment? Is that what you do generally?" She says, "Yes it is". She generally doesn't speak about it or address it to anyone. So I say, "What happens when you do that? Does that work well for you?" And she identifies that it doesn't work very well.

My next question is "What gets in the way of you letting your husband know that you feel resentment?" This is a key step because what she is going to say is, "I'm afraid if I do, something is going to happen." Fear gets in the way. She is afraid she might lose him or he might react to her in some way, but she doesn't know how because she's never really done it.

It may go back to relationships in the family of origin where she learned to internalize feelings. So I'll say, "For you to express your resentment might mean taking a risk".

I might then have her rehearse using an empty chair, or with me acting as her husband. A next step may be to invite her to come up with the real issue that she has with me — not as the pretend husband, but as the counsellor.

To encourage that I'll say, "I think it will be important to identify a concern you have with me. See if you can take the risk to face me with it. It will be important to your therapy, and I'm not fragile." I'll give her that reassurance.

And I might even give her the three-part assertiveness statement that we'll go over later on. She'll try it on, fill in the blanks and address an issue to me, and then I'll congratulate her when she does that.

The next step will be to encourage her to take the risk to address an issue to somebody outside the office. And when she's able to do that I'll congratulate her. So this is a brief outline of working with behaviour change utilizing the idea of moving the client from lowest risk to greatest risk.

STRUCTURE OF THE COUNSELLING SESSION

Speaker To begin the second session with your client, start by identifying the goals. So I'd begin by saying, "What I'd like to do today is be very clear about what you want to achieve in your counselling, and what your goals are". The client will respond, then I'll say, "Which of those is the most important for you, in your counselling?" He will identify a goal and then I'll say, "How long in your life have you struggled with that goal, or that problem, or that issue?" That will take you into the body of the counselling session because he is going to take you back to the origins of the problem.

As he begins to talk about origins, I'm going to say, "What are you feeling right now as you're talking. Fear, guilt, sadness, annoyed, some other feeling?" Reach for feelings and use the feeling list. Reach for a validation, "Is it OK to feel that?" Give the client an invitation to talk, "Say more about that feeling."

"How has that affected your life?" That's an insight intervention. Sometimes the goal presented in counselling is to address a past event such as a death or sexual abuse for example. When the distant past is presented, the process is to explore the past event and the painful feelings and then to explore what the client has done with the feelings, exploring patterns of adaptation or coping to the present time. We might normally think of saying, "How has that affected your life?" and that wording is OK. To say, "What have you done with the pain?" gives the client a sense of choice and power.

Generally speaking, when you're working with symptomatic problems as goals or issues, you're going from recent history to a time farther back in time maybe to early life to explore the origins. Then you're going to work your way back up to the present. And so you're going to then say, "What do you do with those feelings, does that work well for you? No? What might you do differently that might work better?"

That's the process in a nutshell. "What are you feeling as you're talking? What have you done with those feelings? Does that work well for you? What might you do that will work better? Try it on right now." See if you can think of a way for your client to try on the behaviour change in the session itself so that you can then congratulate him, and acknowledge his progress.

In bringing closure, you're going to provide a summary of what the client has talked about in terms of feelings, themes, and issues. For example, "So today you've been talking about feeling afraid to let your husband know about your resentment. And you've related that to a pattern that goes back to parents ignoring your needs, and you've been able to feel the anger and sadness about not being supported by your parents. You've recognized that in order to get your needs met, you will need to take a risk to express feelings to your husband." Sometimes validate the client's work by saying, "You've done a lot of work today, facing difficult feelings and experiences." Then you're going to elicit an evaluation of the session, "What has this been like talking about these things and doing this today?" It's very important to say that so that the client can give you feedback, for her benefit. And then invite the client to return, "I wonder if you are wanting to continue and take this a little bit further in another session?" Finally, set the time, "What would be a good time for you?" This brings a focused close to the session, and sometimes it is important to say, "Maybe we can stop now," even sharper focus.

Remember, if you are at a loss of knowing what to say to your client, use the reflective statement followed by the invitation to talk or to say more, with the occasional reaching for a validation from the client for painful feelings. As follows:

1. "So what I hear you saying is, you feel...because..."

2. "Is it OK to feel that?"

3. "Say more about that."

An entire session can be carried on with these three brief and simple interventions.

A REVIEW OF THE COUNSELLING PRACTICE SESSION

Speaker Okay let's talk about what this counselling practice session was like for you. Anyone like to start on it? Comments and questions about that?

Response I felt when I was counselling with Guy, I don't know if I touched something in him that got him angry. It seems like I did — that there's some kind of tension because of that. Do you feel that or is that just me?

Response *Before you answer, Guy, as the observer I noticed Merv you were spending some time asking questions. Then you got on to asking about the family to see how that would fit in to help make sense with what you were going after. You did a lot of paraphrasing. I thought that maybe you didn't use enough silence when you were asking him a question and then you made almost an interpretive reflection. You may not agree with that, but I thought Merv, that you had your own agenda to pursue, and it was frustrating for the client.*

And there was the frustration because you kept telling him what to do. It was interesting because you wanted to fix it. You wanted to fix it today, and he wasn't ready. He had no interest in it. And I just saw you didn't give much of a chance to explore the feelings and just be with that for a while.

Question *Is that how you felt, Guy?*

Response *Yes, I perceived you, Merv, as wanting things to go a certain way and that's not where I wanted to go. So my frustration was with you not understanding me. That was my frustration. I didn't feel that we were exploring what I wanted to explore. We were exploring what you wanted to explore.*

Speaker A very important point to be made is that when a counsellor asks too many questions, it will tend to direct the session. Whereas, if you make reflective statements and the client is allowed to direct, reflections enable the counsellor to follow the client. Questions lead the client where the counsellor wants to go. So you can keep that in mind as a general principle.

Questions lead the client, and reflections follow the client. And be careful to avoid interpretive reflections, sometimes ironically called advanced empathy or advanced listening.

Question *I'm wondering if you were counselling someone and they've had problems in childhood, do you ask how the other members of the family are feeling towards that or do you just keep it directed on the client?*

Speaker Okay, it's a good point. If you're doing assessment, you can sort of explore how the other siblings have sort of coped with growing up in that family or what the outcome has been for them. That sort of thing.

But when you're into a counselling session, it's important to focus on the client's own experience because there's a tendency for many clients to use discussion about other people besides themselves as a defense. So clients would love to maybe talk about how a brother or a sister has dealt with something or what their problems are, or what the husband's problems are, or what the children's problems are, instead of talking about what his own feelings and his own difficulties are. So it's OK to do that very briefly for assessment only and then bring the focus right back to your client by saying, "What has that left you with?"

Question *Actually it's the same as the first question here. If you're concerned with something going off track, that's probably when you'd do some directing questions. Am I correct in that?*

Speaker If you sense that the client is going off track, you can make a summary reflection. "A moment ago you were talking about such and such, and now you're talking about this." And just saying that will call his attention to having changed topics. And they might say, "Oh, I guess I did go off track there," and he might bring himself back on. Or you can say, "I wonder if there's a link between those two things," or, "I wonder which is easier for you to talk about...," and then have him talk about what's more difficult. These kinds of statements help to focus the session.

Question *So it's a process of bringing awareness to the person, of what's happening.*

Speaker Exactly.

Response *So you're not really directing, you're just making a statement there.*

Speaker There is some directing or encouraging the client to talk about what's more difficult.

Response *And then there will be questions then.*

Speaker Then you may want to invite him to talk about what's more difficult to talk about, then he'll start again being more on track. Then you can go for feelings, and things like that.

Question *What if the client asks the counsellor how he feels about what the client is saying?*

Speaker As a counsellor I might make a reflection for example, "So maybe you would like for me to give you some assurance." And so I'd make a reflection but I wouldn't answer the question for the client. Often you can understand the client's question to you as a question she is asking herself. I would tend to want to put it back to the client by saying, "What do you think? Did it work for you?"

Response *That's one to watch for then as the counsellor — to be aware of that.*

Speaker Absolutely. And not to answer questions, as a general rule.

Response *Yes.*

Speaker Think of a way to turn it around. And usually the way I do it is make a reflection, and then ask him the same question he asked me.

Question *You don't find the clients get agitated with that?*

Response *Well Brenda didn't when I turned it back to her.*

Speaker It depends on how you do it. If you do it abruptly or lack sincerity....

Response *You can say it's none of her business (laughing).*

Speaker Sometimes what the client wants is approval. And that might be part of an old pattern of not being able to find the approval within himself. He is looking too much for approval outside of himself. You can point that out as maybe being part of the pattern and say, "So I hear you wanting some approval, and I wonder if this might be part of an old pattern."

Response *I was observing and I didn't talk. But I was observing Rob and John. They came to a kind of stalemate. It seemed like it got to the point where it became mechanical because it was what you the instructor were expecting from us instead of flowing more naturally. Do you understand what I'm saying?*

Speaker Yes.

Response *So we just, kind of everybody stopped and looked at each other. I tried to follow the process and say things the way you suggested, and then I got stuck and didn't know where to take it or what to do next.*

Speaker Okay. And it makes sense in this situation in that because the repertoire of skills is very limited for you. Otherwise you wouldn't be counsellors in training. It makes sense for you to get stuck and not have the tools to go where you need to go with a client. That's understandable. The fact that you struggled with the process and to come up with what to do next, sounds like progress. To learn to do counselling is learning a new language. To recognize when you are stuck and to mentally search for the next statement or effective wording, is what you must do in order to incorporate new behaviour and skills. It's exactly what the client is doing to grow and change. There needs to be confusion and anxiety in the process of recognizing old behaviour and deciding to do something different that works better.

Speaker The definition of a professional counsellor is this. A professional counsellor is someone who intervenes intentionally with a predictable beneficial outcome for the client. In other words, everything you are saying and doing with your client, you do it as a deliberate statement or choice because you know that it's going to have a therapeutic, beneficial outcome for your client. You can predict that. This is also the definition of a therapeutic intervention.

So when I say, "What are you feeling right now while you're talking?", I know what's going to happen when I say that. When I say, "Let yourself feel that right now", I know what's going to happen. I can predict the result of saying that. I know it's going to benefit my client.

Question *How long does it take to get to the point where you know the outcome of every situation.*

Speaker It takes time, it takes experience, opportunities.

Question *Where do you get all the opportunities to do all the practise before you work first?*

Speaker There are a variety of possibilities.

Question *Do you make mistakes — throw away mistakes on them?*

Question *The variety of ways, what are they?*

Speaker How do you get the opportunities?

Response *Yes.*

Speaker By taking courses. Counsellor training courses, and by doing volunteer work in counselling settings for counselling services, crisis agencies — what have you. The yellow pages is a place to look - let your fingers do the walking.

It sounds as though you are asking about when you will be ready to do counselling as a profession. That's very individual but assuming there is enough progress in one's own process of recovery, confidence level increases with an adequate knowledge base combined with opportunities to use the skills.

Response *In my counselling session, I think I was offering suggestions to the client or advice maybe — I'm not to sure how to phrase it. And I kind of listed things as options or choices. I know there's a fine line somewhere in that area where if the person is looking for examples and not necessarily looking for validation or confirmation, but they're looking for an example. How would you deal with that?*

Speaker Looking for an example of what he can do?

Response *Yes, exactly.*

Speaker So the way I would approach that with a client is to say, "What are your options? What are your choices? Let's make a list." If you're to do it very, very deliberately and in a very structured way I'd have him get out a sheet of paper and number 1 through 8 and say, "Let's make a list of different possibilities", and try to elicit those from the client. And then I'd add my own ideas at the end. And then I'd say, "As you look over that list, what looks most workable to you? What do you think is going to work the best?" Then let him choose.

Response *Yes, that makes perfect sense because if they make the choice and it just so happens to be one of their choices, it kind of empowers them as well.*

Speaker Exactly. If the client can create the options, it empowers him and supports his own creative ability, and that's something he can take with him from the session. Eventually, this person who is being dependent on you, won't need you. He can nurture himself, validate himself, take care of himself, make his own decisions, and be his own person, an individual in relationships while accepting the individuality of others.

Chapter Three:

Loss and Grief Counselling

Speaker Our discussion of loss and grief counselling is a continuation of The Counselling Process and Therapeutic Interventions. We said that everyone has a tendency to repeat or perpetuate aspects of painful conflicts and losses. A primary objective of counselling therefore is to help the client face and integrate the painful feelings of those experiences. Every conflict is a loss because conflict creates distance in relationships, but not every loss is a conflict. The death of a loved one is not a conflict, for example.

Let's begin now to talk about losses, and then in a later chapter we'll talk more about conflicts, specifically how to work with the client, and how to deal with conflicts in his or her relationships, past and present.

TYPES OF LOSSES

First of all I want to review the types of loss that we experience, the goals of grief counselling, painful feelings around loss and grief, the unfinished business of loss, and the behaviour decisions of grief, and then we'll look at some therapeutic interventions.

Loss is part of the human condition. There's no way we can avoid loss. It's something we experience from the time we're born to the time we die. We experience losses every step of the way throughout our lives, such as the loss of a job, loss of health, and loss of relationships through a break up or through death, to name a few.

Because we are bound by time, every passing moment is a loss, but not every loss involves grief. We need to distinguish between loss and grief. Loss is a word that refers to an event in which something that we had or were attached to was lost. It can also refer to something that we needed or wished for, but never had. So loss doesn't necessarily have to do with attachment or having had something. There's a saying that you can't lose something that you've never had, but I disagree with that. I think you can have an experience of loss of something that you needed but never had.

Question *Can you give us an example?*

Speaker Parental caring is a good example. If I never got the caring I needed from my father, that was a loss, even if I never had it in the first place.

Question *So an unmet need itself could be considered a loss?*

Speaker Exactly.

Question *Is need relative or is there some kind of objective needs list?*

Speaker Well, Abraham Maslow came up with a hierarchy of needs that we have at different stages of our lives as we develop. And the primary need that we're working with, with many clients, is the need for closeness and caring. Everybody needs that. Every child needs and deserves that as he grows up. That's a primary loss that we're helping the clients to grieve.

Loss is referring to the event, grief is the emotional reaction to the event. I'd like to make a list of types of losses that people experience and which we will identify during the assessment and work with as we proceed in the counselling relationship. Because unresolved loss is a primary root of problems frequently presented in counselling, it is very important to have an understanding of the broad range and variety of losses which we experience. So let's develop a list of common losses as they occur in order, during a life cycle from birth to death.

BIRTH AS A LOSS

First of all, how is birth a loss? It's a loss of the safe, secure environment that we were in. Our needs for warmth, and nourishment were met, and we were cushioned by that water around us so we didn't have to worry about being jolted, jarred, and bumped so much.

Question *Isn't loss tied to a new beginning as well? You can't have a new beginning without a previous loss.*

Speaker That's right.

Response *It's like life and death — its the same thing really because you can't have life without death.*

Speaker Exactly. Often you can't say hello until you've said goodbye. That's something else. We'll say more about that later on.

So when a child is born it cries to have its needs met. It didn't have to cry before, but at birth now it has to cry to get itself changed, to get fed, to get warm, to get put to bed. There's quite a radical change that comes with birth. Who else loses when there's a birth?

Response *The mother.*

Speaker Alright. How is that a loss for Mom?

Response *I'm thinking about my daughter — I really enjoyed being pregnant with her. Lying in bed at night and feeling the baby move was such a wonderful feeling that's hard to explain. She was born at seven in the evening and the next day when the doctor came in to make his rounds, I was weeping. I explained to him that I was happy she was born and that she was there, but — even now I get choked when I think about this — it was like she had been mine, my own, and now I had to share her with everybody.*

And all of a sudden she was out in the world, and there were other people standing over her and being around her all the time. It was just like she wasn't mine any more. And I really wept over that for about two or three days after. It took a long time.

And the doctor couldn't understand it. He said, "You're the first patient I've had who has said that". He said that, "Everybody's so glad the baby is out." I really missed her after that. I had to put my arms around her to hold her.

Speaker So that was a real experience of loss in the way you're describing it. Maybe that sense of loss after birth leads to bonding with the child because you said you had to hold her after that. Yes, alright. And in another sense that's a loss for a Mom and for Dad.

Response *Especially with the first born, it's a loss of a certain type of relationship between the parents because now there's the third individual.*

Speaker Exactly. They're no longer two, now they're three. And the special one-on-one relationship that was there before has really changed. The attention goes to this demanding entity constantly needing to be changed and fed and so on. And sometimes couples find that the loss of what they had previously is so difficult to accept that the marriage does not survive. Especially if, for example, the father married mother to get caring needs met, and now he's no longer getting that caring because the attention is being diverted to someone else. He might try to get it from somewhere else. And so relationships can break down with a birth. What would be the next loss for the baby as its growing up?

Response *Weaning.*

Speaker Some mothers find that to be a loss as well. They don't want to let go. I've heard of mothers nursing babies until they're six or seven years old.

I don't really have any sort of opinion about that. I haven't seen evidence that it has any detrimental affect for the child or the mother. So I wouldn't say that it's healthy or unhealthy to hang on to that. It depends on what the child's experience is.

Question *Wouldn't you say that having a child is just a single experience of loss because from day one the dependency of the child on the mother is constantly becoming less and less so. So it's turned into a gradual experience of loss.*

Speaker Yes, all the time. Certainly there is a loss of independence. Many mothers and many fathers experience that loss of freedom and independence because they are so tied to the responsibility of raising the child.

Response *My partner had a client, or a patient in yesterday. The man asked if she had children and when she said no, the man said, "What's it like having an evening to yourself?" So he was experiencing that kind of loss.*

Speaker Yes, you feel the loss of freedom with parental responsibility, but then when the child is gone you feel the loss of the child and the emptiness that goes with it.

Response *You can take it as gain because then you have a baby and then the baby has babies, then all the way around it can be more of a gain than a loss.*

Response *In one way it's a loss but you gain all the time.*

Speaker That's right. So the same experience can have a double edge. It can have two sides, the gain aspects and the loss aspects. Being able to recognize the gain as well as grieve the loss, is a key to moving forward, growth, reconstruction of life. What's the next loss after weaning?

Response *When the child has his own mobility there's the loss of having to carry him around. Is that a significant one?*

DEVELOPMENTAL CHANGE AS LOSS

Speaker So you are focusing on the loss experienced by the adult parent. Yes, perhaps there will be a degree of loss more or less for different parents. Certainly there will be, as the child grows up and needs the parent less and less. The more needy or child-like the parent is, the more difficult it will be for the parent to let go and allow the child to develop.

As we focus on the child's experience, any developmental change is a loss because the child no longer gets waited on as much. Because it can walk, it has to accept a little bit more responsibility for itself.

Toilet training is a loss. Around this period of skill development, the child may experience a frustrated or abusive parent which conveys a message that the child is not OK. This loss of self-worth may impede development into the next stage.

What comes after that for a child?

Response *Going to school.*

Speaker Perhaps leaving home to attend day care or pre-school classes. A painful separation may indicate a difficult adjustment to surviving on one's own without the parent. Going to school, yes. Then passing from one grade to the next and leaving teachers, classmates, learning opportunities, and environments behind. In fact moving from one grade to another is parallel to moving from one developmental period to another because when adequate skills are not learned in an earlier grade, the child has difficulty acquiring skills in the next grade.

What are some other losses along the way there? Remember your own experiences.

Response *Loss of friends.*

Speaker Loss of friends, yes. Young families are highly mobile, and the child's friends may be members of young families that move away, or the child's family may move. As we said during our discussion of Clinical Assessment, a child may learn that it is not worthwhile investing too much of himself in friendships if he has been moving frequently, and this can become part of a pattern of distancing and witholding feelings.

Response *Just referring back to the pre-schooler, maybe for the youngster there is a loss of staying in the home environment all the time. Now he's having to go out and interact.*

Speaker That's right. Loss of the safety and security of home may be scary.

Response *A mother going back to work could be a loss.*

Speaker Yes, the mother going back to work, maybe being replaced by a babysitter or a nanny or somebody.

BIRTH OF A SIBLING

Speaker A major loss can happen with the arrival of a sibling. The oldest child or the previously born child occupied a special role as the only child or the last born. Now there is someone to compete for the special attention that the child received. In my own family that's the basis of the rivalry. My oldest is a girl who has said at times that when her brother was born "he took my life away". So it's a very significant loss that sets up an experience of unresolved grief and conflict that can sometimes remain into adult years. What comes after that?

Response *Puberty.*

Speaker All right, yes. Puberty, the loss of innocence maybe. First sexual experiences such as sexual exploration or abuse even before puberty might constitute a loss of innocence for a child. But in itself, puberty brings on physical changes which move the child toward adulthood. For the female child in dysfunctional families, the onset of menses sometimes precedes the loss of father's affection or an experience of abuse when father views her as an opportunity for sexual gratification. What else?

Response *Just going back a bit, I remember going away to school as a loss of being able to decide for myself what I was going to do that day. Teachers would tell me what to do.*

Speaker Yes, so there was a loss of independence, and maybe a reaction against life being more structured by the teacher/parent figure. What else?

Response *Dating.*

Response *When my daughter starts dating, that will be a loss for me in that she's getting affectionate with someone else.*

Speaker You would feel loss as a parent. Her affection has been diverted — you're not getting it all, is that what you're saying? And for some young people maybe dating is a loss because it represents growing up. It's another milestone, so it's a gain which can be made difficult depending upon what has transpired in the parental relationship. The overly critical, dominating opposite sex parent coupled with a passive same sex parent, can make the thought of dating a frightening prospect, and the distant or sexually abusive opposite sex parent can result in the child's difficulty withholding sexual involvement because of the need for parental caring and approval.

Response *It's a loss of childhood, doing adult things too early, maybe having a teen pregnancy.*

Speaker That's right. And if there is an abortion or adoption of the child, additional loss occurs. In terms of adult experience occuring prematurely, something similar happens to people who have to go to work too early. This person may become a martyr figure, one who continues to suffer the loss of his or her own needs into adult life.

What's another loss after that?

Response *Graduation.*

Speaker Yes, and what happens then?

Response *Leaving home to go to university or to work, leaving friends, breaking up relationships.*

Speaker Not at home, out on your own. And then what happens after a person leaves home, what do they do next?

Response *Find someone else.*

MARRIAGE AS A LOSS

Speaker Yes, and perhaps become attached, maybe get married.

Response *They experience the loss of single life, of freedom.*

Speaker Yes, so there is marriage. Have ever wondered why people cry at their weddings?

(Laughter)

Maybe it's because they are grieving the loss of their single life, their childhood, their freedom, their parental relationship.

Question *Are you talking about the bride and the groom crying?*

Speaker That's right. I couldn't complete my vows. I got stuck in the middle. It was too much.

(Laughter)

Response *My best friend bawled her way through her entire ceremony.*

Speaker That's right. We use tears to express strong emotions, and feelings of loss can be very strong. Marriage illustrates how a loss can also contain the element of gain or vice versa. People console parents by saying, "You haven't lost a son. You've gained a daughter."

I'd been single for 28 years. That was a big piece of life to put behind me. What comes after marriage?

Response *You lose your single friends, at least that happens to a lot of people.*

Speaker Yes, lose your single friends. And what happens then?

Response *Divorce. (Laughter)*

Speaker We've skipped over having children. With children there's a loss of the couple relationship which sometimes is not recovered until the children leave home, and maybe not even then. That's a loss that we've already mentioned and then many people get divorced after they've had the children. Having children is a gain and a loss, and divorce may be a loss and a gain. What else?

DEATH OF A LOVED ONE

Response *By now, somebody close to you must have died.*

Speaker Right, you've probably had deaths of grandparents, maybe friends. And then your parents die, and you lose something of your frame of reference. I am who I am because I know my parents live over there in Marion, Ohio. And when they die, it's as if I'm not from Ohio any more. I can already project that. My parents haven't died yet, but I wonder — where will I go to visit? I won't go back to Ohio.

Response *I've been experiencing the loss of the rest of my family since my parents died. All the other relatives are on their own, unless I reach out. My parents had connected us all.*

Response *There's a loss of family ties which can be very significant.*

Speaker So what's the next loss? You've been divorced, you've been unemployed, maybe you had illness....

Response *Retirement.*

Speaker Retirement, exactly.

Response *Somewhere around middle age there is a loss of youth. The medical evidence suggests this begins in the early twenties. The body starts to go down and there's a loss of energy.*

Response *You could lose your teeth.*

Speaker Yes, loss of teeth, loss of hair, possible loss of virility, going through menopause, and so on.

ADDICTION AS A LOSS

Question *What about the loss a person experiences giving up smoking or drinking?*

Speaker Yes, there can be the loss of habits or addictions. Alcohol or drug addiction is itself a loss because of the lost years of closeness with family members and the lost years of experiencing life's challenges and opportunities. The addict is in a cloud, and his personal growth is arrested. The recovering addict often speaks of the experience of learning to live again as if he is starting over or as if he is learning to walk all over again from an earlier age. The addiction resulted in a loss of skill development, so that in recovery it is as if the person starts where he left off, in the period of adolescence for example, or earlier because the addiction began in order to cover the stress of already delayed development resulting from the loss of parental caring.

So addiction is itself a loss, and when recovery comes another loss occurs which is the loss of the use of the substance. If the emptiness is not acknowledged and validated and then used as a therapeutic trigger to do something different, a relapse may occur. One of the keys to relapse prevention is a proper grieving of the addiction combined with replacing the substance with something healthy, as well as engaging in a process of integrating deeper core issues which preceded the addiction. There may be a loss of friends, the beer buddies, so it's important to replace the repeated dysfunctional family with a supportive group of friends, that is, a "functional family".

Response *There are also losses that occur on a societal level. It seems to me that there's a loss of innocence now with environmental awareness. We can't go on doing what we are doing.*

Speaker We have lost the belief in unending resources. We don't have that kind of freedom anymore. We have to watch ourselves.

Response *That's a loss of ignorance.*

Speaker You can also think of it as a loss of innocence.

Response *Moving from one town to another can be a major loss.*

Speaker Yes, that's a good point. Or maybe it's an attempt to cope with a loss which occurred in the previous town.

For some people who move from one culture to another there is also a loss of culture. This is especially true when the culture is very different. For example, second generation children of immigrants from India are often caught between the parental traditional culture and the Western culture of peers. The resulting alienation from both cultures may result in depression and suicide.

The suicide of a family member or the homicide or abduction of a family member, are also very significant for those who are left or who survive. We will address the painful feelings of these losses in a few moments.

Response *What about house fires?*

Speaker Loss of property, financial loss, and bankruptcy may be significant.

Miscarriage is a loss not often acknowledged. A bond has occurred because parents choose a name and visualize the appearance or sex of the child, perhaps speak to the child, plan for the child's birth. This bond is even more possible today perhaps because of technology which allows parents to see the unborn child on a screen. Abortion is a loss which may develop from the pressure of family members or circumstances and which is connected to the conscious decision or choice of the parent.

Adoption is a loss. We may have been adopted ourselves or perhaps gave up a child for adoption as a birth parent.

Adopted people often repeat the experience of rejecting or of being rejected, repeating the pattern of loss that occurs with adoption.

As we grow older, a spouse or partner dies, and this loss of the loved one may result in the surviving spouse's decision to stop living. The three most difficult losses are the death of a parent, the death of a child, and the death of a spouse.

With aging comes the loss of our faculties, possibly terminal illness and facing our own death.

Some of the other losses that we haven't mentioned might be loss of the family of origin by going into foster care, loss of a pet, loss of puppy love or the first partner, child death and crib death.

The death's of pets and of grandparents are important for the child's learning about the validity of grieving, both by observing the healthy grieving of adults and by receiving support for his own pain.

The death of a child is especially difficult because the parent grieves to some extent for many years thinking about the lost child, as he or she sees other children achieving various milestones of development such as walking, talking, puberty, dating, graduation, marriage, grandchildren, and so on.

Something else I want to point out now is that the various types of loss can be divided into three broad categories which often overlap. These are: 1) the loss of people through death and break-up of a relationship, 2) the loss of roles such as parent, child, employee/worker, spouse, and others, and 3) the loss of health, ranging from brief illness to chronic debilitating illness or injury.

PAINFUL EMOTIONS RELATED TO TYPES OF LOSS

It's important to point out that the intensity of our grief varies according to the type of loss, and the degree of emotional bonding or investment in what was lost. Also, the specific painful feelings associated with grief may vary or predominate depending upon the type of loss. As far as intensity, the degree of pain associated with losing your keys is going to be less than losing a child, for example.

Grief itself is a combination or mosaic of specific and distinct emotions, and the type of loss may help us to understand the specific emotion which stands out or is stronger than others. Also, that specific, predominant painful emotion may hold the key to the client's progress in moving through grief, because the strength of that emotion and the client's difficulty in coping with it, may explain why the client is stuck. That predominant emotion then may need to become the focus of treatment in grief therapy for complicated bereavement.

Think of fear, anger, guilt, sadness, emptiness, low self-worth, and despair — the seven primary painful feelings. Which of these feelings do you imagine might stand out with the suicide of a loved one? What do the surviving family members feel?

Response *Guilt.*

Speaker Guilt is often predominant above the others. The grieving person may feel all the others strongly but guilt is primary because it's a feeling that, "I could have said or done something or should have observed something."

Often the key to grief counselling for family members and friends after a suicide, is to identify and work with the anger toward the loved one who committed suicide. The guilt is easier than the anger for family members to present and identify, so guilt is used as a defense to cover anger.

What about the empty nest? When the last child leaves home? What is the predominant feeling?

Response *Emptiness.*

Speaker Yes, because the absence of the child combined with the loss of the parenting role, may leave a terrible emptiness. I had a female client who suddenly became very preoccupied with church activities when the child left home. The husband complained that he missed her because she was gone so much of the time. The key was for her was to share her grief with him so that they could support each other and become closer as a couple rather than for her to separate as she was doing.

What about adoption? What does the adopted person feel deep down?

Response *Low self-worth.*

Speaker Yes. Often well-meaning social workers tell the child or adoptive parents tell the child that the natural mother loved the child and that giving the child up for adoption was the most loving thing the mother could do because the birth mother knew she couldn't care for the child. This sounds very nice and consoling but often it goes in only on an intellectual level. On a feeling level, the adopted person may feel low self-worth, rejected, abandonned, unloved and unloveable, as well as angry, sad, empty and the other feelings.

The importance of grief for the adopted person is expressed by the growing Parent Finders movement, where adopted people and birth parents meet together and talk about ways to find the person they have lost. On the side of the birth parent, the predominant feeling is often guilt, and anger toward people or circumstances that forced the adoption.

What about a crib death?

Response *Guilt.*

Speaker Guilt, yes. Parents believe they could have done something to prevent the death, not realizing that the baby may have had immature respiratory development. Guilt is predominant usually in the death of any child as well as in miscarriage and abortion. Parents being parents naturally feel responsible for the child, born or unborn. In abortion, the guilt often comes from having chosen to abort even if the parent intellectually believes it to be right. The parent may associate the child with himself as a child, containing part of himself or herself, or can not escape the belief that a life was taken.

What about bankruptcy?

Response *Despair. Low self-worth.*

Speaker Low self-worth. People kill themselves because their self-worth is attached to their financial resources which are lost. What's the point of living if you have no worth?

What about retirement? What would be a primary feeling there?

Response *Emptiness.*

Speaker Emptiness, yes, and low self-worth. Maybe you put all your energy, your self, into your work. Your sense of usefulness, purpose, and value have been in that basket, and now you're retired and its all gone.

Response *People tend to identify themselves with their role and if that's a really strong role and it ends, they might not know who they are anymore.*

Response *For people who are forced to retire, there's a lot of anger.*

Speaker Yes, absolutely. So the key in treatment is to support the grief, then help the person to diversify, develop other interests, and it takes time.

Response *Life as you know it has drastically changed.*

MULTIPLE LOSSES

Speaker One loss often results in multiple loss. For example, I have a client who had a brain tumour about eight years ago. She underwent surgery, and as a result she lost her job as a supervisor for a major firm. She lost her husband who couldn't cope with her resulting disability. She had to go into a group home so she lost her independence, and she had never had any children so the prospect of having children was lost. She had impaired memory, impaired vision, impaired speech, and had to use a walker to get around. She had multiple physical losses and the losses of roles and relationships.

Parenting is another example. When your children leave home, you not only lose them but you lose the role of being a parent. And that kind of ripple effect may be true of a number of types of losses.

Another example of multiple loss occurs when an earlier unresolved loss results in subsequent losses. The child who grows up in a dysfunctional family, repeats the loss of caring in adulthood in his own nuclear dysfunctional family.

The child from the alcoholic family, repeats the addiction in adulthood. The child who loses mother at age eight, marries but remains emotionally detached from her own children, and so loses the closeness with them.

GOALS OF GRIEF COUNSELLING

Let's go now to reviewing the goals of grief counselling briefly, which is to deal with the seven most painful feelings.

Response *I guess those are the bottom line painful feelings that can possibly be felt and everything else is a derivative of them.*

Speaker Yes, every other painful feeling can be related to those. For example, anger is at the root of resentment and frustration, fear is the source of anxiety and insecurity, and emptiness gives rise to abandonment and loneliness. Shame is a combination of fear and guilt. It's a fear about what other people might think if they knew, and even if they don't know, it's a fear of what they would think about me if they knew.

There are three goals in grief counselling. The first and fundamental goal is to identify and experience the range and intensity of painful feelings which constitute grief. We're going to help the client to identify the feelings cognitively, and then to experience the full range from fear to despair as well as the intensity of the painful feelings related to his loss, or losses.

The second goal is to identify changes or maladaptive behaviour decisions which are related to the loss. This goal is very important in cases of complicated loss, which occurs when the painful feelings have not been dealt with in a healthy way. Instead of being expressed and shared, they've been defended against and protected, resulting in very maladapted behaviours. By maladaptive we mean ineffective or unworkable or unhealthy behaviour decisions. When we see these behaviours continuing over years, over a long period of time, then we're seeing this as a complicated bereavement experience of our client.

"Decisions" is an interesting word because the behaviour choices, or ways of coping with the pain, are often done unintentionally or unconsciously, but they are decisions none the less. A person can re-decide, can make different decisions about that pain and how to cope with it, how to deal with it.

The third goal of grief counselling is to complete unfinished business, and to say goodbye in order to say hello. It's difficult to say hello to new life experiences until we say goodbye to old painful ones, and by goodbye we mean letting go. Saying goodbye, and letting go, and learning acceptance, which is a commonly used term, all mean the same thing.

Saying goodbye really encompasses all three objectives for grief counselling. A person hasn't completely grieved, or said goodbye, or let go, until he has worked through the pain, identified and changed the behaviour decisions, and finished the unfinished business.

You can see that these goals correspond to the counselling process as we've been discussing it. It's simply a reiteration of what we've been talking about.

As we're talking about loss and grief today and tomorrow I'd like for you to be thinking about your own losses. These could be deaths of loved ones, break-up of relationships, loss of parental caring are among the more difficult ones.

Question *Once you've identified a loss and the person can express the sadness, how often do you go back to that loss? It seems to me that a person could experience those feelings surrounding a loss indefinitely just by putting themselves back in that place again. How do you know when enough is enough?*

Speaker There are two different views. The cognitive school says you don't really get rid of the pain, you just know all about it. You become so familiar with it that it no longer has power over you. And the only way to know all about it is to experience it. There's no other way. So there is a point at which cognitive therapy must include grieving, otherwise there's no true knowledge of the pain.

The other school of thought which is represented, for example, by people who use psychodrama, is that when you express the pain it's possible to release it, and to purge yourself of it. It might take a long time for that catharsis to be complete, but eventually the pain will be completely gone.

I tend to think it's a combination of both. There is a catharsis effect, and some of the pain is released, but then there is also the cognitive aspect of gaining knowledge which comes from experiencing the intensity of the pain that takes the power away from it.

Response *You've faced the fear of the pain.*

Speaker That's right. I'm no longer frightened of it. I know about it and I've accepted it as mine, and as OK, as valid.

PAINFUL FEELINGS OF LOSS

Now let's go on to looking at the specific painful feelings. The first and fundamental goal of grief counselling is to identify and experience the range and intensity of painful feelings. It's going to be important for us to review these feelings, to understand what each feeling may be about, and to suggest some therapeutic interventions for working with each painful feeling.

FEAR

Fear is the first of the seven painful feelings. We also need to realize what the fear of painful feelings is about.

Imagine a successful executive of a corporation who has never experienced any tragedy in his life, any major loss. He has a wife and three kids and he gets a phone call that one of his children, a six or seven year old child, has just been hit by a truck and killed in front of the house. The child came home from school and crossed the road in front of a gravel truck coming from a nearby construction site, and was killed. Now this man has a lot of responsibility to provide for his family and to keep his company going, and since he has experienced a tragic loss he goes for counselling. It's very difficult for him to engage his pain, because he's afraid of what?

Response *He's going to crack. He won't be able to keep his life together.*

Speaker Yes, exactly. So he's afraid of falling apart and of not being able to get on with all of the things he has to do.

Response *He needs to maintain the image of the corporate person.*

Speaker That's right. And to continue with his heavy responsibilities. So not having experienced intense grief before, he doesn't know that it's not going to cause him to fall apart. In fact he doesn't realize that if he doesn't allow himself to grieve, then he's going to fall apart. It's going to be just the opposite of what he's afraid of. So we need to help that person get past the fear, and the way to do that is to encourage him to talk about the fear, to validate the fear, to reflect how scary it might be, and then invite him just to say a little bit about it.

I find that is a very effective approach when working with the very blocked, resistant client. Invite him to say just a little bit about the little bit of fear that he might have. And once he feels supported with that, then he can go on to another painful feeling.

ANGER

Some grieving people find it easier to access anger than their sadness. They'll use their anger to defend against their sadness. They feel strong with anger but weak and vulnerable with sadness. Generally the person who finds it easier to access anger in grief has an aggressive personality. He is usually outspoken, direct, and opinionated.

In working with the very angry, grieving client, we can validate that anger for as long as he needs it to be validated. Draw it out and encourage him to express it, entitle him to that anger.

If we're able to validate or support a person's anger, what feeling comes next?

Response *Sadness.*

Speaker Sadness, yes. The sadness will come out more easily if the anger has been properly supported. Now with the passive individual, who accesses sadness more easily, we need to help him express the anger. The passive individual feels guilty about anger and is afraid of its destructiveness. So to reach for anger we can use the word cheated, or another word that the person feels safer with.

So we can say, "I wonder if you feel a little cheated? Your husband has died, you expected you'd be able to retire together, you were looking forward to that. And now he's gone. I wonder if you feel just a little bit cheated about that?" And often times what I find is if I minimize a feeling and use the word cheated with that individual, he'll maximize and say, "Yes, I feel really cheated". And I'll say, "Go on and say more about being cheated." In fact he is talking about his anger, but he is just not using that word.

Try to find words that don't offend the client or that don't trigger the guilt or fear around anger. Try to use other approaches and other words. Let me suggest some other approaches.

You can say things like, "What are some why questions? If you're to ask why questions about the death of your father, or the death or your child, what would they be?" What are some of those why questions?"

Response *Why did you die?*

Speaker Yes, why him?

Response *Why did they leave me?*

Speaker Why did they leave me, yes.

Response *Why not me?*

Speaker Why not me? Why him? What else? Why did God let this happen? Often the anger is directed at God. Alright, so then I'll say, "What's the feeling that goes with that why question? Fear, anger, guilt, sadness, emptiness?"

Response *I guess if it was a child people would ask why a child died? Why not an older person?*

Speaker Yes. Why not someone who'd lived his full life? Why a child? Anger is what goes with that question — the outrage, the sense of injustice, the unfairness. Often times your client will come up with anger. Then you can invite him to say more about the anger. And you can validate it, support it.

Another thing we can do is say, "Talk about the lost hopes and dreams." Lost hopes and dreams are about being cheated because those hopes and dreams can't be fulfilled now that this death and this loss has occurred. There's a sense of feeling cheated about that. Another thing I might do to draw anger is to design a statement for my client to repeat. I might design a why question or a blaming statement.

For example in the case of an abusive parent, in working with loss of parental caring and closeness, I might suggest the statement, "You didn't care about anyone but yourself. You didn't care about me, all you cared about was the bottle." Try on that statement. I might say it without any affect in my voice.

You can tailor a statement, invite your client to repeat it, and then reach for a feeling. "What's it like saying that? Does that fit? What feeling comes up when you say that? What choice words do you have for this man?" Go for choice words in reaching for anger, if your client has them in his vocabulary. Choice words refers to name-calling, for example, "monster", "stupid", etc. The passive client might not have choice words in his vocabulary.

Response *Some of these words could possibly be very coarse and powerful.*

Speaker Yes, allow emotion to be expressed. Name calling, things like that are okay. I'm talking here about the client who has been severely abused and mistreated. We need to have a way to vent that anger in a therapeutic way.

Question *So you don't really want to escalate it but you want to allow this person to feel that it's okay to feel angry?*

Response *You give them some tools.*

Response *Put on the boxing gloves.*

Speaker Yes, that's the idea. When I'm starting to bring out anger and sadness with a client, I might also say, "I wonder if you're using that anger to defend against another feeling." Or, "I wonder if that anger is easier than the sadness." Or if a client identifies both anger and sadness I'll say, "Which of those two feelings is easier for you to express?"

She might have identified anger as a primary feeling, and I might reach for a little sadness. She might have owned a little sadness and then I would say, "Which one is easier for you to feel?" And which ever one she chooses I'll invite her to talk about the opposite one.

Question *What's the reason you pick the opposite?*

Speaker Because it's the one she doesn't want to talk about, and the key to a person's progress is invite her to explore whatever is most difficult.

GUILT

Guilt is one of the primary reasons that people develop very maladaptive behaviours. A person who feels very guilty doesn't believe that he deserves happiness, and so what does he think he deserves?

Response *Punishment.*

Speaker Punishment goes with guilt, so I might want to explore with the person how much guilt he feels? Maybe a little bit, a lot? This is the same technique I might use exploring any feeling. How much anger do you feel? A little bit, a lot, a medium amount? I want to gauge how much of that feeling he are aware of inside.

If he feel a lot of guilt, or he identify a feeling of guilt I'm going to say, "I wonder if you're aware of how you might be punishing yourself."

And then I'll say what some people do. "Sometimes when people feel guilty they won't let themselves be happy, they'll be depressed, they'll be stuck in their life. They won't let themselves get on with their life. They won't let themselves experience enjoyment, they won't let themselves be close to people, they won't let themselves really welcome the challenges and opportunities that life has to offer. And I wonder if you're aware of how you might be punishing yourself in some small way?"

So again use that minimizing technique, because it's easier for people to think of small ways sometimes and then that opens up other areas of awareness. So a person will choose and then I'll say, "I wonder if you're going to give yourself a life sentence?" That's making use of exaggeration. In other words, take that metaphor to its ultimate conclusion, or to it's extreme, which could be something like a life sentence of punishment by means of depression.

For example, I had a client who lived a rebellious life, and then his mother suddenly died of a heart attack. He blamed himself for his mother's death and he became chronically depressed after that for a number of years. When I saw him in treatment I explored the guilt with him, and I said, "I wonder how you might punish yourself? I wonder if maybe depression is a way you might do that?" And he acknowledged it. And he went on saying that he didn't deserve to be happy. He felt that his life style was a cause of his mother's death. And so I said, "I wonder if you're going to give yourself a life sentence?" And he stopped and the wheels were turning and he made a new decision. He pulled back from the guilt.

With the extreme or the exaggerated intervention, a person will pull back from the exaggerated possibility. He'll say, "No, I'm not going to take it to that extent." This client started making real changes, real improvements in his direction. When people feel really guilty, they won't allow themselves to get on with their grieving. They'll remain stuck in it and that's their punishment.

They won't let themselves work through their sadness and their anger, or other painful feelings, because hanging on to the guilt is a way of hanging on to the person who died. Sometimes I'll put it to a client that way. I'll say, "I wonder if hanging on to that guilt might be a way of hanging on to Mom?" And often times he doesn't realize it, he hasn't thought of it in those terms. When you put it that way it helps him to decide not to hang on.

I've heard clients say, "I don't want to hang on any more." That that implies giving up, letting go of the guilt. You can use that with anger. "I wonder if hanging on to that anger is a way of hanging on to the man you divorced? Hanging on to the fight might be a way of hanging on to your ex-husband. Hanging on to the fight might be a way of hanging on to Dad."

Response *The thing I always hear is, "How do you let go?"*

Speaker And I say, "By doing exactly what you're doing today. Talking about your feelings, putting it into words, by doing exactly what you're doing and I encourage you to keep doing that. What's it like doing that today? Talking about your pain." And he'll say, "It's tough."

SADNESS

Speaker I mentioned that some people use anger to cover sadness and others use sadness to cover anger. So sadness is not necessarily the core feeling, although often for the person who's very angry, it's important for him to get to his sadness.

And for the person who's very sad, especially if she appears to be stuck in her sadness, over a long period of time — weeks, months, or maybe years. Maybe it's because she hasn't dealt with her anger, and she hasn't dealt with her guilt.

EMPTINESS

So then we come to emptiness. Emptiness is something a person might feel constantly. But often times a person will fill the emptiness, or attempt to fill that empty feeling or that void with the other painful feelings. It's easier to feel anger than that agonizing emptiness or that sense of the void, that abandonment, that loneliness.

Often times, early on in grief counselling, that person might identify feeling empty, and the way I might work with that is to say, "What goes into that emptiness? Would it be empty sad, empty angry, empty frightened, empty guilty, empty what?" I'll associate another feeling with the emptiness.

And I might work with the emptiness on its own, and just invite the person to talk about the emptiness. He might talk about a loved one he lost, who had been in his life at the dinner table, or in bed with him if it's a partner, a spouse. She has come to the door at the same time on schedule for so many months or years, and now that person is gone and so there are empty spaces at the table, in the bedroom, at the door.

When a child dies there is tremendous emptiness because that child has occupied so much of the parents' time, and has contributed so much to the noise level. The child leaves a deafening silence that's very agonizing. We need to help a person identify what the emptiness is about and then validate that.

Now the emptiness might become more apparent to a person as he gets support and is able to put these other painful feelings, the anger or sadness, into words. As he is letting go of that anger or sadness, the emptiness might still be there and it might be even more obvious to the person. And most especially, I find that clients report feeling empty when I invite them to talk about letting go or saying goodbye to the loved one.

For example, I sometimes use the empty chair to invite a person to talk to a loved one about saying goodbye, and I then explore the feelings that he is left with. I say, "What's it like, what are you feeling inside as you say goodbye and as you talk about saying goodbye to your father or your child? What feelings come up? Fear, anger, guilt, emptiness, despair?" And nine times out of ten he chooses emptiness because that's what's left if you're going to say goodbye to somebody, that empty feeling.

Now if a person has done a fair amount of grieving, I'll work with that emptiness in a therapeutic way by saying, "Maybe you're at a kind of crossroads in your grief. You can either fill that emptiness with the old pain, your old ways of being stuck and not getting on with your life, not letting yourself be close to other people, or you can begin to fill that emptiness with the challenges that life has to offer, taking risks to get closeness, allowing yourself to enjoy pleasurable experiences in life." Which way do you think he'll go on this crossroad?

That's a cognitive technique that allows the client to make a conscious decision about what she is going to do or what way he is going to go.

TIME-FRAME FOR GRIEVING

Question *What kind of a time frame are we looking at? I mean you can't say it's been three months, it's time to do something. But roughly, how long do people need to grieve?*

Speaker It really depends. If you lose a child you might grieve for years. To assess that we're looking at the individual's ability to function. Is this person able to go back to work, able to get on with the important aspects of his life? Or is he still doing things that are getting in the way of family, social relationships and work?

Has there been some grief that appears to be getting in the way? Depending upon the type of loss, such as the loss of a family member, we might expect a person to grieve intensely. If he was emotionally bonded to someone he might grieve intensely for maybe a year. He might be able to get back to work after a month but the pain of that grief might hang on for considerable time, even for years to come.

Response *I know of a situation where a woman married a man, who disclosed to her after two or three years of marriage that he was homosexual, and then he ended the relationship. She didn't appear to go through any grieving process at all. She went back to work the next day and two months later she met another man. They got married and had kids, and I'm not aware of her going through any process like this. Is it likely to happen later on?*

Speaker Alright, that's a good question. Grief will only be experienced as an intense kind of experience if there's been bonding. If there hasn't been significant emotional bonding...

Response *It's not as much of a loss.*

Speaker It's not as much of a loss, that's right. And if he was homosexual it's understandable that there might not have been much intimacy, or closeness, or bonding. It might have been some other kind of relationship, more like a brother and sister rather than husband and wife.

Question *So it has to do with how much is invested?*

Speaker That's right. A woman came up to me after a talk I had given and said that when her mother died she didn't grieve. And she wanted to know why, because other people grieve. She wondered why she wasn't upset. I asked her, "Were you close to your mother?" and she said, "No." She had never been close all those years. And I said, "I wonder what feelings come up inside you when you think about all those years of not being close to your mother?" That's when the tears welled up in her eyes. That's what her grief was about. It wasn't about her mother's death, it was about the loss of closeness during her lifetime.

LOW SELF-WORTH

A person might feel low self-worth, especially if she is experiencing feelings of guilt, because when a person feels very guilty she does't feel worthwhile, she doesn't believe she deserves to go on living.

A person might also experience low self-worth if he comes from a dysfunctional family and now has experienced a tragic death of a loved one. He may feel as though he didn't really deserve to have that person be alive for him.

Low self-worth sometimes happens when people bargain, often times with God, over the life of the person who died. So you might hear about a person saying, "I'm really the one who should die. Don't let that child die. Take me, God." So in that kind of bargaining the implied message is, "I'm not as worthwhile as the child."

A person might then become very depressed, and isolate himself or deprive himself of enjoyment in life because he doesn't feel worthwhile or deserving.

In cases of sexual abuse, low self-worth is connected to shame or to feeling dirty. What do you do with something if it's dirty?

Response *You chuck it out.*

Speaker You throw it away. That's another kind of loss that we haven't yet talked about. Sexual abuse and assault is a very significant loss. Feeling dirty or feeling shame is closely related to that.

DESPAIR

Despair and hopelessness are the sum total of these other painful feelings, and as a person is engaging in the grief process and getting support and validation, often that despair will diminish. The despair might appear early on along with fear, but as the safety of the counselling relationship increases and the therapy alliance improves, despair often times diminishes along with the fear.

Despair often goes with confusion. A person may have a lot of painful feelings inside that he has not identified, especially early in the grief process. He feels despair because he has the intensity of all that pain but he hasn't been able to sort it out. So as you work with him throughout the process and identify the distinct feelings and help him work through them, the confusion and the despair diminish.

Question *If a person has suffered tremendous losses throughout his lifetime, do you feel that the coping process is easier for him?*

Speaker It depends on how he has dealt with those previous losses. If he has coped with his previous losses in an unhealthy way by burying feelings, or by dumping feelings, or by distancing himself from others, that can become a pattern in relationships.

For example, some people won't say goodbye — they'll just leave and you'll wonder where they went. And it may be that that's related to their way of not letting go or their style of dealing with loss and separation from an earlier experience in life. Often times when a person experiences a tragic loss it will bring up his previous losses. And if there seems to be difficulty establishing and maintaining intimate relationships and getting on with life goals, it may be due to unfinished business with a previous loss.

UNFINISHED BUSINESS OF LOSS

Speaker As we discuss unfinished business, we're referring to unspoken words. These are things that the grieving person did not have an opportunity to say to the loved one, or if he had the opportunity he didn't use it. Some examples are unspoken apology, unspoken forgiveness, and unspoken unresolved anger and conflicts which really belong in a group because apology and forgiveness have to do with resolving conflict.

Maybe the client didn't say, "I'm sorry, will you forgive me?" or didn't say, "I forgive you" for something, and so that becomes unfinished business. Maybe the client wished that he could have heard the person who died say, "I forgive you" or, "I'm sorry for the way I treated you" for the abuse or whatever. But the person died before that conversation could ever be experienced.

It may be that certain issues were avoided and maintained as secrets, and so that becomes unfinished business. As we're talking about these areas of unfinished business I'd like you to think about how they would apply to the client who's loved one is still alive but might have these words waiting to be spoken, and about your own relationships and people in your life that you have unfinished business with.

There might be unspoken affection and caring, not having said, "I love you, I care about you, I'll miss you when you die." Unspoken affection and caring also includes not reminiscing with a loved one about all the good times they had together and all the tough times.

In some families it's very difficult for people to say "I love you" to each other. It's something that we have to do regularly for it to be part of us, part of our communication. And if we lapse into not saying it and a person dies, after years of not having said it to him, a person might be left feeling what?

Response *Guilty.*

Speaker Guilty. Feelings of regret.

Response *To do that with someone — with another family member, what if you really don't love him?*

Speaker What gets in the way of loving him?

Response *Well you are with friends because you choose to be but you're with family members because of blood ties.*

Speaker I would ask the client what gets in the way of her love for that family member. What would get in the way?

Response *Anger or fear.*

Speaker Anger, conflict, abuse — those kinds of things. Maybe there were years of distance because of alcoholism, infidelity, passivity, chronic conflict or criticism, absence due to workaholism. Whatever creates distance may prevent the kind of bonding that makes expressions of affection possible.

There might be unspoken goodbyes, if a person dies and the client didn't have a chance to be with him. He might have died suddenly or maybe he died in a distant location. And so a person is left feeling regret. When there is significant unfinished business, there is complicated grief often times. It increases the sadness and the regret and the guilt, so it makes grieving much more difficult and intense.

We can also speak of unspoken loss of closeness, which is really to do with unresolved issues, unresolved conflict, but never being able to talk to the loved one about the closeness that was missed. And so that becomes unfinished business. If a person can address the unfinished business before the loved one dies, then it makes the grieving much easier.

Question *What if it's not a loved one but somebody who has been in an abusive relationship with them, and there is no love lost between them?*

Speaker When I say loved one I mean that in a very broad sense. It could mean significant other or any family member. And if it was an abusive relationship then that means that there is this area that is unspoken or unresolved, or unfinished.

Response *I know a woman who had been sexually abused, and when she went to counsellors and therapists this always came up, the unfinished business she had with her parents because her mother didn't step in and stop the abuse. And she followed through on going and talking to her parents because she felt the counsellor wanted her to but it didn't do anything for her.*

Speaker What was she expecting?

Response *Well I can't say what she was expecting, but I would guess that she was expecting her parents to start the relationship on a different level perhaps. She might have been expecting to have a relationship with them.*

Speaker If that was what she expected then its understandable she would say nothing changed. When I suggest a client go talk to parents about unfinished business and unresolved issues, it's very important to make clear to her that she is doing this in order to verbalize the issues for herself, not to change the parents. In fact what she may find is that the parents are not going to change. They're not going to be any different. And how will that leave the client feeling?

Response *Frustrated.*

Speaker Frustrated, yes, and empty and sad. The client then is faced with having to grieve the reality that the parents are closed rather than open.

Response *That was her report after she went there. It was like she had never left home. Everything was exactly the same. She presented her issues to them, and they just went on with life, nothing changed.*

Speaker They didn't show any more understanding or caring. It was just the same as it always had been.

Response *So that could be a loss then, the death or loss of the relationship, or maybe of the longing to have that relationship.*

Speaker The longing to have the understanding and the openness, the support, and caring. That's right.

Response *So the client goes for her own benefit, not to change the parent or to get understanding from the parent.*

Speaker The client goes for the client, exactly, not for the parents but to take care of her own pain and grief. Now the reason that people don't address unfinished business is because of a protection racket, which is precisely the same thing the person does to himself around his own pain. The individual who has come through painful life experiences might protect himself from the pain by using what?

Response *Denial.*

Speaker Denial and a variety of other defenses that you have a list of. A person doesn't face family members and significant others with unfinished business. It's probably because of the protection racket which is made up of the fear and the guilt: there is the fear of hurting, and the fear of being hurt. If I bring this up, if I mention this I'm going to cause my dying loved one more suffering. It's going to upset them, or from the perspective of the dying person, if I tell my family members that I'm dying it's just going to make them hurt more so I won't tell them to make it easier for them.

In reality it makes things much more difficult not to tell them. But there's a protection racket because of the fear of hurting or being hurt. I won't go to my father because I'm afraid if I do he'll just reject me again and he'll tell me not to talk like that or not to bring that up now after all these years. There's that fear and that guilt, the fear that if I say something and it hurts the other person, he will be hurt in some way and then I'll feel guilty about what I said. I'll regret it and so I'm not going to say it in the first place.

Response *I think ultimately it's finally coming to terms with the loss of the closeness. There never will be a relationship with that person, and pursuing anything is futile. This is my experience with my father anyway.*

Speaker Okay, so if you go to your father to tell him how you feel, your purpose in doing it would be what?

Response *To protect myself.*

Speaker It wouldn't be to protect yourself, but to take care of yourself, to get that stuff from the inside of you to the outside so that you can say I've said what I needed to say and he did what he did. He did what he had to do, or what he chose to do, and I did what I had to do for myself.

Question *So that's an acceptance, right?*

Speaker Yes. Now it might involve another level of grieving when you are faced with the reality that he's not going to be any different. He's going to be just as rejecting as ever.

Response *He may even become more hostile.*

Speaker Yes, that's possible, but it's more likely he'll just be as hostile as before.

Question *What do you do now that you've brought up the unfinished business but there's no positive response? Then there's something else that you have to deal with, isn't there?*

Speaker That's right. It's a grief. But you see it's not something new. It's something that has been there all the time. The reality of the closed parent has been your experience all those years. It's not something that just happened now that you've faced him with it. What's happened is maybe you are realizing for the first time what the relationship is really like, so it allows you to get on with grieving the loss of caring.

Response *For an example, my oldest brother is old enough to be my father, and I've always looked at him like a father since my dad died several years back. He really reminds me of my dad. I would like to have done things with him like I could have done with my dad. We've never really had a chance to be close because I have felt that whenever I've been around it's exactly like it was with Dad. He doesnÆt acknowledge my presence when I'm in the room. So if I went and I told him that I know what his reaction would be. For me to have to go tell him that and to see his reaction would hurt me even more.*

Speaker Have you ever done it? Have you ever gone and told him and expressed these issues to him?

Response *Exactly how I feel?*

Speaker Yes.

Response *Not really, I guess because of that fear. We only get together maybe once a year. But you know, different times where I have made an attempt to talk to him he just shoos me off like I'm still a little snot-nosed kid.*

Speaker We'll work more with this very area of difficulty a littel later on, because it really is important to work with a client to assess what his style has been in approaching family members.

Response *You can give people information and then they can choose to change, but you can't make them change.*

Speaker You can intimidate them. You can frighten them into submission, but that's not really change.

Response *In other words it doesn't matter if they buy into what I'm saying, at least I've expressed it. I'm getting better without banking on the other person loving me more as a result.*

Speaker Exactly. Now if you find that the parent or family member is open to you, then there might be a chance that you can gain something for the rest of your lives together. And if you find that he or she is just as closed as they ever have been, even if you approach them in a caring, non-dumping way, then that means that it's time to get on with your grieving and let go. Even if there is openness and support from the parent now, there is still a need to grieve the missing years, the lost caring for all the years past.

Response *You have to take the risk. That's what I've had to do to move on.*

Speaker That's right.

Response *It's amazing what happens sometimes when you take a risk. You think something terrible is going to happen and it never does.*

Speaker It's the child in us who is so frightened and so caught up in a protection racket that we remain in that child ego state. That's why we recommend that when the client is ready he approach the people that he has unfinished business with. Doing that allows him to grow up into his adult self.

The child who is either very frightened or very abusive and dumping does the same thing with the parent that the parent perhaps did to the child. The child gets caught up in a fight, or runs away.

It's the adult who can face and express the issues in a straightforward caring, sharing kind of way rather than a dumping way. So when a client can do that, he has taken an important therapeutic steps toward growing into his adult self.

Question *Are there ever any families where the child leaves home without unfinished business?*

Speaker Some are pretty close to that but there's no such thing as a perfect family. But if you look at the continuum between the closed, abusive family and the open nurturing family, there are many families on the open, nurturing end.

Response *I guess I'll never get to work with them.*

Speaker That's right. You won't see those families or individuals from those families in counselling.

Response *Grow your own.(Laughter)*

BEHAVIOUR DECISIONS OF LOSS

Speaker Let's look at behaviour decisions in grief counselling. As we said earlier in discussing the counselling process, the behaviour decisions are related directly to the pain.

Painful life experiences can result in unhealthy, ineffective behaviours and in destructive attitudes or beliefs about self and others. When a person has strong pain in grief that pain often results in certain kinds of decisions.

Let's consider the loss of an intimate relationship. Two people have been going together, and they've been very emotionally bonded. They've developed hopes and dreams about their life together, getting married, having a family, and growing old together, and then one person dies, or decides to leave the relationship. The other person might decide never to get too close to anyone again.

I had a client who was in a relationship with a young man and they were going to get married, but she got cold feet and delayed their plans. He came over that night at about two o'clock in the morning to try to talk to her, to try to change her mind. He was crossing the street and was struck by a hit-and-run driver and killed. She was left with tremendous guilt. When I saw her in counselling she made comments like, "I don't think I can ever find anyone like him. I don't think I'll get close to anyone again." So she made the decision we are talking about: "I will never get too close to anyone."

A woman whose mother died when she was a child got married and had children of her own, but she always maintained a certain distance, an aloofness from them. She made that same kind of decision and adopted the belief, "If you invest too much, get too close, you might lose again and that will hurt." People often conclude that intimacy isn't worth the risk. Guilt might go with that decision as well. "I will punish myself; I don't deserve to be happy; I don't deserve to be close."

As I'm working with a person to identify his behaviour decisions I might, in a similar way that I give a person a feeling list, give him a list of decisions that people often make. I ask him if he can identify what decision he would have made and then invite him to talk about it. These behaviour decisions constitute life patterns. They could be attached to a death or to an abusive dysfunctional family of origin experience such as alcoholic parents, abusive parents, workaholic, or distant emotionally unavailable parents. The client's thinking may be along the lines of: "I will run away, I'll move to another town. I'll move out of this house where this death occurred, where this person who I cared about died. I can't face being around his belongings. Too many memories are here so I'm going to go somewhere else. I'll run away from the pain."

What people don't realize is that the pain isn't in the house, it's up here in the head. You can't run away from that. The client can try by using his defenses, and in so doing he is running away, unable to get on with his life.

A child who experiences a tragic loss might say, "I won't grow up, I'll just stay stuck where I am." A woman whose father died when she was ten and was 38 when I saw her, was really still a ten year old, emotionally and socially. The man she married was a father for her. She was his child. She couldn't go out of the house because she was agoraphobic. She had a fear of public places. She had to be escorted wherever she went. She never drove a car or worked outside the home. She had a child but the child was more a sibling than a son.

Speaker A person may also try to rejoin the lost loved one. What's the ultimate way of rejoining?

Response *Suicide.*

Speaker That's right. We need to be alert to any possibility that the client is not safe with himself or herself. A less extreme way of rejoining the lost one is to look for her in another person: This could be someone who resembles the partner physically or behaviourally. The client I was speaking of earlier, who found someone who was a father-like figure to her, had made all of the maladaptive decisions. She found her dead father in the man she married. She wouldn't grow up and get on with her life. Her father had died of a heart attack the day after he climbed a hill looking for her, and so she felt tremendous guilt because she thought it was her fault for leaving the house. She punished herself by staying stuck in her grief. She wouldn't allow herself to have friends. She wasn't close to anybody except in this safe role as a child of the man she married.

Enshrinement is a way to join a lost person by maintaining the loved one's belongings just as they were. I had a client who disassembled his brother's room and reassembled it in his own apartment, and then he would go in there and experience his brother's presence. In his case that kind of enshrinement was due to a very dysfunctional family in which parents were alcoholics and distant. He and his brother had formed a very close relationship. The enshrined loved one is also idealized. However, idealization can occur without enshrinement.

Idealization is when a person tends to see the dead person as perfect, as having no flaws. This might also be a way of protecting against anger or resentment toward the loved one. One way we can begin to help a person remove the idealizing defense is to have him talk about what might have annoyed him just a little bit. Use that same principle of going for the little bits of resentment or irritation, or annoyed feelings. As long as the loved one is up on a pedestal, it becomes a way of hanging on to him or her.

Question *So they're not ready to say goodbye?*

Speaker The client is not ready to say goodbye. And we find that as soon as the client is able to achieve a more balanced picture of a loved one, he is able to get on with the grieving. Often it's protection against anger.

Question *Isn't there a little bit of enshrinement in our society with markers on graves, or is that more a positive thing? I'm thinking of people who go and visit graves. Is that hanging on to a person?*

Speaker It's not the kind of unhealthy behaviour that we're talking about, and there's almost always some degree of enshrinement when someone dies. Frequently people will maintain the belongings of the loved one. They might even keep a place for the loved one at the table. It may become a problem when it continues on for a very long time, for months or years. Keeping the cremated remains may not be a problem by itself, for instance, but the key is if you see other dysfunctional behaviours, such as difficulty getting on with social and occupational life, that indicate the person is stuck.

Response *We also have memorial services and markers where no one is buried, and graves for the unknown soldier and the like. Some people go back again and again to talk to and grieve for the lost person.*

Speaker That's right. The disadvantage of not having a body is that some people find it difficult to accept the reality of the death without it.

THERAPEUTIC INTERVENTIONS

What I'd like to do now is suggest some therapeutic interventions you might use, especially in relation to the death of a loved one.

One of the things I might say in the beginning of the session would be, "Talk about this person. What was he like?" With that statement we're helping the person to reconstruct images and memories of the person. It's a very broad open-ended intervention. "Tell me about the good times you had together." When a person responds to that, he is coming up with memories, pictures in the mind about things that happened. What do you imagine might occur as the client begins to talk about the good times?

Response *They might feel loss.*

Speaker Yes, the loss of the good times. He might begin to feel sad because as he begins to talk about the good times, he realizes that the good times are gone. There won't be any more good times. So sadness often comes up.

"What didn't you like about him even a little bit," is what I might say if a person is idealizing. Another way to work with idealizing is to exaggerate the idealization by saying, "So your father was absolutely flawless and perfect. Is that what you're saying? Never said an unkind word, never offended anyone?"

Question *What if they agree with you?*

Speaker The client may agree, so it might not work. Another approach is to say, "I wonder what feeling might come up if you began to look at the flaws." The idealization is about the fear of letting go, sometimes the fear of emptiness. The loved one was needed too much in life, so the tendency is to hang on to the loved one in death.

Sometimes idealization is used to cover up a secret associated with feelings of fear, guilt, and shame. One of my clients who was chronically depressed, idealized a son who died in a car accident. I said to her, "Was he drinking when he died?" She wept as she acknowledged the truth. Mentioning the unmentionable secret allowed her to take the son off the pedestal and to get on with her grieving.

"Talk about the illness." The illness may have been a very difficult period of time, with a lot of suffering. A person might have a lot of feelings recalling that, a lot of mental images and memories about the suffering person.

Response *Some people are dying, waiting for death, for years.*

Speaker That's right, yes. There might be a feeling of relief when the loved one finally dies.

"How did he die?" This may get into the area of things that the person would prefer not to mention, like suicide. The fact that the person may have committed suicide may have been glossed over or covered up in some way. But as the client describes how the death occurred, you may as a counsellor wonder if this was a suicide. You might say, "Have you ever thought that maybe he committed suicide?" Mentioning the unmentionable is often important in order to free up areas of grief.

Response *Would you use the word suicide, or would you ask if they maybe harmed themselves?*

Speaker No I would say suicide. I want to mention the unmentionable.

Next I might have the client talk about what it was like being there when the loved one died. "Were you with him when he died? What was it like?" Have the client describe those last moments. That's going to be emotional and may facilitate the grieving. There will be again mental images, memories that come up.

Every once in a while as a person is talking and answering our questions, we need to be saying things like, "What are you feeling right now as you're talking?" Reach for those feelings periodically. A person can get into just story telling. Grief counselling is not just about relating experiences. It's about experiencing the feelings of grief that go with those memories.

If the client wasn't at the deathbed, you might ask, "How did you hear about the death?" This brings up memories about the time and the place that he heard the news of the death.

You've heard me refer to these mental images and memories that come up. Those are inevitable and we can use them therapeutically by tapping into them. You can say, "I wonder if you can see him in your mind as you're talking about him. Tell me what's happening." As I go for the mental image, I use the present tense. "Tell me what you see in your mind right now. What's happening? What else is happening?"

I had a client who didn't really grieve over her husband's death until I had her recount in detail the last moments of being with him in the hospital room. He died of cancer, and I said, "Tell me who is in the room with you. Is it just you and your husband? Describe the furniture in the room. And tell me what's happening during the last hour that you're with him. Are there doctors and nurses coming in and out?" She began to relate those movements and images of the last moments, and she went into a sort of hypnotic state. I find that when I have the client use the present tense it's as if she is put back into that time and she re-lives it. As she began to describe every detail, she finally came to his last breath. As soon as she mentioned that, that's when she broke down and cried.

That was the breakthrough for her. Up until that time she had a lot of feeling, but it was almost all anger directed at doctors and nurses. She couldn't get to the sadness until that point.

"What was the funeral and burial like for you?" Have the client discuss and describe that, and again have him describe the mental images that come up around that. And when a person cries we need to say, "Just let yourself feel that. It's okay to cry, just let it out. It takes courage to face the pain." Talking about the loss of hopes and dreams helps to get at the anger of feeling cheated.

What are some why questions? Have the client come up with some why questions. Why him? Why did God let this happen? Why now? and so on. That helps the client access the anger.

Now to get the behaviour decisions and life patterns proceeding from a loss, we can say, "How has your life been affected by his death?"

A person might say in response to that, "Well, I haven't felt like going anywhere. I don't care to visit friends like I used to."

What the client is telling us is that he has made a decision not to get close to others right now. And we can say it in another way, "If he had lived, how do you imagine your life might be different?" You're asking the same thing but in reverse. She might say, "We would be having a good time visiting and travelling." What she's telling you is she would be getting on with her life. She's saying she made a decision not to get on with her life. I would reflect that back to her.

Question *What if it's just the opposite? What if she said her life would be miserable because he treated her badly?*

Speaker That points to a loss of caring and closeness before the death. It may be that there are feelings of relief around the death that she feels guilty about, so you could explore that.

To get at unfinished business we could say, "What do you wish you had said to him before he died?" or simply, "What was left unsaid or unfinished — what things do you wished you had said but didn't get a chance to?"

And then you might give her a list of possible unfinished business by saying, "Sometimes people don't get a chance to say I'm sorry or I forgive you, or I love you. It could also be that they didn't get a chance to talk about the coming death to the loved one. They didn't take the opportunity to reminisce about the good times and to say good-bye. I wonder if you're aware of what you might have wished you could have said, but didn't. I wonder if there are some unresolved issues that you wish you could have cleared up." See whether the client is able to identify and explore that. Areas of unfinished business often are not acknowledged or identified until the counselling process has continued for some time.

Response *If the client was in denial right up until the time the person died, then they wouldn't have thought of things to say.*

Speaker That's right, and in exploring the circumstances you're going to identify the unresolved issues.

Speaker With the empty chair technique, I used to more commonly invite clients to say goodbye to a loved one, but at some point I decided to invite the client to talk to a loved one "about" saying goodbye rather than to simply say goodbye. I find it has the same effect. It still elicits the emptiness. If I see that a client is very stuck in the grief I'll say, "I'd like you to try on saying goodbye. See what it feels like." If a person reports difficulty saying goodbye, or says he doesn't want to, I won't pressure him. What I'll say is, "Maybe it's too soon to say goodbye. It's not easy to let go. It's not something you can hurry or rush. It takes time."

I find that when I do that with people, it's easier for them to say goodbye and let go. It's one of those paradoxical interventions. I'll say, "Maybe it's important for you to do more grieving" and support an extension of the grieving process. Are there any questions about any of these points?

Response *I'm thinking of an aunt and uncle who wouldn't let go of their son who had been dead for 20 years. Whenever I visited their apartment or house there was this huge picture of him in their den, but no large pictures of anybody else. All I had to do was accidentally say anything about him or mention his name and my aunt broke down. She might have been helped by hearing, "Maybe you're not ready to say goodbye yet."*

Speaker That might be a helpful thing to say to her. "Maybe you need to do more grieving. Maybe you're not ready to say let go, and that's okay. It's okay not to let go yet. It's okay not to say goodbye."

Question *So it's okay if people just continue to grieve?*

Speaker But when you say that it has a paradoxical effect.

Response *If you give them permission to hang on, then they're more likely to let go.*

Speaker Yes, it's like you flow with the client's resistance. You don't confront it. If you try to knock it down, it's only going to make it stronger.

Another thing I find that works to facilitate grieving is to talk about the cemetery. Just say, "Have you been by the cemetery?" That facilitates a lot of grieving. What do people do when they go to the cemetery?

Response *Talk to the loved one.*

Speaker The person talks to the loved one, either out loud or in his mind. He might straighten up or clean up the grave site.

There was a woman who lost her seventeen year old son. He committed suicide by hanging himself under the sun deck. She went to the cemetery at least once every single day to seek forgiveness, to express her guilt and sorrow. She felt very much to blame for his death. And she did contribute to it in some very significant ways. She was emotionally abusive, and a very harsh disciplinarian.

THE EMPTY CHAIR TECHNIQUE

So when we use the empty chair, we are actually doing something very similar to what a person does when they go to the cemetery, but we're using it as a deliberate technique. So I'd like to go through the process and just describe how you would introduce the use of the empty chair. It is a particularly powerful technique for helping a person to address unfinished business.

There are three principles to observe in using the empty chair. First of all, I won't introduce it until about the third or fourth session because it's very important to have a strong therapeutic alliance first. You need to have developed safety and trust in the relationship because it's usually quite different from what people are use to.

The counsellor also has to feel comfortable and confident with the technique. That is true of any technique, but especially of the empty chair. If the counsellor is not confident, the client may feel like a guinea pig and feel unsafe.

The third principle is that the empty chair is especially useful in working with the heavily defended client simply because his usual defenses are designed for talking to you. He has no defenses for talking to empty chairs. Also, keep in mind that using the empty chair may overwhelm some clients with too much emotion. If this appears to occur, tell the client, "Maybe it's important to slow down and grieve a little bit at a time. There's no hurry."

I might introduce the empty chair by saying, "I'd like to suggest an exercise to help you explore your feelings a little bit further. Is that something you want to do today?" The person will give his permission and then I'll get up and bring an empty chair directly in front of him. I'll place my chair right next to the client's chair and a few inches back from the front of his chair, so I can still talk comfortably with the client, but I'm outside of his peripheral vision.

Then I'll warm up the client to the exercise a little bit further by having him provide a physical description of the person that he is going to be addressing — the one who died.

I'll say, "To begin this exercise I would like for you to imagine...." I use the word imagine, not pretend, because pretend has connotations of a child's game. I'll say, "I'd like for you to imagine that your mother is sitting here right now and to help us to begin to imagine her..." and here I use the word "us" to join the client in imagining, "...I'd like for you to begin to describe what she looks like. How tall is she? Is she thin, medium weight, overweight? What colour is her hair? Is she wearing glasses?" And I'm using the present tense. That makes the image more real for the client. "What is she wearing right now? How would you describe the shape of her face? Does she have any jewellery?"

When I have a clear enough image myself, which is how I assess whether the client is able to imagine the person, I'll say, "I'd like for you to begin to speak to your mother and say anything to her that comes to mind. Anything at all is fine." To the very resistant client I'll say, "Just say something very brief, just a little bit of something." Again it's the concept of saying just a little bit. At first a client might say something to me like, "I don't know what to say." I'll say, "Say that to your mother." That's a way to get a person started.

Once the client gets started he can go from there. I'll say, "Go on with that." If there is any sign of tearing, or emotion, or conspicuous silence, I'll say, "Let yourself feel that right now. Stay with the feeling."

And when a client identifies a feeling I'll have him report it to the loved one instead of to me. He might report it initially to me, and then I'll say, "Tell your mother about the sadness," or the anger, or whatever it is.

If a person asks a question of a loved one, I'll have him sit in the loved one's chair. I'll say, "I want you to sit in Mom's chair and respond in her characteristic way. Respond the way you think she would." And then when he is finished speaking for Mom, have him return to his own seat and respond to her.

It's especially important to do the reversing when the client says, "I'm sorry", because "I'm sorry" implies the need for forgiveness. So if a client says, "I'm sorry for..." then I'll say, "Sit in your mother's chair and respond in her characteristic way to your apology." And I'm going to be listening for whether mother is forgiving or not.

If mother cannot be forgiving, maybe that's mother's characteristic way. The client is faced not only with the death as a loss, but the lifetime relationship as a loss because if mother was unforgiving in life, that indicates the loss of caring and closeness. So there's a double level of loss that the client needs to come to terms with, the death and the lifetime loss of parental caring.

Speaker If the parent comes across with forgiveness, who is really forgiving who?

Response *The client is forgiving himself.*

Speaker That's right.

To explore unfinished business, I may say, "What are some areas of unfinished business?" I explore that and continue to help the client to verbalize the unspoken words. In closure I'll be saying, "I'd like to bring this to a close in just a few moments. I wonder if there is something that you need or want to say before we close, that you'd regret not saying, or something you have been witholding for any reason." That gives a person one final opportunity to say something else. Then we close. I'll say, "Perhaps we can close the exercise right now" and then I'll turn to the client and say, "What I'd like to do now is just take a few minutes talking about what it has been like doing this?"

This last question leads to a review or debriefing or processing of what the exercise was like, and sorting out feelings and insights and whatever came out of that exercise. The important therapeutic principle here is to put into words anything that may have been stirred up, so that the exercise feels finished. Any questions or comments?

Question *What happens when someone asks for forgiveness, and when they get in the empty chair and respond as the loved one, they can't forgive?*

Speaker That might be the reality, because the client knows the loved one's characteristic behaviours which is to be unforgiving.

Question *So what if there is no forgiveness?*

Speaker Then the client is left with having to work through that. It means the client needs to face the loss of caring and to grieve it.

Response *That's a client holding on still, isn't it?*

Speaker Well, it means that the client is left with the guilt. He is not going to get forgiveness from the other person. He can give himself forgiveness, but the question is whether or not hanging on to the guilt means he is hanging on to this person. What punishment does he think he deserves? Not what punishment does he really deserve but what punishment does he think he deserves? Is he going to give himself a light sentence? Because ultimately it comes down to whether the person can forgive himself.

Question *What about the person who idealizes the parent and has a parent responding unrealistically and forgiving him without dealing with the reality of the situation?*

Speaker Well, if the client has idealized the parent, the parent has probably been a person who is easy to idealize. In other words, he probably was a forgiving person, but also had other flaws that the client has overlooked or has glossed over. The client is ignoring those flaws as a way of hanging on. I might say, "What may have annoyed you slightly?" Or I may use exaggeration by saying, "So he was perfect and never made a mistake." The client will most likely retract the idealistic claims. Once the client identifies anything about the loved one that was annoying or less than perfect, I will focus on that and explore the client's feelings about it.

Response *What do you do if a client is very resistant and can't think of things to say to the person being imagined in the empty chair?*

Speaker In that case I'll say, "Yes it seems ridiculous to talk to an empty chair. It's not something you do every day. Try it anyway and see what happens."

This approach validates the resistance yet refuses to give it power. Another approach which I find is most effective is to say, "Talk to me about your mother..." for example, "...what was she like?" The idea here is to engage the client in talking to you briefly about the person in the empty chair. Then simply wave your hand toward the empty chair and say, "Tell that to your mother."

OPENING THE SESSION

I want to point out a couple of things about the opening of the grief counselling session which distinguishes it from other types of counselling sessions.

If we're working with someone who has identified some type of a goal or problem that he is experiencing now in his life, we would be working from present experience back to the original loss or conflict, working through painful feelings, then bringing it back up to the present again to help the client gain insight into patterns of behaviour which spring from the past loss. In other words, if the client starts with a presentation of current struggles or symptom behaviours, you would go from the present to the past, then to the present again.

When you are working with grief, a person is going to identify the past loss, and you're going to move from the experience of the loss forward in time to the present as you explore the effects of the loss and grief on the life of the client.

As you begin your practice sessions, I'd like for you to begin by asking your client what loss he or she would like to talk about today, and then proceed by using the interventions we've been talking about, especially helping the person identify and experience any emotions related to the loss. Then you could explore how that loss or those emotions have affected his or her life. You can also explore some behaviour decisions or patterns that come from the loss. Does anyone have any question?

A REVIEW OF THE GRIEF COUNSELLING PRACTICE SESSION

Speaker I'd like to talk briefly about what this experience has been like, and I'd especially like for you to talk about what your counsellor did that you thought was most helpful.

Response *I thought John had a lot of empathy and let me say what I wanted to say. I felt he didn't push me in any way. And he made me really feel good. He never suggested anything that I may have not been feeling. He just let me flow with it and I felt it was really good.*

Speaker Alright. You didn't feel directed?

Response *No I didn't.*

Speaker Someone else?

Response *I liked hearing the reflective statements, just to make sure that what I was saying was on track and also that I was clear in what I was saying.*

Speaker Okay, so you found reflective statements very helpful.

Response *Yes.*

Speaker Was your counsellor supportive?

Response *Very. Also, I like to wander off the topic sometimes, but it's more satisfying when you feel like something is being done to keep things focused.*

Speaker Alright, your counsellor looked for links between topics that you were talking about.

Response *I felt very comfortable with Mike, and that was very helpful.*

Response *Would you mind telling me what I did that led to your feeling comfortable?*

Speaker So was it the warmth or the gentleness, his non-threatening affect?

Response *Yes. He was non-threatening. And it was reassuring to hear him say things like, "Are you comfortable with this, do you want to carry this on?"*

Speaker I might just comment that when you ask a client if he is comfortable, that might be a way of checking out whether or not he feels safe enough. In fact your client may not feel comfortable at all, and it may not be to his benefit to feel comfortable. So the word "safe" may be more accurate. "Do you feel safe enough?" or, "What's this like doing this so far today?" Let your client respond to that. Someone else?

Response *As a counsellor I discovered I was still over-directing. So when I was counselling John, I ended up telling him what to do.*

Speaker And you're becoming aware of how you get into directing.

Response *Yes, especially by listening to them reflect back what I said. I'm not making them safe. I understand the discomfort that can come through the growth, but I have to make it safe for the client.*

Response *I found that the issue I thought was the important one turned out to be a cover for something else. It started out as loss of childhood and really it was why did I lose that childhood, and who was the person responsible, and that really is the loss. I'd always dealt with it intellectually before but focusing on the visual images helped my emotions to start coming out.*

Speaker Okay. So you were defending against the real loss?

Response *I didn't think so at the time, but yes, that's quite possible.*

Speaker So working with the mental images and memories was helpful. If a child has lost his childhood, there is an adult who is responsible for that. Adults are responsible for children.

Response *That was the conclusion I came to.*

Response *I had the same experience — the original loss we were going to talk about became something much more important. It was interesting what the client will get around to if you just hang in there with him, and give him safety.*

Speaker The client will lead you to the core issue.

Response *That's what I felt happened.*

Response *I felt with John that we explored every feeling. He'd say something like, "Did it make you feel angry?" We got right through it. I was really impressed.*

Speaker One comment about the phrasing of an intervention. Rather than say, "How did that make you feel?" we need to say, "What are you left feeling?" When we imply or say, "How does that make you feel?" how might the client feel?

Response *Somebody else controls the emotions.*

Speaker Alright, we're saying the client is powerless, a victim of circumstances or of others.

Chapter Four:

Communication and Conflict Resolution Skills

Speaker Let's move on to communication and conflict resolution skills. As we begin this topic, we need to look at a few general truths about conflict.

GENERAL TRUTHS

Conflict is something that can't be avoided no matter how hard we try. It's inevitable because people are individuals with different views, feelings, experiences, and ways of perceiving things. And so the object is not to eliminate conflict, but to try to work with conflict so that it has a positive outcome, such as bringing people closer, or creating new ideas, new possibilities.

As we're working with the individual client, we're seeing a person who has difficulty with communication and conflict. Those difficulties are a major part of his life patterns that often come from a dysfunction family of origin, such as significant unresolved conflict in the parental relationships, or from significant unresolved losses. The client may be overly passive or overly aggressive, or a combination of those behaviours. His ways of relating are unintentional, unconscious compulsions, and often he doesn't know a healthy alternative to reacting out of emotion or habit.

We're going to be assessing the client in terms of five communication styles: passive, assertive, aggressive, passively aggressive, and destructive.

PASSIVE COMMUNICATION STYLE

So let's just define these terms briefly and then go from there. How would you define passive style?

Response *Tries to avoid a conflict.*

Speaker Yes.

Response *They are very agreeable. You won't pick up a sense of what they're feeling.*

Speaker Yes, you won't really know what he is feeling.

Response *He's almost a non-person.*

Speaker Yes, you don't really get to know him.

Response *Is that the doormat type of person?*

Speaker She might be a doormat. She might be agreeable as someone said, or apologize prematurely. She will avoid conflict at all cost. She keeps things nice. She won't express her own true feelings. It's as if she has capital N-I-C-E etched on her forehead. She might not be able to make eye contact very well. Her body language will be demonstrated by maybe slouching in her seat, not being able to sit up straight and look a person in the eye.

The person who has a passive style is behaving as if he doesn't believe that he has equal worth to others. He behaves as if he's not entitled to his own feelings and views, and isn't entitled to be treated with respect. If you call him names or put him down, he won't stand up for his right to be treated with respect. He might just put his head down, or tuck his tail between his legs, so to speak. He might even agree with the person who labels him, or calls him names. He might also put himself down, call himself stupid.

AGGRESSIVE COMMUNICATION STYLE

How would we define aggressive style?

Response *Pushy.*

Speaker Pushy, alright.

Response *Loud.*

Speaker Loud, dominating.

Response *Inconsiderate. They want what they want.*

Speaker He wants what he wants and he might even order you to get it for him or do it for him.

Response *Demanding.*

Speaker Obnoxious in a demanding, ordering way.

Response *These things come out easier.*

Response *We all know these people.*

Speaker There is nobody like that here, of course. We've been on the receiving end of these personalities.

Question *Are you saying we don't have personalities?*

Response *I heard there are only seven or eight really nasty people in the world but they move around a lot.*

Speaker So he might accuse and blame other people. Point the finger. The aggressive individual behaves as if he alone has worth, and you don't. He behaves as if he alone is to be treated with respect, but he'll treat you with disrespect. He'll behave as if only he is entitled to his feelings and views. So he'll dominate the time. He'll interrupt you if you are talking or he just won't leave you any room for your point of view. He'll insist that he's right and you're wrong.

Now deep down the aggressive individual is very insecure and afraid, and has low self worth. He has very low ego strength. If he had a stronger sense of himself, he wouldn't have to be so pushy.

Question *Would I be correct in saying that sort of person is often labelled as egotistical?*

Speaker Yes, that's right. An aggressive person is often egotistical. In reality he has a very weak ego.

PASSIVELY AGGRESSIVE COMMUNICATION STYLE

A variation on aggressive style is passively aggressive style, which is demonstrated by the indirect or passive expression of hostility.

Question *When protesters lie down in front of whatever they're protesting, or refuse to move, is that passive aggression?*

Speaker Sure, passive resistance is passive aggression. When I was in the army I was told to scrape the wax off the floor and to strip the floor in the hallway. Well, I was in there against my choice. I was drafted, and I was a conscientious objector, so when I was given that task, I deliberately worked on one square inch for the whole day. I accepted the task, but not gladly.

Response *It might take a while to finish the floor.*

Speaker That was passive aggressive behaviour. I resented being forced into the army and being given those tasks. Deliberately burning the toast at breakfast is another example. Sabotaging, undermining, talking about people behind their backs are all passive aggressive behaviours.

Question *So people don't really speak their feelings?*

Speaker They don't speak them directly. They may use a punitive silence, or refuse to speak to somebody for a long period of time.

Question *The cold shoulder?*

Speaker The cold shoulder is passive aggressive, and so is walking away from a person when he's talking to you or yawning in his face, things like that.

DESTRUCTIVE COMMUNICATION STYLE

Destructive style is characterized by hitting, throwing, name calling, threats, yelling and screaming. It includes any behaviour which is destructive of property, of self-esteem, or physically of a person's body. Name calling is a good example, and so is using judgemental terms to demean a person. "Where were you when they passed out the brains?" Sarcastic put-down's are destructive because they imply a label of stupidity, ignorance, or something like that.

Question *Is this type generally resulting from very dysfunctional homes where there is physical or mental violence, or sexual abuse?*

Speaker It might result from that style being exhibited or demonstrated in the home.

Question *In that type of environment you might find any of those styles.*

Speaker Right, you might find all these styles prominently displayed in a dysfunctional home except for assertive style. You might not see that one too much.

ASSERTIVE COMMUNICATION STYLE

Let's talk about assertive style, which is being able to be clear, direct, brief, and non-judgemental.

The assertive individual behaves as if he believes everyone is entitled to his or her feelings and views. "You're entitled to your view, I'm entitled to my view," and therefore he is brief. He'll state his case but he'll want to know what your point is too — he'll give you equal time. He'll be clear about his feelings. He'll say what he feels using feeling words. "I feel annoyed." "I feel sad." "I feel afraid when you do this." And when he describes your behaviour he's not going to use judgement, he's just going to give a non-judgemental description of your observable behaviour. "You don't take accurate phone messages..." not "You're so inconsiderate..."

THE ORIGINS OF COMMUNICATION STYLES

As we look at the development of these styles, we can see that some of the unhealthy behaviours — the destructive styles on so on — are modelled on what was experienced in the family of origin and some are a reaction against experiences in the family of origin.

If in the family of origin there is a lot of violence, a person might decide that anger is no good because anger is only destructive, so he'll develop a passive style to keep his anger in. But then he might have explosive outbursts at times because if he keeps his anger in about things, the tension may build up to the point where he can't take it any longer and then he just spews out all kinds of name calling or other destructive behaviours. And then that only proves to him that anger is no good so he stuffs it all again and goes through that cycle.

If a person grows up with two passive parents who don't fight and then he finds a partner who's very aggressive, what is he going to do with that? What's that going to be like for him?

Question *He'll feel harassed, he won't have any sense of control.*

Speaker He won't know what to do with that because when he was growing up he didn't see anybody deal with conflict in a healthy way. He didn't see his parents dealing with issues openly. He experienced them being silent or avoiding conflict, and so he would be in a loss. He wouldn't have the skills or the ability to cope with strong anger coming out.

Response *It's the same way with two aggressive people. That's the only way they know how to deal with stuff.*

Response *In my home that was the norm, and if I'm visiting your house and you and your wife start to argue, I will have to leave. I'll excuse myself because I'm very uncomfortable with that. I'd go to great extremes not to have that happen. I don't raise my voice in our house.*

Speaker Okay, so you've made a firm decision about anger.

Response *It's no good.*

Speaker It's no good. So you've gone the opposite way.

Response *And I come from both passive and aggressive in the same house.*

Speaker You might be capable of both passive and aggressive styles, then.

Response *I am. I've been the doormat and I've also been the bully.*

Speaker Alright. So as we're working with the client, we want to try to understand the story behind his style, to try to help him understand it and gain insight into it, and then we want to help him develop a broader repertoire of styles and skills for communicating and dealing with conflict.

There are three primary skills that we want to pass onto the client. The first is to help him express his feelings and views in a more assertive way. Then we want to help him to listen to the feelings and views of the other person because even the passive individual doesn't necessarily do that very well. He might be wandering off somewhere else while someone is talking to him. Thirdly, we need to pass along problem- solving skills to the client so he can learn how to reach an agreement with another person without taking power or controlling, because the aggressive style and the passive style are both very controlling and powerful styles.

The passive individual is very powerful in his use of silence and other passive aggressive behaviours. And the aggressive person tends to be very powerful by demanding, ordering, and intimidating people. If we want to help our clients give up power and move beyond power in relationships, we need to help them learn new skills.

EXPRESSING FEELINGS AND VIEWS: PAST AND PRESENT

Let's first take a look at expressing feelings and views, both past and present. We really want our client to learn to express himself fully about issues in relationships past and present, throughout his lives.

We talked about that unfinished business when we were doing grief counselling. The same applies to communication styles and skills.

And so as we pass along assertive skills, one of the things we are going to do is introduce the three part assertive statement, which is, "I feel _______, when you _______, because _______." In the first blank, we put in a feeling word — annoyed, sad, furious, venomous, perturbed, irritated. Choose a word that matches the level of the feeling that the person has. In the "when you" blank the person provides a non-judgemental description of observable behaviour. In the "because" blank he clarifies the effect on his life, of the other person's behaviour.

"I feel frustrated when you don't put gas in the tank and you leave it on empty because then I have to stop by the gas station and fill the tank, and then I'm late for work."

"I feel really cheated when you don't follow through on the the tasks we agreed that you would do because then I'm left with more work."

"I feel frustrated when you don't phone to let me know you are going to be late because then I lose valuable time waiting."

I'd like you to form a statement using that format. And I'd like for you to think of a relationship in which you had some issue, minor or major, past or present, which you can make a statement about.

It could be in relation to a loss of parental caring and closeness, or unresolved conflict with a parent. Or it could be something that happened with an acquaintance very recently, or with a friend over a relatively minor issue.

Question *Do you use this for expressing positive feelings?*

Speaker Yes. You can use the same format.

Response *That would be to reinforce the behaviour.*

Speaker That's right. It enhances closeness, and I think that's a very important point that you're making because people often times have much difficulty giving and receiving good things — strokes, things like that. It's important though to address issues. Positive experiences aren't issues. So take some time and fill in the blanks with an issue, rather than with a compliment.

Response *I feel empty when you don't phone because I worry.*

Speaker Okay now, put "worry" up in that first blank. "I feel empty and worried when you don't phone." Can you think of a practical effect on your life? If you end up putting a feeling in the last blank bring it up into the first blank.

What's a practical effect when she doesn't phone? What do you do with your time? Are you able to plan your time? Does it affect your planning or organizing?

Response *I waste my time worrying.*

Speaker So it could be, "because then I can't get on with other tasks".

Response *I think that's it.*

Speaker Okay, someone else?

Response *I feel hurt and disrespected when you don't listen to me because then I don't get to finish what I have to say.*

Speaker Right. Are you a little angry? Frustrated?

Response *Yes.*

Speaker Would it be okay for you to put the word frustrated or the word annoyed in that sentence? Alright, someone else?

Response *I feel ripped off when you weren't there for me because I feel we could have done so much more as father and son.*

Speaker Okay, good.

Response *That's using a feeling word: "because I feel we could have done so much more...."*

Speaker Well, he's using the word feel to mean think, or believe, and that's fine. Okay, someone else.

Response *I feel anger when you get out of bed because I don't get as much time to be alone with you. I'm thinking about my husband.*

Speaker Okay, speaking to your son. Good. Someone else?

Response *I feel very uncomfortable when you ask me a question because I don't always have an answer.*

Speaker Uncomfortable what? Uncomfortable anxious? Uncomfortable frustrated?

Response *I also wrote frustrated above it.*

Speaker It's best if we can think of specific feeling words, and that's why I'm working with you on it. It's easier to avoid a feeling word by using a vague general word and then we end up not being as direct and clear as we could be.

Response *I always feel awkward when you ask me a question because I don't always have an answer.*

Speaker Okay, alright. Someone else?

Response *I feel upset when you go shopping and you don't buy the foods I want because my health is very important to me.*

Speaker Alright. Upset what? Upset angry? Upset anxious?

Response *Upset anxious.*

Speaker Alright, good.

Speaker What do you imagine the passive person struggles with when he attempts to become assertive? What gets in the way?

Response *Fear.*

Speaker He struggles with fear and guilt. The fear is of hurting or being hurt, of saying something that's going to hurt the other person, or of experiencing a negative reaction. When the feared thing happens, he feels guilty about not having prevented it from happening. The end result is the protection racket.

The passive individual prefers to avoid stating the issue clearly. He might allude to it, probably in vague and general ways. Now what the client needs to understand is that passivity, or any one of the other styles of communicating, might be appropriate in a given situation.

The bottom line is to choose the style as a conscious, deliberate decision, rather than as an impulsive reaction. For instance, if I'm talking with a policeman or an employer, I'll usually choose to be passive or possibly even apologetic.

As a counsellor you need to restrict your personal style somewhat. I wonder if you've ever expressed anger to a client? Not only do we not say, "I love you" to a client or, "I care about you," we also don't express anger to a client.

Response *You wouldn't direct any strong emotions toward the client?*

Speaker I wouldn't express anger or affection, no. I wouldn't tell a client that I'm angry or frustrated with him, even in a low tone of voice, because the statements of a counsellor are powerful.

Now, although I wouldn't express anger or frustration, there might be times when I choose to be assertive. Sometimes I will interrupt a client by saying something like, "I'd like to see if I understand what you're saying."

Response *Do you raise your voice?*

Speaker No, not when interrupting. But I will raise my voice with a client passively, as a way of joining or taking sides with him as he is talking about his anger toward somebody else. "You have every right to feel that. Say more about that." I'll do it as a way of encouraging him to raise his voice and bring out his anger.

Response *But they're doing the driving?*

LISTENING TO FEELINGS AND VIEWS: PAST AND PRESENT

Speaker The client is doing the driving. Okay. Let's look very quickly at the next skill, which is the reflective statement. It's easy to remember it, and have the client remember it, as the opposite of the assertive statement.

The assertive statement is, "I feel _______ when you _______ because_______." The reflective statement is, "So you feel _____ when I ______ because________." And then we just add a perception check at the end. "Is that what you're feeling?" "Is that what you're saying?" "Do I understand you?"

Essentially, the reflective statement reflects feeling and meaning. When we make a reflective statement, and when our client does, we might want to point out to her that it's better for her to overstate than to understate the speaker's point. In other words, when we make a reflection, it's better to reflect just a little bit more than what the speaker has said. You might even reflect the implication of what the speaker has said.

Often times, the speaker does not say what the practical effect on her life is, she'll only point out my behaviour. In that case, when I make a reflection, I'm going to reflect how my behaviour has affected her life, even if she hasn't stated it. That's to help her feel fully understood. If I understate her case in my reflection, what's going to be her reaction?

Response *They'll think you didn't quite understand.*

Speaker I didn't quite understand, so what might she feel?

Response *Alone?*

Speaker She might feel alone or she might feel very frustrated. She might increase her own anger or resentment, whereas if I'd overstated and if I'm sincere and not sarcastic in my reflection, she is going to feel very supported. Her resentment or hostility will tend to diminish.

In a conflict, it's important to exchange a series of reflective statements. Use them to clarify the issues to be resolved, and if the other person doesn't know about reflective listening, and most times he won't, we can still elicit a reflection, so that we can feel understood. You can do this by saying, "Let me know what you think you heard me say, because until I know that you understood what I've said, I don't think we can go any further with this. I have to know that you understand my point of view.

Response *What if the person reacts with, "Do you think I'm stupid, that I didn't hear you?"*

Speaker I'd say, "I'm not saying you're stupid, what I'm saying is that I need to know that you understand what I'm saying. I need to know that you understand me. So, can you tell me? I think you can understand, I just need to know what you understand. I need to hear it. And I need to understand your point of view. I need to let you know that I understand it and what I understand. Because unless our issues are clear to each other, then we can't begin to problem solve." This is the first step to resolve a conflict.

FIGHTING BEHAVIOUR

A conflict may degrade into a fight. The definition of a fight is when one person is unwilling to listen to the point of view of the other. And it only takes one person who is unwilling to listen to the point of view of the other to have a fight. It could be a silent fight or a verbal fight, I could use a wall of words to keep from listening to you or I could use a wall of silence.

It's very important for fighting behaviour to be recognized early on, and there are two things you can do to deal with it. The first is to keep the fight fair. As long as there are no threats, name calling, put-downs, or physical expressions of anger such as hitting, pushing, or throwing things, it's within fair limits.

The second way to deal with fighting is to recognize that as much as we may want to resolve the issue, we may be too angry or frightened to begin to be reasonable at all. At those times it's very important to say, "I can't talk about this now, but I'll talk about it this evening or when I feel I'm ready to talk about it." And if it's the other person that's refusing to talk, or in any case after that period of distance, it's important to come back to the other party and say, "I'm ready to talk about this if you are." And at that time you could sit down and make assertive and reflective statements.

PROBLEM-SOLVING SKILLS

Clarify the issues and then move it to the next step, which is to say, "What are we going to do?" That's the question we must ask in order to move to the problem solving phase, which is essential to the resolution of the conflict. You have to get around to saying, "What are we going to do about your issue, about our issue, about my issue?"

At that point you can begin to problem solve. If you use a highly structured method of problem solving, you might get a pencil and paper and make a list of issues — your issues and my issues — and prioritize them. "I'll circle my most important issue, and you'll circle yours. We'll flip a coin to see whose issue gets dealt with first." Take that issue and start brainstorming solutions.

This is a highly structured problem solving process. Structure is the key to maintaining safety in conflict, especially if the conflict is emotionally intense and there are multiple, confusing issues to be dealt with. I believe it's important to use a written process. You also need to give the feelings time to settle, because when people try to resolve things early, they get bogged down and begin to react emotionally to things that are said. Let me give you an example of how I would work with an individual for crisis intervention and looking at choices and options.

A STRUCTURED PROCESS

Speaker At the top of a sheet of paper, I'll list the numbers one through five. That has the advantage of allowing a person to generate the issues. If I only put number one down first and ask, "What's your first issue?" he or she will have a harder time.

If I list numbers one through five, the wheels will start turning and they start thinking, "Well, I guess there's more than one, so I'm going to start thinking of all the possible issues." That makes it easier to come up with the first one.

When they've come up with about five different issues, then I'll say, "Which one of these is the most important issue to you?" Then I'll bring that issue over to another sheet of paper and write it down at the top of the sheet, and below it write the numbers one through eight. Then I'm going to say a number of different things to the person to help her generate creative options and begin problem-solving.

The key to brainstorming is to write down whatever comes to mind without discussion, because as soon as you start allowing discussion of pros and cons, of advantages and disadvantages, or start evaluating an idea, what happens to creativity?

Response *It just stops the creativity. It's not so spontaneous.*

Speaker Yes. You deflate your creativity.

Response *I'm not sure I understand this. Do you brainstorm before the most important issue is chosen?*

Speaker No. You prioritize the issues by saying, "Which issue is the most important to you?" So let's say, the issue is what to do about mother-in-law. Let's take an issue with couple counselling.

What to do about mother-in-law? "Here is a list numbered one through eight, and I'd like for the two of you, speaking as a couple, to think of eight different possible solutions to the problem you're having with mother-in-law", which in this case is his mother. Now as I'm generating creative options, the first thing I'm going to say is, "For number one let's write down what's happening right now."

Now the situation is that mother-in-law flies in from Toronto, and he picks her up at the airport in Vancouver. He leaves her with his wife, knowing that they don't get along, and then he takes off to his second job. He's a workaholic, he has two jobs. The last time this happened, she took him into the back room and they had it out. She threatened to leave him for doing this. It wasn't the first time. She'd had enough.

So, they're in crisis, they come in, and I go through the brainstorming process with them, to problem-solve this. There's an urgent need for hope, for some solution, some beginning of an agreement for an approach to this issue. At the beginning I'll say, "So, what's happening now is always a choice. You can always keep doing what you're doing."

The next thing I'll say is, "What's the opposite of what's happening now?" And, that will generate the next option, the next choice. "You can always do the opposite of what's happening now which is send your mother home."

Now, to stimulate another option — but which really depends on the kind of issue you're dealing with — is to say, "Think of a past success," because that person might have had a positive experience in the past that he can draw upon and bring forward and apply to this situation. "Think of something that you did around this issue of mother-in-law that worked, either permanently or temporarily, at some time in the past." And in this case, she said, "Well, she decided to go on a short visit with him to her relatives, which meant that he had to stay there with his mother."

The fourth is this: "Think of the ideal fantasy. What's your fantasy of what you would like to see happen?" This wording comes close to number five. "Think of something that sounds silly or ridiculous." Now, in this case the daughter-in-law thought of, "Hang mother-in-law" and they did just what you did, they laughed when she mentioned that. So this has the benefit of bringing humour into the conflict and lightening it up. Also, when you invite people to think of something silly and ridiculous, they often take the censorship off their minds, bringing up more creativity, so that they can come closer to a reasonable idea than they would if they had continued to censor their thoughts as being silly or ridiculous. I'm giving them permission to be silly.

Something I may say to increase creativity is, "Think of the worst possibility." The worst possibility would be: let her move in. Well, that's an option. Actually, in this situation they were on a roll and the husband thought up, "I'll build a suite for her," which is similar to letting her move in.

And then another statement to the couple is, "Imagine you are someone you respect. Someone whose advice or wisdom you admire. What would that person say?" In this case it was his father who had died when his son was 10, which by the way is the key to why the daughter-in-law and the mother-in-law didn't get along. The daughter-in-law took her boy away, who took father's place when father died. So father would have said, "Son, why don't you stay there when mother visits? Don't leave her with your wife and take off." So, there was another very valuable option. And then I would say to the couple, "There's always an option you haven't considered. Look at all of these you have been able to come up with, and think of one you haven't yet considered." And while they are thinking of these choices, you say things like, "Excellent," "Well, that's it, let's write that one down," "All right, very important," and so on.

Response *You do the writing down?*

Speaker I write them down on newsprint, on the wall. And as I write I'll encourage them. I'll keep the wheels turning. I'll say, "You've come this far and there's something I want you to always keep in mind, and that is that there's always an option you haven't considered, so keep thinking." Then I write another one down. Then near the end of the process I say, "I can think of a possible solution to this that you haven't thought of and it may work very well." And they'll look at me and say, "Well, what is it?" and I'll say, "I won't say now. Keep thinking."

So that's kind of a teaser, but it keeps the creative wheels going, because they work harder to come up with this really good idea that they haven't thought of. And nine times out of ten, they'll come up with an excellent idea which wasn't what I was thinking at all.

Response *Do you ever say to them, "Well, we'll probably come up with an option today. You might want to come back next week and we'll keep going."*

Speaker No. The couple will be able to reach an agreement in that session, and it's very important that they do, especially in a crisis situation. But at some point, if they don't reach an agreement based on what appears, I'll encourage them to keep working on it. I'll put the solution that I had at the very end, say at number nine or number ten.

REACHING A BASIC AGREEMENT

The next step is to invite each of the parties to select three out of the eight or ten options that he or she believes is the most workable and most realistic towards resolving the issue.

I'll have them make a private selection by writing the numbers of the options they like on a little slip of paper. In this case, he chose three, four and six, and she chose four, five and six. So whatever choices they overlap on, forms their basic agreement. I'll take their little slips of paper and I'll say, "You've both chosen number four and number six".

Response *Looks like you hang the mother-in-law! (laughter)*

Speaker It's really surprising how many times the couple will choose the same three options. They could not have done it earlier by speaking to each other, but writing it down is a highly effective approach.

If they don't overlap in their choices you have three different alternatives. One approach is to ask each person to look at the other person's choices and to identify the one that is least objectionable. A second approach is to encourage them to brainstorm more options. A third approach is for each person to come up with his own list of solutions. Then you have them trade their lists and choose from the other person's list what they would find most acceptable. Again, that helps to begin to form a basic agreement. A final point here is that once a basic agreement has been formulated, ask the client or couple, "When will you implement the agreement?" If you don't help them identify when to actually use the plan they've agreed to, it won't happen.

Also, remember that no agreement is carved in stone. Tell the couple that if the agreement doesn't work, it's OK to go back to the process for problem-solving. Rigidity leads to conflict, and flexibility leads to resolution. If Plan A doesn't work, try Plan B, then Plan C. This same process applies to the individual's relationship with himself as much as with another person. As long as the individual or the couple remains open, the resolution of conflict is possible. Questions or comments about problem-solving?

Response *What did the couple decide to do?*

Speaker In this case they decided that Jane would try to talk to mother-in-law about the problems between the two of them. She was afraid to do that initially, so I modelled a possible approach about how she could begin the conversation by saying, "There's something I've wanted to talk with you about for a long time, but I've been afraid to because I was afraid of how you might take it or afraid it might get messy." I suggested she just leave it at that and see how mother-in-law would respond, see if she is able to be open about the difficulties.

Nine times out of ten the other party will be open when it's put that way. Because you will notice that rather than anger being presented, fear is identified. Generally, if I say I feel angry or frustrated, the other person will be defensive, whereas if I say I feel scared, or sad, or lonely, the other person will be open. Also, the other person's curiosity is increased and he will say, "Well, what is it?" and that's the opening. Sometimes he will say, "Well sure, let's sit down and talk about it."

Okay, anything else?

Response *Yes, this has to do with the process. Does the statement of the issue or problem have to be well defined and specific?*

Speaker What I prefer to do is to keep the issues stated generally, so I would say, "What to do about mother-in-law", because that allows for many different sorts of ideas or thoughts whereas if you have a very narrow issue, that makes it much more difficult for creativity to work. Creativity seems to need more room.

Response *But is this always towards certain, specific solutions?*

Speaker Yes, it will result in a narrower focus, but you have to start out broad... go broad to narrow. It's like beginning from the least contest, least confrontation, the same type of principle.

THE ENACTMENT EXERCISE

Speaker In this session I'd like us to go over the enactment exercise which is the primary technique for exploring the client's current style of communication and for helping the client to try on and adopt new healthier ways of communicating.

It has three advantages. First, it allows the client to vent feelings, to release painful emotions, to express things that she wouldn't feel safe enough expressing to the person she is in a relationship with.

Second, it helps the client gain insight into her styles of communicating and ways of relating and helps her to increase her empathy for the other person with whom she is relating.

And then, third, it helps the client to try on new behaviours, new ways of relating, new ways of communicating, which she can then bring into her relationships outside the counselling session.

The enactment exercise has the advantage of allowing you to see how the client relates, rather than having him or her just tell you about the way he relates and what his relationships are like. With the enactment exercise you can see it happening in front of you.

What I'd like us to do is go over the enactment exercise step by step and then I'll provide a demonstration with a volunteer. So I'd like the volunteer to be thinking about a relationship and some kind of an issue that you have, minor or major, or some type of conflict that you might have with somebody in your life — past or present.

Alright. I might introduce this exercise at a point at which the client is talking about a problem in his relationship. I'll have him discuss that for a while and give him a summary of the issues and problems experienced.

Then I'll suggest the exercise. I'll say, "What I'd like to suggest is that you try an exercise that will help you to explore ways of communication you've tried in the past that may not have worked so well. Then we'll use the exercise to help you discover some new ways of approaching this person that you might try some time in the future. Is that something you'd like to do?"

I give the client the choice whether he wants to go to this step or not, and then I bring the empty chair in front of him and then I position my chair at an angle and a little bit to the rear of his, near him. Place the empty chair about four feet from the client's chair.

Then I say, "As we begin this exercise, I'd like for you to imagine that this is the other person's chair." Let's say my client's name is Helen and she's going to be doing an enactment exercise with Bob who is not present. I'll say, "I'd like you to imagine that's Bob's chair and that will always be his chair and this will always be your chair. And so, to begin this exercise, I'd like you to sit in Bob's chair so I can interview you as if you are Bob."

That interview of the client as the other is the warm-up to the exercise. It's very important to have that warm-up. With the empty chair exercise in grief counselling, the warm-up is the physical description of the person who has died. In this exercise I have the client sit in Bob's chair and I begin to ask a series of questions that are important for this interview and which you might want to make note of.

I start out by saying, "What is your name?" and the client responds with, "My name is Bob." And then I say, "How old are you?" "What is your occupation?", "What is your marital status? Are you married, single, divorced, separated?"

Then I'll take it to another level of depth and I'll say, "What's it like being married, Bob?" So I might repeat Bob's name, so that Helen is reminded who she is speaking for. And as I'm asking her details about herself as Bob, she's getting more and more into feeling what Bob feels. And I might actually make that suggestion earlier on that, "As I'm asking you these questions, I want you to try to imagine what it's like to be Bob and to feel like Bob."

So I'm saying, "What is it like being married? What is your personality like? Are you a passive, laid back kind of guy, Bob, or are you an aggressive, outspoken kind of a man? How would you describe yourself?

How do you deal with your anger? Do you keep it inside? Do you let it all hang out? What do you do with that?" And when he talks about his occupation, I might say, "What's it like doing that kind of work for that long?" or if he's unemployed, I might say, "What's it like being unemployed?" And I might make reflective statements to help Helen get more in touch with what Bob feels by saying, "So maybe you're feeling a little down about not being employed for that length of time?" and things like that.

Then I'm going to say, "So you're married to Helen. Bob, I'd like for you to tell me a little bit about Helen. What is Helen like in your point of view? Describe her personality and tell me about your marriage. What's your relationship like?"

So, as I'm asking these questions, Helen is getting more and more into Bob's point of view and what he's feeling, so she's developing an empathy for him. Empathy is increased when you put yourself into the other person's shoes, and that's exactly what she's doing. This is going to be very interesting for her and for me as a counsellor.

I'm doing this for two reasons. One is for Helen to gain some insight and empathy for Bob, and the other is so that I can observe what Bob is like, because eventually I'm going to become Bob so that Helen can relate to him in the exercise.

Response *Do you often get an accurate picture of the other person, or is it just someone else's interpretation of what they are like? Like if you meet Bob later on, will you know him because she has been him?*

Speaker Well, all it can be is her perception. But I can encourage her to be as accurate as possible by saying, "I'd like for you to respond in Bob's characteristic way." I use the word characteristic or I say, "...in Bob's usual way." But that's only within her perception. That's all it can be. And it's her perception of Bob that she has to cope with. So from that point of view it ultimately doesn't matter how accurate it is really.

Then I'm going to say to my client, "I want you to get out of Bob's chair now and sit in your own chair now and be yourself." And then I'm going to say, "Helen, I'd like for you to imagine that this is an opportunity for you to talk to Bob about your issues and concerns that you talked about earlier, when you summarized your relationship. I want you to speak to him in your characteristic way. You can begin any way you like. Just begin. Open a conversation and take it from there".

So Helen will begin and as Helen is talking to Bob, I'm going to be observing her style in terms of whether it's passive, aggressive, assertive, or passively-aggressive. I'm going to be looking at whether she's beating around the bush, whether she's bringing in destructive name-calling, or put-downs, judgements, or sarcasm, whether she's being very apologetic or passive, things like that.

Then I'm going to say, "Now I'd like for you to sit in Bob's chair and respond in Bob's characteristic way." Now as soon as Helen gets up and sits in Bob's chair, I'm going to slip into her chair and repeat her last line.

I don't have to remember everything she says, only the last phrase or last sentence. That helps to provide a transition for the dialogue. It maintains continuity.

As she responds as Bob, the counsellor in me is assessing Bob's style. Is Bob coming across in a passive, aggressive, assertive, passively-aggressive or destructive kind of way? I'm also assessing whether Bob is generally open or closed. For instance if Bob says, "I don't have to hear this," that's a closed style. But if Bob says, "So tell me more. Go on," that's an open style.

Response *At what point did you say you assess the client's style?*

Speaker When she's being herself. And when she's being Bob I'm assessing what Bob is like. The purpose of the exercise is to get the client to understand both sides of the issue, and the feelings that come up around it. The conversation can go back and forth for a while. So when Bob seems to be finished, I'm going to stand up out of Helen's chair and say, "Now I'd like you to sit in your own chair and respond to Bob" and then I'll sit over in Bob's chair and repeat Bob's last line to provide that transition and continuity.

And Helen will respond as herself and, again, I'm observing what Helen's style is. Is Helen reacting emotionally to Bob? Is she starting to get frustrated now? Is she starting to cry? What's happening? Is she becoming passive or aggressive? Is her style changing in those ways? I'm going to be assessing that. So Helen speaks and when she seems to be finished, I'll stand up and I'll say, "Now respond as Bob," and I'll come over and sit in Helen's chair and repeat Helen's last line.

Speaker The role reversal process will continue for a long enough period of time so that I can assess the nature of the interaction.

Are they getting stuck in the struggle? Is this going nowhere? Is the conflict increasing? Or is it reducing? Is Helen able to be open to Bob, or is she closed to Bob, as well as Bob being closed to her?

Also, whenever Helen is in Bob's chair and expressing Bob's point of view, I'm going to be listening for Bob's general theme, because I'm going to invite the client to be herself once I have a good grasp of that theme and then I'm going to sit in Bob's chair and stay here.

There's not going to be any more role reversal after this point. I'm going to repeat what's most difficult in what Bob has said, what seems to be most difficult for Helen to hear. What causes her to struggle the most? It might be silence, or it might be, "I have no interest in hearing what you have to say" and I'll just keep repeating that over and over again in different ways. "I don't care what you have to say." "I don't understand what you're saying." "I can't hear what you're saying." "I wish you would go away."

I will expand on and maybe even exaggerate Bob's theme, because I want to see what my client's coping skills are. Is she reacting with frustration or is she able to reflect Bob and be open to Bob?

Now, when I've seen enough, I'll sit in the counsellor's chair and I'll say, "I'd like to stop the exercise now and give you some feedback about how I saw you communicating with Bob. Would that be okay?" This is an important part of the exercise.

In order for me to give her helpful feedback, I need to be well versed in what passive, assertive, aggressive, passive-aggressive and destructive styles are, because that's what I'm going to give her feedback about.

I'm going to talk about whether I saw her coming across with hard feelings rather than soft feelings — hard feelings being anger, frustration, soft feelings being sadness, fear, guilt, emptiness, loneliness, hopelessness.

If I find that my client has strong feelings coming up during the exercise, I might actually stop the exercise at that point and slip over here to my counsellor's chair and give her support. I say, "Just let yourself feel that right now." Because what often happens when a client is encountering a closed other party, she begins to grieve. She begins to grieve the loss of the closeness and caring. She might not realize that that's what it is, but that's what she's doing.

Now sometimes the tears are angry tears, so I don't assume that they are sad tears. They might be tears of frustration, or tears of guilt or some other kind of tears, so I'll sort out what the tears are about and I might make a comment like, "Maybe it feels to you as if you've lost Bob. You've lost closeness and caring, is that what's happening? Is that what the sadness is about? Is that what the pain is about that you're feeling right now?" If the client acknowledges that then I'll support and validate the feeling.

And then, if I'm seeing that the client can benefit from trying on a new approach, I'll say, "What I'd like you to do is have you sit in Bob's chair and be Bob and I'll sit in your chair and demonstrate a way that you might communicate with Bob. We'll see what that feels like or looks like."

The client then sits in Bob's chair and we start the conversation from the top. I demonstrate the new skills, the different ways of communicating, the assertiveness, the reflective listening, the problem solving that Helen hasn't been able to use yet. She's going to experience what it feels like being the other party and having these approaches used. And she's going to experience the effectiveness of it on the receiving end.

When I've finished, I'll sit over here in my counsellor's chair and I might say to Bob, "What was it like when Helen spoke to you in this way, Bob?" And Bob's going to give a validation, maybe. He's going to be able to give a positive report. "It feels pretty good. It feels better than what you have done in the past."

Then I'm going to say, "I want you to sit over here and be yourself, and I'm going to be Bob once again, and I'd like for you to try on some of these approaches." Now, before she actually tries them on, I might take some time to review some of those approaches. We'll go over what I did that was different and then invite her to try those techniques on with me being Bob.

When she's finished I'll sit over here in my counsellor's chair and say, "What was it like doing that?" And that'll give her an opportunity to validate the new approach, the experience of trying new ways. And then I'll say, "When do you think you might actually try these approaches with Bob in a face-to-face meeting?" Now, it's very important to nail down a time, because if you don't nail down a time, what's going to happen?

Response *Nothing.*

Speaker Nothing. That's right. So I might say, "Do you think you'll do this tomorrow? Monday? Tuesday? What time? In the morning at breakfast? In the evening at supper? At seven or eight in the evening? I'd like you to nail down the hour." Then we'll talk about a time when we can meet again and review how it went.

Now, another thing I might have to review with a client is, "What is it like thinking about facing Bob in this way? What feelings come up in you when you think about actually doing this?" It might be important to review what sort of feelings might get in the way of the client implementing the new approaches. What do you imagine is the feeling that most often gets in the way?

Response *Fear.*

Speaker Fear. Exactly. When we identify fear, I say, "It might take a bit of a risk for you to do this and it may be that you're not quite ready. That would be understandable. It's okay to not be ready to do something like this because it might be a big step. Does it feel like a big step to you?"

You get a sense of how big a step it is for the client, and if necessary you arrange for more practice before he takes that step. If a client doesn't feel confident enough, he might end up repeating his old patterns or his old styles and either dumping on the person, as he has in the past, or withdrawing in his old ineffective way.

Are there any questions about the exercise?

Response *I'm wondering how far into the counselling process you would do this? Is there a rule of thumb or do you just do it when it seems appropriate?*

Speaker As with the empty chair, you need to be sure there's a strong enough therapeutic alliance for the client to feel secure. But generally speaking, it's something that has to happen towards the latter stage of the process because, with this type of intervention, we're talking about behaviour change.

In other words, we're introducing it at a time when the client has already worked through her core, painful issues to a large extent. She understands something about how her old ways of relating are connected to her pain, and now she is ready to take the risk and try something new and different.

Response *So it's letting them feel comfortable before you proceed with this exercise.*

Speaker Right. Make sure he is feeling safe enough in the counselling relationship. You're also introducing it at a point in the whole process of counselling when he can benefit the most. In other words he has already worked through the pain that he has traditionally reacted to and have been ineffective in dealing with. He has either dumped out of his rage and anger or withdrawn out of his fear and guilt. Once he works through the rage and the fear then he is ready to take a reasonable risk without it being too scary.

Response *And you keep checking with them that it's okay. That's what I'm realizing. You've always got to check with the client to make sure that she is okay with this decision. It's up to her to make the decision.*

Speaker To see if he would like to do this...that's right.

Response *Is there a lot of protection?*

Speaker Of the other person, initially? There is in the case of the very passive client. A client that's very passive is generally very protective.

Response *How would you work past that point so that they can be a little more objective?*

Speaker The key to working with the protection racket is to help the client identify the fear and to use the feeling of fear that comes up, not as a signal for withdrawal as she has done characteristically, but as a signal to move forward into another behaviour.

Response *So you change that behaviour right there?*

Speaker Exactly. You can use the cognitive therapeutic intervention here. You help the client arrive at a cognitive awareness of the signals that indicate the old behaviour is happening. For the passive person the signal is fear. She may feel shaky, get panicky inside, she begins to hyper-ventilate, and so on.

Now, traditionally, that old pattern had resulted in withdrawing. So you can use that fear now as a signal for the client to take a risk, to advance forward and do something different.

Response *So there will be quite a bit of core issue work before that. When I went through this exercise in my mind, I found that I was a little bit nicer to my partner when I changed the roles. I wouldn't deal with my emotions and my objections.*

Speaker You were being protective.

Response *I was being protective. So I had to go through that exercise to see what happens.*

Speaker Generally, the passive person needs to have an opportunity to express more of his anger... to own that and express that.

The aggressive person, the person who's used to dumping his anger on the other party, that person needs to express more of the soft feelings that are under the anger. His anger and frustration are only on the surface. Under that, there's the sadness and the fear. It's being expressed in anger. So the aggressive person needs to be able to report his sadness and his fear, and what he may find is if he is able to report that, the other party will open up. The reason for the conflict is that the aggressive party has been too aggressive and too angry. That's caused the other party to shut down.

Response *There's no hand held out.*

Speaker That's right. There's no open hand. There's a closed fist. So for the aggressive party, the key is to have him report his sadness. "I feel really sad when you do that." Or, "I feel afraid when you do that," instead of, "I feel so frustrated." It might be risky and scary to report a sadness and a fear because the aggressive party feels vulnerable. He is afraid of being criticized.

A REVIEW OF THE ENACTMENT EXERCISE PRACTICE SESSION

Speaker Let's briefly discuss what it was like doing the enactment exercise.

Response *Fantastic. I like the idea of role reversal because I've gone through this process before, but not the same type of structure. I was able to identify what the real issues were, and I was learning something more for myself.*

Speaker So, you're talking about gaining insight.

Response *More insight, but more insight into myself this time, as to how I communicate. The role reversal is good that way.*

Response *I became aware of the real need to validate and express support for one another. It became really clear that when that isn't happening with the client, the frustration builds. But, then again, when it does happen, it becomes a much more open relationship.*

Speaker Yes, because the client feels accepted. And it's also tied to a client's self-worth, I think. Hopefully, the client's going to reach the point where he can validate himself more and more. What else?

Response *I think managing the pace is really important.*

Speaker Keeping it slow enough?

Response *Slow enough...at the right speed.*

Speaker That's right. So you see where the confusion is if the pace is too fast, going from one chair to the other?

Response *Yes.*

Speaker Also, the slow pace is important to help a person get in touch with feelings.

Response *And it would give the counsellor time too. I mean, because you're dealing with two personalities, you need that time to keep everything straight.*

Speaker The counsellor really has to think about two or three or four things at the same time.

Response *I gained a lot of trust in myself through this process. A couple of days ago, I felt very insecure and very unable to counsel. After working through these classes, and doing these processes, I feel very confident that I do know what I'm doing and I do pay attention to my intuition. That is a good part of it...and the guidelines were excellent for me to follow. It was very satisfying.*

Response *Is it necessary for it to always follow in the sequence you outlined? I thought the structure of the exercise would be flexible.*

Speaker No. There is some flexibility there. But for training purposes, I think it is necessary to follow the guidelines as closely as possible. Once you learn the process, then you can change it. Use your creativity to benefit your client.

Response *This has also helped me to be more empathic. I mean, I used to have some trouble understanding how my clients felt when they told me how they felt. It's easier now.*

Response *One thing I did feel was, that I didn't feel directed by you. I felt that you just let me take things my way.*

Response *Yes. I had lots of fun with this.*

Response *Yes. So did I.*

Response *I mean, this stuff really works! And I found myself... as you say, "I felt angry... How angry? Sad angry? Sad?" It's neat to try this stuff on. You know and, here, it was a little awkward, but it was neat to be able to try it on, and you kind of just went with it.*

Response *Well I had fun with it because I could feel the range of emotions. I guess, maybe I've had a bit of an advantage because I'd gone through some of that process, but not as much really. It's just that I decided to have fun with it because it is psychodrama and you can do what ever you want...*

Response *But you let it go too, though. I mean you took off the brakes. Like I mean you went through that whole thing very together...*

Response *I don't think I would have been able to take the brakes off that easily if I hadn't had the days before. I think you do build up to that point and if you're doing the counselling, the same thing, you probably have maybe 2 or 3 sessions before you can let go of the brakes as counsellors.*

Speaker Okay. Once you get into using it as a client, the client almost wants to do it more. Because when he first does it, it's like having a dream and not realizing you're dreaming, and not knowing you have the power to change this dream. But then, once you learn that you can change this dream, you can do whatever you want in it because it's a lucid dream.

And, you can be lucid in that way with enactment exercise. You can do almost anything you want. Experiment, play with it... go for broke.

Response *There's a possibility, at least this is what I've found, that there might be cases where the conflict may not be resolved by contacting that other person but by resolving it within the person himself. And, that's what Merv seemed to come to. He didn't need to contact the other person, he could really take care of it within himself. And I thought, "Yeah, that's the process... just working itself out within... the way it needs to.*

Response *It takes care of the guilt too because you don't feel guilty about dumping baggage on your carpet.*

Response *You can dump it right here. You can dump it during the exercise.*

Response *And, you were talking about taking risks. Well I've taken the risks as much as I can do. It's a different situation... and it's like, I don't have to go and do this with somebody else, because I've already done this with my counsellor and me, and I feel okay with it the way it is... because I've done all this other stuff and it doesn't work anyway. So that was — a light bulb comes up and I say, "Wait a minute. I don't have to go out and keep chasing..." The line that I use is, "When you chase something it goes away, so if you let it go it may come back to you." Well that happened to me the other day and I never thought about it until this afternoon. So, once I let go, I had a riot.*

Response *So you can do your releasing in a counselling session. You don't have to go and dump on the person.*

Response *That's right. That part... to be rejected. Part of you still wants to be rejected. That's my pattern. It's always been, to get rejected.*

Chapter Five:

Couple Counselling Strategies

Speaker Our next topic is an extension of Communication and Conflict Resolution Skills. In moving to Couple Counselling, perhaps I could begin by saying that I find this to be one of the most interesting kinds of counselling to do, because it's an opportunity to see how people relate first-hand.

I don't just get the report of how they relate to somebody else. And it's not simply role playing, in which I'm looking at the client's perception of how the relationship is. I get an opportunity to see how things actually are — what the communications skills are actually like.

THE STRUCTURE OF COUPLE COUNSELLING

When you are doing couple counselling, you are actually working on two levels.

The first level is communication skill training. When I see the couple, I'm assessing them as to whether they're coming across to each other in a passive way, an aggressive way, or an assertive way. I'm looking at their listening abilities. I'm looking at their problem solving abilities.

I usually spend four or five sessions just on communication skill training, because I find that most of the problems that couples present could be solved by the couples themselves if they had adequate communication skills. Also, the problem is with process and communication rather than the content of the issues involved.

Response *Would you extend assessment that to families, generally?*

Speaker Yes. I would say that would be true for families as well.

The second level that I work with couples on is to help each of the individuals in his or her individual life patterns, because those patterns are interacting with each other in such a way as to create or exacerbate problems.

In the structure for couple counselling, which I'll elaborate on later on, the first five sessions are devoted to Communications Skills Training, and that's referred to as Phase One.

Phase Two is when I may meet with the couple as individuals one week, and then as a couple the following week, and then as individuals the next week, and then as a couple the week after, alternating as long as that phase lasts.

When I meet with them as individuals, I'm helping each of the partners to identify his or her life patterns that are being brought into the relationship from their past life experiences. And then, as I meet with them as a couple, we refer to our communication skill training and also share the insights they gained from their individual sessions. That enables each person to take responsibility for his own contribution to the problems, rather than blaming the other person, which is where they started. Any questions or comments about that process?

Response *When you're helping individuals gain insight into their life patterns, do you always do that on an individual basis? Does it ever come up when both are present?*

Speaker Well, when I see them as a couple, they have an opportunity to share those insights into themselves and into their life patterns with each other. Certainly, it does come up in the first session when I do the assessment, and I'll talk more about that in a few moments.

Response *Can you talk about a time frame on this? You mentioned that Phase One would be about five weeks. How long is Phase Two?*

Speaker Phase Two is longer, usually about 12 weeks, generally.

Response *If someone comes in to talk with you and they're having trouble communicating with their spouse, do you suggest couple counselling, or do you wait a little, while this one person works through his problem first?*

Speaker If the problem is that one person wants out of the relationship, I'll want to have a meeting with the spouse as soon as possible, let's say the very next week, so that I can assess as much as possible the dynamics in the relationship which are contributing to the problem.

Response *Would you continue with one person if all of a sudden the spouse didn't want to come for counselling?*

Speaker Yes, I would. Because I believe that if one person changes, that relationship's going to change.

RELATIONSHIP DYNAMICS

Alright. Let's talk about relationship dynamics very briefly. When I see a couple in my office, I'm assessing them in terms of three different source scenarios.

One possibility is that one person has a generally aggressive style and the other has a generally passive style. That's the most common scenario.

It seems that passive people are attracted to aggressive people, and vice versa. Part of that is the compulsion to repeat unresolved conflict with an aggressive parent or unresolved loss of parenting and caring. And part of it is an attraction to someone who has a quality that the other one wished he or she had. Each person is looking for a balance in himself by choosing someone who has that other quality of aggressive style or passive style.

The second scenario is to find two people who are fairly passive. The third is two people who are generally aggressive in their styles.

In all those situations, you're going to have conflict, and you're going to have dysfunction. You're going to have ineffective ways of coping with issues and problems that arise from the relationship.

Response *It seems to me that the only relationship that would have a good start would be between two assertives.*

Speaker That's right, two people who have strong adult egos.

Response *What if one person wishes the other had a quality that's lacking in himself?*

Speaker Right. When you have a passive person and the other aggressive, sometimes one of the reasons that he is attracted is that the other person has a quality that the one partner wishes he had.

Response *So the passive person wishes he was more aggressive?*

Speaker Right, that may be part of his or her attraction to that person. And the aggressive person wishes he or she could be more calm and cool and collected, more laid back and relaxed. Of course these are generalizations. A passive person, for instance, is not always relaxed, but could be full of tension.

Another way we could understand relationship dynamics is to use transactional analysis concepts. In TA terms, each one of us has three parts of ourselves — the parent self, the child self, and the adult self.

Dysfunctional and co-dependent couples have strong child egos or strong parent egos within themselves, and very weak adult egos. So, our goal is to strengthen the adult egos in the partners.

Let's define the ego states a little more specifically. The parent part of us can be divided into the nurturing parent and the critical parent. Another term for the critical parent is aggressive behaviour.

The aggressive style is synonymous with the critical parent because the aggressive person is telling people what to do and that's what a critical parent does. "Clean your room. Eat your food. Get a haircut."

Response *Take a hike. (laughter)*

Speaker Now the person who comes from a very dysfunctional family in which there was abusive parenting, a lot of critical parenting, is likely to have a large critical parent inside him. He is probably capable of critical parenting the person he's with in an intimate relationship.

It's also possible for the person to have too large a nurturing parent inside her. In other words, she's too giving. She neglects her own needs and she's willing to look after this other person completely.

Sometimes it's a combination, as in the person who wants intensely to look after the partner but does so in a critical way. She doesn't come across in a soft, nurturing way. But the person who gives too much or who's too controlling is going to create a dysfunction in her own relationship and she's not going to be getting her own needs met. She's not looking at herself. She's trying too hard to look after the other person.

The child ego can be divided into two parts. It can be the fun-loving, adventurous or free child — a spontaneous child who likes to explore and have fun. And then the child can be rebellious, passive-aggressive, shy, fearful, or irresponsible. Irresponsible overlaps with fun-loving sometimes. Maybe he's having too much fun.

So a person who comes from a dysfunctional family is going to have a large child and a large parent inside him, and the adult will be small. Picture a small circle around the adult, and large circles around parent and child. What we often find in couples is that one person has a large, critical parent and the other person has an irresponsible or passive child in him. And the nature of that relationship is going to be conflictual. The parent resents the child and the child resents the parent.

And then there's the possibility of having two childlike people in a relationship. Both of them are irresponsible, they're both messy, they don't clean up after themselves. They each expect the other to look after him or her and to carry the conversation. Maybe each person is passive and fearful, so both sit in silence.

Question *Are dysfunctional adults more likely to be the responsible child or the rebellious child?*

Speaker Individuals who have a large critical parent are often times coupled with an irresponsible, passive, or fearful child. And the more aggressive or critically parenting one parent is, the more passive or passively aggressive the other one becomes, the more withdrawn. And the more withdrawn the child becomes, how does that affect the critical parent?

Response *He or she becomes more critical.*

Speaker She becomes even more critical because what is she feeling with this passive partner?

Response *Anger.*

Speaker Yes, frustration and anger. So that only increases the critical parent reaction so you have an ever-widening gap between these two people.

Response *So one wants to control and the other one doesn't want to be controlled.*

Speaker Well, in fact they are both controlling in a way. The passive style is just as controlling in a passive way as the aggressive style is in an aggressive way.

Response *The child might be saying, "I'm going to take the toys and leave." I think that's controlling.*

Speaker Yes. He's going to take the marbles and go home or he's not going to speak, for example, and he uses that as a weapon.

Response *I remember you saying a couple days ago that they are both very powerful positions to be in.*

Speaker Yes, they are power-hungry, power-seeking positions or behaviours. It's the adult that gives up power. So what we're trying to do is to take our couples beyond power and helping them to find a way of relating without control, without power.

Response *So power becomes the currency of the relationship.?*

Speaker I'm not sure by what you mean by currency

Response *Well that's the way business is done. I did this for you, you have to do this for me kind of thing.*

Speaker Yes. I gave. I did all this for you and I expect something in return. I want some caring in return. I expect for you to do some things for me. So it's not unconditional caring.

Response *The win-win situation is preferable, I think.*

Speaker That's preferable and that's what the adults are able to do. That's what you want to bring your clients to.

Response *That sounds like a first date. I did this for you, now I expect something back...*

Question *The couple who are both critical parents, that's really quite volatile, isn't it?*

Speaker Absolutely, and what are they going to be doing to each other? Criticizing each other, a lot of heavy ordering around.

Question *Is that where most of the physical abuse happens?*

Speaker Well, in most wife battering situations you have an abusive parent ego and then you have the fearful child, the doormat child ego, who keeps getting beaten. There are situations where you might have two critical parents going at each other.

Response *On equal terms then, it really isn't what we usually think of as abuse. In battering one wins all the time, physically anyways.*

Speaker And if they're both battering they're both losing. Alright. If you have two children, two childlike people you are going to have conflict. It might be underground, it might be silent conflict, so if you see these people in counselling they'll both be sitting there but not saying much. They're both afraid to say much.

Response *So you bring out the toys, right?*

Speaker Yes, you bring out the toys. (laughter) They seem to need a lot of parenting from me as the counsellor. They need me to look after them, to do the work, to draw them out or expect me to tell them what to do. Well, if you have two parents or two children you're going to have conflict, and if you have a parent and child you're going to have conflict.

Question *Can you pigeon-hole somebody and say they're always the parent or would it depend on the type of person? Could you have a client who sometimes attracts the passive person and tends to be more parent-like, and then maybe in another situation end up being the child in a relationship, or do people tend to stick to one style?*

Speaker Certainly people can relate differently to different people. A person who is generally passive with his aggressive partner might be aggressive at work with subordinates or with the children at home.

Well, we might find some people who flip within the relationship itself. For example they might go through a period of time where one person is the angry critical parent ego and then there's a big blow up because the passive person decides he doesn't want to take it any more, and the parental partner decides, "This is no good. This is destructive. I'm tired of being the bad guy. I'm going to keep my anger to myself for a while and be the easy-going one." At the same time, the passive one is angry about being stepped on and takes on the critical role.

But because there's a need to maintain a level of hostility in a relationship, the other person will probably start piping up. Often chronic conflict is something each person is familiar with in the family of origin, or it is a means of getting close or of making contact. Maybe they are uncomfortable or frightened of sustained harmony or intimacy because of unresolved conflict or grief in the family of origin.

Question *Could somebody take on different roles depending on who they were relating to? Like with their mother they might be like a child or with their friend they could be like a parent.*

Speaker Yes, but the bottom line is still the same, which is that he is not able to achieve the intimacy he wants.

Response *Maybe their roles changes within the sexual relationship or depending upon circumstances. Is that a possibility?*

Speaker Yes, if one person is passive in the sexual relationship, and not verbalizing her needs, she might be aggressive in the other aspects of the relationship.

Response *That's what I was wondering. Do you treat both together or do you just look at each aspect of life separately?*

Speaker You could look at how their ego states are changed depending upon where they are, whether they're in bed or sitting down to breakfast. What ego state are you in then? So yes, ego states can change depending upon the circumstances.

Response *Because it may be acceptable to be passive within the sexual relationship, but not in the rest of the relationship. That seems like some kind of split that would need to be addressed.*

Speaker It's being in a different ego state at different times, yes. And the bottom line is to choose the ego state that you want to be in as a deliberate intentional decision rather than as an unconscious complusion to repeat a pattern of behaviour. So the adult can decide when he wants to be a fun-loving child, or when he wants to be passive, or when he wants to be critical, or when he wants to be nurturing, and he will do that as a deliberate, conscious, intentional decision.

The person who fluctuates between child and parent, or remains generally a child or generally a parent is doing that as an unconscious compulsion or habitual kind of behaviour. It's not a conscious choice.

It becomes dysfunctional because then the individual is not the master. He's being swept along by significant unresolved conflict and losses from his own past. His painful feelings are really mastering him.

So the goal of our counselling with couples is to enable them to relate to each other deliberately and intentionally by being more fully aware individuals.

Response *How do we distinguish between emotional reactions which are based in present reality and which emotions come from our past?*

Speaker If the emotional reaction appears to be exaggerrated or out of proportion to what is being described as present reality, then it may be something unconsciously brought forward from the past.

For example, a man reacted in rage when his wife asked him a question and then said, "Never mind. I figured it out." I said, "What did she do that pushed your buttons?" He replied, "She cut me off, didn't care what I had to say." I said, "What other important person in your life cut you off and didn't care about what you had to say?" He then identified his father who was an alcoholic. This client went on to say, "I used to hate my father but I don't any more."

This illustrates how the rage toward father is being denied and then is triggered by the behaviour of the wife. So the key is to look for the exaggerrated emotional reaction as a signal of what pain is being brought forward from the past to the present situation which bears some resemblance to it.

He's going to react impulsively out of his child or out of his internalized parent reacting angrily, or reacting to withdraw in his passive style, out of fear. Reacting out of fear or out of anger.

Response *Or no reaction to it like in childhood there's no reaction some time. The child, like you said, withdraws.*

Speaker No reaction is a reaction.

Response *That's what I meant. That's the other side of the reaction. My decision is to make no decisions. That's how I used to put it years ago. I was making a decision but never thinking that I was.*

Speaker I want to make one more point about ego states. When some people come into counselling they say, "Well, I wasn't this way until I married her." What the client is alluding to is that there's a possibility that he may have been transformed from an adult ego into a child by the partner acting like a parent.

If somebody tells you what to do or criticizes you, then you find that you don't want to cooperate with him. You become passively aggressive. Maybe you watch T.V. more. It might mean that you're being transformed into your child. But what it probably means is that you didn't have a very strong adult to begin with, even if you thought you did.

But we can take that concept and apply it to the possibility of changing a relationship if you work with only one person. If you can strengthen the adult ego in one person, then that person might have the ability to transform the partner. When an issue comes up the adult is able to be assertive, to reflectively listen to the other person, in other words treat him as an adult rather than as a parent treats a child.

The adult is able to facilitate a problem-solving process around issues instead of telling the other person what to do. The adult is going to say, "What are we going to do? What are some approaches or solutions that we can come up with together to resolve this issue? I'm ready to problem solve this whenever you're ready." He won't be going to the partner like a critical parent and dumping on her, calling her names, or putting her down, or telling her what to do. He is going to give up power by using the problem solving process. By treating the other person like an adult, then he is going to be able to help the partner move out of the child ego state.

The problem solving process is what I mean by moving beyond power. It's where both people are contributing to possible solutions, and through that problem solving process they're arriving at a mutual agreement: an agreement in which both win. And so that way one person can transform the relationship. On the other hand, if the other person comes from a very dysfunctional family of origin, it may not be possible to make a difference by strengthening the adult. Any questions or comments about this?

Question *When we're looking at the adult who becomes the child, would that be the kind of person who has a hard time saying no?*

Speaker Well, the over-nurturing parent has a hard time saying no.

Question *So is it a conflict to do with the child's upbringing?*

Speaker Yes, because the nurturing parent, the person who feels too responsible for other people and wants to take care of them, can't say no to their demands. In effect the over-nurturing parent, is operating from the child ego state because she is still looking for the parental caring and approval that she missed. She hopes for appreciation and caring, and with this ulterior motive for looking after others, she is frequently disappointed, becomes the martyr, and ends up repeating the familiar feelings of sadness, frustration, rejection, low self-worth, and emptiness associated with the loss of parental caring. But she keeps trying and giving, to her own detriment, because she can never get from others the caring that she missed from parents.

PROBLEMS FREQUENTLY PRESENTED

Now let's look at some problems that are frequently presented in counselling. Communication is a process issue, others are content issues.

Earlier I made the distinction between process and content. A good analogy to use is comparing the process to the vehicle and the issues or the content to the passengers who ride in the vehicles. If the vehicle is not functioning, if there is something wrong with the engine or the tires or the brakes, then the vehicle isn't going to be able to get the passengers to the destination, which to extend this analogy is resolution or agreement. So to have a well functioning vehicle, or process, we need assertiveness, reflective listening, and problem solving skills. We need effective communication skills. When we have those skills in place we have a well running vehicle that can take anybody wherever he or she needs to go.

This is the reason that couples usually need to focus on communication skill development. If they can communicate effectively, often these other problems can be resolved by the couple themselves. However, very often we find that the content issues, such as household responsibilities for example, are the tip of the iceberg and that below the surface issue is the need to control or to distance the partner because of unresolved issues stemming from dysfunction in the family of origin or from unresolved conflicts and losses from early days. These unresolved issues are resurfacing in the couple relationship and making communication difficult.

Response *I wouldn't think that alcoholism would be very common, at least with the people that I hang around with.*

Speaker Well it is common. It is quite common.

Response *I think the others are more common.*

Speaker Well, actually you might put a circle around alcoholism. I see that quite frequently as well. With couples I use a structured intervention process that we deal with more in the advanced course.

Question *Do you think infidelity can always be addressed? At that point a person may have made a strong decision not to stay in the relationship.*

Speaker Let's go down this list in order and I'll come to infidelity and suggest some approaches. What I'd like to do is suggest some strategies that help to resolve some of these content issues.

1. Communication Problems
2. Physical Abuse
3. Time Spent Together
4. Finances
5. Household Responsibilities

6. Infidelity

7. Alcoholism

8. In-Laws

9. Sexual/Romantic Issues

10. Intelligence/Cultural Differences

For example, time spent together. I see this frequently in situations in which couples work opposite shifts. They don't see each other during the week at all. He works during the day, she works at night or vice versa. And then they don't meet, they might see each other on weekends. The problem that comes in here is that they have to get to know each other all over again. They expect too much of the other person. They expect that the other person should know what they need when really they don't because there is so much time that's intervened. They have to get re-acquainted. They have to be patient with each other.

So couples in this situation need to spend quality time with each other and put their relationship on the front burner, make a date with each other, and keep their dates.

Response *It's funny you should say that because Karen and I were just talking about our fairly busy schedules. We do spend a fair bit of time with each other but she said even when we have kids and we take a day off, then that is our day. We take the phone off the hook. It's very positive that way.*

Speaker And that's very important because if you don't see each other you're going to become alienated and estranged from each other.

Finances. This is often a control issue. One partner is in charge of the money and maybe they're using only one account, or if there's more than one they're all in his name. So this becomes a major issue for many couples. A strategy for dealing with this might be what?

Response *A joint account.*

Speaker Okay, it might be a joint account. What else?

Question *Can they get special training, like go to some kind of workshops?*

Speaker Yes there might be things like that. What else?

Response *Let the other person have more control over the finances.*

Speaker Yes, and how might that be arranged?

Response *Make it so that one person doesn't write all the cheques or pay all the bills.*

Speaker Right, we're talking about access to money.

Response *There should be consensus on how much money is to be spent on what and who's going to be responsible for doing that.*

Speaker Okay, when I've experienced this as being a difficult issue, one person is in control of the money.

Response *But the one who has control is going to have to be willing to give up a bit of control.*

Response *A lot of control.*

Speaker They're going to have to share access. I think one of the things that works best is separate accounts. She has her personal expense account; he has his personal expense account. The same amount goes into each personal expense account each month, and then they have a joint account for the family expenses.

People lose sight of the fact that they can have as many accounts as they like. They could have eight banks, or eight accounts at one bank. There are a lot of financial options out there for people to have equal access to funds.

Another thing that often works well is to set a ceiling above which there needs to be agreement. In other words if you're going to spend over a hundred dollars we need to agree on that expense. Anything under a hundred dollars we don't even need to talk about. We can just go out and spend freely.

Response *Each person can have their own personal account.*

Speaker Yes, there could be a spending limit on their own personal accounts, and especially on the joint account.

Response *I have a couple of friends who have similar problems and there is just no way on earth they could get this organized.*

Speaker Maybe they need counselling. Alright, household responsibility. What's the solution here?

Response *Share the duties.*

Speaker Share the duties. This is a real problem for traditional men. The traditional men think that it's the his place to work outside the home and hers to look after everything in the home. So he works 9 to 5 and she works 9 AM to 10 PM, or 9 AM. to 11 PM, or 7 AM to 11 PM. With the man who has a traditional view, I'll hold up the mirror and say, "So let me see if I can get this right, your job goes from 9 AM to 4:30 PM and her job goes from 7 AM to 10 PM. Is that what you're saying?" I'll reflect that reality back to him and out of that he'll just stop. The wheels will start turning and you can see him just mulling that over and then often coming out of it with something like, "Well, I guess that doesn't seem quite fair."

Response *So what's your point? (laughter)*

Speaker Once they agree that there needs to be more fairness, then I suggest that they make up a list. The way we do this is have each person take a sheet of paper and then they cooperatively develop the list. I'll say, "What's going to be number one on the task list? Okay, both write down laundry by number one on your own sheets of paper. Number two, what's the next task? Meals. Number three, discipline and child care. Number four, vacuuming. Number five, cleaning up the bathroom. Number six, straightening the bedroom. Number seven, doing the shopping. Number eight, banking. Number nine, writing out checks and paying the bills. What's number ten? Have I said them all?"

Response *Cleaning the litter box.*

Speaker Pet care.

Response *Number 11, garbage. Number 12, car care. Number 13, yard care etc. I've had couples come up with 50, 60 or 70 tasks.*

Response *A lot of problems seem to arise when there is not enough money, so people are frustrated because they can't get ahead, they're not buying what they want or even having what they want.*

Speaker That's an access issue.

Response *But that could be for both because only one salary isn't going far enough. That's sometimes a great struggle because the working spouse doesn't think the spouse who's staying at home is doing a fair share.*

Speaker There's the issue of income. Who's going to generate it? And then there's the issue of outgo or outflow of expenses. How are the expenses going to be looked after? Who's going to do the bill paying and how much spending is going to be done? How do we decide who spends how much for what?

That's one category of finances, and the other is how are we going to decide where the money comes from? Those are important and difficult issues.

Response *So I guess if you list objectives, if you have goals set you want to meet on your own and say you're not the breadwinner in that situation, then you put your goals down and discuss them with the person. "This is what I'd like to do" and then come to some kind of compromise. "Can we do a trade here or something?" Those things would be listed so you have something concrete to deal with.*

Speaker Exactly. Making lists is the key to learn.

Response *Making lists is a good idea.*

Speaker We were talking about household responsibilities. They make out a composite list on two separate sheets of paper and then I say, "Now I'd like for you each privately to put your initial by the tasks you would prefer to do." And when they've done that I have each person read off what he or she stated as preferences so that the other person can mark them on their list. In this way the preferred tasks are being distributed, and that gives them an opportunity to see which tasks neither one wants to do. Then they'll divide those up. Now they've created a balanced list of responsibilities.

Response *It's also a good idea to trade off some tasks.*

Speaker Alright. Alternating tasks you're saying.

Response *That really helps. I've seen this in households particularly where there are single parents, and when the children can join in the single parent isn't overwhelmed doing both parents' roles.*

Speaker Exactly.

Response *That's a great idea.*

Speaker Child care. So for example, one parent might be doing the child care, especially when there are small children. If parents alternate, it's better to do it for a week than for one day. If you try to alternate days, it gets confusing trying to remember whose turn it is. You also get less of a holiday to look forward to.

Meal preparation is another one that works well when you alternate. I don't have to worry about doing any meals next week because that's your week. I think it works well in that situation I've just described for one person to do the child care during the week and the other person does the meal preparation. It's hard for one person to do both child care and meal preparation. If you've ever tried it you know how crazy it gets. If you're trying to make meals and the kids are coming in and they want looking after, you can't get the meals done. It takes a lot longer so it's a lot more stressful.

Response *That seems like quite a departure from the old standard of how to run the family. I know of a situation, that's common I suppose, where the father goes outside to work and the mother occasionally has worked outside but primarily around the house. But the situation is that the mother does most of the disciplining with the children, and she does the household chores and he doesn't know how to cook for himself. So if she's not there he is pretty well helpless. And then when retirement comes up the guy doesn't know what to do with himself. He doesn't know how to take care of himself and he's been very dependent. So it's very important that there is that kind of sharing.*

Speaker If she were to die before him he would die soon after. Of starvation (laughter).

Response *Exactly, that's amazing how often you see that. Although realistically I suppose starvation isn't the cause. But your children will also pick up those things and feel, "Hey, Dad never had to do dishes around the house. Why should I?"*

Speaker They learn their roles from their parents.

Response *They learn their roles, right.*

Speaker Alright, another thing is not to cooperate too closely on tasks.

For example I had a couple decide she was going to take care of putting clothes into the machine and he would take the clothes and put them into the drier. What happened was she didn't get around to putting them into the washing machine so it created a new conflict. He couldn't do his task unless she did hers, and so they finally decided that one person would do all the laundry and then the other person would do some other major task to balance it all off.

Question *Are you assuming that people have worked through the communication problems first? Couldn't something like conflict over household responsibilities could just grow out of the communication problem.*

Speaker Yes, but once the couple learns the communication skills then they still need to problem solve these issues. And sometimes they need help to create strategies because they have perhaps never been in a problem solving mode in their communication. They're learning to walk in that kind of way. So they might need some help to think of some creative options and deciding some of these things.

Now with infidelity, we're looking at a very destructive situation in a relationship. You see the person who's had the relationship or the extramarital affair and they're coming in for counselling often times because the one who's been offended really does want to make the relationship work, but they're hurting so much because of the affair that they don't know what to do. They don't know how to resolve this thing. What do you imagine these people are feeling?

Response *Guilt.*

Speaker Who's feeling guilty?

Response *The "guilty party".*

Speaker The other person might be feeling guilty too.

Response *The other person for not having met that one's needs.*

Speaker Yes, feeling that she did not meet his needs.

Response *Or they wonder what's wrong with them?*

Speaker That's right, there's low self worth there. Those are feelings of inadequacy on the part of the one who was offended. What else is the outcome here?

Response *Anger.*

Speaker Anger, yes a lot of anger.

Response *Resentment.*

Response *Lack of trust.*

Speaker Lack of trust is the major stumbling block to couples recovering their closeness. Exactly. And so that's really where the focus needs to be. You might need to work with the offended party to verbalize the anger. Often times the person who has had the affair wants the other person to be angry with him and to express that anger. So you might spend some time helping that person release the anger, and sort out what the guilt is about. And the person who has been offended cannot extend forgiveness as long as there is a lot of anger and resentment. Once she has taken care of her anger and resentment maybe she can extend forgiveness, but she will still be left with a lack of trust. I find that most often mistrust is the core issue with infidelity.

The thing that the person who's been hurt needs to hear is the following: "I love you and only you, and I will never do this again." She needs to hear that repetitively, several times a day for days to come. She needs to be regularly reassured of the commitment. There has to be a reaffirmation and a restatement of a person's love for the other. It's not, "You're my best girl, you're number one." (laughter)

Now if this is the second or third time I'm wondering about whether the person who's been offended is a doormat type of person, a martyr type who has been attracted to an anti-social personality. The person who has multiple sexual partners or repeated affairs is often times an anti-social personality.

Response *They're destructive.*

Speaker Yes, a destructive person. He's violating the rights of the other. There's a boundary around that relationship that comes with the commitment, with the marriage contract. It's an agreement to stay together and to be together for life. And when there is an affair, there's violence done to that boundary, and in order to restore the boundary there has to be reassurance of love and a restatement, a reaffirmation of the commitment that was stated at the very beginning of the relationship.

Now most often, I find the person who's had the affairs is an irresponsible type, if not an anti-social type, and he refuses to make that commitment. He says basically, "Well I don't know what's going to happen in the future. I can't say what will happen, I can't predict what I might do." So if the person is unwilling to make that affirmation of commitment, you're not going to be able to restore trust. You're wasting your time.

Question *How do you help the partner if the other partner is stuck in it and won't leave — the doormat.*

Speaker Alright, I'd like to speak about that also in relation to the first item listed, which is physical abuse. When you work with a person who has been repeatedly offended physically, or emotionally with repeated infidelity, it's very important never to recommend that the person leave the relationship.

Never tell her to leave but only present her with the options. Her choices are for example, "You can stay in this relationship the way it is, continue to allow yourself to be beaten, or to be in a position where he or she is having more affairs. Or you can leave this relationship, or you can try to get both of you into counselling, or you could separate and continue in counselling in the mean time, either the both of you or individually. Or you can file charges against him in the case of beating or assaulting. What do you think you'll do?" So you outline some of the options but you always put the choice to the client.

Whether you're seeing them individually or as a couple, you let them sort out what they're going to do if there is a reoccurrence of this abuse.

If there are children involved and there's beating going on, you want to always find out if the children are being beaten too and sometimes they are.

Question *If they are you have legal responsibility to report that to social services, don't you ?*

Speaker That's right. That was just what I was going to make sure everyone knew about. You are legally obliged, in fact anyone who knows about child abuse is legally obligated to report it to police or social services.

Speaker What might happen if you tell a woman who is being beaten to leave her husband?

Response *She'll defend her husband.*

Response *She'll leave the counsellor.*

Speaker She might.

Response *He might come after her.*

Speaker Yes, say it again.

Response *He might come after her.*

Speaker Yes, he might come after her. He might kill her.

Response *He may come after you too.*

Speaker He might come after her. That's right, exactly. So I don't want to take responsibility for her being beaten or killed. I want her to take responsibility for her decisions. I once counselled a separated couple; the woman had decided to leave her husband. During one session he offered to take her home. She really didn't want to go with him, because she was afraid of him. She finally gave in and went, and I got a phone call within the next hour from her. She was crying, very upset, and saying that she had been raped by him. He had dragged her by the hair down the steps into the bedroom, tied her up and raped her.

So I said, "What are you going to do?" I said, "You can either do nothing," — and she said, "He's still there still in the room," — "or you can make a report to the police. What are you going to do? Maybe there are some other options open to you. What do you think you'll do?" She decided to make a report. So that's the kind of approach we need to take.

Question *Do you support them in their choice? Say you presented those options and she said she wanted to leave but didn't know where to go, do you offer alternatives as to where she could go?*

Speaker While not telling a person what to do, I would encourage her and even say, "If you decide to leave I would certainly support you in that decision".

Or I might say, "If you decide to make a report I would certainly support that decision." And then I might even go further and say, "If you decide you want to leave, here are some of the things that you can do to prepare for that," and then give her information about a shelter that she can go to without leaving any trace of her whereabouts.

I had a client who I actually used this process with, and I said to her, "You know, often women are battered up to six times before they finally leave, and she said "Well, that's not going to happen to me." I used paradoxical intention, and indeed she left the first time and never went back and felt tremendous relief and improvement in her situation. She went to Victims Assistance and they provided additional counselling to help her make that move.

Now let's go through some of these other issues, and then I want to talk about crisis intervention, which is very important.

Sexual issues are fairly common in couple counselling and usually take on two forms. The one is to hear a person say, "I don't love him any more and so I don't think we should stay together." What she means is, "I'm not in romantic passion any more," and I talk with them to clarify and define that. In other words, the flame has flickered from the time they first knew each other.

The reality is that romantic passion loses its spontaneity within the first three years of a relationship. I haven't heard of it lasting longer. Before that point it's spontaneous, you don't have to work at it. Afterward it needs to be deliberately worked at. For some this comes as a sad realization, for others it comes as a relief to know that what they're feeling isn't strange, it's the norm. And the reason that it's the norm is that habituation and familiarity cause that spontaneous romantic passion to diminish.

Response *There are no surprises any more.*

Speaker You can develop or experience that spontaneous romantic passion with any new person because there is the unfamiliarity and curiosity there. Romantic passion isn't a problem.

So this is where affairs come in. A person gets attracted to somebody else and she crosses that boundary by expressing her attraction to the other person. It's one thing to feel attracted to somebody and it's another thing to express it verbally or otherwise to that person. The moment you do that you cross the boundaries of your relationship. The spontaneous passion will last a while in the new relationship and then decrease significantly. And so it's important to explain to couples that the romantic passion is expected to diminish, and if you want to recover it you have to deliberately work at it and intentionally create romantic situations and encounters.

Now the other aspect of sexual problems that I often see is when the aggressive critical parent comes into the sexual relationship — "You're not doing it right." There isn't anything that will destroy a sexual moment of intimacy more than criticism or judgement. When there is any pressure or expectation brought into it, you can forget it. So the key there is to remove all expectation and pressure, remove it from yourself and take it off your partner too. Don't put expectation on him, don't put expectation on yourself.

View sexuality as something that is much broader and inclusive than intercourse. Gentle touching is sexual, saying flattering things or letting your partner know how she excites you, verbally letting her know that, is sexual. So sometimes it's important for couples to just be able to be together without having intercourse, showering together or being naked together without intercourse, and I might give them that assignment.

It's also important to take away the expectation of an orgasm. Have intercourse without an orgasm, you don't have to have an orgasm to have sex. And if you make orgasm your goal and if that's your expectation and you work too hard at it, that's the surest way not to have it. So the key principle is remove the pressure and remove the expectations.

Response *I read something along this line where a couple came in for counselling and the man was expressing he was no longer sexually aroused by his wife. The counsellor gave them the assignment of going to bed expecting not to be aroused. So he went to bed and he had to struggle with himself to not be aroused. Out of that came the arousal.*

Speaker Okay, so he took the pressure off and took the expectation away. The paradoxical approach again. Any questions about that?

CRISIS INTERVENTION WITH COUPLES

Speaker Alright, let's talk about crisis intervention of couples. I see a couple as being in crisis when they're in a fight in my office, or when one of them says, "There are so many problems, I'm having so much trouble, there's so much stress that I can't take it any more." They might also say something like, "I'm about ready to ditch the marriage. I can't take it and I'm going to have to get out of this. I'm going to have to commit marital suicide here, kill our marriage." Maybe that's marital homicide, I'm not sure.

And so when I see a couple is in that situation, if they're in a fight, I stand up so that they can focus on me and I say, "What I'd like to do is stop what's happening right now and make sure that we focus very clearly and carefully on the very important issues that each one of you is trying to express." So I validate the importance of each person's issues and I go to the newsprint on the wall.

I'll put Bob's name at the top and the numbers one through five, Helen's name and the numbers one through five under it and I'll say, "Bob, what's one of your issues? One of the things that's upsetting you, annoying you, angering you about what's happening in your marriage. Let's write that down. What's another thing, another issue, number two? Excellent." It's important whenever they state an issue to commend it, to validate it, and see if we can come up with five. Do the same for Helen.

And then I'll say, "Bob, which of your issues is most important to you? Which one do you need to be resolved above all others. And Helen, what's your most important issue that you need to be resolved above all others?" So that's prioritizing each person's issues. Next I say, "How are you going to decide whose issue is going to be dealt with first?" I observe the interaction to see who's going to insist or who's going to defer. Often the aggressive party defers, you know the magnanimous bravado of the aggressive party. Or the passive party might defer as well.

Response *They might get in another fight over who goes first.*

Speaker Yes. So I'm observing. I'll give them feedback. I'll say, "You know it's interesting how you made that decision. Another option would have been to flip a coin, that way neither one of you would have needed to decide or be in control about whose issue would be dealt with." So I bring the issue over and have them problem solve it.

Write the issue right at the top of the next page of newsprint, write the numbers one through eight in advance, and then brainstorm options the way we discussed yesterday. When they come up with an idea write it down. Spur them on with some statements that stimulate creative thought and ideas, generating ideas and options. When they up with eight, have each person choose three of the eight privately, just by jotting down the numbers down of the options. And then I take the slips of paper and correlate the responses and where they overlap is their basic agreement.

Now it's very important to do this with couples who are in crisis. In other words, set aside your assessment as you do with the individual in crisis. If the couple is in crisis in the first session, do only a very brief assessment, then go right into addressing the issues that are creating this crisis and see if you can problem-solve it because this is a couple in despair.

You need to instill hope before that first session ends or you're probably going to lose them, and they may not come back. And so when a couple is in a fight they're in despair, they're upset, they don't know what's going to happen or what they're going to do. They're feeling hopeless but as soon as you involve them in the problem solving process what are they feeling?

Response *That they're getting somewhere.*

Speaker They feel they're getting somewhere, they're feeling hope. Remember the couple we discussed yesterday, who were sorting out what to do with mother-in-law. They were laughing and feeling very hopeful midway through this process. They had a strategy, a plan of action that they felt very good about.

Question *Do you ever have a situation that arises where they don't agree on anything independently, when you get two sheets of paper and you look and none of them match?*

Speaker Yes, and in that situation another option or approach is to have them come up with their own private list of options and then exchange their lists and choose from the other person's list the alternatives that each person finds least objectionable or most desirable. So that way they can begin to work at an agreement.

Flip a coin to see whose primary issue will be dealt with first and once we've finished that we go for the other person's primary issue. I may or may not have time to do both person's primary issues in one session, I may only have time to do one issue. But at least they see the results of it and they have hope enough to come back for another session and work on the other issue.

I find it works better if they work on the other primary issue with me instead of trying to work on it themselves because they don't get to know the process well enough. So I go over the problem solving process with a number of issues enough times, just over and over the process until it becomes part of them, until they become so familiar with it that the next time they have an issue come up in their marriage, they'll know what they can do. They'll know what works and they won't need to go to a counsellor. My objective is to work myself out of a job, and help people become more self-reliant.

THE FIRST SESSION

Now I'd like you to take a look at the outline of couple counselling. We'll expand this outline more in the Couple and Family Counselling Skills course. But this gives you the general structure in terms of what happens in initial assessment and how much family history we go over, because in the first session I do a brief individual assessment of each partner with the other person there.

I first ask questions about the relationship: length of time together, previous couple counselling, previous separations. Then I review each persons's idea of problems in the relationship. I use reflection and explore how long specific problems have existed in the relationship.

It's important to remain neutral and to draw out the unmotivated partner in a way that helps him feel supported. In other words if he feels pressured into coming to counselling I will say, "I wonder if this is the first time you have felt pressured by Helen to do something you didn't want to do," and, "It makes sense you would feel annoyed about being here."

Then I go over individual histories including family history and identify what each person's parents' marriage was like in terms of the way they dealt with conflict and expression of affection.

I have each person describe his parent's personalities and his relationship with each parent. I make statements like, "You're no stranger to conflict. You know what conflict is about; you're an expert when it comes to conflict. You grew up in a family where there was a lot of conflict," if that was the case. Or if the opposite was the case I might say, “So you don’t really know anything about conflict because you grew up in a family where conflict was avoided. It sounds like you perhaps don’t know much about what to do with anger when it gets expressed or directed at you. Is that accurate?”

So in other words, I make connections in terms of what the client knows about or doesn’t know about based on what the family of origin was like. “You know what it’s like not to be close to people because you’re telling me the family you grew up in was not a close family. You weren’t close to people who were important to you, so it’s no surprise that you’re having trouble achieving intimacy and closeness in your marriage.” Or I’ll say it like this, “So you’re saying there wasn’t much communication in your family, and that sounds familiar, something like you were saying about your relationship now."

I make a direct connection between then and now because I’m going to want to point out to them, as I outline this structure, that there may be a need to take a closer look at those core issues from the family of origin if it becomes necessary to pursue Phase Two.

I will also ask the question about the person’s role in the family of origin, because the victim role, responsible child role, invisible role, or other role may be extended into the couple relationship. Then I will ask about three things the person would have wanted to change about the family of origin if he had magical powers. This identifies core unresolved issues, and I will ask, “I wonder if you can imagine how your life might be different or how you might be different today if those things had been different in the family you grew up in.”

Finally, I will explore sexual and marital history, previous meaningful relationships, divorces, personalities of partners, and look for patterns in choice of partners and reasons for relationships ending.

USING CLOSURE TO INCREASE MOTIVATION

In closure I say, “So now I’d like to recommend a way to proceed in counselling. What I’m hearing is a need to improve your communication skills. So I’m recommending a series of four or five sessions which I refer to as Phase One. In Phase One we’ll begin in our next session with learning how to express feelings and problems in a way that communicates clearly. In the session following that I will introduce exercises to improve your ability to listen to each other on a deep level. And then in the next session we’ll use a very effective process that will allow you to resolve nearly any issue that arises from day to day. Then two weeks after that session, we will meet to bring all the skills together and see how you make them work. After each session, I'll give you an assignment to help you practice the skills during the week."

Notice that Phase One focuses on skill building. Many couples make adequate progress with just Phase One. However, I'm also going to discuss meeting for a follow-up appointment one month later, and then I'll describe Phase Two which motivates the couple to work hard to make the skills work in Phase One. There's a motivating factor in providing this kind of structure. I'm motivating them to maintain their gains, to not lose the progress they've made.

To introduce the idea of the follow-up session I'll say, "I'd like us to suspend our meeting for a month and establish a one month tentative appointment. And if things are continuing to go well and you're using your communication skills that you've learned, then you can phone two days ahead and cancel that appointment."

Now that motivates them to maintain their gains, to continue to use the communication skills that they've learned. And it's the tentative appointment one month down the road that does the trick.

Then I'm also going to say, "If you find you can't make the skills work well for you I'll recommend Phase Two, in which I'll meet with you individually, and then as a couple, and then as individuals, and then as a couple for 12 or 16 weeks. Because it may be that you have issues from your past before you ever knew each other, that are working inside you in a way that undermines your ability to use the skills that you know about. So in Phase Two when I meet with each of you individually, I'll help you increase your awareness of what you may be unconsciously bringing into this relationship from your past. Then when we meet as a couple the next week, each of you can share your insights and then we can work more on communication skills."

STRUCTURE CAN BE COMFORTING

I will say, "Does this sound like something that will work for you?" Couples are relieved to hear that the process will be structured, time limited, and aimed at achieving specific practical goals. Sometimes they will say, "Could we start with Phase Two, since we'll still be working on communication skills then anyway when we meet as a couple?" This is an optional structure which I may present without describing Phase One and Phase Two, especially with highly motivated couples or couples from dysfunctional backgrounds who appear to be operating significantly out of unresolved conflicts and losses from pre-marital or family of origin history and who need to gain insght into themselves.

Work on unresolved conflicts, losses. ↑

Otherwise, I want to increase motivation to make the communication skills work. Let them know that if they don't make the skills work they're looking at Phase Two which means more time, and more money. Now if you don't have these motivating factors, couples often times don't give their best effort. Motivation contributes to 95% of the progress people make. That's just a sneak preview of the Couple and Family Counselling Skills course.

Appendix A: Course Handouts

CLINICAL ASSESSMENT

Counsellor's Name: ______________________ Client's Name: ______________________

Date of Birth: ______________________ Phone #: (   ) ______________________

Date Admitted: Month______ Day ____ Year______

Identification: As we begin today, I would like to take notes to help me make an assessment of problem areas. Would that be okay with you? Everything will remain completely confidential.

- What is your age?
- What is your marital status?
- Client's sex/race/ethnic identity
- What are your children's names and ages?
- What is your employment? How long?
- Do you live alone or with someone?
- Do you have any religious affiliation?

Mode of Admission: Who referred you and when?

Presenting Problems: What problems and concerns bring you to counselling? How have you been feeling?

History of Presenting Problems:

- How long have you been feeling this way? (for each feeling or problem)
- What happened at the time you began feeling this way?
- What happened at the time you decided to come for counselling?
- When have you felt like this in the past and what happened?
- Since you have been feeling this way, do you feel worse or better now?

Past Medical/Counselling History: Now I would like to ask you a series of questions to help me get a broader understanding of your situation. Would that be okay?

- Surgical: Any previous surgeries? Age? Complications?

- Medical: Any health problems? e.g. epilepsy, diabetes, etc.

- Psychiatric: Any previous counselling? Ages, reasons, treatment.

- Obstetrical:
  - Any miscarriages, abortions, postpartum depressions, etc.?
  - What age did you begin menstruating?
  - Any venereal diseases?

Family History and Relationships: Now I would like to ask you some questions about the family you grew up in. Is that okay?

- How many brothers and sisters do you have?

- Which one are you in the line of birth?

- How many years separate you from the others nearest you?

- What are your siblings' work and marital situations?

- Who were you closest to when growing up?

- Are your parents still living? What was your age at their death?

- Describe your father's personality and your relationship to him when you were growing up. Were you close, not so close, distant?

- Describe your mother's personality and your relationship when you were growing up. Were you close, not so close, distant, affectionate?

- Was your family like others around you economically and socially?

- What was your role in the family when you were growing up? Think of a word, e.g. peacemaker, black sheep, victim, outsider, assistant parent, invisible, baby, etc.?

- Describe your parents' marriage. Were they affectionate? How did they deal with conflict?

- Was anyone in the family or extended family ever hospitalized for emotional reasons or commit suicide? Any mental retardation?

- How did family members relate to each other?

- How were feelings of anger, sadness, fear, and guilt expressed?

- Describe the who, how, and why of the discipline you experienced.

- What personality features do you have which your parents also have?

- Who was there for you when you were hurt?

- What messages about your worth and the worth of others, was communicated by each parent both verbally and nonverbally?

- How old were you when you left home, and why did you leave?

- If you had miraculous power to change the family and your childhood experience in any three ways, what would you choose?

- If your family experience had been different in the ways you mentioned, how would your life be different today?

Personal History: Now I would like to ask you some questions about your life apart from your family. Is that okay?

Birth and Developmental

- Do you know if your mother had any problems with your birth?
- Were you a planned pregnancy?
- Did your parents ever tell you what kind of baby you were? Easy? Difficult?
- Any experience of bed-wetting after early childhood?
- Did you learn to walk by age one and talk by age two?
- Any long high fevers or convulsions as a child?

School and Intellectual Development

- What was the first day of school like?
- How many moves and school changes occurred during school years?
- Describe your relationships with teachers.
- Describe your relationships with peers.
- Do you believe you achieved your best in school?

Social Development

- Did you have a group of friends during the first six grades?
- Did you have one or two very close friends as a teenager?

- Did you tend to be a follower or a leader with friends?

- How old were you when you first dated?

- Do you have friends now? Or acquaintances?

- Do you have a satisfactory network of friends, family, groups?

- How would you describe the types of people you associate with? (What is your role with friends and acquaintances? Helper, victim, other?)

Occupational History

- How old were you when you first went to work?

- What types of jobs have you had and how many?

- Why have you left your jobs?

- What has been your role at work? Helper, invisible, responsible, victim, other?

- How have you gotten along with bosses?

- Are you feeling fulfilled and satisfied in your work?

Hobbies and Side Interests

- What are some of your side interests and activities?

- Has there been any change in your level of interest lately?

Sexual and Marital History

- Describe your personality during the early teen years. (Shy, disinterested, outgoing with opposite sex?)

- What were your feelings about menstruation or wet dreams?

- What was your first date like for you?

- How old were you with your first sexual experience? (Or first intercourse?)

- How many sexual partners have you had over time?

- What is your sexual preference or orientation?

- Describe your partner's personality and your relationship.

- Describe previous meaningful relationships, personalities, and why they ended.

- Describe the family including how you, your partner, and the children relate to each other.

Alcohol and Drug Abuse History

- What about your use of alcohol and drugs? How much and how often?
- Why do you use it?
- How long have you used it and what changes have occurred?
- Has your use of this gotten in the way of work or family and social relationships and responsibilities?
- Has anyone ever objected to or commented about your drinking (or use of drugs)?
- If use has been a problem, you are required to discontinue use for 30 days before your counselling can begin.

Legal Difficulties

- Have you had any past arrests, warrants, charges, suits against you?

- Any outstanding debts?

Functional Inquiry: Could you ask your doctor to send me a report of your recent physical examination? If you haven't had one within six months, have another one.

General:

- Allergies - Any allergies?

- Medications - What medications do you use? Why? How long?

- Appetite and Weight - Any changes in weight or appetite? Any dieting? Any vomiting?

- Sleep - Any problems getting enough sleep?

- Energy - What has your energy level been like?

Systems:

- Head and Neck - Have you ever injured your head or neck?

- Respiratory - Any problems breathing?

- Cardiovascular - Any heart or chest pain?

- Gastrointestinal - Any problems with bowels?

- Genitourinary - Any problems urinating?

- Locomotor and Integumentary - Weakness or stiffness in joints?

- Central nervous system - Headaches or shakiness?

Personality:
- How would you describe your personality?

Mental Status:

General Behaviour and Appearance

Talk

Sample of Talk

Mood - Anxiety, Depression, Suicidal and Homicidal ideas

- If you were to rate your mood on a scale of 0-10 with "0" meaning that life's not worth living and "10" meaning that life is great and you're feeling optimistic about your present and future, where would you put yourself right now?

- Have you ever had suicidal thoughts at any time in your life? How old were you? What happened?

- Have you ever had thoughts of wanting to kill someone?

(Record information regarding intent and commitment to talk rather than act on suicidal or homicidal thoughts.)

- How nervous or tense do you feel right now, on a scale of 0 to 10?

Cognition

- Orientation - What's my name? Today's date? Where are you?

- Delusions and Misinterpretations
  - Do you believe strangers are out to hurt you?

  - Do you think people are always talking about you negatively?

  - If you walk into a room of people laughing, do you think they are laughing at you?

- Hallucinations - auditory and visual
  - Do you hear voices other people don't hear?

  - Do you see things other people don't see?

- **Compulsive Phenomena**
  - Are you a perfectionist? (If yes, ask the following)
  - Do you have set routines, which if interrupted is very upsetting?
  - Do you check and re-check the stove, locks, lights?
  - Do you have unwanted thoughts repeating in your mind?

- **General Information** - Now I want to ask you some questions to see how well you are remembering and concentrating.
  - Who is the Prime Minister?
  - Who is the Premier?
  - Name three capital cities in Europe.
  - Name five large cities in Canada.

- **Intelligence** (Counsellor will record basic impression: below average - average - above average)

- **Memory** - "How has your memory been lately?"

- Attention and Concentration - How well have you been concentrating lately?

- Babcock Sentence - Repeat after me: "The one thing a nation needs in order to be rich and great is a large, secure supply of wood".

- Proverb Interpretation - What does this proverb mean to you, "People who live in glass houses shouldn't throw stones"?

- Judgment - Have you been able to make day-to-day decisions?

Client's Etiologic Formulation: Having reviewed much of your background, I'm wondering if you might have just a little bit of insight or some understanding of the story behind the problems you began talking about today or about what makes you tick.

Client's Goals: If you were to continue your counselling, what would you hope to achieve or what would be your goals in counselling?

Client's Evaluation and Motivation:

- What's this been like today talking about yourself and your situation?

- Would you like to do this again and pursue your goals in counselling?

Formulation:

- Diagnostic (Give evidence for disorders or personality traits or features, from the DSM IV)

  Axis I

  Axis II

  Axis III

  Axis IV

  Axis V

- Etiologic Formulation

Psychodynamic Goals:

Plan of Treatment:

Prognosis:

Authorization for Release of Medical Information

I,_____________________________________ , residing at ________________________________

____

do hereby grant authorization to ____

____

for the release of any medical information concerning me. I am fully aware and agree that this information will be used solely and confidentially by ________________________

____

in the determination of appropriate services to be rendered to me.

Signed ______________________________

Date ________________________________

Witness______________________________

Date ________________________________

- -

Authorization for Release of Medical Information

I,_____________________________________ , residing at ________________________________

____

do hereby grant authorization to ____

____

for the release of any medical information concerning me. I am fully aware and agree that this information will be used solely and confidentially by ________________________

____

in the determination of appropriate services to be rendered to me.

Signed ______________________________

Date ________________________________

Witness______________________________

Date ________________________________

Progress Notes	No ____________ Name ____________________

Date		**Medical Referrals & Signatures**

SUICIDE PREVENTION PROCEDURES

Suicide Assessment Questionnaire

- What has your appetite been like?
- What has your sleeping been like?
- What has your energy level been like?
- What is your mood using a scale of 0-10, "0" being life is not worth living, and "10" being life is great and you feel confident and optimistic?
- If the response indicates less than "5" say, "Have you had any suicidal thoughts?"
- If the answer is affirmative say, "Have you thought how you might kill yourself?"
- Are you safe with yourself?
- Do you live alone or with someone?
- Other factors which contribute to a high risk profile are:
  - over fifty years old
  - male
  - unemployed
  - living alone
  - means of committing suicide are effective and available
  - major stressors are present: bankruptcy, marital problems, death, major illness, or injury
  - unusual euphoric mood and tidying up personal affairs following severe depression or crisis

Suicide Prevention

- **Suicide Contract** - If the answer to the question 'Are you safe?' is affirmative, say "Can you agree to talk to me personally before you ever carry out a plan to kill yourself?"
  If the answer is "I don't know," or "No," and if the person is not already hospitalized, say "I'm recommending that you go to a hospital emergency room. Will you go?"
- **Office Setting** - If the person responds negatively say, "If you are unwilling to go, I will have to ask the police or RCMP to accompany you."
- **Phone Setting** - If the person responds negatively say, "I'll phone you back in a few minutes."
  - After phoning the police and giving them the specific statements of the suicidal person, they will go to the individual's address and accompany them to the emergency room.
  - Phone the suicidal person and engage in conversation until the police arrive.

Suicide Follow Up

- Refer the person if you feel you would be unable to help him or her.
- During weekly visits, assess and document suicidal thoughts until they are no longer reported for at least four weeks.
- Re-affirm the suicide contract made above.

ETIOLOGIC FORMULATION

This is a summary of factors from categories in the assessment which may have contributed to the presenting problems. It includes strengths and healthy ways of coping as well as negative factors and problems. The term "etiologic" means the story or understanding of the "origin" or "beginnings" of the client's problems.

Categories in Formulation

- ***lines 1, 2, 3:*** Family History
- ***line 3:*** School and Intellectual Development
- ***lines 4 and 5:*** Social Development
- ***lines 5 and 6:*** Presenting Complaints
- ***lines 7 and 8:*** Strengths
- ***lines 8 and 9:*** Hereditary, Genetic, Biological Factors

Example

1. Mr. Z is a 35-year-old, single, Caucasian man who came from a family in which the father

2. was an alcoholic, verbally abusive, and often absent, while the mother was overprotective

3. and "smothering." He experienced many moves in early years.

4. He had difficulty making friends and describes himself as a "loner" during teenage

5. years. He now states that he is unable to meet people, is afraid of women, has

6. difficulty holding a job, and feels hopeless about the future.

7. His strengths include intelligence, and motivation since the loss of a common-law

8. relationship, to look at changes. There do not appear to be biological, hereditary, or

9. or genetic factors affecting this case.

Notice that the order of appearance in the formulation are first, factors from Family and Developmental History; second, Presenting Complaints; third, Strengths (with mention of precipitating factor); and finally, a statement about Hereditary, Genetic, and Biological Factors. The order of mention proceeds generally from early to recent history.

EXAMPLES OF ETIOLOGIC CATEGORIES IN FORMULATION

	Biological	**Psychological**	**Sociological**
Predisposing	Family history of alcoholism, depression, schizophrenia, epilepsy, Alzheimer's disease Huntington's chorea, neuroticism Congenital disorders, i.e. Down's syndrome Congenital abnormality, i.e. cleft lip Hyperactivity	Pattern of childhood avoidance, fears, enuresis, etc. Physical and/or psychological abuse in childhood	Chaotic family background - fighting, alcohol, frequent moves
Precipitating	Recent illness, surgery, injury Childbirth Medications Alcohol and/or drugs	Feeling rejected after argument Narrowly avoiding dangerous situation, i.e. car accident Recent mishap or assault and/or rape	Recent separation / marriage Leaving parent's home Change of residence
Propagating	Chronic physical illness, i.e. renal failure, rheumatoid arthritis Deafness Mental retardation Continued need for medications to treat other conditions, i.e. cortisones to treat ulcerative colitis	Fear of rejection so avoids closeness Ongoing physical/mental illness or handicap	Ongoing court cases: criminal, divorce, custody, compensation, etc. Worker's compensation Poor work history
Protective	Good physical health High intelligence	Active and outgoing Successful Resourceful Likable	Good marriage Good work history Supportive family and/or friends

INTAKE

Name:______________________________ Age: _______ Date of Birth: ________________

Identification:

Accommodation, occupation, educational level, marital status, religion

Referral Source:

Presenting Problems:

Onset, duration, severity, if recurrent

Acting Out Behaviour:

Alcohol/drug abuse (past and current), suicide attempts, other self-violating acts, prostitution, gambling, punctuality in jobs or school, frequency of job changes and residential changes, use of prescription and non-prescription drugs and frequency of use, extent of use of non-prescription drugs, e.g. Aspirin.

Family History:

Brief information on family relationships and other significant relationships, present social support and degree of dependency.

Previous Treatment:

Medical, psychiatric, reasons for hospitalization, duration of inpatient or outpatient treatment, brief information on treatment received i.e. meds, E.C.T., etc.

Functional:

Sleep, appetite, eating disorders, any active diseases that may interfere with treatment, energy level and any changes.

Mental Status:

Appearance, abnormality of talk and speech. Mood - any changes in mood. Suicide risk; previous attempts, current thoughts, commitment not to act on thoughts. Hallucinations or delusions, if present; duration, severity, current state, concentration, memory, and insight.

Goals and Motivation to Change:

What are the goals and expectations of counselling in the patient's mind and in the therapist's mind. Motivation and attitude to change. Willingness to participate in all aspects of the program. Ability to handle confrontation, psychological mindedness - trial interpretation.

Legal Problems:

Past, present, and pending.

BACKGROUND INFORMATION

Please complete these forms as fully and accurately as possible. All information will remain confidential and will be used to benefit you in your counselling. If more space is needed, please use the back of the page.

Date: Month ___Day __ Year ______
Last Name:_______________ First Name:__________Middle Name:________
Address: _______________ City: __________Postal Code: ______
Phone #: Home (__)__________Work: (__) __________

Emergency Notification: Name: ____________________
Address: _______________ City: ________ Phone #:(__)__________
Relationship: (e.g. spouse, mother, father, friend, etc.) ____________________

Date of Birth: ____________ Age: ___ Sex: ❑ Female ❑Male

Marital Status

- ❑ Never Married
- ❑ Married
- ❑ Separated
- ❑ Divorced
- ❑ Widowed
- ❑ Widowed, remarried
- ❑ Divorced, remarried
- ❑ Common-law
- ❑ Other

Racial Origin

- ❑ White
- ❑ Negro
- ❑ Treaty Indian
- ❑ Metis
- ❑ Inuit
- ❑ Semitic
- ❑ East Indian
- ❑ Oriental
- ❑ Other

Religion

- ❑ Anglican
- ❑ Baptist
- ❑ Greek Orthodox
- ❑ Jewish
- ❑ Lutheran
- ❑ Roman Catholic
- ❑ United Church of Canada
- ❑ Other, Evangelical?
- ❑ Other
- ❑ no religious affiliation
- ❑ Do not care to say

Yearly Income

- ❑ $0-$4,999
- ❑ $5,000-$9,999
- ❑ $10,000-$14,999
- ❑ $15,000-$19,999
- ❑ $20,000-$29,999
- ❑ $30,000-39,999
- ❑ $40,000-$49,999
- ❑ $50,000 plus

Yearly Family Income

- ❑ $0-$4,999
- ❑ $5,000-$9,999
- ❑ $10,000-$14,999
- ❑ $15,000-$19,999
- ❑ $20,000-$29,999
- ❑ $30,000-$39,999
- ❑ $40,000-$49,999
- ❑ $50,000 plus

Education

- ❑ Grades 1-3
- ❑ Grades 4-6
- ❑ Grades 7-9
- ❑ Grades 10 or 11
- ❑ High School
- ❑ Technical School
- ❑ Community College
- ❑ Some University
- ❑ University Degree
- ❑ Postgraduate Degree

Usual Occupation: ____________________
Current Occupation: ____________________

Current Employment: (Check the one category that describes you best)

❑ Employed, full-time
❑ Employed, part-time
❑ Full-time student
❑ Part-time student
❑ Retired
❑ Housewife
❑ Unemployed

Who told you about "*Counselling Services*":

❑ Doctor's or psychiatrist's office (e.g. receptionist/nurse - you have never seen the doctor or discussed your problem with them.)

❑ Doctor (name)________________________
❑ Psychiatrist (name) ________________________
❑ Hospital (name) ________________________
❑ Relative (e.g. spouse, father, mother, friend, etc.)________________________
❑ School
❑ Friend, relative
❑ Nobody

Have you previously been admitted to "*Counselling Services*"?

❑ Yes ❑ No When? ________________________

What problem brought you to "*Counselling Services*"?

What other significant problems or stresses are you facing at the present time?

Have any of the following happened in your life in the past year? Check all that apply.

1. ❑ Vacation
   ❑ Minor legal problems
   ❑ Small bank loan

2. ❑ Began or ended school (Technical apprenticeship/college/university)
   ❑ Argument with neighbour/boss
   ❑ Change in work hours

3. ❑ Death of close relative
   ❑ Jail term (duration ______________)
   ❑ Divorce

7. ❑ Change in residence
   i) How often in past year __________
   ii) How often in past 5 years _______

4. ❑ Change to different line of work
   ❑ Death of close friend
   ❑ Pregnancy
   ❑ Child leaves home

5. ❑ Severe illness in self or family
   ❑ Bankruptcy
   ❑ Marital separation
   ❑ Birth of child

6. ❑ Multiple death of family
   ❑ Devastating natural disaster (e.g. flood, tornado)
   ❑ Other ________________________

Has any member of your family other than yourself seen a psychiatrist, psychologist, social worker or counsellor at any time?

❑ Yes ❑ No

If yes, specify which member and nature of the problem.

Which family member	Nature of problem

Have YOU ever seen a psychiatrist, psychologist, social worker or counsellor at any time?

❑ Yes ❑ No

If yes, specify who you saw and the nature of the problem.

Who did you see	Nature of problem

Have you ever been hospitalized for an emotional problem?

❑ Yes ❑ No

If yes, how many times? ______________________

Where	When	For how long (please check)?	
		Less than 24 hrs	More than 24 hrs

Are you or any of your family taking any medication prescribed by a doctor at the present time?

❑ Yes ❑ No

If yes, specify who, the type of medication and reason for taking it.

Who	Medication	Reason for taking it

Are you taking any medication NOT prescribed by a doctor, such as aspirin, sleeping medication, laxatives, antacids, diet pills, wake-up pills, etc. at the present time?
❑ Yes ❑ No

Medication	Reason for taking

Have you had a period of heavy alcohol or drug abuse, past or present? Please describe.

Has any member of your family had a period of heavy alcohol or drug abuse, past or present?
Please describe.

Did your parents feel that your birth and early development (learning to crawl, walk, talk) was normal?
❑ Yes ❑ No
If no, why not?

Was there anything unusual about you or your life during the time you were in grade school and high school?

How old were you when you began working?

Approximately how many jobs have you had since you began working?

List your last three places of employment starting with the most recent or current place:

Present or most recent employer	Position	Length of stay	Reason for leaving

Please list the members of your family.

Immediate family:

Name	Sex	Age	Living with you now Yes	No	Deceased	If not, where do they live	Current or usual occupation
Spouse							
Children							

Parents and/or stepparents:

Name	Sex	Age	Living with you now Yes	No	Deceased	If not, where do they live	Current or usual occupation

Brothers and sisters:

Name	Sex	Age	Living with you now Yes	No	Deceased	If not, where do they live	Current or usual occupation

State date(s) of any significant relationship(s) in your life (i.e. marriage, common-law union) starting with the most recent or current:

Approximate dates of marriage / union / significant relationship From	To	Reason for end (e.g. death, divorce, significant relationship ended)

More General Questions

Have you or any member of your family had any legal problems?
❑ Yes ❑ No
If yes, please describe.

Is there any other information you feel would be helpful to us?

What kind of help are you expecting to receive from "*Counselling Services*"?

Women Only

Date of last Pap smear: Month____ Day ____ Year __

Any problems with your menstrual cycle?
❑ Yes ❑ No
If yes, what?

How many pregnancies and/or miscarriages have you had? Abortions?_______

Describe any problems with the pregnancies.

ATTITUDE QUESTIONNAIRE

Name:________________________________ Date:____________________

Please indicate how each of the following statements applies to you by circling the appropriate number using the rating scale from 1 to 5, after each statement. Please mark *every* item.

1. How often do you feel inferior to most of the people you know?
1. very often
2. fairly often
3. sometimes
4. once in a great while
5. practically never

2. Do you ever think that you are a worthless individual?
1. very often
2. fairly often
3. sometimes
4. once in a great while
5. practically never

3. How confident do you feel that someday the people you know will look up to you and respect you?
1. not at all
2. not very
3. slightly
4. fairly
5. very

4. How often do you feel to blame for your mistakes?
1. very often
2. fairly often
3. sometimes
4. once in a great while
5. practically never

5. Do you ever feel so discouraged with yourself that you wonder whether anything is worthwhile?
1. very often
2. fairly often
3. sometimes
4. once in a great while
5. practically never

6. How often do you feel that you dislike yourself?
1. very often
2. fairly often
3. sometimes
4. once in a great while
5. practically never

7. In general, how confident do you feel about your abilities?
1. not at all
2. not very
3. slightly
4. fairly
5. very

8. How often do you have the feeling that there is nothing you can do well?
1. very often
2. fairly often
3. sometimes
4. once in a great while
5. practically never

9. How often do you worry about criticism that might be made of your work by who ever is responsible for checking up on your work?
1. very often
2. fairly often
3. sometimes
4. once in a great while
5. practically never

10. How much do you worry about how well you get along with other people?
1. very
2. fairly
3. slightly
4. not very
5. not at all

11. Do you ever feel afraid or anxious when you are going into a room by yourself where other people have already gathered and are talking?
1. very often
2. fairly often
3. sometimes
4. once in a great while
5. practically never

12. How often do you feel self-conscious?
1. very often
2. fairly often
3. sometimes
4. once in a great while
5. practically never

13. When you have to talk in front of a group of people your own age, how afraid or worried do you usually feel?
1. very
2. fairly
3. slightly
4. not very
5. not at all

14. When you are trying to win a game or sport and you know that other people are watching you, how rattled or flustered do you get?
1. very
2. fairly
3. slightly
4. not very
5. not at all

15. How much do you worry about whether other people will regard you as a success or a failure in your job or career?
1. very
2. fairly
3. slightly
4. not very
5. not at all

16. When in a group of people, do you have trouble thinking of the right things to talk about?
1. very often
2. fairly often
3. sometimes
4. once in a great while
5. practically never

17. When you have made an embarrassing mistake or have done something that makes you look foolish, how long do you usually keep worrying about it?
1. very
2. fairly
3. slightly
4. not very
5. not at all

18. Do you find it hard to make small talk when you meet new people?
1. very often
2. fairly often
3. sometimes
4. once in a great while
5. practically never

19. How often do you worry about whether other people like to be with you?
1. very often
2. fairly often
3. sometimes
4. once in a great while
5. practically never

20. How often are you troubled with shyness?
1. very often
2. fairly often
3. sometimes
4. once in a great while
5. practically never

21. When you are trying to convince other people who disagree with your ideas, how worried do you usually feel about the impression you are making?
1. very
2. fairly
3. slightly
4. not very
5. not at all

22. When you think about the possibility that some of your friends or acquaintances might not have a good opinion of you, how concerned or worried do you feel about it?
1. very
2. fairly
3. slightly
4. not very
5. not at all

23. How often do you feel worried or bothered about what other people think of you?
1. very often
2. fairly often
3. sometimes
4. once in a great while
5. practically never

COMPLAINT QUESTIONNAIRE

Name:______________________________

Instructions:

Below is a list of problems that people sometimes have. Read each one carefully and choose one of the numbers that best describes how much the problem has bothered you during the past week, including today. Place the number in the box to the right of the complaint. Do not skip any items. The example below will show you exactly how to mark your answers. If you have any questions, please ask your therapist.

Example

How much were you bothered by:
__2__ Body aches (moderately)

Answers

0 Not at all
1 A little bit
2 Moderately
3 Quite a bit
4 Extremely

_____ Headaches
_____ Nervousness or shakiness inside
_____ Repeated unpleasant thoughts that won't leave your mind
_____ Faintness or dizziness
_____ Loss of sexual interest or pleasure
_____ Feeling critical of others
_____ The idea that someone else control your thoughts
_____ Feeling others are to blame for most of your troubles
_____ Trouble remembering things
_____ Worried about sloppiness or carelessness
_____ Feeling easily annoyed or irritated
_____ Pains in heart or chest
_____ Feeling afraid in open spaces or on the streets
_____ Feeling low in energy or slowed down
_____ Thoughts of ending your life
_____ Hearing voices that other people do not hear
_____ Trembling
_____ Feeling that most people cannot be trusted
_____ Poor appetite
_____ Crying easily
____ Feeling shy or uneasy with the opposite sex
____ Feelings of being trapped or caught
____ Suddenly scared for no reason
____ Temper outburst that you could not control.
____ Trouble getting your breath
____ Feeling afraid to go out of your house alone
____ Blaming yourself for things
____ Pains in your lower back
____ Feeling blocked in getting things done
____ Feeling lonely
____ Feeling blue
____ Worrying too much about things
____ Feeling no interest in things
____ Feeling fearful
____ Your feelings are easily hurt
____ Other people being aware of your private thoughts
____ Feeling others do not understand you or are unsympathetic
____ Feeling that people are unfriendly or dislike you
____ Having to do things very slowly to ensure correctness

Example

How much were you bothered by:
__2__ Body aches
(moderately)

Answers

0 Not at all
1 A little bit
2 Moderately
3 Quite a bit
4 Extremely

____Heart pounding or racing
____Nausea or upset stomach
____Feeling inferior to others
____Soreness of your muscles
____Feeling that you are watched or talked about by others
____Trouble falling asleep
____Having to check and double-check what you do
____Difficulty making decisions
____Feeling afraid to travel on buses, subways, or trains
____Hot or cold spells
____Having to avoid certain things, places or activities because they frighten you
____Your mind going blank
____Numbness or tingling in parts of your body
____A lump in your throat
____Feeling hopeless about the future
____Trouble concentrating
____Feeling weak in parts of your body
____Feeling tense or keyed up
____Heavy feelings in your arms or legs
____Thoughts of death or dying
____Overeating
____Feeling uneasy when people are watching you
____Having thoughts that are not your own
____Having urges to beat, injure, or harm someone
____Awakening in the early morning
____Having to repeat the same actions, such as touching, counting, washing
____Sleep that is restless or disturbed
____Having urges to break or smash things
____ Having ideas or beliefs that others do not have
____ Feeling very self-conscious with others
____ The idea that something serious is wrong with your body
____ Feelings of guilt
____ Feeling uneasy in crowds, such as shopping or at a movie
____ Feeling everything is an effort
____ Spells of panic or terror
____ Feeling uncomfortable about eating or drinking in public
____ Getting into frequent arguments
____ Feeling nervous when you are left alone
____ Others not giving you proper credit for your achievements
____ Feeling lonely even when you are with people
____ Feeling so restless you can't sit still
____ Feelings of worthlessness
____ The feeling that something bad is going to happen to you
____ Shouting or throwing things
____ Feeling afraid you will faint in public
____ Feeling that people will take advantage of you if you let them
____ Having thoughts about sex that bother you a lot
____ The idea that you should be punished for your sins
____ Thoughts and images of a frightening nature
____ Never feeling close to another person
____ The idea that something is wrong with your mind

Handouts for Chapter Two:

Counselling Process and Therapeutic Interventions

OUTLINE

Qualities of the Counsellor

- Self-awareness
- Empathy, genuineness, warmth
- The saviour syndrome
- The use of one's own feelings
- Unconditional positive regard
- Providing support

The Counselling Process

- Initial assessment and movement toward awareness
- Creating a safe enough environment: therapeutic alliance
- Expressing feelings, needs, and views
- Rest or withdrawal from action
- Moving through the cycle of resistance, pain, insight, and change
- Consolidating self-worth, success, creative ability, empowerment
- Closure

Therapeutic Tasks

- Assessing the individual or family
- Validating and supporting the painful emotions
- Generating insight into behaviour patterns
- Motivating reintegration or reconstruction of life or preparing for death

Assessment Skills

- Initial and ongoing assessment
- Understanding the story behind "presenting problems."
- Goal setting

Reaching for Feelings

- Using the feeling list
- Gestalt methods for expressing emotions
- Validating painful feelings
- The use of emotional blocking, resistance, and defense mechanisms
- The empathic reflective statement
- Supportive statements
- Specific approaches for primary feelings
- Completing unfinished business

Generating Insight

- Using the tentative interpretive reflection
- The use of backtracking
- The exploration of early ways of coping
- The use of transference phenomena
- The use of exaggeration and minimizing
- Increasing self-worth through validation and affirmation

Motivating Reconstruction

- The use of alternately validating and challenging
- The use of individual responsibility
- Increasing creative ability and empowerment
- The use of communication skills with gestalt techniques
- The use of risk-taking and assignments
- Closure skills

THE ECLECTIC APPROACH TO COUNSELLING AND PSYCHOTHERAPY

The use of particular models and skills is determined by the needs of the individual, the counselling process, and the ability of the counsellor. This simple chart attempts to relate specific models to aspects of the counselling process.

The sign "+" indicates which models and interventions are used to achieve therapeutic goals by a particular counsellor. Your chart may look different.

	"Working Through" the Feelings	Understanding Patterns	Changing Patterns
Decision Counselling		+	+
Psychodynamic Therapy	+	+	+
Behavioural Therapy		+	+
Existential Therapy		+	
Person-Centred, Modern Rogerian	+	+	+
Gestalt Therapy	+	+	+
Logo Therapy		+	
Cognitive Therapy		+	+
Reality Therapy		+	+
Transactional Analysis		+	
Family-Marital Therapy	+	+	+
Community-Psychoeducational		+	
Feminist Therapy		+	
Psychodrama	+	+	+
Rational-Emotive Therapy		+	
Strategic Therapy		+	+
Structural Therapy		+	
Problem-Solving Therapy		+	+
Communication Therapy	+	+	+
Hypnotherapy	+	+	+

BASIC COUNSELLING SKILLS

Stage Setting:

Positioning

- Why - To maximize the comfort of the other person in order to obtain the most information.
- How - By sitting at a 90 degree angle, not face to face, and a distance of 20 to 36 inches.

Engaging in the Medium of the Other

- When - The other person seems initially comfortable or unwilling to express himself verbally
- How - Parallel what the other person is doing nonverbally
  example: staring out the window

Attending

- When - Not to distract but to let them know you are listening
- How - By leaning forward, frequent eye contact, head nods, and verbal cues, such as uh-huh, yes, etc.

Engaging Feelings:

Reaching for Feelings

- How - By verbalizing nonverbal behaviour;
  describing feelings people generally experience in similar situations
- When - Feelings are expressed but not verbally;
  no feelings are expressed in the situation that generally evokes feeling;
  feelings expressed are not congruent with the feelings that such a situation generally provokes

Waiting out Feelings

- How - By remaining silent
- When - After you have just reached for feelings, when verbal behaviour stops abruptly or when nonverbal behaviour signals "time-out"

Getting with Feelings (understanding)

- How - By making a congruent statement or noise
- When - The person expresses feelings in words and the person acknowledges that feeling you reached for is the feeling he is experiencing

Reporting own Feelings

- When - Your report may shed light or help the person contact his own feelings.
  example: "I feel a little tense right now. Does anyone else feel that way?"

Reaching for a Feeling Link

- How - Asking if anyone has a sense of feeling of a person or by asking if others have felt this
- When - The feeling is expressed and more than two people are present

Engaging Information:

Reaching for Information
- How - By asking open-ended questions to get more facts or by asking close-ended questions to get specific details
- When - Reach only when uncertain about the facts

Partializing
- How - Divide the problem into parts by making a list
- When - The problem has many facets or there are different problems at the same time

Providing Information
- How - Explain that the opinions are yours
- When - If the information increases knowledge, not already available, and only if the information is relevant (facts, opinions, ideas)

Recasting Problems
- How - By providing alternative definitions asking client if these might be valid to him
- When - Client's definition of the problem is not the only definition

Running out Alternative (for action)
- How - By listing possible courses of action
- When - The information increases knowledge not already available, and only if the information is relevant

Pointing to Possible consequences
- How - By giving positive and negative consequences
- When - Alternatives have been suggested

Managing Interaction:

Checking out Differences
- How - By stating the assumption and asking for confirmation
- When - Interpretation is appropriate

Giving Feedback
- How - By repeating the essence of client's statement and asking if that is accurate
- When - The message received is not clear

Making Connections between Discrete Facts or Events
- How - By asking if the facts or events are related
- When - Client does not connect, you infer a connection which places a different perspective

Summarizing
- How - By describing information or feelings
- When - A series of discussions, at beginning, during, and at the end, when things seem confused and the focus is lost

Amplifying a Subtle Message

- When - More than two people are present;
  nonverbal behaviour indicates feelings;
  others do not notice
- How - Verbalizing nonverbal behaviour to the group

Toning Down a Strong Message

- When - More than two people are present;
  a highly affective message (yelling);
  others cannot deal with the message at that level
- How - By verbalizing the essence, or asking the person to verbalize the essence, or restating the message without the affect
  example: "Do you understand what he is saying to you?"

Redirecting a Message

- When - Person directs message to another party than the intended
- How - Move your hand to the appropriate person, ask person to address appropriate person.

Talking in the Idiom of the Other

- When - Person uses an analogy or parallelism or expresses his feelings directly
- How - Use the same symbols
  example 1: Analogy - it takes a spider a whole week to make a web and you can wipe it out in a second
  example 2: "I have a friend who has this problem..."

Engaging Barriers:

Referring to Purpose

- How - Restate the purpose and indicate its difference from what is happening
- When - Observable behaviour differs from purpose

Pointing out Obstacles

- How - If you know the obstacle, note it; if not, ask what's getting in the way
- When - Prerequisite: You have already referred to the purpose and it failed

Challenging the Taboo

- How - By mentioning the unmentionable word or phrase or idea
- When - Sudden silence or verbal diversion

Confronting with contradictory reality

- When - The information provided by the other person is inaccurate or the verbal expression of feeling and nonverbal expression contradict
- How - By presenting information to counter the distortion
  example: "But you are frowning."

THE COUNSELLING SESSION

Opening the Session

Unstructured Openings

- Smile and nod to signal the client to begin.
- "Where would you like to start today?"
- "What would you like to talk about today?"

Structured Openings

- "What's been happening?"
- "Maybe we could start by talking about what's happened since we last met."
- "What I'd like to do today as we begin, is to focus on what your goals are and what you would like to achieve in your counselling."
    - Reflect the client's goals.
    - Then say, "Which of these is your most important goal?"

Working Through

- If the goal or topic seems to be a symptom of a previous painful life experience, continue by saying, "How long in your life have you struggled with this?" Then say, "Talk about what was happening in your life around the time the problem seemed to begin."
- If the goal or topic seems to be a painful life experience, e.g. death of father, continue by saying, "Talk about what happened."
- **Identify feelings** (if not already engaged): "I wonder what bits of feelings might be coming up inside right now as you're talking. A little fear, guilt, anger, sadness, or some other feeling?"
- **Engage feelings:** "Take some time with silence right now and just let yourself feel whatever feeling is there inside. That's important."
- **Validate feelings:** "Is it okay to feel angry (sad, fear, etc.)?"
- **Invitation to talk:** "Now say more about the sadness (or other feeling). What's it about?"
- **Insight intervention:** "What have you done with the feeling? How has it affected your life?"
- "I wonder if you know how your life might be different if you didn't struggle with this."
- **Change intervention:** "Does the way you've handled the feeling work well for you?" "What can you do differently that might work better?" If the client is resistant say, "It's understandable that you wouldn't be ready to change yet."

Closing the Session

- **Summary reflection:** "So today you've been talking about (topics, themes, insights gained, feelings engaged, decisions to change, assignments, etc.)."
- **Validation intervention:** "You've done a lot of work today."
- **Evaluation:** "What's it been like doing this and talking about these things today?"
- **Invitation to return:** "I wonder if you'd like to do this again and take it a little bit further."
- **Appointment:** "Is this time OK for you next week?"
- **End point intervention:** "Maybe we can close now and I'll see you next time."

INTERVENTIONS FOR PARTS OF THE COUNSELLING PROCESS

I. "Working Through" the Feelings

- What are you feeling right now as you talk?
- Are you feeling fear, sadness, guilt, anger, emptiness, low self-worth?
- Say more about that feeling.
- What were you feeling just when your voice dropped?
- What are the tears about?
- Just let yourself feel that right now.
- Just stay with that feeling right now without saying anything.
- I wonder if maybe you feel just a little___*(feeling word)*___
- That could leave a person feeling ___*(feeling word)*___
- Just say a little bit more about that.
- It takes courage to face that pain.
- That's it, just let more of it out.
- What is the fear about?
- What is the most difficult thing for you to talk about?
- I want you to imagine that your (significant other) is sitting here.
- What are you feeling as you recall that memory?
- How much of that feeling do you have? A little, medium, a lot?
- Is it okay to feel that? I believe it is okay.
- You have every right to feel that.
- What choice words do you have for him or her?
- So maybe you feel just a little annoyed or cheated. Is that accurate?
- So you feel _______ when_______ because _________ . Is that what you're saying?
- I want you to exaggerate the way you feel right now.
- I wonder if hanging on to that feeling is way of hanging on to that person.
- What unfinished business do you have with that person?
- What is your fantasy of that person?
- What has that event left you feeling about yourself?
- What have you done with that feeling(s)?
- What goes into the emptiness?
- You can either fill the emptiness with old feelings or with new feelings for people and for life experiences.
- What feeling gets in the way when you try to do (or say) that?
- What is it about this person that pushes your buttons?
- So you are hypersensitive or have an exaggerated feeling of when that happens. Is that accurate?
- How has the guilt affected your life?
- Talk about the time when you experienced that feeling the most.
- What is it like for you when you feel that?
- What feeling is under or beside the feeling you just talked about?
- It certainly is understandable that you would have those feelings with what you have been through.
- Which of those two feelings is harder to talk about? Talk about it.
- How much of that feeling do you have on a scale of 0-10?
- What can you do to feel more or less of that feeling?
- I wonder if you are letting that feeling get in the way of your therapy.
- I wonder what you'd feel if you didn't make a case for that person.
- Talk about the last time you felt that way, and the time before that.
- How safe do you feel?
- How do you feel toward me? It is important to your therapy.
- What is it like saying that? Is it OK to feel that?
- How long will you hang on to that feeling?

II. Understanding Patterns

- Maybe it's too soon to let go of that feeling(s).
- What is the story behind that behaviour?
- What gives it meaning or allows it to make sense?
- Is that the first time this has happened?
- What was the last time something like this happened, and the time before that?
- What characteristics of this person seem to push your buttons?
- What significant person in your life had characteristics similar to this person?
- What did you do to cope with what happened as a child?
- What is your way of coping with a similar event now?
- What kinds of men or women are you attracted to?
- What was your role in the family you grew up in, and where do you see this role being repeated?
- What do you do to make distance?
- What is the pay off or outcome of that behaviour?
- I wonder if you have some insight or some handle on what makes you tick?
- What do you do when you feel that?
- It makes a lot of sense that you would relate in that way.
- If your family had been different in some way, how do you imagine your life would be different today?
- Which parent are you most and least like and why?
- How do you express your various feelings?
- Do you see yourself as generally passive, aggressive, or assertive?
- How much giving and taking is there in your significant relationships?
- What is the purpose of your life?
- If your life were a play, would it be interesting, boring, sad, funny, provocative?
- What aspects of unresolved losses and conflicts are you still experiencing?
- If your life were a book, what would the title be? If the chapters covered periods of your life what ages would be for Chapter One and what would the title be? Chapter Two?
- What similarities do you see among the people you have mentioned?
- What is the link between what you are saying now and what you were saying before?
- What characteristics do you see in me that remind you of someone significant in your life?
- So far you have been talking about several topics. What is the connection among these?
- I can see a connection here, and I'm wondering if you can see it.
- How has that experience affected your life?
- What punishment do you think you deserve? How do you punish yourself?
- What age do you feel inside?
- What do you do when you're under pressure?
- So you become aggressive when your spouse does not talk, and he or she reacts by talking less?
- How much of your feeling belongs to your mother or father, and how much belongs to this situation?
- Are you modeling your parents or reacting against them?
- What is your contribution to the problem?
- So you are a "Survivor" of difficult experiences.
- Hanging on to this behaviour may be a way of hanging on to your "significant other."
- Maybe it's too soon to change this behaviour. You've been doing it for a long time.
- How do you protect yourself and others?
- What do you think too much about?
- What are your positive and negative thoughts? Make a list.

III. Changing Patterns

- It's understandable that you wouldn't be ready to change yet.
- Is what you're doing working well for you?
- What could you do that would be different?
- What are your choices? List as many possibilities as you can without evaluating them until you've exhausted the list.
- What would be the opposite of what you are doing?
- Think of a choice that sounds ridiculous or silly.
- In thinking about choices in our lives, there's usually a choice we haven't thought of.
- Rehearse or practice the desired behaviour change: e.g. Complete the three-part assertiveness formula, "I feel ____________ when you __________ because ________ ", directed toward me as your counsellor.
- Imagine your (significant other) is sitting here. Say the things you would like to say in your visit with them.
- Imagine I'm your (significant other). Tell me things you feel but wouldn't want to say for fear of hurting me or of being hurt by me.
- What gets in the way of your doing what you know works best?
- Maybe you will need to take a risk to find out what works.
- You've been struggling for a long time with these problems, so change may not be experienced overnight.
- Maybe you need to grieve some more. Maybe it's too soon to let go or say good-bye.
- What do you think you will do?
- It's going to be very important to your counselling that you develop your own strategy.
- You have an opportunity now to repeat an old pattern or to try something new.
- I want you to try to increase the problem.
- Each time you repeat the old behaviour give yourself a consequence.
- Each time you engage in desired behaviour give yourself a reward.
- Visualize, draw, sculpt, dramatize, write about, and verbally explore the desired behaviour.
- Set a goal with a time for implementing. When will you do it?
- Follow these steps:

  What have you done?
  What are your choices?
  What works best?
  What will you do?
  When will you do it?
  Can you do it here and now?
- Maybe a multifaceted strategy could be created with stages or steps.
- When you think about doing something new, what feelings come up in you?
- One option would be to take a small step first.
- Congratulations for taking that step. What you did was courageous. Progress!
- You've been working very hard at changing.
- No doubt you are motivated and want to change or you wouldn't be here.
- You will have to work very hard at changing.
- How much do you want to change?
- If you don't experience change, what could be the consequences?
- Make a list of affirmations.

COUNSELLOR ASSESSMENT EXPLANATION

This assessment may be completed every two weeks, to determine whether or not and to what extent your counselling needs are being met. You may feel that something is missing in the counselling relationship or that your counsellor is doing a "good enough" job. Communicating your needs is only fair to you and to your counsellor, and may help achieve wellness in other relationships, past and present.

Two questions to ask yourself as you complete the assessment are: 1) Are you "dumping" or underestimating your counsellor's qualities and abilities? and 2) Are you "protecting" or idealizing your counsellor's qualities and abilities? Two other related questions are: 1) What other significant people in your life have you tended to "dump" on or struggle with? and 2) What other significant people in your life have you tended to "protect." If you indicate that a particular counselling aspect was "N/A" or not applicable, was it because the counsellor did not provide something that you wanted or needed? If so, maybe you are protecting the counsellor at your own expense. What other significant people in your life have you protected from your painful feelings related to unmet needs?

Counsellor Aspects

1. **Came across with sincerity:** Did you feel that the counsellor was genuinely interested in your problems, feelings, and life experiences?
2. **Provided accurate empathy:** Did you sense that the counsellor was able to experience or connect with the emotions you were having?
3. **Had non-possessive warmth:** Was the counsellor able to be nurturing through voice tone and facial expression without being overwhelming or smothering?
4. **Demonstrated unconditional positive regard:** Was the counsellor non-judgmental and leave you feeling that you and your problems are of the greatest importance and value?
5. **Conveyed understanding of my problems:** Was the counsellor able to state your problems from your perspective and fully reflect your feelings and views?
6. **Drew out my feelings:** Did the counsellor help you to identify and experience the range of emotions you were having?
7. **Supported my feelings:** Did the counsellor say or do things to help you stay with or let you feel certain emotions?
8. **Helped me feel safe in counselling:** Did the counsellor provide a non-distracting atmosphere and appear to know what to do?
9. **Helped me get past my fear and resistance to facing difficult feelings and life experiences:** Did the counsellor help you to feel safe with yourself in order to explore the painful feelings related to certain experiences? Did the counsellor seem to be aware of ways you protect yourself against the pain?

10. **Helped me gain new insight into my life and old behaviour patterns:** Did the counsellor say things that helped you become aware of unhealthy ways of coping with stress and relating to yourself and others? Did he or she also help you to understand the origins or causes of these patterns?

11. **Helped me create new choices:** Did the counsellor say things to stimulate your ability to create or think about a variety of coping skills, approaches, and ways of relating to yourself and others?

12. **Helped me experience new ways of relating and coping:** Did the counsellor provide modeling of healthy ways of relating as well as opportunities, tasks, or assignments for trying on new behaviour?

13. **Helped me feel validated:** Did the counsellor say things that left you feeling that your painful emotions, old ways of coping, and fluctuations in progress were valid, OK, understandable, or made sense?

14. **Helped me feel empowered and hopeful:** Did the counsellor say things that helped you develop a sense of direction, mastery, confidence, choice?

15. **Helped me define my goals in counselling:** Did the counsellor help you clarify what you want to achieve in counselling, and help you remain focused on your priority goal?

16. **Helped me assess my achievement of goals:** Has the counsellor reviewed your progress, helped to clarify expectations, and helped you to validate and consolidate your gains?

When you have completed the assessment including questions 17 and 18 (see Counsellor Assessment Form), you may want to briefly give your counsellor feedback on what has been most helpful, least helpful, or what could have been better. The ability to give clear, direct, non-judgmental feedback is an important goal for counselling.

If you find this frightening or difficult, then this may be a key to your therapy, and it might be important and helpful for you to explore and "work through" the story behind this difficulty. If giving critical feedback comes easy for you, was it too easy and do you tend to be overly critical or aggressive in significant relationships? If so, then exploring and "working through" the story behind this behaviour, may be important to your relationship wellness in your social, family, and work life.

Sometimes counselling may focus on aspects of your life which you believe has little or no relevance to your problems. Maybe you have talked about your distant past with this counsellor and would like to focus more on what is happening now, or vice versa. Maybe you have worked on painful emotions and would like to gain more insight or understanding of your life patterns, or vice versa. Maybe you have done a lot of talking and would like to explore choices for taking action. Your counselling experience may change or become stagnant, provide something worthwhile, or become unproductive. Can you identify what you want? Can you provide input on how to achieve what you want? If so, you have taken a step toward wellness. When you seek something different in counselling, ask yourself, "Am I wanting something that is good for me, or am I wanting to protect myself from the pain or difficulty that I must face in order to let go and get on with my life?"

COUNSELLOR ASSESSMENT FORM

Dates ______________________________ Counsellor ______________________________

Indicate your degree of satisfaction with your counsellor for each aspect of the counselling relationship on a scale of 0-10. Zero "0" means you were "not at all" satisfied and ten "10" means you were "completely satisfied." If you think this aspect of counselling did not apply or was not important to you in this session, simply designate "N/A" in the blank.

Counsellor Aspects	**Satisfaction Rating**
1. Came across with sincerity	______
2. Provided accurate empathy	______
3. Had non-possessive warmth	______
4. Demonstrated unconditional positive regard	______
5. Conveyed understanding of my problems	______
6. Drew out my feeling	______
7. Supported my feelings	______
8. Helped me feel safe in counselling	______
9. Helped me get past my fear and resistance to facing difficult feelings and life experiences	______
10. Helped me gain new insight into my life and old behaviour patterns	______
11. Helped me create new choices	______
12. Helped me experience new ways of relating and coping	______
13. Helped me feel validated	______
14. Helped me feel empowered and hopeful	______
15. Helped me define my goals in counselling	______
16. Helped me assess my achievement of goals	______

17. Describe in your own words what your counsellor did that you experienced as ***most helpful***.

18. Describe in your own words what your counsellor did or did not do that you would ***like to be different*** in the future to benefit you the most.

FEELING LIST

Fearful
Tense
Anxious
Afraid
Nervous
Worried
Concerned
Scared
Insecure

Angry
Frustrated
Annoyed
Irritated
Perturbed
Ticked Off
Livid
Outraged
Furious
Seething
Venomous
Aggravated
Insulted
Resentful
Indignant

Guilty
Ashamed
Judged
Damned
Convicted
Condemned
Undeserving
Sentenced
Disgraceful
Villainous
Remorseful
Contemptible

Low Self-Worth
Demeaned
Rejected
Worthless
Useless
Inadequate
Insignificant
Unimportant
Ignored
Left Out
Humiliated
Despicable
Pathetic
Shy
Timid

Sad
Dejected
Depressed
Melancholy
Sorrowful
Dismal
Despondent
Blue
Down
Gloomy
Glum
Forlorn
Low

Lonely
Empty
Abandoned
Void
Hollow
Nothingness
Aloneness
Sunken
Desolate
Bleak
Withdrawn
Detached
Aloof
Distant
Desolate

Despair
Hopeless
Agony
Anguish
Helpless
Defeated
Destitute
Sterile
Deficient
Lacking

Drained
Depleted
Spent
Exhausted
Burdened
Consumed
Devoured
Tired
Used
Abused
Dissipated
Discounted
Weary
Dead

Relaxed
Tranquil
Placid
Serene
Collected
Quiet
Composed
Soothed
Sedate

Worthwhile
Useful
Valuable
Functional
Effective
Helpful
Okay
Important
Self-esteem
Valid

Hopeful
Optimistic
Encouraged
Heartened
Eager
Reassured
Supported
Strengthened
Able
Empowered

Fulfilled
Accomplished
Complete
Satisfied
Secure
Whole
Settled
Perfected
Contented
Sated
Intact
Definite

Motivated
Inspired
Stimulated
Activated
Actuated
Triggered
Prompted
Fired Up
Determined
Committed

Confident
Assured
Sure
Certain
Positive
Safe
Stable
Convinced
Definite
Empathic
Graceful
Balanced
Grounded
Calm
Brave
Proud

Happy
Cheerful
Delighted
Glad
Pleased
Fortunate
Ecstatic
Elated
Jubilant
Thrilled
Bright

Energized
Aroused
Excited
Exhilarated
Captivated
Fascinated
Enthused
Wild
Delirious
Electrified
Charged
Ready

New Words

____
____
____
____
____
____
____
____

SOME COMMON DEFENSE MECHANISMS

- Denial
- Rationalizing
- Displacement
- Intellectualizing
- Projection
- Interjection
- Retrojection
- Over-talking
- Red herrings
- Somatic complaints
- Sublimation
- Repetition compulsion
- Philosophizing
- Confusion
- Anger
- Silence
- Vagueness
- Deletions
- Religiosity
- Distancing
- Controlling
- Reaction formation
- Eyes closing
- Idealizing
- Blaming
- Avoiding the first person "I"
- Addiction
- Emotionality
- Changing Topic

COUNSELLING SKILLS CHECKLIST

Directions: When observing a session, write the verbatim statements of the counsellor under the correct heading below.

Assessment Interventions

Reflective Statements

Identifying Feelings

Engaging Feelings

Validating Interventions

Insight Interventions

Change Interventions

PERSONAL ISSUES AND GOALS

Unresolved Issues/Unfinished Business

- ______________________________
- ______________________________
- ______________________________
- ______________________________
- ______________________________

Old Patterns, Effects of Unresolved Issues

- ______________________________
- ______________________________
- ______________________________
- ______________________________
- ______________________________

New Patterns, Goals for Change

- ______________________________
- ______________________________
- ______________________________
- ______________________________
- ______________________________

Handouts for Chapter Three:

Loss and Grief Counselling Counselling

TOPICS FOR LOSS AND BEREAVEMENT TRAINING

By Dan Keeran, M.A., M.S.W., R.S.W.

A. Training Philosophy:

The more choices you have, the more creative, confident, and effective you can be in your helping role.

(Theory)

B. Types of Loss

Death of a loved one	Addiction / Recovery
Crib death	Divorce
Miscarriage	Dismissal
Abortion	Unemployment
Suicide	Empty nest
Homicide	Retirement
Terminal illness	Bankruptcy
Abduction	School Failure
Sexual assault	Adoption
Paralysis	Foster care
Disability	Amputation
Brain injury	Birth Defect
Epilepsy	Heart condition
Mastectomy	Blindness
Infertility	Leaving home
Hysterectomy	Breakup
Parental abuse/neglect	

C. Goals of Loss

1. To identify and experience the range and intensity of feelings related to the loss.
2. To identify and to change maladaptive behaviour patterns related to the loss.
3. To complete unfinished business and to say good-bye or let go of the loss.

D. Feelings of Loss

1. Fear
2. Anger
3. Guilt
4. Sadness
5. Emptiness
6. Low self-worth
7. Despair

E. Unfinished Business

1. Unspoken apologies
2. Unspoken forgiveness
3. Unresolved anger and conflict
4. Unspoken affection and caring
5. Unspoken good-bye
6. Unspoken loss of caring and closeness

F. Behaviour Decisions Of Loss

1. I will never get close again
2. I will not get on with my life and accept responsibility
3. I do not deserve happiness: I will punish myself
4. I will find a way to keep or join the lost person

A BRIEF LOSS GROUP IN A PSYCHIATRIC DAY HOSPITAL

By Daniel M. Keeran, M.A., M.S.W.

Founder of the Counsellor Training Institute, Mr. Keeran is a private consultant to health care administrators and professionals in areas of grief counselling, team-building, and conflict resolution. He resides in North Vancouver, British Columbia.

This is a short report on the psychodynamic goals, treatment approaches, and results of a bereavement group within a psychiatric day program. The "Loss Group" meets for one hour per week, and each patient attends the group a total of six times in consecutive weeks in a four-month program. Patients attend a variety of groups every weekday from 9 a.m. to 4 p.m. except Friday when groups end at 1 p.m. The size of Loss Group fluctuates from eight to fifteen people depending upon changes in the program census.

The psychodynamic goals of Loss Group are:

- to verbalize and experience the range and intensity of painful feelings associated with an identified loss; feelings of fear, guilt, anger, sadness, and emptiness
- to gain insight into and to change maladaptive behaviour patterns and attitudes linked to the loss, and
- to complete unfinished business and say good-bye or let go of the loss.

The treatment approaches within the Loss Group include a number of therapist interventions with predictable beneficial results for the group members.

Opening Statement

The therapist often begins the group with a brief statement about loss. For example: "Everyone born has experienced some type of loss. It could be the death of a spouse, parent, child, or close relative. It could be loss through divorce, the loss a job, the loss of physical ability due to disease or injury, or even abortion, or adoption, or miscarriage. Instead of a caring and understanding parent, you may have had a distant or abusive and uncaring one, which is another very real kind of loss.

Loss brings the pain of sadness, anger, guilt, and emptiness, and our natural response is to often deny or run from these feelings because none of us likes pain and loss hurts. Today, we're going to face the pain of loss because it is through facing our pain that we can often free up energy needed to get on with our lives."

A statement of this kind presented empathically helps provide a sense of safety and permission needed for working through grief. Reference to the universality of loss coupled with the focused goal of "facing the pain," allows each member to feel part of a cohesive group. To "face the pain" implies courage which promotes further support from the therapist. The therapist's initial talk also provides a warm-up to the intense grief work to follow.

Linking Statements

As the group begins, the therapist makes statements linking members with similar feelings; "John and Robert are both feeling very sad right now," or "What you're feeling John, is very much like your sadness, Bob." The therapist builds up support by saying, for example, "Who else feels the guilt Jean was talking about?"

Empathic Skills

As group members relate issues of loss, the therapist uses his empathic skills to provide permission and safety for the expression of grief. Empathy is the prime therapeutic element, along with a sincere, warm voice tone and facial expression. Empathy is the ability to feel the emotion of the grieving person which enables the therapist to provide effective support for specific feelings. Empathy is especially present in the therapist's specific supportive and reflective statements.

Supportive Statements

Grief work is facilitated by supportive statements which maximize the sense of safety and permission within the group.

Examples include: "It's OK to cry. Just let it out - that's good. It takes courage to face the pain. Just stay with the sadness right now. The sadness is there now, just feel it. This is a safe group." Statements like these addressed to an individual who has taken the risk to share grief, encourage others to take similar risks.

Reflective Statements

The aim of reflective statements are to convey understanding and acceptance of the patient as well as to facilitate their own insight. For example: "You feel cheated because he died just when you were getting to be close" or "You feel deserving of punishment because your father climbed the hill looking for you and died of a heart attack the next day". When the bereaved hears themself, they may hear something different and gain perspective if the therapist provides an accurate reflection of the feeling and meaning of the patient's statement. When the feeling is not labeled by the patient, the therapist provides the label along with a paraphrased version of the statement. This allows the patient to decide whether his initial statement is tenable while feeling accepted and understood and therefore supported at the same time.

Exploring Feelings

The therapist may help patients explore feelings by saying, "What other feeling is there beside the (sadness)?" If the patient is very angry and hostile, the therapist may initially support it by asking the patient to elaborate on the feeling and to repeat angry statements. But if the anger appears to be a cover for sadness, the therapist may say, "Which is easier to feel, the anger or the sadness?" or "What feeling is under the anger?"

The therapist may challenge guilt verbalized by a patient as a way of hanging on to the loss through a life sentence of self-punishment by loneliness and depression. It is often necessary to deal with the guilt before other feelings in order to clear the way for working through grief. As a means of self-punishment, the very guilty person will resist grief work, becoming a sacrificial monument to the loss.

Feelings of fear may be associated with a fear of facing the pain of loss, closeness, facing the future alone, or new unfamiliar responsibilities. Emptiness may be reported at any point, especially when considerable grief work has occurred and the bereaved is letting go of the loss. At this juncture, the therapist may say, "You are at a fork in the road. You can either fill the emptiness with the old pain and patterns of behaviour, or you can fill it with new ways of relating and new people."

Feelings of grief or the loss itself may be denied. A 38-year-old woman stated in group that her father was not dead although he had in fact died when she was ten. The therapist labeled and supported her denial by saying, "So for you your father is still alive. You're in the stage of denial and that's OK. It's just important and valuable for you to know where you are in your grief." With this support from the therapist, the woman moved from denial into other aspects of her grief.

The therapist may also support the denial of specific feelings which then results in the patient exploring those parts of his grief. Sadness may present as the predominant or exclusive feeling which could mean that anger is being denied. Anger and hostility may present as predominant serving as a protection against the pain of sadness and guilt. The therapist may say in support, "You feel very sad and that's easy for you to express. For other people the anger is easy. It's just helpful to know where you are in your grief."

Being careful to listen, observe, and reflect what is said and heard, the therapist knows which feelings to explore, facilitate and support. In the process of facilitating, however, the therapist may clarify that patients should not invent feelings but simply become more aware of existing feelings. When a patient has difficulty identifying or recognizing what they are feeling, group feedback can be elicited by the therapist.

Reaching for Anger

Angry feelings are often viewed as unacceptable by people in our society. Rather than confront the resistance to identifying anger to the loss, the therapist asks the patient if they feel cheated or believe the loss was unjust or unfair. The bereaved is much more likely to admit feeling "cheated" than "angry" and can be asked to explore this in terms of with whom they are angry. Regarding the anger toward the deceased, the therapist may state, "What shouldn't the deceased have done?"

The therapist may reach for anger by asking the patient to verbalize "why" questions, saying, "What 'why' questions do you have about this (or for the lost person)?" Examples of responses are: "Why did he kill himself? Why did it have to be her? Why didn't the doctor save her?" The therapist can then focus the feeling by saying, "What feeling goes along with that 'why' question?"

A review of lost hopes and dreams may facilitate feelings of anger. The reality that one will not enjoy a retirement with a spouse who has died, that having a family will never happen, or that a child's developmental milestones will never be seen, are often associated with feelings of sadness, disappointment and anger.

Sometimes the bereaved idealizes or enshrines the lost person as a way of remaining emotionally attached. The therapist may direct the bereaved to discuss something he only slightly disliked about the lost person. This discussion prepares the bereaved for viewing the lost person more realistically, which may lead to more open expression of anger, and has the effect of dethroning the lost person so that progress toward letting go can proceed.

Use of Silence

The appropriate use of silence allows crying until the need to weep has subsided. The therapist then invites the bereaved to "put the tears into words." This silent time is not interrupted with questions or interpretations but may be supported by empathic statements encouraging the expression of sadness or anger. The therapist is careful to protect the patient from distracting comments of other group members during this period of grieving.

Use of Deletions

Sometimes the therapist makes use of what is not mentioned by the bereaved. The name of the lost person, the words "death" or "dead," and the cause of death (e.g. suicide or drinking), are often laden with emotion, and the mere mention of these realities can help facilitate grief by addressing aspects of denial. Deletions may be more apparent near the beginning of treatment than toward the later stages of grief work.

Key Words

A woman related the death of her six-year-old son who died in hospital after being dragged two blocks under the rear wheel of a city power truck. She spoke without affect and with little variation in her voice until she mentioned the power truck at which point she stopped briefly, as if to check her feelings, then she proceeded with the reporting style. The therapist noted the words and phrases which immediately accompanied her moment of silent emotion and spoke them to her at a later time when he wanted to facilitate her grief work. When others were sharing their losses, the therapist said to her simply, "There was a power truck." At this point, she wept freely and was able to verbalize her grief. Key words and phrases from the patient's vocabulary are those noted to be connected to grief as the bereaved discloses the loss. These key words are repeated by the therapist when he wishes to facilitate grieving.

Mental Imagery

Frequently, as in the above example, the key words are associated with a mental image of events and circumstances around the loss of memories of the lost person. As the woman related the day of her son's death, she was able to form mental images of people and objects. When a patient stares during a group discussion, this may be a cue that they are observing mental images related to the loss. They may or may not be talking during this staring behaviour. The therapist uses this opportunity to facilitate grief by saying, for example, "You seem to be staring into the distance as if you are seeing something in your mind. Tell us what you see." When mental images are verbalized they often carry emotional significance, and facilitate grief. It is sometimes helpful to recall the day of the death and the moment of hearing about the death. A therapist may continue the imagery by saying, "What's happening next in your mind? What are you feeling?" A resistant patient can be assisted in describing a mental image such as, "Are you standing or sitting? Is the door open or shut ? Is the weather sunny or cloudy?" These questions help the patient get more into the images and thus more into the repressed aspects of the loss, both memories and feelings.

Identifying Maladaptive Patterns

The therapist explains that "the work of letting go of a loss involves not only grieving but recognizing and changing behaviour patterns connected to the loss, ways of relating that haven't worked, and attitudes or ways of thinking that keep one from being all that one can be."

A group meeting can be used to specifically focus on identifying patterns. Smaller groups or triads, can be used to explore patterns with suggestions from the therapist who states for example: "When we experience a loss, sometimes we make decisions that don't work well for us. These decisions may be conscious, or unconscious and unintentional. For example, "I won't get close, or I won't accept responsibility and get on with my life, I will punish myself, or I will find the lost person (by marrying her, etc.)." Now we will break into small groups, and I want you to talk about how your most difficult loss has affected your attitudes and relationships."

After a period of about thirty minutes, the group reconvenes to share the various patterns while the therapist directs feedback in terms of distancing behaviour, for example, observed by others. An adopted girl alternated complaints of being left out followed by withdrawn, nonverbal behaviour, and this was pointed out by group members as being parallel to her feeling of being left out by both adoptive and natural parents.

Patterns are sometimes identified when grief is being expressed. When guilt is verbalized, the therapist may say, "How do you punish yourself?" or

"What punishment do you feel you deserve?" When anger is identified, the therapist may ask what happens to the anger or who gets the anger, which may reveal patterns of conflict or other distancing behaviour. Sometimes a patient will express regret or anger about a behaviour pattern which resulted in lost relationships, as in the case of a man who recognized a pattern of setting himself up to be rejected, repeating his experience growing up with an abusive, uncaring father. In recognizing this pattern, the patient acknowledged feeling very angry toward the father and himself. The therapist stated, "Are you angry (sad, lonely) enough to change?" This use of re-decision has the effect of affirming a desire to change maladaptive behaviour, which had positive results for the patient described.

The Empty Chair

The empty chair is sometimes used as a warm-up to grief work, a tool enabling patients to identify feelings around a loss, and a vehicle for exploring unfinished business in terms of issues or verbal expressions not articulated prior to or at the time of the loss. Expression of love and caring for the lost person, unresolved anger, statements of apology or forgiveness, reminiscing about past experiences with the lost person, and talk about saying good-bye, can be directed to the lost person as if present in the empty chair.

The therapist may introduce the empty chair by stating for example, "Sometimes in this group we use the empty chair as a tool for exploring loss, and so today I want you to imagine seeing the lost person in your mind and imagine yourself saying something to him/her that has seemed unfinished. It may be some unresolved issue, apology, statement of forgiveness or caring - whatever you want to say to this person. Then I will ask each of you to make a statement to the lost person as if he or she were sitting right here in this empty chair. Just take a silent moment to think of what you want to say. Then I will tell you when to start."

After a minute or two of silence, the therapist states, "Now we will start on this end with Bob, and I want you to tell us the first name of the person and his or her relationship to you, then make a statement to the person as if they are sitting here." The therapist must be aware of time constraints with this exercise and intervenes with a question such as, "What are you feeling right now as you talk?" When the patient identifies a feeling or feelings, or if he spontaneously grieves, the therapist may suggest, "Just stay with that sadness (or other feeling) and let yourself feel it." When everyone has participated in the empty chair exercise, the therapist changes the focus from the empty chair to the group by saying, "Let's continue to share our feelings and support each other." The empty chair invariably elicits strong feelings of grief, and so the therapist may say, "There's a lot of sadness, anger, and guilt in this room right now. Let's just keep talking and supporting each other."

The empty chair is also useful for exploring guilt toward the lost person in the empty chair. Following expressions of guilt, either the therapist or the bereaved sits in the empty chair and speaks as the lost person in offering forgiveness or in clarifying reality: "I would have died even if you had come to the hospital. You didn't make me die. You didn't know I was going to die then. I was sick a long time. I forgive you."

A person facing the loss of physical ability can be asked to imagine the injured or diseased part of the body in the empty chair or to imagine the complete, whole self sitting in the chair. Statements of the bereaved to the empty chair are usually of intense anger and sadness.

After considerable grief work has been accomplished, the bereaved may be asked to address the lost person on the subject of saying good-bye and letting go. To prevent premature closure of grief, the therapist asks the patient to talk "about" saying good-bye rather than saying good-bye. When patients choose to say good-bye or discuss letting go, using the empty chair, the effect is often a feeling of emptiness. At this juncture, the therapist reminds the patient of two choices in relation to his/her emptiness (reviewed under Exploring Feelings) and may say, "Now that you're letting go and saying good-bye, can you choose to say hello to life, to people, and to closeness?" This question guides the bereaved toward re-decision.

Group members may arrange the empty chair in the centre of a semicircle, taking turns to address it, while the therapist leaves his or her own chair empty after introducing the exercise. A variation is to form a tight circle of chairs including or excluding the empty chair following the warm-ups in which each patient in turn addresses the lost person. If included, the empty chair remains available to anyone who wishes to use it.

Closure

The group meeting ends with a statement by the therapist encouraging members to continue working on their losses, commending them for their courage to face the pain, or summarizing the predominant feelings expressed or patterns identified in the group.

Evaluation and Research Findings

A research and evaluation team of psychologists with the program collated ratings of treatment benefit patients provided at the point of discharge. They also conducted an analysis of an open-ended ranking by patients of the groups they found most helpful while in the day program. A third method of evaluation were the observations of team members attending Loss Group.

Of fifteen separate group series offered in three phases of the four-month program, Loss Group was rated as one of three most valuable groups, including Communications Group and Psychodrama Group. Patients' written evaluations substantiated the therapist's effectiveness in mobilizing affect and encouraging attainment of treatment goals. Research team personnel noted his sensitivity to patient needs, empathy for and ability to elicit affect, and ability to provide support for patients as they grappled with personal issues. The therapist was said to have a good grasp of patient dynamics and appeared able to apply his knowledge productively.

LOSS OF A CHILD

By Daniel M. Keeran, M.A., M.S.W.

The loss of a child is given attention here because it is one of the most common and most difficult types of loss to accept. The painful feelings associated with this loss are difficult to defend against and parents commonly experience depression, heaviness, and distancing behaviour. This chapter focuses on loss from the parents' perspective, while the experience of siblings is addressed in "Loss of A Sibling." Multiple losses, of closeness in relationships and employment, can result from a difficult adjustment.

Varied Circumstances

Circumstances related to the loss of a child include age, order of birth, sex, health from birth, relationship to the parents, lifetime expectations for the child, nature of the child's illness or injury causing death, parent's marital status and relationships among family members at the time of death. Other types of loss include permanent mental or physical disabilities such as Down's Syndrome, spina bifida, cerebral palsy, etc.

Painful Feelings

Painful feelings may vary according to the circumstances related to the child's death. Generally guilt, along with other painful emotions, may be quite prominent especially if the child is young. At this time the parents would naturally feel responsible for the child's health and safety. When death occurs, especially if it is sudden through accident or Sudden Infant Death Syndrome, parents are stricken with grief wondering if there was something more they could have done to prevent the death. Some thoughts may include "if only" thoughts:

- "If only I had watched or looked in on the child more frequently."
- "If only I had seen the child cross the street."
- "If only I had taken the child to the doctor sooner."
- "If only I had not used alcohol or drugs during pregnancy."

Guilt may linger if a teenager was estranged from the family at the time of death. In one situation, the teenage son had been adopted as an infant when the natural mother, who was single, died of cancer. Before the mother's death, a sister promised to adopt and raise the child as her own, but the boy who was not close to the adoptive family, developed additional behaviour problems during adolescence and died suddenly in a motorcycle accident. The adoptive parents felt guilty, believing they had failed the natural mother as well as the child.

The parent's marital status at the time of the child's death, whether they were in conflict, separated or divorced, may induce guilt for somehow contributing to the child's accident or lack of will to live.

Guilt may also stem from the perception of having disciplined the child too severely or not enough, not spending enough time with the child, not being affectionate enough, not loving the child enough, not visiting the child enough during the illness, and not being with the child at the time of death. These thoughts may be associated with feelings of failure and low self-worth as a parent, and depression can become a form of self-punishment.

Guilt may overwhelm the bereaved to feel undeserving of closeness and caring. Anger may then be used to keep people at a distance through irritability and criticism of others. Another expression of anger occurs when guilt is projected onto others as in the case of a young father who was hundreds of miles away at the time of his infant son's crib death. Upon his return he learned about the death and blamed his wife who was already experiencing extreme guilt. She in turn blamed the husband for being gone. Mutual projection of guilt is common and often results in the breakdown of the marriage. The reality of this dynamic underscores the importance of the couple grieving together in a way which allows them to put the guilt and other specific emotions of grief into proper perspective.

Anger may be felt toward the child for not being more careful in the case of an accidental death. A parent may feel guilty for feeling angry and protect the child with excuses or explanations for their behaviour preceding the death. If a teenager died while drunk or on drugs, the parent may want to avoid this information, or blame themself as a way of hanging on to the dead child.

A parent may use anger to protect the more vulnerable feelings of sadness, fear, and emptiness. The father, as a male in a society where sadness and other feelings are associated with feminine weakness, may focus on feelings of bitterness and resentment toward the health care providers or God. "Why did my child have to die? Why not someone who has committed murder? Why an innocent child? Why, God?" Statements of injustice or unfairness are common as anger is sometimes safer and easier to express than sadness, and a parent may become stuck in the anger as a way of hanging on to the loss.

Fear of painful feelings can become a block to further grief work especially if the emotions of grief are intense and unfamiliar. The fear related to a child's death may become a fear of losing a child who remains or the fear of getting close to them, which can result in the loss of that relationship. If the fear results in overprotecting the remaining child, the parent-child relationship is distorted through excess dependency where the child loses other experiences and relationships important to his social development.

Sadness is often thought to be the core feeling in grief, and in the death of a young child the sadness is strong because of the emotional bond which begins even before birth. The sadness is often linked to the hopes and dreams parents have for the child to mature and succeed in career and family life. When these expectations are interrupted by death, the sadness is renewed whenever they see their child's peers graduating from high school, getting married, and achieving other developmental milestones. Recalling the child's birth and early memories may evoke intense sadness as would longing to hold the child again or to see their smiling face or hear their laughter.

Emptiness and loneliness are sometimes the most agonizing feelings in the death of a child. The child may have occupied much of the parent's time and energy whether the child experienced a lengthy illness or simply lived a normal life. The parent fills an active role as mother or father for the child, and when the child dies, the role is gone leaving a tremendous void. The silence can be unbearable without the child's familiar clatter and clutter, frequent demands and requirements for care and discipline, and endearing and provoking behaviours. Gone too are the opportunities to touch, kiss, hug, and cradle the child, and to experience his presence in many ways. It seems preferable to feel the intensity of sadness and anger than the emptiness, so the tendency is to hang on to the grief as a way of filling up the empty space. This may be the source of the need to continue grieving and the accompanying resistance to letting go and saying good-bye.

If the child is born with or later develops a ***physical or mental disability,*** parents may feel guilty, inadequate, and

low self-worth as well as angry with God or feel cheated. In some cases, parents will project guilt and anger onto each other for the child's condition. The feelings of guilt and inadequacy are associated with believing there is something wrong with one's genes. A parent will review his or her life in a natural attempt to understand why the disability occurred, and associate guilt with taking drugs, smoking, drinking, being injured, and other experiences before or during pregnancy. As with the child who died, parents of a disabled child may feel painful emotions for many years when they see non-disabled children passing through the usual life stages.

Unfinished Business

Much of the painful feeling associated with the loss of a child is linked to unfinished business or unspoken words. If the parent feels guilty or responsible for the death or for something lacking in the relationship, it may be important to say the ***unspoken apology*** to progress with grieving. A common experience is of the parent who frequently criticized the child before a sudden death and is left feeling guilty about that aspect of the relationship. In another, a father is overwhelmed with guilt in feeling responsible for his son's drinking and death, following an argument where the son attended a drinking party and was killed in a car accident. Often, guilt comes from parents taking too much responsibility for the child's behaviour, and if the child, now wiser, could speak from the dead, he would say, "It wasn't you. I'm the one who decided to go drinking and driving."

Distance sometimes occurs between parents and children, particularly in adolescence, and a death at this time may leave regrets about not having expressed ***affection and caring***. Family members take their love for one another for granted, or feel uncomfortable saying, "I love you. I care for you." When death occurs, parents sometimes feel guilty for not having made these kinds of statements, and they become unfinished business.

Unspoken anger may prevent the expression of affection and caring and may be directed toward the child or those perceived to be the cause of the death. A mother whose son was killed in a motorcycle accident, felt anger toward her son for not wearing a helmet as well as toward the driver of the vehicle that struck the boy. Rather than face the anger toward these people, the anger seemed to be directed toward the husband, surviving children and insurance agents. She tended to explain away or protect the son and the driver of the car. When she owned the unfinished anger toward the son and the driver, her anger toward family members and insurance agents was significantly reduced. She was able to properly direct the anger and place it in perspective with other feelings.

Unspoken forgiveness cannot be extended to the child unless the anger is talked through first. Conversely, anger sometimes requires the ability to express forgiveness before the anger can be further resolved or finished. The child may die before conflict can be resolved and the grieving parent may need to put the unspoken anger, apology and forgiveness into words, to complete this important area of unfinished business.

Unspoken good-bye is often another source of guilt. The child who died suddenly or after a lengthy illness may provide no opportunity or too many opportunities for saying good-bye prior to death. In the case of a lengthy illness, the death may not have been certain or its timing predictable. Statements of affection and caring which could have been made at the time of saying good-bye become related issues of unfinished business. The primary feelings of grief, including anger, sadness, guilt, emptiness, and fear, may be tied to unspoken good-bye. Anger may linger toward the child for dying unexpectedly, cheating parents out of the opportunity to say good-bye and making them feel responsible for not taking advantage of previous opportunities. Emptiness may also result from an unspoken good-bye and a sad yearning to speak one last time with the child. A fear of missing good-byes with the surviving children may lead to a need to always have them near.

Behaviour Decisions

Whether or not behaviour decisions associated with the loss of a child are conscious and intentional, many are identifiable.

"I will never get close again."

Sometimes this decision comes from the fear of losing again and cripples relationships with other family members. Parents lost their 8-year-old daughter to heart and lung failure after a lengthy illness from pneumonia and asthma, after which the mother became silent and withdrawn from a surviving 10-year-old son, while the father increased his drinking. They grieved separately and remained distant throughout the son's growing years and he has continued difficulty achieving closeness in relationships in his adult life.

Another way of distancing is to substitute caring with material things. The experience of grief after losing a child may be so painful, a parent may remain emotionally aloof for fear of being hurt again through the death of another child. Yet a sense of guilt may motivate a parent to show caring, but through material things: money, gifts, trips, schooling, etc.

In some instances, anger and criticism or irritability may create distance in relationships with the spouse and surviving children. This criticism may arise from any pretext or elicit disapproval of the surviving child's choice of friends and social activities. This behaviour combined with the fear of losing the surviving child tends to limit the child's activity or involvement outside the home. The child may feel resentful for being restricted or may adopt the parent's fear of the outside world. In either case, further distancing behaviour is established in the child's ways of relating.

Anger may be used to distance the spouse through increased criticism or blame for the death of the child. Distancing may also result from a preoccupation with the dead child, as a parent continues a mental review of the child's life and death and hangs on to painful, perhaps unspoken, feelings. Thus, the bereaved parent's emotional energy is taken up with or devoted to the dead child, with little energy available for the closeness needed in relationships with the living. Sometimes, this distancing carries over into relationships at work which also require emotional involvement.

"I will not get on with my life and accept responsibilities and challenges."

This behaviour decision is manifested in a parent's difficulty fulfilling usual responsibilities and activities. A mother driving her three preschool children and the child of a friend arrived at a railroad crossing where the sun blocked her view from an oncoming train. Two of her children and her friend's child were killed. Three years after the deaths, the mother was still unable to put her life back together. She remained depressed and could not maintain employment.

"I do not deserve happiness I will punish myself."

At times, this decision stems from guilt for feeling somehow responsible for the death or for weakness in the relationship with the child prior to his or her death. Guilt makes the parent feel deserving of depression and heaviness in life and they become like a monument to the dead child. A mother whose teenage son was killed in an automobile drag race accident, was unable to manage the behaviour of a younger daughter and was plagued by self-deprecating thoughts around memories of her son's death. She experienced low self-worth and felt she had failed as a mother in raising her children. The father had similar feelings about himself and his wife and left the family.

"I will find a way to keep the lost child."

In the struggle with painful feelings a parent may deny the child is gone and enshrine them by keeping his belongings in a special room as if the child will return or is there, but invisible. The agony of emptiness can lead to this denial and enshrinement, so the parent feels better believing the child is still alive.

Enshrinement is sometimes associated with idealizing the dead child where the parent insists the child was perfect. The child is elevated to a pedestal, contributing to distancing behaviour with the surviving children who may feel unable to measure up. The idealized child may be called upon for advice so that the bereaved parent can communicate with them at any time.

The parent may see the dead child in other children and seek to befriend them as a way of being closer to his or her own child. A parent so preoccupied may also transpose the image of the lost child upon the surviving child. A parent who lost her 18-year-old daughter to hepatitis, tended to overprotect her 10-year-old daughter who at 23, lacks a sense of her own identity, is self-critical, and maintains daily contact with her parents long after getting married. The father had developed a drinking problem shortly after the older daughter's death and was not close to the surviving child, who also developed hepatitis at 18. She stated feeling unaccepted for who she was and whether she was seen by her parents as being anyone other than the child who died.

Counselling Scenario

A single mother about 38, with two daughters aged 13 and 11, seeks counselling for prolonged grief and chronic depression in dealing with her son's death. Two years ago, a city utility vehicle struck six-year-old Guthrie on his bicycle and dragged him for two blocks as he was pinned under the rear wheels. He was conscious but died of severe injuries two days later with his mother at his side.

She spoke of traveling to India and would smile and laugh about escaping to some part of the world. But her voice became a monotone while relaying her son's death, and she drifted into unrelated issues as if to escape the pain of her loss.

Eventually, she was able to talk in more detail about feelings related to Guthrie's death. Initially, she felt sad about missing her son, and spoke with affection and caring about happy memories, descriptions of the boy's personality, and aspects of the relationship. These topics facilitated a great deal of sadness and crying about lost hopes and dreams and of never being able to see and hold Guthrie again. As more circumstances of Guthrie's death were discussed, she expressed guilt for not checking the child's safety and anger toward the driver of the power truck. Once the mother faced the pain of her son's death, she appeared less anxious and depressed and her distancing behaviour of over-talking was also less frequent.

The example of counselling skills used with the mother is taken from a period of her most intense grieving.

line 1	Counsellor:	"Talk about Guthrie."
line 2	Mother:	"I don't know what to say."
line 3	Counsellor:	"There was a power truck."
line 4	Mother:	(cries) "Yes, and took my Guthrie." (cries)

line 5 Counsellor: "That's it, just let it all out." (silence)

line 6 "Say more about the tears. What are they about?'

line 7 Mother: "Guthrie was my baby. I loved him so much." (cries)

line 8 Counsellor: "Just let yourself feel that right now." (silence)

line 9 Mother: "I nursed him until he was two. We were so close."

line 10 Counsellor: "Go on."

line 11 Mother: "Well. He was the only boy, with two big sisters." (smiles) "He loved to play. There were so many happy times."

line 12 Counsellor: "Tell me about one of the happiest times."

line 13 Mother: "That would be Christmas. I can still see his expression when he came into the living room and saw the Christmas tree and all of the ornaments." (smile turns to tears) "Christmas is so empty without Guthrie."(cries)

line 14 Counsellor: "Just cry right now. You miss him so much." (silence)

line 15 "Are the tears sad tears or angry tears?"

line 16 Mother: "Sad...mostly...some anger."

line 17 Counsellor: "Talk about the anger. What's it about?"

line 18 Mother: "The truck."

line 19 Counsellor: "What about the truck?"

line 20 Mother: "It's not his fault. He couldn't see Guthrie."

line 21 Counsellor: "Who's fault?"

line 22 Mother: "The driver." (silence)

line 23 Counsellor: "Say more about the driver."

line 24 Mother: "He felt terrible. He came to the house after the funeral and he just felt terrible."

line 25 Counsellor: "Does that take away what you feel?"

line 26 Mother: "No."

line 27 Counsellor: "If the driver was standing right here right now, what would you feel like saying to him?"

line 28 Mother: "Why weren't you looking harder? You killed my boy."

line 29 Counsellor: "Say it again a little louder."

line 30 Mother: "You killed my little Guthrie!" (cries) "Why him, God?" (cries)

line 31 Counsellor: "What feeling goes with that 'why' question?"

line 32 Mother: "Anger. It's not fair."

line 33 Counsellor: "Say more about the anger, about fairness."

line 34 Mother: "He was just a little boy. The driver said he was sorry. So what!" (cries)

line 35 Counsellor: (silence) "Just cry now. Uh-huh."

line 36 (silence) "It takes courage to face the pain."

line 37 (silence) "You're entitled to your anger and sadness."

line 38 (silence) "It's not easy to say good-bye and let go of someone you love so much."

line 39 Mother: "But I don't want to let go."

line 40 Counsellor: "It's much too soon. What you've been doing today is very important as difficult as it is, and I encourage you to keep talking about your feelings just as you have been doing."

Discussion Of Skills

Most of the skills used in the counselling scenario include invitations to talk, supportive statements, use of silence, and exploring feelings. Beginning with a specific invitation to talk about the child and using his name in line 1, the counsellor breaks through some initial resistance by using key words, "power truck," in line 3. The key words are emotion-laden and clearly, but indirectly, refer to the child's death. When the mother cries, a supportive statement is used to give permission for the grieving (line 5), followed by an invitation to explore the tears (line 6).

In line 8, the counsellor supports the crying by directing the mother to focus on the feelings. The use of the words "right now" in the supportive statement help the mother feel safe just to feel without talking. Notice the burden to talk is with the bereaved, and so in line 10 the counsellor simply invites the mother to continue. An alternative would be to use memories by saying, "Can you see him nursing in your mind?"

When the mother refers to happy memories in line 10, the counsellor invites her to recall a happiest time, which quickly reduces her to tears as she feels the emptiness of Christmas without her little boy. After supporting more of the grief in line 14, the counsellor explores feelings around the tears with the intention of reaching for anger in lines 15 and 17.

At this point the mother seems reluctant to discuss anger, then directs it toward the truck while indirectly protecting the driver (line 20). The counsellor makes use of this deletion and leaves the mother with no choice but to mention "the driver." After being invited to say more, the mother still protects the driver by focusing on his feelings in line 24, but the counsellor redirects the discussion to what the mother feels (line 25).

In line 27 the counsellor suggests the mother visualize the driver and address him. She then makes some angry statements which she is asked to repeat in line 29, with the intent of reaching for more anger. Notice that instead of discussing being angry at God, the counsellor concentrates on the feeling associated with the "why" question (line 31). Having reached for and remaining focused on the anger, the counsellor invites the mother to elaborate on this feeling in line 33 leading to a stronger expression of anger in line 34. The counsellor supports her crying in line 35 followed by a supportive statement defining the expression of feelings as a strength (line 36).

The counsellor acknowledges the mother's entitlement to her feelings which provide validation of her grief (line 37). By this time the counsellor has begun closure and suggests the primary goal and direction of counselling while supporting the difficulty of the process (line 38). The mother resists the stated goal, and the counsellor supports her resistance by acknowledging and validating her involvement in the counselling process (line 40).

Handouts for Chapter Four:

Conflict Resolution and Communication Skills

YOU CAN'T AVOID CONFLICT - How Well Do You Manage It?

By Daniel M. Keeran, M.A., M.S.W.

This article was first published in British Columbia's BUSINESS EXAMINER, June 1986.

Conflicts within management and between supervisors can lead to positive or negative outcomes. Tension from mishandled conflict costs money and wastes time through lowered morale and decreased performance, but when handled properly, conflict produces motivation, cohesiveness, team spirit, creative planning, and career satisfaction. Because people are unique individuals with various feelings and views, conflict is common and normal to interpersonal relationships. Therefore, the goal is not to eliminate conflict but to utilize its positive potential. Unresolved issues at home and work can interact to compound the stress felt by members of the team. There are four primary steps to positive conflict in relationships both in the family and on the job:

1) Asserting the issues,
2) Supporting the issues,
3) Developing creative options, and
4) Making a contract.

The goal is not to eliminate conflict but to utilize its positive potential.

Asserting the issues

The first step is to put the issues into words in a way that can be heard by others. The passive approach is to avoid the issues in order to keep things nice while the aggressive style is to engage in name-calling, threats, sarcastic put-downs, and judgmental terms. The aggressive approach may also include arguing and dominating the discussion. Whether the style is passive or aggressive, the result is to keep the conflict unresolved.

When asserting your issues, keep the following principles in mind:

- State your feelings as well as your thoughts. Feelings may include fear, frustration, annoyance, and irritation, as examples.
- Express your feeling as a choice, not as an impulsive reaction. You may not be able to control the sense of feeling angry as it wells up inside you, but you can choose how the anger comes out of your mouth.
- Use the assertive "I" statement: "I feel annoyed when you don't keep the agreement we reached last week, because I lose valuable time." This statement includes three parts: a disclosure of you feeling (annoyed), a non-judgmental observation of the other person's behaviour (when you don't keep the agreement), and the practical effects on your life (I lose valuable time).
- Avoid name-calling, threats, and other put-downs.
- Express your issue when you are first aware of it or as near that time

as possible and address it to the person with whom you feel annoyed.

- Broaden your feeling vocabulary with synonyms of "angry" and choose a word corresponding to the level of anger you are feeling. Examples include: perturbed, annoyed, frustrated, ticked-off, furious, livid, venomous, fed up. The person who is generally passive or aggressive has a poor vocabulary of feeling words, so this needs to be developed.
- Avoid blanket comments such as "I don't like you," or "You always... never... " Rather, point out the specific behaviour you don't like and give the person some credit.
- While feelings of anger need to be put into words appropriately and briefly, your issue should focus on content or meaning. Focusing on your anger may result in being delayed by a struggle, so define the issue in terms of the facts as you see them.
- Avoid threatening gestures such as pointing your finger or pounding the table as you assert your issues.
- Avoid telling people what their ulterior motives are, bringing up the past, or comparing the person to others as a put-down.

Studies have shown that middle managers have more difficulty asserting issues to upper management than to subordinates. We tend to be aggressive with subordinates and passive with superiors. Subordinates must risk themselves in spite of their fear and direct their issues appropriately having weighed the consequences through an assessment of the degree of permission and safety. The degree of permission for raising issues can be assessed by observing the reaction of superiors to others who have expressed grievances or simply by asking, "May I offer you some negative feedback or criticism?"

Supporting the issues

If organizational health, team spirit, and job satisfaction are to be maintained, managers and supervisors must be careful to provide a sense of safety and permission for offering negative input. Employees and subordinates who do not feel safe to raise issues may undermine management by complaining behind their backs and by poor work performance and absenteeism. Supporting the issues raised by others is the most important aspect of conflict resolution for managers. Here are some important points for establishing an atmosphere of safety and permission for expressing criticism.

- Let individuals and groups know that you want to hear their ideas and criticisms.
- Schedule a weekly meeting for "Conflict Resolution" or "Creative Planning." For personal conflicts, make yourself available to mediate in situations too difficult for individuals to handle alone.
- When criticism is being directed at you, use silence and wait out the intensity of feelings being expressed. Avoid interrupting, reacting defensively, or returning charges.
- Ask the critic to say more and to elaborate on his or her concerns.
- Be sincere in you verbal and nonverbal expressions.
- Lower you voice in responding to an intensely angry critic.
- Acknowledge the critic's entitlement to his or her feelings and views, and let him/her know you respect and value the feedback.
- Be willing to consider elements of truth in what your critic is saying: "You may have a valid point. I want to give this further consideration."

- Most importantly, convey an understanding of the critic's feelings and meaning by stating his case back to them. Most of his or her anger is due to not feeling understood, and when you are able to convey and understanding of his point, much of the need to press the point is taken away. For example, someone says, "I never get a holiday when I want it. I'm always the last to choose." A supportive statement would be, "So you feel quite annoyed when you are left with the last choice of holiday time because of the inconvenience of that time. Is that what you're feeling?"

This kind of response to an angry statement is also known as empathic listening or reflective listening, and it includes three parts:

1) stating the feeling of the speaker (quite annoyed)
2) stating the meaning of the speaker (when you are left with the last choice of time...) and
3) checking out the accuracy of your reflection (Is that what you're feeling?).

You should continue to use empathic listening as long as the other person is intensely angry. Use the other approaches in combination with this skill. Supporting the issues requires practice in order for it to come across in a sincere way as a part of your spontaneous response.

Approaching a conflict may follow this course:

1) You assert your issue.
2) Wait for a response.
3) Support the response.
4) Assert your issue.

The idea is to alternate assertive and supportive statements until both of you feel understood by the other. Supporting does not mean agreeing. Once both parties feel understood by the other, the next step is to develop creative approaches.

Developing creative approaches

During this stage of the process, the positive approach to anger and issues begins to produce even more positive results. After the issues have been asserted, supported, and understood, you can lead into developing creative options by saying, "What are we going to do about our issues?"

This is a time for being factual and unemotional. During this phase, you should call for brainstorming without critical comment or evaluation of suggested alternatives. Even call for options which may sound ridiculous and list them on a sheet of paper or chalk board. Listing the solutions helps to keep the discussion objective and unemotional. You will want to structure this time in proportion to the intensity or complexity of the conflict because structure contributes to a safe atmosphere. list as many ideas as possible.

Then review the list of alternatives and discuss the practical advantages and disadvantages of each one.

Dividing into small groups may demonstrate objectivity when the groups separately arrive at similar conclusions about the alternatives.

In some situations, agreeing to disagree may be an option particularly when the issue is not requiring cooperative action but rather has to do with philosophy, beliefs, or personal tastes. Otherwise, the goal is to agree on one alternative.

Making a contract

Once you have agreed on one alternative, the next step is to make a contract which may be verbal and informal or written and signed. When the contract is informal, one or both parties may simply say, "I will agree to use the alternative we arrived at." The contract will/may include a reference to fair fighting or disrespectful name-calling and put-downs. For example, if the conflict was destructive, this should be raised as an issue: "I resent your calling me stupid because I'm not given the respect I deserve." The verbal contract in response would be, "I apologize for the put-down, and the next time we disagree, I'll be more assertive." Notice that the contract may include an apology, and this is especially appropriate when you slip into destructive expressions of anger.

When the contract has been made the conflict is resolved for the time being. The conclusion of positive conflict is a synthesis of ideas and from this comes a renewed sense of cohesiveness. The worth of team members is affirmed, and the sense of security and job satisfaction is increased.

Three humanitarian principles provide the foundation for positive conflict:
1) everyone is entitled to his or her feelings and views
2) everyone has equal worth and dignity, and
3) everyone deserves to be treated with respect.

Conflict checklist

In order to assess difficulties you are having in a conflict situation, ask yourself these questions:

- Did I express my issue assertively rather than passively or aggressively?
- Did I stay in the empathic listening mode as long as my critic was very angry?
- Did I look at alternatives objectively and unemotionally?
- Did I recognize resurfacing anger and attend to it?
- Was I able to reach agreement on one alternative or agree to disagree?
- Did I offer apology or forgiveness sincerely?
- Was a contract made whether formal or informal?

If you answer "no" to any of these questions, you may be able to determine why the conflict still feels unresolved.

Conflict training

Managers and staff in business and professional settings can gain confidence in facing conflict constructively when the principles and skills are clearly understood and practiced. The model developed by the Counsellor Training Institute provides the sense of mastery in otherwise frightening situations because parameters and approaches to conflict are well defined and practical. Sometimes conflict goes underground because people are afraid either of their own loss of control and lack of verbal skills or of the reaction of superiors and peers. An "Assessment Questionnaire for Organizational Conflict" can be completed anonymously by management and staff followed by a variety of training experiences.

CTI MODEL FOR POSITIVE CONFLICT:
Principles and Skills for Interpersonal Relations

I. Anger:

- Expressing one's own anger

II. Assertiveness:

- Expressing one's own needs and feelings

III. Empathic Reflective Listening:

- Being open to others' needs and feelings

IV. Conflict Management and Resolution:

- Being open to others' anger

Principles:

- Everyone has equal dignity and worth.
- Everyone deserves to be treated with respect.
- Everyone is entitled to his or her feelings and views.

Definition:

- Communication is being open with your own needs and feelings as well as being open to the needs and feelings of others.

I. Anger:

- Expressing one's own anger

Review why it is important to express anger:
To be fair to yourself and to others
- To keep from getting depressed
- To keep from exploding
- To keep from displacing the anger
- To let others know their behaviour is affecting you
- To clear yourself to prepare for the resolution of conflict

Review the myth and reality of expressing anger
- *Myth #1* - Anger is effective in changing the other person.
  Reality - Express anger to take care of yourself.
- *Myth #2* - Expressing anger will automatically reduce it.
  Reality - Venting anger may increase it.

Review principles for the appropriate expression of anger.
- Assess the degree of permission and safety.
- Express anger at the time to the person with whom you are angry.
- Sharpen your words; sound angry.
- Use the assertive "I" statement: "I feel angry with you because..." Avoid blaming, "you" statements.
- Don't label, hit, throw, threaten, use sarcastic put-downs. Avoid destructive expressions of anger.
- Say what you don't like about the person rather than writing them off as in "I don't like you" or "I hate you."
- Avoid blanket statements saying, "You always...never..."
- Avoid judgmental terms: "You're wrong, dumb, stupid, selfish, lazy, inconsiderate, irresponsible, etc."
- Express anger as a choice, not as an impulsive reaction.
- Broaden your feeling vocabulary with synonyms of "angry" and choose a word corresponding to your level of anger.

Anger vocabulary exercise (list synonyms):

Empty chair exercise.
Comment on your statement, your style, your ease or difficulty, etc.

II. Assertiveness:

- Expressing one's own needs and feelings.

Review why it is important to be assertive:

- As antidote/preventative for depression
- As a way to enhance self-confidence
- As a way to enhance closeness
- As a way to take care of yourself and avoid being the martyr
- As an alternative to being passive or aggressive

Review principles for assertive expression:

- Making statements about "I" - "I need, feel, want, think, like, disagree..."
- Being non-judgmental, nondestructive, non-threatening, but nonetheless clear and direct about one's feelings and views.
- Having a voice tone which is firm and certain.
- Having a body language which conveys certainty: sit straight, make eye contact.
- Use three part formula: "When you _________ I feel _________ because _________"
- Say "no" without feeling guilty, or "yes" if this is what you want. ***Know*** what you want and ***say*** it.

Review the three-part assertiveness formula:

- ***Behaviour***: "When you don't respond... (state other's behaviour non-judgmentally)
- ***Feeling***: ...I feel frustrated..., (disclose your feeling)
- ***Effects***: ...because we can't resolve things." (clarify the effects on your life)

Review characteristics of passive expression:

- Avoiding eye contact
- Soft voice tone, brief responses
- Avoiding the issues to keep things nice
- Agreeing or apologizing when not appropriate
- Preoccupation with fear of hurting or being hurt (protection racket)
- Vague or general terms; lack of clarity

Review characteristics of aggressive expression:

- Interrupting
- Blaming and accusing, "you" statements
- Dominating the discussion, not allowing space for other views
- Pointing, pounding the table
- Constant eye contact, staring
- Ordering; angrily telling others what to do

Review characteristics of passively aggressive expression:

- Withdrawing into angry silence to punish

- Talking negatively about others
- Yawning and ignoring others, frowning while denying the issues
- Uncooperativeness, walking out, arriving late, etc.

Comment on the difference between aggressive and assertive expression:

- Aggressive - denies other's entitlement to feelings and views
- Assertive - acknowledges everyone's entitlement to feelings and views

Comment on the difference between aggressive and destructive expression:

- Aggressive - uses domination and accusation
- Destructive - uses methods which demean and destroy the other person's self-esteem and sense of safety

Give a comparative listing of characteristics of three styles of fighting:

Destructive	*Aggressive*	*Passive*
shouting, screaming	interrupting	angry silence
name-calling	accusing	undermining
threats	pointing	uncooperativeness
sarcasm	dominating	ignoring
judgmental terms		sabotaging
hitting		
throwing objects		

Review the common denominator of all fighting behaviour:

- Unwillingness to consider others' views and to resolve the issues

Review the effects of destructive fighting:

- Using fear and put-downs, destroying others' self-worth, property, and the relationship itself

III. Empathic Reflective Listening (ERL):

- Being open to the needs and feelings of others

Review why it is important to use ERL:

- To clarify and identify the issues
- To diffuse hostility by conveying acceptance and understanding of others' feelings and views

Review principles for ERL:

- Frequent eye contact
- Forward leaning
- Head nods
- Sit at 90 degree angle
- Sit at 20-36" distance
- Attending sounds, "uh-huh, yes"
- Sincere facial expression and voice tone
- Paraphrase, summarize, reflect meaning of speaker; state the other's case back to him/her accurately
- Reflect the feeling of the speaker even if not stated
- Check out if reflection is accurate; e.g., "Am I hearing you correctly?"

Review how not to use ERL:

- Avoid parroting, repeating the other's exact words.
- Avoid sounding mechanical and insincere.
- Avoid stock phrases.
- Avoid sounding patronizing or condescending.
- Avoid coming across as a counsellor or therapist.

Review the three-part ERL formula:

- ***Reflect feeling:*** "You feel frustrated...
- ***Reflect meaning:*** when the supplies aren't there, because you can't do your work.
- ***Check accuracy:*** Is that what you're saying?"

Comments on ERL exercises:

- Dyads speaking and listening:

- Dyads doubling:

- Role reversal with opponent:

- Role reversal with class member:

IV. Conflict Management and Resolution:

- Being open to another's anger or hostile criticism.

Review why it is important to be open to another's anger:
- To convey other's entitlement to be open to another's anger
- To reduce hostility in a conflict situation

Review factors which reduce and increase anger in a conflict:

Reduce	*Increase*
Use silence, wait out feelings	Interrupt the speaker
Ask opponent to say more	Return charges, criticism, "you" statements
Use empathic reflective listening	Impulsively react, defend, explain, or assert
Use low voice	Threats, put-downs, pointing
Be sincere in verbal/non-verbal expression	Raise your voice
Be willing to consider elements of truth in other's views	Understate the speaker's issue
Acknowledge other's entitlement to stated feelings and views	Ordering
Attend the speaker	Use sarcastic tones
Overstate the speaker's case	Tell speaker what he/she is really thinking, real motives, push your assumptions
In fight, use distance until adrenaline settles	Bring up the past
	Compare the speaker to others as a put-down
	Ignore the speaker

Review the approach when:
1) only the other party is angry, 2) only you are angry, and 3) both you and the other party are angry:

a) Display openness, use ERL
b) Assert your feelings and views
c) Alternate ERL and assertive statements until both feel understood

Review the approach when:
1) only the other party is in a fight mode, 2) only you are in a fight mode, and 3) both you and the other party are in a fight mode:

a) Label the fight, state willingness to talk when other party is ready
b) Fight fairly, get finished, then distance
c) Fight fairly, label the fight, then distance

Review why it is important to allow distance after a verbal fight:
- Adrenaline in the body inhibits rational thinking and problem solving.
- Distance allows time for the adrenaline to settle.

Review the two most common difficulties in facing a conflict:
- Raising the issues.
- Getting past the fight, managing the anger.

Review the steps for resolving conflict after the anger has been reduced:

- Identify issues, brainstorm solutions and agree on one or agree to disagree.
- Exchange apology and forgiveness if appropriate.
- Make verbal contract(s).

Review steps for developing creative options:

- Brainstorm 5 to 8 alternative solutions without critical comment.
- Privately select first and second preferences.
- Share preferences and discuss advantages and disadvantages of each.
- Agree on one alternative.

Review the appropriateness of agreeing to disagree:

- When issues are philosophical, matters of personal taste, or different recollections of a past event; not when issues have to do with cooperative action.

Review factors for creating an atmosphere for the safe airing of grievances in the workplace:

- Set aside time for expressed purpose of airing negative feedback.
- Welcome feedback without reprimand or reaction from management.
- Focus attention on the recording of issues on newsprint or chalkboard.
- Structure the time and the process with written reports, anonymous written responses, voting, etc.

Describe a structure for utilizing negative feedback in a group:

- See "Structure for Positive Conflict in Groups" (p. 358). Also use small groups to brainstorm alternative solutions and agree on one, followed by results reported to the large group and collated for a final vote by the large group.

Checklist for assessing/processing conflict management and resolution:

- If there was a fight, were you fair?
- Did you present your feelings and views assertively, rather than passively or aggressively?
- Were you able to stay in the empathic listening mode until the other party felt understood?
- Were you able to look at alternatives objectively?
- Were you able to identify resurfacing anger and attend to it?
- Were you able to reach agreement on one alternative or agree to disagree?
- Were apologies and forgiveness sincerely exchanged?
- Were verbal contracts made?

Comments on re-enactment of conflict scenarios:

- What is your characteristic style in receiving criticism?
- What is your characteristic style in giving criticism?
- What feelings interfere with your being assertive?
- What difficulties do you have with empathic listening?

What are your goals for changing the way you handle conflict situations?

- ____________________
- ____________________
- ____________________

STRUCTURE FOR POSITIVE CONFLICT IN GROUPS

* 1. Facilitator states purpose of meeting as providing opportunity for safe airing of grievances regarding policies and managerial style and for developing creative options where possible.

2. Facilitator asks group members to raise specific issues and concerns. These are listed on newsprint or chalkboard so that everyone can participate in refining or rewording the issues.

3. The facilitator asks group members to prioritize the issues by simple vote.

4. Facilitator asks group members to brainstorm five to eight possible solutions or approaches to the number one priority issue, and these are listed on the chalkboard.

5. Group members are asked to write down the suggested solutions and then are instructed to circle the numbers of first and second preferences.

6. The facilitator collates the preferences on the chalkboard followed by open discussion of the advantages and disadvantages of final preferences.

7. Facilitator asks group members to select a final solution by majority vote.

8. Follow steps 4 through 7 for priority issue #2.

* Facilitator should be assertive, skilled at reflective listening, and acknowledge entitlement in order to establish safety and permission for airing grievances.

CTI MODEL FOR POSITIVE CONFLICT MANAGEMENT & RESOLUTION

Management

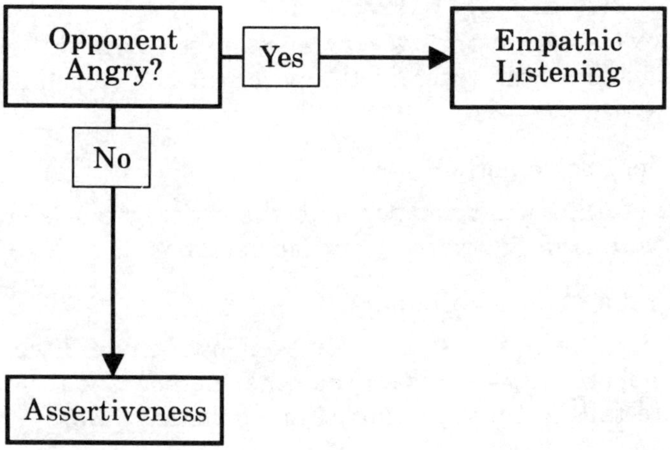

Resolution

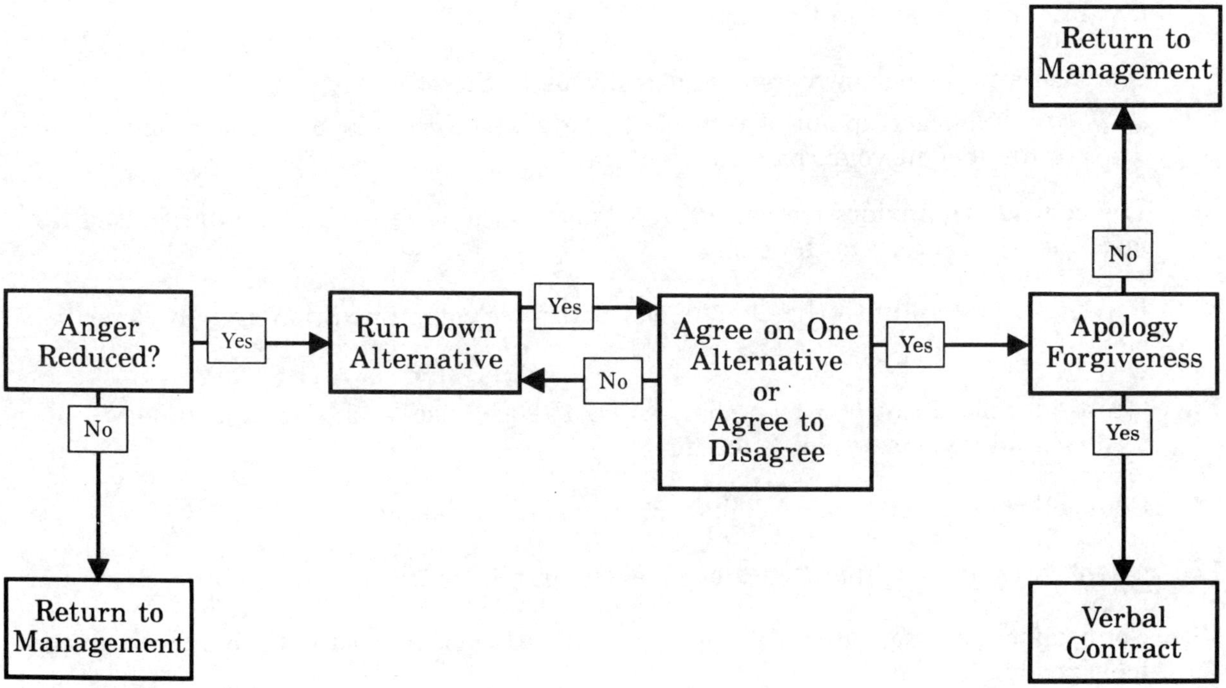

ENACTMENT EXERCISE

1. Invite the client to summarize the issue(s) or conflict in the relationship.
   - e.g. "So talk a little bit about the conflict you are having. What's it about?"
2. Suggest the exercise.
   - e.g. "I'd like to suggest that we try an exercise that will help to explore the way you have communicated in the past and how you might try to communicate in the future."
3. Interview the client as the other.
   - *say:* "First of all, I want you to sit in the other person's chair so that I can interview you as if you were the other person."
4. Client addresses the other as him/herself.
   - *say:* "Now I'd like you to sit back in your own chair. I want you to imagine this is an opportunity to talk to the other person about your issues, and I want you to talk to them in your characteristic way."
5. Client responds as the other with the most difficult response for the client face to face.
   - *say:* "Now I want you to sit in the other person's chair and give the response that is most difficult for you to face."
6. The counsellor provides transition by sitting in the client's chair and repeating the last line of the client to the other.
7. Client sits in his/her own chair and responds to the other.
   - *say:* "Now get up out of that chair, be yourself in your own chair, and respond to him/her in your characteristic way."
8. The counsellor provides transition by sitting in the other's chair and repeating the last line of the other to the client.
9. Repeat #5 and #6 until the client's characteristic communication style becomes clear.
10. Counsellor sits in his/her own chair, stops the exercise, and gives the client feedback on style or explores feelings.
11. Counsellor demonstrates workable communications options.
12. Client tries on new approaches or grieves the relationship.
13. Counsellor discusses possibility of facing the other at a specific time or wait until feels ready.

Handouts for Chapter Five:

Couple Counselling

COUPLE COUNSELLING OUTLINE

Introduction

Session #1:

The Initial Assessment:

- Identification: Ages, years married, occupation, children
- Presenting Problems: What are the problems that bring you here today?
- Problem History: How long have you had each problem? Precipitating factors, fluctuations, previous counselling, separations, previous marriages.
- Brief Stress Status: How much stress are you experiencing now? Use scale from 0-10.
- Individual Assessment: Past History, Family History, Personal History
- Describe outline of the structure to follow (Phase I & Phase II)
- Close with assignment to read article or listen to tape on "Resolving Conflict."

Crisis Intervention (If a high stress rating is given or conflict is open)

- Brief couple and individual assessments
- Identify and prioritize issues on newsprint
- Problem solving priority issue of each partner
- Describe outline of the structure to follow (Phase I & Phase II)
- Close with assignment to read article or listen to tape on "Resolving Conflict."

Phase I

Session #2:

Assertiveness Skill-Building

Session #3:

Listening Skill-Building

Session #4:

Problem-Solving Skill-Building

Session #5:

Consolidating Skills After Two-Week Interval

Session #6:

Tentative Appointment After One-Month Interval

Phase II

Alternating individual and couple sessions begin if communication skills are not being used.

RESOLVING CONFLICT

By Daniel M. Keeran, M.A., M.S.W.

Conflict is common and normal in marriage because people are individuals with unique feelings and views. Therefore, the goal is not to eliminate conflict but to handle it in a way that has a positive rather than a negative outcome. This chapter will provide a basic model and essential skills for resolving conflict in marriage. You will learn the following:

- How to get past the fighting stage
- Raising and identifying issues appropriately
- Listening to the other side
- Reaching an agreement

Conflict is frightening to many people because it has traditionally been discouraged and regarded as bad. In many families, marital conflict is denied, avoided, or hidden behind closed doors so that the children are not able to learn from observing how conflict is handled. In other cases, the conflict is so unmanaged that children learn only to fear the experience when parents lose control of emotions.

Getting past the fight

The two most difficult steps in the process for resolving conflict are to raise the issues appropriately and to get past the fight. The old saying, "It takes two to tangle," is a myth simply because **fighting occurs when only one person refuses to listen to the other person's views**. This may occur in two ways: by using silence to punish the spouse or to avoid the issue and by dominating or abusing the spouse.

Nothing can be resolved as long as the couple is in the fighting stage. Therefore, it is best to recognize the fight as soon as it begins and allow a cooling off period so that the adrenaline can settle. Then the couple should resume discussion as soon as possible so that issues are not left hanging.

It is worthwhile to distinguish "fair" fighting from "destructive" fighting. In destructive fighting, there is behaviour which is damaging to the other person physically, one's self-worth, property, and the relationship itself. **Destructive behaviour** includes name-calling, put-downs, sarcasm, threats, judgmental terms (e.g. lazy, wrong, bad, irresponsible, inconsiderate), hitting, throwing things, and screaming and shouting. In **fair fighting**, there may be interrupting, finger pointing, accusing, and sharpening one's words. So it is important to keep the fighting stage fair if it must occur at all. **Destructive behaviour should be raised as an issue to be resolved. It is like a cancer to a marriage.**

To recognize the fight beginning in yourself, ask these questions:

- Am I carrying on or pushing my point, not allowing the other person to speak?
- Am I reacting defensively to explain or justify myself?
- Do I repeat my issue without taking it to a resolution?
- Do I withdraw into an angry silence?
- Do I state my issue before giving my understanding of an issue previously expressed by my partner?
- Do I try to "get back" at the other person with counter charges, abusive language, silence, sabotage?

If you are able to answer "yes" to any of the above questions, then you can pinpoint a goal for change and select alternative approaches. Remember, emotions may well up inside without your control, and you can decide how to express them. If you're not in charge of your anger, who will be? So express anger as a choice, not as an impulsive reaction.

As soon as you feel the adrenaline surge through your heart and lungs and **you begin to lose the ability to state the other person's view**, you may want to break off the exchange by saying, "I'm not able to talk about this right now but I'll let you know when I'm ready." Or conversely, you may observe that your spouse is unable to consider your views, and a similar statement would be appropriate.

It is common for a couple to experience fantasies of divorce and of being single again following a severe conflict. However, it is important that the normal degree of distance not become too lengthy or extreme; e.g. a spouse may leave the house, but moving to a hotel would be extreme. The more extreme the distance, the more difficult the resolution. When there is physical abuse, the abused spouse should move out and seek couple counselling as soon as possible.

Raising and Identifying Issues

The following principles or guidelines are important for expressing issues in a way that can be heard:

1. Assess the degree of permission and safety for raising your issue. If the consequences would be too costly, e.g. abuse, then safety is low. Observe how the person interacts with others, or perhaps ask the person if you can offer some feedback. If the answer is, "Well, that depends," then safety is questionable.
2. Express your feeling of anger with an "I feel" statement: "I feel annoyed when you don't put gas in the car and leave it on empty for me, because then I lose time when I have to stop for gas in the morning."
3. Be clear, direct, and brief as in the above example, without judgmental terms.
4. Provide a factual description of your spouse's observable behaviour.
5. Provide a factual description of the practical effects on your life resulting from your spouse's behaviour.
6. Always raise name-calling and put-downs as a violation of your human right to be treated with respect: e.g. "I resent your calling me names, because I am not being given the respect I deserve."
7. Express your anger as near the time you feel it as possible, to the person with whom you are angry. Some people save up issues and dump them all at once or get back with the occasional put-down. **Express your anger and** let it go, then get on with resolving **the issue**. If you are angry with your spouse be careful not to take it out on the kids.
8. A principle worth repeating is: Express your anger as a choice, not as an impulsive reaction. Choose how and when the emotion of anger comes out of your mouth.
9. Sound angry, sharpen your words or accent them for emphasis.
10. Broaden you feeling vocabulary of words synonymous with "angry" but which may describe various levels or degrees of anger. For example: furious, perturbed, livid, irritated, outraged, annoyed, frustrated.
11. Avoid blanket statements such as: "You always....never," or "I hate you." Give the person some credit and point out specific behaviour rather than writing the person off.
12. Avoid being too passive or too aggressive and destructive. The passive approach is to avoid the issue to keep things nice or be uncooper-

ative like; burning dinner, being late, remaining silent. The aggressive approach is to interrupt, point, bring up the past, compare the spouse to other people (e.g. her mother) as a put-down, push your assumption about what your spouse is really thinking or what his or her real motives are.

Fear and guilt are the most common blocks to asserting one's feelings and views. The fear of hurting or of being hurt leads to a protection racket where avoidance results in more distance in the relationship. Reacting violently to an issue raised by a spouse gives them the message that feedback is not allowed.

Listening to the Other Side

Identifying the issues in a conflict often works well with an assertive statement if you are the one who is angry. If your spouse is the angry party, an empathic statement may work well to identify his or her issue(s) and to **reduce the anger by conveying acceptance and understanding**.

The empathic statement is an attempt to **state the other person's issue** including his or her feelings and meaning. For example: "So you feel furious when I don't do an equal share of the household responsibilities, because it makes more work for you. Is that what you're feeling?" The listening spouse tries to hear feelings not expressed and tries to convey an understanding of how the angry spouse's life has been affected as well as the reason being stated. The empathic statement is a sincere attempt to state the other spouse's case back to them. **This lets the angry spouse know that you are wanting to identify his or her issue**. As a result, the angry spouse may not feel the need to push the point.

Other listening principles include the following:

- Use silence, wait out the feelings of the angry spouse.
- Sincerely ask the spouse to say more or to elaborate.
- Keep your voice low. An ancient proverb says: A soft voice turns away anger.
- Be sure to make eye contact and give the spouse indication that you are listening and regard his or her views as worthwhile.
- Be willing to consider elements of truth in what your spouse is saying, not giving false agreement, but to say, "Maybe I need to think about what you've said."
- Tell your spouse you value his or her feedback.
- Acknowledge your spouse's entitlement to their feelings and views.

The goal of the listener in all these approaches is to give maximum permission to your spouse's expression of the issues so that it can be identified for resolution.

Sincerity is essential to empathic listening. If there is any hint of sarcasm or insincerity in one's voice tone or facial expression, the effect will be to increase rather than reduce the conflict.

Reaching an agreement

Common practice is to fight over the same issues without taking them to the point of a workable agreement. Especially when the issues are intensely emotional or complicated, it is helpful to refer to a model which provides steps to follow and which one can use to pinpoint the area of difficulty. The steps are as follows:

- Get past the fight and silent period by saying, "I'm ready to talk now if you are."
- Identify the issues using assertive and empathic statements as described above.
- Each spouse writes down his or her issues and privately decides which is most important.

- The couple decides whose "most important" issue will be dealt with first.
- Both spouses will write down the issue and list below eight possible approaches or solutions. These will be suggested without evaluation or discussion, and both spouses will write the same points on his or her own paper. It is sometimes helpful to include what's happening now, the status quo, its opposite, and even approaches that sound silly. These suggestions help stimulate creative thinking. And remember, there is always an alternative you haven't thought of.
- Each spouse will privately circle three of the eight numbered approaches that they believe are most workable and realistic.
- Each spouse reads off the numbers of the three approaches selected, and where the numbers overlap, an agreement has been reached.

The above approach has been proven to be effective in over 90% of couples seeking marriage counselling through the writer's private practice.

Here are some further guidelines. Couples often focus on past events or issues and carry on the struggle over the recollection of details. Rather, the discussion is more productive when the focus is on current and future behaviour or practice. Another very important point is that a resolution or agreement can occur even if the issue presented is false. Therefore, much arguing over the accuracy or validity of an issue can be avoided. The issue can be viewed as a hypothetical situation which can still be resolved so that a standard of behaviour or practice is affirmed.

Apology and forgiveness are important if destructive fighting has occurred such as name-calling and put-downs. One option for issues, related to philosophical views and personal taste, is to agree to disagree. But if the issue has to do with cooperative action, agreement on one approach is necessary.

Bringing it Together

Minor conflicts can often be resolved without using pencil and paper, but when the issue is complicated and emotional the above structure saves time and energy in the long run. The following dialogue will demonstrate the process for resolving conflict and some of the major skills:

Her: "I feel quite annoyed when you just sit and watch TV after work because then I don't get to talk with you."

Him: "So maybe you're feeling left out and angry when I don't talk with you more after work. Is that what you're feeling?"

Her: "Yes. It's as though you don't want to be with me."

Him: "So you feel lonely and sad sometimes. Is that what you're saying?"

Her: "Uh-huh."

Him: "You're entitled to your feelings. Tell me more."

Her: "Well, I just think we've become more distant. We don't spend time together ... just talking about how the day went."

Him: "So the issue is spending time together. Is that what you're saying? Let's make a list of possible solutions, since this is an everyday problem."

Her: "I'll get two sheets of paper and two pencils. One for each of us."

Him: "Number one through eight. Here's the first idea...."

Both spouses mention ideas and these are written down without evaluation or discussion. The list looks like this on each sheet of paper:

Issue:

- The wife feels angry and sad because she does not spend time talking with her husband.

Suggested Approaches:

- Continue watching TV and not talking to wife.
- Talk to wife every minute of the time.
- Make appointments to talk.
- Have one evening out per week together.
- Have one evening per month together.
- Talk every day about how the day went.
- Watch only news and documentaries on TV.
- Watch no TV when wife is home.

Each spouse then privately circles the number of three approaches which they think is most workable, realistic, fair, and reasonable. Finally, each spouse shares the numbers selected, and if the spouses choose the same number(s), agreement has been reached. If not, spouses then choose which of the other spouse's selections they have the least trouble with, and the couple discusses advantages and disadvantages of those two approaches. If the couple still cannot agree on one of the suggested approaches, the next step is to brainstorm more approaches, keeping in mind that there is always an alternative you haven't thought of.

Review Questions

1. What is the common denominator of fighting behaviour?
2. What is fair fighting as opposed to destructive fighting?
3. What can you say to break out of a fight situation?
4. Give an example of an assertive "I feel" statement using the formula.
5. Give an example of an empathic statement using the formula.
6. What element is essential to an empathic statement?
7. What does an empathic statement accomplish?
8. What behaviour increases conflict and tension?
9. What is the concept of entitlement?
10. What should you do if your spouse is physically abusive?
11. How can spouses arrive at possible approaches to an issue?
12. According to the model described, what is the final means of reaching an agreement?

ASSERTIVENESS EXERCISE FOR COUPLES

Choose a word from the anger vocabulary in #10 (see page 365) and complete this sentence directed to your spouse: "I feel ____________ when you ___________ because ______________________ ." For an example, review #2 (see page 365). Do not say more than this one sentence, and the spouse may not respond to the statement at this time. So look at your spouse, think of something you slightly dislike about them, then formulate your single statement.

When each of you have completed the exercise, discuss the following questions:

- Did you feel hurt or angry by what was said to you?
- Was anyone destroyed? Did anyone turn into a 'grease spot'?
- Do you feel just a little bit guilty for making your statement?
- Did you break the rule and react to your spouse's statement?

LISTENING EXERCISE FOR COUPLES

Remember, empathic listening does not mean that you agree with your spouse, only that you accept and understand how the speaker feels. Here is an exercise to help you practice your empathic listening skill. Follow these steps:

- Decide who will be the speaker and who will be the listener.

- For five minutes, the speaker will elaborate on the issue expressed in the "Assertiveness Exercise" or choose another issue.

- The listener completes the following sentence during breaks in the speaker's comments: "So you feel ______________, when I ______________________, because ____________________________. Is that what you feel?"

- The listener should not ask questions or lead the conversation in any way, except to say, "Say more about that."

- The speaker should allow frequent breaks, e.g. every two or three sentences.

- Reverse speaker and listener positions after five or ten minutes.

- After each person has been the listener, talk about whether or not you felt understood by your spouse.

Appendix B: Counselling Practice Supplement

COUNSELLING PRACTICE NOTES

By Daniel M. Keeran, M.A., M.S.W.

The Counselling Practice Development Course offered at the Counsellor Training Institute, is relevant to independent practice as well as employment in service agencies. Among the topic areas for the course listed here, notes for the last three topics are provided in this article:

1. Creating and Building a Professional Image
2. Basic Business Requirements
3. Generating Clientele: Developing Creative Strategies
4. Brochure Writing
5. Ethical Standards and Legal Issues
6. Fee Assessment and Professional Contacts
7. Client Relationships: Initial Contact, Determining and Maintaining the Length of Counselling, Evaluation of Progress, and Closure

In this review an effort has been made to describe challenging scenarios which are frequently encountered in a counselling practice and to provide practical suggestions of actual words to use with clients.

Ethical Standards and Legal Issues

The threat of a law suit brought against a counsellor is minimized if the counsellor adheres closely to clear ethical standards as contained in the CTI Code of Ethics and shared by the Canadian Professional Counsellors Association. An example of a situation which might result in a law suit is failure to take proper steps to assess and prevent suicide. Surviving family members may initiate a lawsuit if they believe the counsellor failed in his professional responsibility. A knowledge of the specific questions to ask in assessing the degree of risk, as well as establishing a suicide contract with the client who has a recent history of suicidal thoughts, are essential. A detailed discussion of the process is given in *Healing Words: The Counsellor Training Course Manual* on pages 82-86. It is also important to document the above in the client's file by recording the specific questions asked by the counsellor and the client's verbatim responses.

In the event of a suicide threat or gesture, the incident must be properly documented. When a client is having suicidal thoughts, the counsellor must ask in every session whether the client has had suicidal thoughts since the last session, until there have been four consecutive weeks in which the client reports no suicidal thoughts. If there is a single report within that time or any time thereafter, or if there is an increase in depressive symptoms, the counsellor must inquire again and continue to do so in subsequent sessions until there have been four consecutive sessions of no suicidal thoughts. These inquiries and the client's responses must be documented in the client's file in the progress notes.

Another situation which might result in legal action is the failure to take steps to warn the victim of possible homicide threatened by a client. A typical scenario is that of the male client who is angry because his fianc leaves him for another man. During a counselling session, he threatens to kill his girlfriend and/or the other man. The counsellor has an obligation to take steps to warn the potential victims, and this may be accomplished simply by phoning the police and providing information about the circumstances. For a discussion of homicide assessment and prevention refer to *Healing Words: The Counsellor Training Course Manual* on pages 82-86. Confidentiality is not required when the client is believed to be life-threatening to himself or others.

A third situation which may result in legal action is failure to report the suspected physical or sexual abuse of a child within 24 hours after hearing the report. Add to this the suspected abandonment or neglect of a child, under eleven years of age, who is left alone without adult supervision. The counsellor may anonymously phone in the report to police or child protective services and must document this in the client's file.

Other situations which could result in legal problems might involve violation of confidentiality which leads to some kind of "personal injury" to the client such as revealing to a spouse that the client had been sexually abused, which then results in a breakdown of the marriage. A similar situation could occur in which the counsellor recommends the separation of a couple or recommends that a client leave a spouse, which could bring about legal action especially if the couple later reconciles and realizes that the counsellor caused the "alienation of affection" between them.

Yet another situation of legal action might occur if the counsellor becomes sexually involved with the client, resulting in the worsening of depression perhaps requiring hospitalization or related to the client's suicide. A law suit may result from any physical contact other than a social handshake; especially with the Borderline Personality who experiences erotic transference and then murderous rage when the romantic feelings are not reciprocated. Another possibility of legal action to be mentioned here, is the introduction of techniques which result in severe regression for the client, such as the use of guided imagery or hypnosis with a client who has been hospitalized for psychosis or major depression.

More recently, numerous law suits have been successfully brought against therapists who lead the vulnerable client into believing that he or she was sexually abused during infancy, resulting in a false memory of abuse which becomes the basis of legal action against a family member as the suspected perpetrator or which at least causes a painful alienation of affection between the client and the family member. Later then, the family members or the client herself who realizes she was manipulated, bring a law suit against the counsellor. The lesson is, always allow the client to initiate the disclosure of sexual abuse; never ask if it occurred and do not directly suggest to a client that it may have occurred.

A further word about confidentiality, with the exception of life-threatening behaviour and child abuse and neglect situations, in order to release information about a client or to obtain information about a client from another professional, the counsellor must have a release of information form signed by the client who thereby gives his or her permission. If a spouse or family member phones to ask about your client, simply explain that "Because of confidentiality I am not even able to acknowledge that the person you named is my client." If a professional phones or writes to inquire about a client, you must have a release of information from that professional person signed by the client. In order to obtain information from another professional person about your client, you must send a copy of the release of information signed by your client. Think of the disclosures of the client as his or her personal property which belongs only to the client.

Two situations which pose special challenges are 1) the adolescent client and 2) work with couples. To work successfully with the adolescent client, an agreement with the parents must be made that the child will have a right to the confidentiality of sessions. In work with couples, when the counsellor is seeing them individually and as a couple, he or she must be careful not to reveal information to the partner. Any revelations must come from the client in these situations.

A special problem in working with family violence is that the counsellor may be wanting to encourage the adult victim of spousal abuse, to leave the abusing partner. The important thing to remember here is that the counsellor must not recommend or tell the victim to leave the abuser. This decision must remain solely the responsibility of the client who is the victim. Rather than say, "I think you should leave him", the counsellor can say, "What will you do?" and "What does staying with him say about the way you feel about yourself?" and "If you were to leave him, what steps could you take?" The counsellor can help the client arrive at the decision to leave but may not directly recommend it. The client remains in charge of decisions, and this also decreases the likelihood of retaliation or blame being directed at the counsellor.

A situation frequently encountered is when the adult survivor of childhood sexual abuse reports that the perpetrator, who was also an adult during the client's childhood, is still alive. If the counsellor suspects that the perpetrator may still be abusing other children, a report must be made for their protection. It may be therapeutic for the client to make the report, but if not, the counsellor should phone in the report within 24 hours.

Fee Assessment and Professional Contacts

Usually in the first phone contact with the client, a determination is made of the amount of the fee to be provided. This may be done simply by explaining to the client that, "My usual fee is $75. Is that something you can provide?" With this approach the words used are important. For example, the word "usual" indicates a norm but also shows flexibility. It says that this is what most people pay, and the client is therefore inclined to want to pay what most people pay. It also indicates what you believe is the value of your hour of service.

In my experience, this is more effective than referring to a sliding scale, because I have found that clients who would normally pay less on a sliding scale, will either pay your usual fee or come very close. People will usually place upon themselves the expectation to pay your usual fee when you remove the expectation by asking, "Is that something you think you can provide?" Already you are giving your client the power and responsibility to decide, which is therapeutic in itself, and at the same time you are upholding the value of your service.

The counsellor may want to employ the idea of a free initial session or a free initial 30 minutes with the option to extend the session for half the regular fee. This allows the client to evaluate the benefit of your service before committing, and it works well for clients who come to you cold without a referral from a professional or an endorsement from a friend.

In terms of the amount of the fee per session, consider the clientele you wish to attract. If your fee is too low for your clientele, they will not come because they will not value your service. For example, if your clientele are high income earners such as lawyers, corporate managers, and other professionals, you may need to charge in the range of $90 to $120 or more per hourly session in 1995. Whatever the amount of the fee, this should be clarified in the initial phone contact with the understanding that payment will be provided at the end of each session and that a receipt will be given in exchange. Say, "You can write a cheque at the end of the session, and I'll give you a receipt." When you state your payment policy simply add, "Is that OK with you?" or "Does that make sense?" This again acknowledges the client's right to offer a different view and gives him power to contribute to decisions.

An occasional problem with regard to fee payment is the client who does not pay at the end of the session as agreed. The client says, "I forgot my cheque book," or "I can't afford to pay you this week. Is it OK if I pay you next time?" It is important not to allow the client to repeat a dysfunctional pattern of being dependent and becoming a victim. An unpaid debt to you creates a barrier of fear and guilt on the client's part and fear and resentment on the counsellor's part. If this occurs, you can use the occasion to generate insights into patterns by saying, "I wonder if this is the first time in your life, you have been in this situation or been in this kind of position in relation to someone."

You may allow the client to go no more than two sessions without paying the balance. If it is not fully paid in the third session, you may want to discuss the client's emotions related to the unpaid amount and arrange for a reduced fee, suggest spacing sessions farther apart, or even offer time reserved for people who can not afford to pay. In any case, the client is engaged in a process of exploring his feelings, thoughts, and then he is engaged in a process of taking action or problem-solving so that the matter is settled and free of anxiety. This becomes a model for coping with many types of issues and challenges in the client's life.

In terms of professional contacts, the counsellor may be receiving referrals from a physician. When a referral has been made by a physician, it may come in the form of a phone call from the physician's office. The appointment is made by the client or on the client's behalf. When the client arrives or if there is a "no-show", the physician's office should be contacted by phone or by letter to let them know whether or not the client appeared for the appointment. Then also at the close of the counselling relationship whether or not it was a therapeutic closure, the counsellor will notify the physician's office by sending a letter briefly outlining the beginning and end dates, number of sessions, areas of progress, and a recommendation that the client attend the physician's office for follow-up.

Also, to maintain a working referral network with physicians, recommend to clients that they visit the physician on a weekly basis during your holiday periods. In addition, be sure to refer clients to their physicians for physical examinations, request a report for the client's file, and as a rule only initiate the discontinuing of medication with the physician's agreement.

Following these procedures with physicians, will generate referrals from new physicians and will maintain a flow of referrals in existing professional relationships. Situations which require referrals back to physicians while maintaining a counselling relationship, would be the need for physical exams, diabetes control, and medication management related to mood disorders. Conditions of schizophrenia and bi-polar disorder may require a referral with the suggestion of a need for a psychiatric evaluation.

Client Relationships

Initial Contact

Return any messages left on your answering machine within the hour if possible. Strike while the iron is hot. The client's felt need for counselling may soon pass as the defenses strengthen. A number of considerations are important to clarify during the initial phone contact. The conversation may go something like this:

Client: "Hello. Is this the Counselling Service?"

Counsellor : "Yes it is. How can I help you?"

1. Scheduling the Appointment

Client: "Your name was given to me by a friend, and I wonder if you have some time available to see me."

Counsellor: "Yes I do. Let me check my schedule. I could see you as early as tomorrow afternoon or perhaps later in the week." Give the client the earliest available time. Again, strike while the iron is hot.

Client: "Tomorrow is fine."

Counsellor: "Two o'clock?"

Client: "Yes. That would be fine."

Counsellor: "What is your name and phone number?"

Client: "My name is Jane Doe. My phone number is 234-5678." Write the name and phone number next to the time in your appointment book. Be sure to write the phone number as you will need this for a no-show or to notify the client if you are ill.

2. Directions to the Office

Counsellor: "Do you know how to find my office? (Or another option is to meet in your home if there is privacy there.)" Directions are given.

3. Assessing the Fee

Counsellor: "Are you aware of my fee?"

Client: "I'm not sure."

Counsellor: "My usual fee is $75. Is that something you think you can provide?" See the explanation for this approach, in the section on fee assessment.

Client: "It sounds a little high."

Counsellor: "How close to that do you think you can come?"

Client: "Would $60 be OK? I think I can afford that right now."

4. Payment Policy

Counsellor: "Yes. What I usually ask is that you provide payment or write a cheque at the end of the session, and I'll also give you a receipt at that time. Is that OK with you?"

Client: "Yes that's fine."

5. Preparing for Assessment

Counsellor: "In the first session, I'd like to take some time to talk about your need for counselling and then I would like to ask you a series of questions to get a broader understanding of your life experience. Would that be OK?" (If the client indicates a crisis situation, the background history may be set aside.)

Client: "Yes. That sounds fine."

6. Cancellation Policy

Counsellor: "If you are unable to make the appointment for any reason, I would like you to let me know 24 hours in advance if possible."

Client: "Yes. Thank you very much."

Counsellor: "You're welcome, and I'll see you then tomorrow at 2 p.m. Bye for now."

Determining and Maintaining the Length of Counselling

The discussion about the number of sessions typically occurs during the first session at the end of the Clinical Assessment. A client may ask, "How many sessions will I need?" The counsellor may respond by saying, "There are two ways to proceed. One is to agree upon a number of sessions. The other is to leave the counselling open ended, meaning that when you feel you are ready to stop you can let me know. Which would you prefer to do?"

Giving the client the opportunity to agree on a number of sessions in advance, provides a reasonable guarantee of the counsellor's availability, helps the vulnerable client feel safe from the fear of exploitation, and encourages therapeutic work to be concentrated and focused within a determined time frame. The explanation can be given that near the end of the 12 sessions, for example, "We can discuss your progress and you can decide whether or not you would like to extend the number of sessions." Another situation which may call for a limited number of sessions, would be uncomplicated bereavement in which case perhaps a few sessions would enable the client to grieve further on his own.

On the other hand, the value of leaving the counselling relationship open-ended helps the client with long-standing problems feel assured of sufficient time to heal. When the counsellor perceives the latter scenario based on findings in the Clinical Assessment, she may want to describe only the open-ended plan.

When a client wants to discontinue counselling prematurely, he or she may present lack of time or finances. If these are in fact excuses, nothing will resolve these issues. The counsellor can offer the option to meet less often or to reduce or even eliminate the fee, but when all offers or suggestions are refused, then some form of resistance or perhaps negative transference is getting in the way. If the client is insistent upon discontinuing, it is important for the counsellor to validate this decision by saying for example, "So what I'm hearing is that you're deciding to stop for now, and I certainly support your decision. If you decide at some point in the future that you would like to continue, I would certainly be available to you."

If the counsellor perceives the client to be in need of counselling, the wording may be as follows, "I would encourage you to continue your counselling whether it's with me or with someone else you feel safe with and have confidence in. In any case I do encourage you to seek help from someone at this time." This approach disconnects the client from you, and lets the client know that you have no financial interest in his or her well-being.

A common situation is for the new client to resist setting a time for the second appointment by saying, "I'll call and let you know." An approach that works well is to say, "What I prefer to do when someone is uncertain is to at least set a tentative time for the next appointment. That way, the time will be reserved for you if you can make it. If you can't make it, you can simply phone and cancel. How does that sound?" This approach establishes the time mentally so that the client expects to return for that specific time.

Another occasion for setting boundaries is when the client does not show for a scheduled appointment and does not cancel in advance. The effective procedure is to phone the client 15 to 20 minutes into the scheduled time and engage in the following conversation:

Counsellor: "Hello, Bob. I just thought I'd phone to see what happened, because we had an appointment for 2 p.m. and when you didn't come I thought I would phone to see what happened and what you'd like to do about your counselling. Are you wanting to make another appointment or what would you like to do?"

Client: "Yes. I think I would. I completely forgot. So many things have been coming up lately."

Counsellor: "So would next week at the same time be OK for you?"

Client: "Yes. That's fine."

Counsellor: "Also since this has happened it might be a time for me to explain that if you're not able to make an appointment and if I don't hear from you to cancel, then my policy is to require payment of the usual fee for the session. I won't charge you this time but only if it happens again. The only exception being if you were unable to phone due to circumstances. Does that make sense to you?"

Client: "Oh, sure. Yes, it won't happen again."

Counsellor: "OK so I'll see you next Thursday at 2 p.m."

The approach here is to phone the client during the no-show appointment. This impresses upon the client the seriousness of the no-show. This occasion is also used to state the policy on no-shows, or the policy can be stated earlier, before the first occurrence. If there are three consecutive no-shows, the policy is to discuss beginning counselling again and inviting the client to phone to schedule an appointment when he is ready to begin and believes he can make his appointments.

To maintain a counselling relationship, it is important to process parts of sessions in which new difficult material is disclosed. This is done by saying, "What's it been like talking about this so far?" and "It's not easy to face these painful memories," and "It's OK to go slowly." There is always a possibility of the client's dropping out when painful emotions or unresolved issues toward the counsellor are not acknowledged, verbalized, and validated.

Another important ingredient for maintaining the counselling relationship is periodic review and refocusing of goals by saying, "What I'd like to do as we begin is talk about your goals and what you want to achieve in your counselling." This keeps the process moving toward meeting the client's identified needs which also permits the evaluation of progress. Keeping each session on track can be done by saying, "I wonder if we're talking about the things you most need to be talking about, and if it seems like we're on track with your goal." This statement helps to determine whether or not the client's priority goal is being addressed.

Evaluation of Progress

An assignment given at the end of a session and reviewed in the next session, also helps to evaluate progress and maintains the relationship by tying one session to the next. A communication exercise to practice, or journalling the session and experiences during the week, are examples of typical assignments. Journalling especially strengthens cohesion within the counselling process as the client continues to work between sessions.

When a client is making progress, it is important to acknowledge this by saying, "Sounds like you've made progress," and "You've taken a big step forward," and "You took a risk and survived," and "Congratulations." Signs of progress may be perceived when the client follows through with recommendations and assignments, when the client reports feeling better and making identified specific changes, and when the counsellor can observe that the client's appearance of posture, personal grooming, and facial expression show increased self-esteem and stable mood.

Some clients may present false progress for various reasons, for example in the case of the Borderline Personality Disorder to avoid abandonment, the Dependent Personality Disorder to please the counsellor, the Anti-Social Personality Disorder to avoid legal consequences, and the Narcissistic Personality Disorder to appear highly competent.

Closure

In the case of the Borderline Personality Disorder, the risk of extreme regression, a suicide attempt, or hospitalization may increase when closure of the counselling relationship is initiated by the counsellor. To avoid the recurrence of abandonment trauma, the Borderline should be prepared for and work through the ending of a counselling relationship far in advance of the end point, with a structured follow-up schedule in place.

In the case of any client who experienced the childhood loss of parental caring resulting in a Dependent Personality Disorder for example, a therapeutic closure after working through the significant core psychodynamic issues, may involve saying "good-bye" to the counsellor. The counsellor may say, "I wonder what this counselling relationship has been like for you." When the client describes the counsellor as being supportive and helpful, the counsellor can say, "What other important person in your life do you wish had been supportive and helpful?" The client may then identify the parents, and the counsellor can say, "So saying good-bye to me may also be a way of saying good-bye to the parents that you wish you had and also a way of leaving home and being on your own." This realization may trigger further grieving as part of saying good-bye, letting go, and becoming more independent.

In bringing therapeutic closure to a counselling relationship, which may be initiated by the counsellor or the client, three areas are important to review in the final sessions. When the client initiates closure, she may say, "I think I'm ready to try making it on my own for a while," and this will be acknowledged and validated by the counsellor. The counsellor may initiate closure by saying, "You know I've been thinking and maybe you have too that you've been making significant progress, and so I'm wondering about the possibility of bringing our relationship to a close some time in the near future." If the client has indeed experienced enough progress, he or she will acknowledge having considered closure or at least spacing out the appointments.

The counsellor may then engage the client in a process of 1) identifying areas of progress including specific insights gained, increased mood and self-acceptance, painful issues faced, behaviours changed, new tools for coping and relating; 2) working through emotions related to ending the counselling such as relief, excitement, exhilaration, hope, fears, anger, sadness, emptiness, low self-worth, despair; and 3) areas for future work in view of the fact that old patterns may re-emerge and that this is normal.

The client who has made adequate progress may be expected to have more of the positive emotions about leaving although some normal grief may be felt around leaving the counsellor. It is extremely important for a healthy separation and closure, for the client to adequately process, verbalize, and validate every emotion related to closure. Discussion about what to do with the emotional and psychological space occupied by the counselling process, may be important for some clients and a support group may be desirable or perhaps an expanded social network which hopefully develops prior to closure. For some clients a tentative one-month follow-up appointment can be set and canceled if not needed, and for others a gradual spacing out of sessions may be needed before the last good-bye.

CODE OF ETHICS

The mark of a professional counsellor is adherence to a set of standards which define responsibilities to clients and related parties. The Code of Ethics must include boundaries between the counsellor and client essential to maintaining the safety of the client and necessary for the healing process. Other articles in the Code of Ethics are for the protection of potential victims and for ensuring the client gets the help that he or she needs.

---

1. I will make every effort to complete a comprehensive standard Clinical Assessment at the beginning of the counselling relationship;
2. If I do not have the skill level to provide the help needed, I will refer a client to other qualified professionals;
3. I will preserve the client's right to confidentiality and will not release any identifying information verbally or in writing without the client's signed permission (excepting the threat of suicide, homicide or suspected child abuse);
4. I will not engage in any relationship with the client other than the counsellor-client relationship;
5. I will not touch a client or convey any message which might be interpreted as expressing sexual feelings for the client;
6. I will avoid statements to the client which may generate false memories of sexual abuse;
7. I will inform the client that mental images which emerge during hypnosis or guided imagery may not be memories of actual events;
8. I will provide a safe, private setting for counselling;
9. I will not require payment of a fee for service before the service has been provided;
10. I will not introduce spiritual concepts unless I am previously known to the client as providing spiritual or pastoral counselling;
11. I will make every effort to relate to the client intentionally for a predictable therapeutic outcome;
12. I will provide a means for evaluation of progress so that the client is not misled or taken advantage of;
13. I will be careful to properly assess, prevent, and document the possibility and potential of suicidal or homicidal behaviour by a client;
14. I will immediately (within 24 hours) report the sexual or physical abuse of a child to the police or other authorized persons;
15. I will not give a client the false hope that the counselling relationship can be anything more than that, or that it can be permanent;
16. I will take direct steps to inform the potential victim of homicidal threats made by a client;
17. I will not use hypnosis or guided imagery as part of the treatment for a client who has been hospitalized for psychosis or major depression;
18. I will not devalue the competence of another practitioner in the presence of a client but will direct any complaints to the appropriate professional disciplinary body;
19. I will avoid expressing anger or reacting emotionally to the client;
20. I will not advise a couple to separate or to end their relationship but will allow each party to make his or her own decision;
21. I will not pressure a client to remain in a counselling relationship against the client's expressed desire to terminate;
22. I am committed to my own personal growth and recovery as essential to being an effective counsellor;
23. I am committed to continuing professional education and to expanding my repertoire of skills and my understanding of counselling practice.

Appendix C:
Glossary of Selected Terms

Theoretical Terms

THEORETICAL TERMS

Descriptions submitted by Bill Halyk, B.A., M.Ed.

The following are brief descriptions of some of the major theoretical worldviews and related terms used in the field of counselling and psychotherapy. They are designed as an introduction to the terms and theories, as well as the representative thinkers and writers. For an in-depth discussion, refer to *Counselling and Psychotherapy: A Multicultural Perspective* by Allen E. Ivey, Mary Bradford Ivey & Lynn Simek-Morgan, the text used in the Models of Counselling and Psychotherapy course at the Counsellor Training Institute.

Cognitive-Behavioural Worldview

The Cognitive-Behavioural worldview sees emotional problems as a result of one's dysfunctional beliefs, which need to be challenged. Negative self-talk is altered by recognizing inaccurate thought patterns and erroneous assumptions. Constructive thoughts reinforce a positive belief system, leading to positive changes in feelings and action.

Contributors: Albert Ellis, Donald Meichenbaum, Aaron Beck

Existential-Humanistic Worldview

The Existential-Humanistic worldview recognizes self-actualization. Clients, with capacity of self-awareness, are helped to use their freedom in developing their uniqueness and identity and accepting full responsibility for choices made. They will recognize factors which block freedom, and ultimately find their own positive direction. Thinking is based on "I am the one living, experiencing; I choose my own being".

Contributors: Rollo May, Carl Rogers, Victor Frankl

Family Systems Worldview

The Family Systems worldview suggests that the problems of the individual are really developed in the context of the family. Treatment aims at modifying faulty or unacceptable behaviour which is always in some way related to others. The entire family is helped to examine the immature and maladaptive family behaviour that has been, and is being, transmitted and encourages cooperative individual effort toward positive relationship changes.

Contributors: Murray Bowen, Salvador Minuchin, Irene Goldenberg, Herbert Goldenberg

Feminist Theory Worldview

Relationships and lifespan issues call for recognition of a woman working within the support of family, extended family, and community. Women, whose contribution has been undervalued and downplayed through male domination, need scope for contributing to a "positive intergenerational family script" and to find their "self" in relationships.

Contributors: Mary Ballou, Nancy Gabalac

Multicultural Worldview

The Multicultural worldview perceives the family and its members in a cultural framework. Analysis of problems of the family must take into account the features of the surrounding community, for example, economic climate, ethnic and racial influences, religious beliefs, and historical and political processes. Individual and family counselling must be supported in the community at large. Counselling modalities must follow the recognized and established norms.

Contributors: Arnold Lazarus, Derald Wing Sue, David Sue

Psychodynamic Worldview

The Psychodynamic worldview understands that the present has its roots in the past. Clients need to know how present thoughts and actions relate to past experiences before changes can be permanent. "What is the story behind the story" is a key question. Losses and conflicts need to be processed.

Contributors: John Bradshaw, Erik Erikson, James Framo

GLOSSARY

Existentialism - Stresses individual responsibility for creating one's way of thinking, feeling, and behaving in the "here and now".

Contributors: Martin Guber, Rollo May

Gestalt Therapy - The person is seen as having the capacity to recognize how earlier influences are related to present difficulties. Gestalt therapy helps him or her make decisions "here and now" based on awareness of moment-to-moment" experiencing.

Contributors: Fritz Perls

Logotherapy - "Healing through reason"; focus is on searching for value and meaning in life.

Contributors: Victor Frankl

Object-Relations Theory - Focuses on intrapsychic developmental stages as the subject separates from and identifies with individuals in his or her environment ("objects"), eventually integrating these objects to form an identity.

Contributors: Melanie Klein, Donald Woods Winnicott

Person-Centred Therapy - Puts the client, not the therapist, in the "driver's seat". The client, if supported by positive, unconditional respect, will resolve blockages, and find his or her own answers.

Contributors: Carl Rogers

Phenomenology - Accepts the reality of the person subjectively experiencing the world.

Contributors: John Bradshaw, Rollo May

Rational-Emotive Therapy (RET) - Assumes that thinking and evaluating is the base for behaviour change. RET is a teaching and directive process by which the clients are helped to reorganize self-statements, and to change the way they feel and behave.

Contributors: Albert Ellis

Reality Therapy - Assumes a control theory whereby people are able to take charge of their lives by gaining confidence and strength and accepting full responsibility for all their actions. Focus is on current behaviour, planning, and commitment. No excuses are accepted and there is no punishment.

Contributors: William Glasser

DIAGNOSTIC TERMS

By Daniel M. Keeran, M.A., M.S.W.

The following terms are defined in the Diagnosis and Treatment of Common Disorders course at the Counsellor Training Institute and are used in class presentations and materials for other courses. For an in-depth discussion, refer to the *Diagnostic and Statistical Manual of Mental Disorders.*

Adjustment Disorder - This is a significant excessive stress reaction due to an identified stressor which occurred within the previous three months. The stress reaction may for example include depression, anxiety, or some form of misconduct.

Agoraphobia - This condition may accompany Panic Disorder and is characterized by a fear of public places or situations with no escape or no help available if a panic attack occurs for example.

Anorexia Nervosa - This is an eating disorder characterized by perceiving one's body as fat although emaciated along with a fear of gaining weight, self-worth based on body weight, denial of seriousness of low weight, body weight less than 85% of normal, and absence of three consecutive menstrual periods.

Antisocial Personality Disorder - This is a pattern of a chronic violation of the rights of others since age 18, with characteristics of Conduct Disorder before age 15.

Avoidant Personality Disorder - This is a pattern of avoiding social situations because of an extreme fear of criticism or of saying or doing something which others might think is foolish, along with strong feelings of inadequacy.

Bipolar Disorders - These include Bipolar I and II Disorders and Cyclothymia which are characterized by episodes of mania and depression. In Cyclothymia, episodes of mania and depression are less severe than in Bipolar Disorders in which manic episodes and major depression usually require hospitalization and treatment with medication such as Lithium.

Borderline Personality Disorder - This is a pattern of intense emotional instability, deep feelings of emptiness, fear of abandonment, clinginess followed by rejection of another, idealization followed by devaluation of another, and suicide attempts following experiences of abandonment and sometimes requiring hospitalization.

Bulimia Nervosa - This occurs outside anorexia and is characterized by binge eating, excessive eating with a sense of being out of control, followed by efforts to lose the food or weight, occurring twice a week for three months. Also, self-worth is associated with body size.

Conduct Disorder - This is a pattern of violation of others' rights or of age-appropriate rules, which occurred in the previous 12 months. The individual must be under age 18.

Dependent Personality Disorder - This is a pattern of submitting to others because of an intense need for approval and the fear of loss of a relationship.

Depressive Disorders - These are mood disorders which include Major Depressive Disorder and Dysthymic Disorder. No mania is experienced.

Diagnostic Formulation - A listing of the tentative diagnoses, DSM criteria for each diagnosis, and information from the assessment which supports the criteria for each diagnosis.

Dissociative Identity Disorder (formerly **Multiple Personality)** - This involves the presence of two or more personalities having distinct and consistent ways of expressing, viewing, and relating to others and which individually control the person's behaviour at different times. There is also an inability to recall significant amounts of personal information beyond simple loss of memory.

Dysthymia - A low level of depression which occurs over a period of two years or more.

Etiologic Formulation - A statement of the negative contributing factors behind the presenting problems and including the client's descriptions of the parental relationships as well as strengths and possible biological factors.

Histrionic Personality Disorder - This is a pattern of excessive dramatic and shallow emotion, a need for attention especially when not the center of attention, imagines relationships to be intimate when they are not, and may engage in attempts to be sexually exciting.

Hypochondriasis - A condition lasting at least six months in which there is a preoccupation with fears of having a serious illness, which continues after reassurances from medical professionals, and which results in significant social or occupational functioning.

Major Depression - Severe depression which may include suicidal ideas and which may require medication and hospitalization.

Mania (Manic Episodes) - Periods of high energy, high mood, inflated self-confidence, poor judgment such as quitting a job, excessive spending, partying all night.

Mood Disorders - These are conditions characterized by a disturbance in mood and include Depressive Disorders, Bipolar Disorders, and mood disorders due to medical conditions and substance use.

Multiaxial Classification (Five Axes) -

Axis I: All disorders except for personality disorders and mental retardation
Axis II: Personality Disorders and Mental Retardation
Axis III: A listing of current medical problems
Axis IV: A listing of stressors
Axis V: A number from 0 - 100 indicating level of psychosocial functioning

Narcissistic Personality Disorder - This is a pattern of an exaggerated sense of one's own importance or achievement, an excessive need for admiration, extreme sensitivity to criticism, lack of sensitivity to others needs.

Obsessive-Compulsive Disorder - An anxiety disorder characterized by either 1) repeating stressful thoughts which are excessive, intrusive, and unwanted and which the person tries to suppress and which are recognized as coming from one's own mind, or 2) repetitive behaviours resulting from the previously mentioned obsessive thoughts or which the person feels compelled to rigidly perform and which, although unrelated and excessive, are intended to prevent a feared event or to reduce the fear.

Obsessive-Compulsive Personality Disorder - This is a pattern of an excessive need for control and order which take priority over closeness in relationships and the needs of others.

Panic Attack - An acute period in which symptoms peak within ten minutes such as pounding heart, dizziness, fear of losing control, and shortness of breath.

Panic Disorder - A disorder in which there have been recurrent unexpected panic attacks with at least one month of continued anxiety resulting from the panic attack.

Paranoid Personality - This is a pattern of fear or suspicion that others are against the individual.

Paranoid Schizophrenia - A severe disorder characterized by visual and auditory hallucinations (psychosis) and in which the individual imagines that there is a conspiracy against him.

Passive-Aggressive Personality Disorder - This is a pattern of resistance or of indirect opposition to the perceived demands of self or others.

Personality Disorders - These are separately defined patterns of behaviour which are pervasive and lasting, which cause subjective distress or social or occupational dysfunction, and which began in adolescence or early adulthood.

Post-Traumatic Stress Disorder - A disturbance exceeding one month in which there is significant social or occupational dysfunction due to having seen or experienced a frightening death or violence and which is re-experienced in psychological ways beyond the control of the individual. This also leads to attempts to avoid similar events, failure to respond to others, and increased fear, vigilance, and defensive anger.

Prognosis - A brief statement of the expected outcome of the treatment plan, i.e. Good, Fair, or Poor; or Fair to Good, or Fair to Poor.

Psychodynamic Goals - A listing of emotional, cognitive, and behavioural tasks related to identified underlying unresolved conflicts and losses. E.g. To work through the grief, negative self-talk, and increased assertiveness needed to resolve childhood loss of parental caring due to early abandonment by father.

Schizoid Personality Disorder - This is a pattern of aloofness from social relationships and a limited variety of emotions or ability to express them.

Schizotypal Personality Disorder - This is a pattern of eccentric behaviour, detachment from others, odd thinking and speech.

Somatization Disorder - A history of many physical complaints from before age 30 which has no medical basis and has led to a search for medical help or to significant social or occupational dysfunction. There has also been a history of pain in four different parts of the body, at least two gastrointestinal symptoms, one sexual symptom, and one symptom of the nervous system.

Substance Abuse - During the same 12 month period, the person continues use although social problems result, legal problems result, or recurrent use in dangerous situations, e.g. driving drunk.

Substance Dependence (Addiction) - During the same 12 month period, the individual has 1) experienced increased tolerance to the substance, e.g. has had to increase the amount of the substance to achieve the desired effect, 2) experienced withdrawal symptoms, 3) attempts to decrease the amount of use 4) substance use continues despite social or physical problems caused by use.

Treatment Plan - A listing of models, techniques, interventions, and referrals intended to help the client.